small group
communication
a reader

SMALL GROUP
COMMUNI-
CATION

A READER

Robert S. Cathcart
Queens College of the City University of New York

Larry A. Samovar
San Diego State College

WM. C. BROWN COMPANY PUBLISHERS
Dubuque, Iowa

Copyright © 1970 by
Wm. C. Brown Company Publishers

SBN 697–04131–X

Printed in the United States of America

CONTENTS

v

PART II. INDIVIDUAL AND GROUP OPERATIONS

PART III. GROUP COMMUNICATION: THEORY AND PRACTICE

PREFACE

This collection of articles, essays, and research reports is intended for the student of small group communication and group discussion. It offers a selection of readings drawn from a wide variety of disciplines and publications designed to acquaint the student with the vast body of small group literature which has been formulated in the past fifty years. The collection presented here is selective rather than comprehensive. It makes available in one place representative articles from psychology, sociology, philosophy, speech, English, and business management which are pertinent to the study of small group communication. The forty-one readings were chosen after weighing and considering many factors and many alternatives. For any one selection included in this volume, the editors reviewed and excluded a dozen or more similar essays or experiments. The editors have purposely avoided pressing the case for any one particular school of thought on small group process. Rather, they have brought together some of the foundation-stone essays and experimental studies which have given impetus to the group discussion movement and the development of Group Dynamics, some of the theoretical essays which most all group discussion texts draw from, and some of the contemporary techniques and experiments which are reforming our thinking and teaching about small group processes.

It is our purpose in presenting this collection to provide students with a conveniently grouped selection of readings that will expose them to ideas and practices which will be supplemental to the materials found in textbooks in group communication. These essays will bring greater depth and understanding of the principles of group communication and a wider variety of techniques and methods available than can possibly be found in the usual textbook. We believe that students of communication should be exposed to the diverse viewpoints expressed in this reader and they should be cognizant of the germinal essays and latest techniques which are presented herein. Although this book has been planned especially for college students and teachers who are interested in small group communication, the editors believe that business and industrial groups, church groups, and all individuals who find themselves involved in group activities will gain ideas and insight from this volume.

The readings are grouped under four headings according to their content and focus. Part I, Small Groups and the Individual, contains eight readings which discuss the nature of small groups and the relationships among individuals and groups. Part II, Individual and Group Operations, presents eleven selections designed to add to the student's understanding of group processes. Part III, Group Communication Theory and Practice, offers twelve articles on the nature of the communication process in small groups and the means of improving group communication. Part IV, Group Leadership, concludes the reader with ten articles devoted to leadership theory, types, and performance. Each part is introduced with an essay prepared by the editors explaining the background, the needs, and some of the research studies in each area along with a brief report on each reading. An extensive bibliography accompanies each Part of the reader giving the student an organized list of references for further study in the area.

The editors are particularly happy to present four original essays written expressly for this reader. The articles appearing here in print for the first time were generously offered by Charles Kelly, Larry Samovar and Edward D. Rintye, Robert Benjamin and Laura Crowell. These essays bring to the student some of the most recent thinking on small group communication and they add immeasurably to the knowledge in the field. The editors are deeply indebted to these authors for their most worthwhile contributions to this reader.

We are also indebted to those many other authors who have given us permission to reprint their published writings. We have tried to present original essays in their entirety wherever possible. We have excerpted where we felt the material was not relevant to the particular area being illuminated or where statistical charts and tables were beyond the knowledge of general undergraduate readers.

A careful study of these readings, in whole or in part, should reward the student of small group communication with a greater understanding and appreciation of the monumental strides that have been made in this century toward a theory of human communication. It should also make him appreciate how much there is yet to be learned about man and his group life.

Robert S. Cathcart
Larry A. Samovar

PART I

SMALL GROUPS
AND THE
INDIVIDUAL

"Modern life is group life," wrote Eduard C. Lindeman in 1924. He was confirming the twentieth century view of man as the social inter-actor shaped by the conditions of group life. Traditionally, man had been viewed as an individual or an isolated unit of society and only incidentally a member of the groups within society; the family, the guild, the community, the class.

It was this traditional view of man and society that produced the classic descriptions for the various forms of social or political organizations; Plato's Republic, Machiavelli's city state, Hobbe's Leviathan, Rousseau's Social Contract, and Locke's social compact. All of these formulations were based upon assumptions about the nature of man and the inherent structure of society. It was assumed that there were only two major variables, man and society. Groups, e.g., the family, were fixed and played little part in the theorizing prior to the nineteenth century. This traditional view has gradually given way in the twentieth century to the view of *groups as society*. Modern sociologists and psychologists, focusing on man's behavior rather than his inherent nature have found it is the primary or informal groups that are the warp and woof of man's daily life. They are the well springs of man's values and attitudes. These small groups are now recognized as the very mechanisms of socialization. Societies are now seen as a maze of interlocking and overlapping groups in which the individual plays various roles.

The study of man and his group life has developed at an ever increasing pace since early in this century when John Dewey recognized the child could not be truly educated apart from the groups which formed his immediate world and psychologist, Floyd Allport, found that experiments with individual behavior were always in-

1

fluenced by the groups the subjects were a part of. The rapid growth of a psychology of groups has developed mainly along two tracks; the political-practical and the theoretical-experimental. The political-practical stream has focused on means and methods of improving group processes operating on the assumption that this would in turn improve society. It has lead to a concern with the processes by which democratic decisions are made, how democratic leadership could be improved, how individual participation could be enhanced, and over-riding all these concerns, the need for improving communication within groups. The practitioners of group process have produced an ever growing array of techniques for understanding and improving groups. They are responsible for the now widely known practices of role playing, feedback, brainstorming, buzz sessions, T-groups, encounter groups and sensitivity training.

It is the political-practical approach which produced the still growing group discussion movement in the college, the community, and the business world. Hundreds of courses and workshops in group communication and group process are held annually, all designed to increase the individual's ability to function more effectively in groups and in turn to make groups more effective contributors to our democratic society. Rare is the teacher or business executive today who does not use group discussion or committees to enhance learning and decision making. Group psycho-therapy has become the leading method of treatment for neurosis and psychosis and the group techniques developed by psychiatrists and psychologists are currently receiving widespread application on the campus and in community in the form of marathon group sessions. The principle behind this approach to group study is summed up by Dorwin Cartwright and Alvin Zander in *Group Dynamics.*

> A democratic society derives its strength from the effective functioning of the multitude of groups which it contains. Its most valuable resources are the groups of people found in its homes, communities, schools, churches, business concerns, union halls, and various branches of government. Now, more than ever before, it is recognized that these units must perform their functions well if the larger system is to work.[1]

The theoretical-experimental track to group study is more recent and is inextricably tied to the growth of the social sciences. Its roots lay in the movement which has produced the sciences of human behavior; psychology, sociology and anthropology. It is a part of the

---

1. Dorwin Cartwright and Alvin Zander, *Group Dynamics: Research and Theory,* 2nd ed., Row, Peterson & Company, 1962, ix.

tradition which holds that man's behavior and social relationships can be subjected to scientific investigation equally as well as can natural and biological phenomena. The social psychologists of this century brought man into the laboratory and developed the techniques of scientific research and statistical measurement which led eventually to the experimental study of groups. The contributors to the theoretical-experimental side of group study are seeking a theory of human behavior based upon scientific experimentation. For the most part they are behavioral scientists who are more concerned with theoretical research than with finding practical answers for the improvement of group functioning.

The scientific study of groups received its greatest impetus in the late 1930's when Kurt Lewin established the Research Center for Group Dynamics where theoretical problems of group interaction were studied, and when Muzafer Sherif developed ingenious experimental techniques for the investigation of social norms. Thus, an identifiable field of scientific study was established which has come to be known as Group Dynamics. "Group dynamics is [that] field of inquiry dedicated to advancing knowledge about the nature of groups, the laws of their development, and their interrelations with individuals, other groups, and larger institutions."[2]

Not all of the investigations of the group dynamicists have been conducted in the artificial atmosphere of the laboratory. W.F. Whyte and Robert Bales in particular adapted scientific techniques of observation and measurement to the field and took their studies into the streets, the classrooms, the board meetings, etc. There they tested theories of interaction and group process. Whether in the laboratory or in the field the researcher in group dynamics is concerned with advancing our knowledge about group life.

We are far from formulating a complete theory of human interaction or group dynamics. However, the student of group communication has today an overwhelming array of theoretical and practical information from which to choose. Experimental research proceeds apace and practitioners are continually evolving new techniques for the improvement of group communication and interaction. It is our purpose here to bring to you some of the more significant theories, principles and practices which have contributed to our knowledge about groups and the part the individuals play in them.

This first chapter is devoted to writings about the nature of groups and what happens to individuals as a result of participation in groups.

---

2. *Ibid.*, 29.

It contains two sections. The first section focuses on Group Theory and presents some of the current thought on what constitutes a small group, why individuals live groups lives, how individual actions are determined by group norms, and what is the role of groups in a democratic society. The second section contains selections which focus on Group Facilitation. The various relationships of the individual to the group is examined through the results of practical experience and experimental studies. Some of the facets explored in the second section are: how do individuals perceive of themselves in groups, on what basis do they relate to other members of the group, what do they risk as group members, and how are cooperation and competition affected by group membership?

In the first selection, Bernard Bass discusses the problem of defining a group and indicates why it is so difficult to find a satisfactory definition. He argues that in actuality a group is any collection of individuals whose existence as a collection is rewarding to the individuals. He discusses group effectiveness and group attractiveness as they relate to his theory of reward. He feels that the effectiveness and attractiveness of all groups can be determined by how interaction difficulties and task difficulties are overcome and goals achieved.

Muzafer Sherif, one of the pioneers in Group Dynamics, and his wife Carolyn discuss groups as they exist in social settings in our second selection. Their ideas are derived from extensive field studies of adolescent groups. They find two earmarks of a group: (1) the structure of interaction and (2) the shared group norms. In the spontaneous groups that people join to gain self identity and support in the everyday business of living, the group values and group norms become so internalized within the individual that he will not deviate even if the group is socially unacceptable. The Sherifs propose that since groups are necessary to every individual's survival, it does no good to condemn groups as such or try to isolate them, rather we should understand group role systems and norms and attempt to provide anti-social groups with desirable values and goals.

The relationship of groups to the larger society is also a concern of Milton Horowitz and Howard Perlmutter in their article on "The Discussion Group and Democratic Behavior." They consider why some groups operate democratically and others do not; assuming that if our society is to be democratic, the groups within it must function democratically. They explore both the anti-democratic and democratic forces latent in every group. Their research reveals there are three groups of factors which operate on each side of the equation; these are interpersonal factors, group phenomena, and personality. In each of these three areas there exists a state of tension between democratic and anti-democratic forces and they would have us understand the variables operating so that the scales can be tipped in favor of democratic action.

The first selection in Chapter 2, Group Facilitation, presents the findings of a medical doctor who derived a game theory of human behavior from his experiences with psycho-therapy groups. Eric Berne, in this excerpt from one of his books, points out that all individuals have biological and psychological needs which can be fulfilled only through suitable group contact. He claims all individuals have "life plans" and "provisional group imagoes" which if they could be fulfilled would provide the individual with the maximum possible satisfaction. Berne sees most of us struggling to fit our group imagoes to real groups. He advances the interesting notion that one's successful adjustment to group reality is determined by the "script" or life plan which each individual carries with him on the subconscious level.

A rather different approach to group role theory is made by Erving Goffman, the Canadian sociologist who is best known for his book, *The Presentation of Self in Everyday Life*. In this brief excerpt from that book, Goffman examines group facilitation from the external side. He develops some unique ideas about groups as teams of individuals who perceive a certain relationship amongst themselves based upon the "face" that the team presents to the outside world. What creates a team is recognition on the part of a set of individuals that cooperation is necessary to maintain a projected definition of a situation. This cooperation consists of presenting a team face while at the same time concealing those things which might damage that face. An example would be the family that appears affectionate and helpful to each other while in public, but vicious to one another when out of sight within their house. To understand such a group, according to Goffman, we would have to be aware of the interactions involved in this presentation of the public face.

The article by Edward Gross is an example of the experimental research that is part of the theoretical-experimental approach to group study. The author, a sociologist, conducted a controlled experiment involving selected groups of Air Force personnel to test theories of social bond, or what holds people together in groups. He explains that this experiment is part of a larger inquiry into integrative forces in small groups, and that his concern will be with only two of the known concepts of group integration: symbiosis and consensus. After describing the experimental procedures followed to isolate and measure certain variables, he presents the results and discusses their implications in light of the findings of other researchers. Gross makes an important addition to our knowledge of group facilitation.

The next article, "Components of Group Risk Taking," is also a research report. The experiment conducted by Teger and Pruitt was conducted in a psychological laboratory on a college campus and uses college students as experimental subjects. It differs from the Gross experiment in two significant ways. The experimenters use a markedly different design for the collection of data and they attempt an experiment which could resolve the differences between two conflicting theories of group risk taking. The authors discuss at length the conflicts between the Wallach and Kogan "Affective Bond" theory and the Brown "value theory" of group risk taking, and the need for an experimental design to overcome the weaknesses inherent in earlier research. The results of this experiment, according to the researchers, tend to support Brown's "value theory" which holds that each group generates a "value of risk" commensurate with the problem to be solved and the cultural norms present. When members of a group find that a decision warrants a risky approach they place a value on risk which causes the group to make a greater risky shift than would any individual alone.

Our final selection in this chapter contains some recent research findings on one of the oldest problems in group study: cooperation vs. competition. As Julian and Perry point out, research on cooperation and competition began as early as 1898 and has been so extensive that there is now a danger of these two terms becoming catchall labels for all comparisons of performances among individuals and groups. What concerns Julian and Perry is that most research into this topic confuses cooperation among individual group members and competition among groups. Thus, they set out to measure how individual cooperation is affected when competition *within* groups is contrasted with competition *between* groups. Their findings are summed up in the statement: "cooperation among group members without the pressure of inter-group comparisons may be a pleasant circumstance in which to work, but it does not necessarily foster high productivity."

The materials in Part I have been selected to aid the student of group communication in his understanding of what makes a group a group and to help him increase his own effectiveness in groups by adding to his awareness of what it is that produces group facilitation.

chapter 1

Group Theory

GROUP EFFECTIVENESS
Bernard Bass

A Lion used to prowl about a field in which Four Oxen used to dwell. Many a time he tried to attack them; but whenever he came near they turned their tails to one another, so that whichever way he approached them he was met by the horns of one of them. At last, however, they fell a-quarrelling among themselves, and each went off to pasture alone in a separate corner of the field. Then the lion attacked them one by one and soon made an end to all four.

—Aesop's Fables (ca. 600 B.C.)

The Concept of Group

The fable illustrates Aristotle's dictum that the object of every association is some good. And for us, what distinguishes a group from a mere collection of people is its purpose. We define "group" as a collection of individuals whose existence as a collection is rewarding to the individuals. Whether or not the group is of importance to nonmembers will not be considered here. Members are held in the group because remaining in it earns for them such incentives as material comfort and security and/or enables them to avoid tissue injury, harm, blame, or other unsatisfying states of affairs which would occur if they left the group.

While other investigators may debate the judiciousness of this definition of "group," there can be no quarrel concerning the meaning of the label. Others may not accept what we choose to call "groups" and what we choose not to call "groups," since at least five distinct types of definitions of groups are available. But each investigator has complete freedom to define and label operations as he sees fit. The acid test of the adequacy of definitions lies in demonstrating their utility and convenience in theory construction and in the evaluation of the theory by empirical operations.

The definition of "group," like others to be offered, is partial; there may be other ways to infer the existence and variations in the concept. Thus, we define "group" by one means, while suggesting that many other means are probably available that will lead to calling certain things "groups," and other things "not groups."

Selection of the Definition

The definition has been selected with a particular purpose in mind. It will permit us to make use immediately of the law of effect to derive our first theorems about group behavior. It will fit with our attempt to discuss leadership as a consequence of reinforcement. It also requires that a minimum of surplus meanings be attached to it and to the definitions that follow. It appears to conform with evidence concerning the origin and emergence of groups and leadership from mere collections of people. It also enables us to deal parsimoniously with animal groups even where the behavior is "built-in." Incentives to action in natural animal groups often concern mutual protection. But the "interaction for security" may be an innate consequence of evolution. For example, when one minnow is caught by a perch, the others disperse. Why? The skin of the killed minnow releases a chemical substance which causes avoidance behavior in the others.

A swarm of moths around a light is a mere collection gathered because all moths are all attracted to the same stimulus. There is no connection between the collection of moths, as such, and the stimulus-response patterns. But the lamb and its mother form a group. While lambs suck instinctively, sucking also satisfies hunger. In turn, the mother gains relief from mammary gland tension.

Similarity of the Present Definition to Others

Our concept of the group is shared by numerous other investigators. "Every group exists as a means of satisfying certain purposes, wishes or interests, of furnishing goods or values, to its members" according to Sanderson. For Deutsch, a group exists to the extent that the individuals composing it are pursuing promotively interdependent goals. According to Cattell a group is an "aggregate of organisms in which the existence of all is utilized for the satisfaction of the needs of each." In Parsons' theory, social systems must provide the satisfaction of the minimum biological and psychological needs of the members of the system. Gibb conceived groups as mechanisms for achieving individual satisfaction through interaction. In the functional school of social anthropology as exemplified by Malenowski, all elements of society are interrelated to meet the needs of individual members and contribute to the survival of the society. Rules, ritual, and magic develop to satisfy needs which cannot be coped with alone by members.

Surplus Meanings 1. *Perceived unity*; 2. *Common goals*; 3. *interaction*

For purposes of definition, the many other characteristics ascribed to groups are surplus. Perceived unity is one of these. Aristotle applied Socrates' test of unity to his concept of group. All members of a group are those who term the group "mine." While many or even most groups, as we conceive them, may have a shared perception of their unity, this is not an essential condition nor does it contribute to our analytical account of group behavior. Sherif found that by making goal attainment dependent on the efforts of both, he could make two competing collections of boys cooperate as one unit, although two distinct aggregates were perceived by the boys. We would describe this situation as one in which the two collections had merged temporarily into one group.

Many theorists have emphasized that members must have common goals to form a group. For example, Freeman stated that persons with common goals unite to realize their goals. Yet we can conceive of collections of persons who share common goals, which collections are not groups and, more important, do not show the behaviors common to what we refer to as groups. The collection with common goals only becomes a group when the collection, as such, is potentially rewarding. For example, a collection of prisoners may all have the common goal of escaping but may regard each other as stool pigeons. The collection builds tensions, and does not increase the promise of escape. The behavior of the collection will be very different from the behavior of a group of prisoners who view each other as potential help in an escape effort.

Others such as Eubank have emphasized that an essential feature of a group is that its members be in definite interaction, usually face to face. Other requirements have been that groups have interlocking roles (prescribed patterns of behavior) and shared norms (common standards of behavior). Yet, as we define "group," the many stockholders in a company may comprise a group viewing each other with alarm if a sudden spurt of stock selling occurs, or with satisfaction if selling is slow despite a falling market. Yet the stockholders do not necessarily play interlocking roles or share common standards or perceive any unity or interact with each other. Any of these "surplus" conditions can vary in amount and degree within groups. However, their presence or absence will not be necessary before we say a collection of individuals is a group.

Cattell gives an example of a collection of persons we find it useful to define as a group, yet the five conditions of definite interaction—common goals, interlocking roles, shared norms, and shared perception of unity—are absent. Two swimmers, each a mile off shore and a mile apart, form a group in that the sight of one swimmer provides security for the other and vice versa. They never interact, may be out swimming for entirely different purposes (one for exercise, the other for excitement), and do not necessarily agree on the roles each plays nor share any standards.

Effectiveness and Attractiveness

Groups vary in the extent they are rewarding to members. The extent they reward is their *effectiveness.* Groups also vary in the extent they are expected to reward. The anticipated goal attainment is the *attractiveness* of the group. A potentially rewarding group is attractive; a group which actually rewards its members is effective.

Groups cease to exist and become collections when their attractiveness approaches zero. With additional effort, the collection itself will disband. (The individuals may remain assembled since it takes some motivation to withdraw, but group activity and change will be minimal at this point.) It is also conceivable that individuals may become satiated with the rewards resulting from membership in a group, resulting in their withdrawal from the group.

Groups displace individual isolated activity because groups tend to be more effective. All other things being equal, humans and their immediate mammalian predecessors would probably have never formed groups—other than mother-child or temporary sex-partner groups—since there is no known direct physiological drive among humans which leads to gregariousness, per se, other than sucking in the infant, mammary tension in the mother, contact comfort, and the sex drive. That the group brings greater rewards (effectiveness) than individuals in isolation is attested to by a large number of experimental comparisons. . . . Although many factors are known which reverse the effect, groups have generally been found superior to individuals.

"Morale" has been used by others to label what we have defined as group effectiveness and/or group attractiveness. For Gordon, morale is the degree a worker is satisfied his needs are being met on the job. On the other hand, Smith and Westen define morale as satisfaction with and desire to strive for the goals of a particular group. Child suggests that morale both involves motivation toward and confidence in gaining the goals of the group (attractiveness) and a "condition of well-being" enabling hopeful effective work (effectiveness). While we will attempt to describe more precisely the phenomena involved, using the more specific concepts of effectiveness and attractiveness, we will infer that groups are likely to be attractive, effective, or both, if described by other investigators as having high morale.

The source of reward or reinforcement may be the *task* or the interaction among members. It may be *immediate* or *delayed* for long periods. The observed goal attainment may be *relevant* or *irrelevant* to the membership. Reinforcement may occur *partially* or *totally*. Groups can be described as varying in task effectiveness, interaction effectiveness, immediate effectiveness, ultimate effectiveness, relevancy of goal attainment, and in the extent behavior in the groups is reinforced partially or totally.

Individual and Group Performance

In Figure 1 we conceptualize group learning or performance by building on the schematic of individual behavior in the face of problems.

When presented with an obstacle in his path to a goal, the single individual attempts a variety of responses limited by his past learning, his brainpower, and situational restrictions. The response yielding the goal will be reinforced. The other responses will not be reinforced. If presented again with the same problem, the individual will be more likely to make the reinforced response and less likely to make the others. The individual will have changed his behavior.

We conceive of two sets of barriers between individuals and their respective goals when the problem requires that they cooperate as a group to achieve their respective goals. First, they usually must "straighten out" the human entanglements to successful interaction; second, they must adequately perform their respective activities yielding completion of the task. Solving the problems of interaction yields rewards, particularly to those who are interaction-oriented, and may be independent of task success and its rewards. But such interaction effectiveness often is necessary before the group can concentrate on task success. Thus, Gibb, Platts, and Miller suggest that before trying to solve a new group's problems, we need adequate "getting-acquainted" periods; we must promote pleasant interpersonal relationships permitting the shift from interpersonal problems to group task goals. Conducive procedural arrangements must be provided. Given a task requiring a high degree of coordination and cooperation, it would appear that group task effectiveness can only occur if first the group's interaction is effective. If relatively little interaction among members is demanded for task success, then it should be possible to observe little interdependence of task and interaction effectiveness. If they are completely independent, however, one may suspect he is dealing with a collection of isolated workers rather than a true work group.

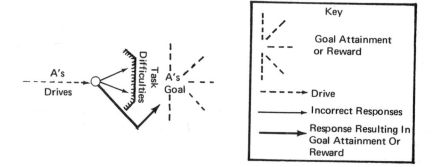

The Individual Problem Solving Situation

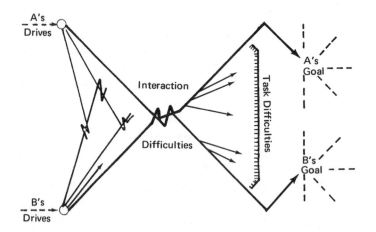

The Group Problem Solving Situation

Figure 1. Individual and group problem solving situations.

Keep in mind the problem of relevancy of goals. The productivity of a group may not necessarily measure group effectiveness if the members are not rewarded for high productivity. Productivity may even be negatively related to effectiveness. We may observe a harmonious, highly interaction-effective group of saboteurs "delightfully" effective in *lack* of productivity. Relevancy will be treated in detail later.

Task Effectiveness

Ignoring for the moment the matter of relevancy of goals, some ways group task effectiveness can be measured include (1) the observed amount members reach their goals with a minimum expenditure of time and energy; (2) the degree of satisfaction members express concerning the group's products and decisions; and (3) the quantity and quality of productivity, rewards earned, and punishments avoided.

Gibb mentions as possible measures to task effectiveness the number of ideas produced, quality of the ideas, decision speed, scores on objective examinations, winning of games in competition with other groups, and satisfaction with the decision. Peterman used this last criterion as a major index of conference task effectiveness. The extent conferees were satisfied with the decisions reached, in turn, correlated .34 with the number of agenda items completed and .68 with a conferee's satisfaction with his own work at the meeting. The more time spent per substantive topic, the less satisfied were conferees with the group's decisions. Total conference time was an ambiguous criterion, for while generally negatively related to satisfaction with decisions, it was positively related in a pleasant, friendly atmosphere. We may be happy to waste time with a group of friends. On the other hand, rapid decision-making may reflect apathy, not efficiency. . . .

Interaction Effectiveness

Interaction effectiveness can be assessed by (1) observed amount of harmony and absence of conflict; (2) expressed satisfaction of the members with the interaction; (3) congruence of actual or perceived relations between members with the relations the members desire.

Massarik, Tannenbaum, *et al.* suggested examining within an organization the formally prescribed relations or interaction, the relations perceived by the members, the actual observed relations, and the desired and rejected relations. Various indices of satisfaction with the interaction, per se, could be derived by contrasting actual and perceived interaction with what is formally demanded and with what is desired. Satisfaction would be low if a large discrepancy existed, say, between desired and perceived interaction.

One method of assessing interaction effectiveness is Bales' interaction process analysis. Interaction effectiveness would be reflected among groups who exhibited a great deal of the categorized behavior described by Bales as showing solidarity, raising others' esteem, giving help and reward, showing tension release, joking, laughing, showing satisfaction, agreeing, accepting, concurring, and complying. Interaction ineffectiveness would be characterized by disagreement, rejection, withholding help, withdrawing, showing antagonism, deflating others' esteem, acting defensive or self-assertive.

In an interactive factor analysis of 490 questionnaire descriptions of air crews, Rush uncovered a *harmony* factor which he described as dealing with the presence or absence of conflict among crew members and the compatibility of relationships, and possibly representing a general or halo factor reflecting whether the rater likes or dislikes the group. Rush's analysis suggests the possibility of obtaining a relatively pure measure of interaction effectiveness by descriptive techniques.

Similar Terms

Conceptions of morale have often included what we mean by interaction effectiveness, usually without the implications of reward assigned to interaction effectiveness. On a more descriptive level also are Hemphill and Westie's concepts of *viscidity* and *hedonic tone* and corresponding concepts by Cattell and Stice. These also contain elements similar to what we mean by interaction effectiveness.

Viscidity has been defined by Hemphill and Westie as the degree to which members of a group function as a unit. It is reflected in absence of dissension and personal conflict among members, by absence of activities serving to advance only the interests of individual group members, and by the ability of the group to resist disrupting forces. Interaction effectiveness has similarities to *synergy,* defined by Cattell and Stice as the ability of a group to resist disruption. If most of the synergy, can be expended on the task, the group shows a high degree of interaction effectiveness.

Hedonic tone is the degree to which group membership is accompanied by a general feeling of pleasantness and agreeableness. It is reflected by the frequency of laughter, conviviality, pleasant anticipation of group meetings, and by the absence of griping or complaining. Hedonic tone, for Cattell and Stice, refers to success, harmony of internal relations, cheerfulness and absence of destructive criticism and complaints.

Relations Between Task and Interaction Effectiveness

We have noted already that task effectiveness usually requires earlier interaction effectiveness. However, each can occur in the absence of the other, and under certain conditions interaction effectiveness may depend on task effectiveness. The dependence of task on interaction effectiveness has been found most commonly.

Task Effectiveness as a Consequence of Interaction Effectiveness

Rush obtained positive correlations between *harmony* and efficiency ratings in combat of the air crews mentioned earlier. Katz and Hyman found shipyard productivity highly related to morale defined mainly in terms of interaction effectiveness. Stogdill and Koehler noted that shipboard morale (again involving satisfaction with interaction) was moderately related to overall efficiency ratings of the ship. Similarly, Goodacre observed more agreement with the leader's solutions, more satisfaction with one's own status, and more pride in the squad, itself, among 13 infantry squads performing well on field problems compared to 13 poorly performing squads. In the same way, Goodrich reported that group productivity suffered when aggression was high in the group. Katz, Maccoby, and Morse found higher productivity among insurance departments where supervisors took more personal interest in their subordinates. Among 14 work groups, Nagle observed correlations of .86 and .63 between the rated productivity of the departments and the extent the employees liked their supervisor and the company. Again, crews rated good by their instructors perceived in projective sketches (which supposedly reflected their own group experiences) more orderly functioning, more interpersonal harmony, as well as more productivity. Closely supporting the generalization that task effectiveness hinges on effective interaction, Berkowitz and Levin noted that among 31 conferences, "low quality" solutions were reached more often among groups "bogged down" in process.

Interaction Effectiveness as a Consequence of Task Effectiveness

Continued *task* failure may produce interaction ineffectiveness. Odiorne contrasted the behavior of operators of ten poorly operating machines with 40 percent down-time (and thus low task effectiveness) with operators of ten machines "down" only 10 percent of the time (and thus with higher task effectiveness). Much greater job dissatisfaction, absenteeism, tardiness, quitting, grievances, and observed arguments with other employees were noted among the operators of the poorly running machines.

The relation of task to interaction effectiveness is purely arbitrary. We can make either dependent on the other in laboratory settings, although in natural groups task success is likely to depend on the earlier attainment of the goals of interaction. But consider how this may be reversed in an animal experiment.

Suppose every time two rats interact by touching paws they earn a pellet of food. Also, they earn a larger pellet if either one depresses a lever. While the rats would be satisfied to merely interact and completely ignore working the lever, they find that the lever must be worked to some extent or the rewards for interacting will cease. It is not difficult to locate human groups where the convivialities and enjoyments of interaction far outweigh the importance of task accomplishment. Task effectiveness is maintained to some minimum extent so that the group can justify its existence, but the main concern is with the satisfactions of interaction. Many volunteer agencies are likely to fit this description. Guetzkow and Gyr noted that conference groups could reach interaction effectiveness at the expense of task effectiveness. Meetings faced with difficulties could achieve a high degree of consensus and good feeling by postponing complex problems, and tackling only simple agenda items. Solution of these simple agenda items gave a sense of task accomplishment, although the major success occurred in achieving satisfying interaction.

Conditions Promoting the Independence of Interaction and Task Effectiveness

Under a variety of special circumstances, interaction effectiveness and task effectiveness may be unrelated.

Goode and Fowler described conditions in a small feeder plant in the auto industry. The work required little skill or coordination. The workers were marginal or handicapped employees unable to get jobs elsewhere. Little training was required and an abundant labor supply was available. The workers produced to a high degree despite abusive supervision likely to promote interaction ineffectiveness and under more normal circumstances likely to reduce task effectiveness. "Produce or get out" was effective with employees under these conditions. Production was rewarding to the employees since they could keep their jobs only if they produced; and if they lost their jobs, they would have difficulty in finding new ones.

A contrary condition is exemplified in the British building trades. Davis found that 60 percent of British building workers were opposed to wage incentive plans (which would mean higher rewards to them for task effectiveness) because the workers felt incentive plans would hinder harmony and good feelings within the group (would lower interaction effectiveness). And the workers were right, for according to Wyatt, while piece rates and bonuses increased productivity and take-home pay among chocolate wrapper girls, they also increased disagreement, stress, and faultfinding. If task effectiveness is increased mainly by increasing the magnitude of the incentives for the group members, it may produce greater tensions in their interaction rather than promote satisfaction with interaction as well as task effectiveness.

The independence of task and interaction is illustrated by a research unit, composed mainly of clerks, which was noted for its pleasant interactions, harmony, and good feelings. Each member's birthday was an occasion for a feast. Its Christmas party was celebrated among the many held. There was only one thing wrong. It did not produce any research. Bitter tears were shed at the dissolution of the unit. The failure to produce, of course, was not due to the harmonious interpersonal relations but rather to the lack of training of the clerks and the lack of suitable direction.

Sources of Bias

Two factors bias the correlation between task and interaction effectiveness. One is the situation in which the group is placed; the other is a matter of the personality of the individual member. Miller reported a marked difference in satisfaction of military personnel with such things as recreation, transportation, and leadership at different air defense sites. The differences did not appear due to the differences in available facilities or in the leadership. Rather, it was a matter of how geographically isolated the sites were. It has been remarked that one could almost perfectly account for the satisfaction of stateside servicemen during World War II by the geographical proximity of their camp to the nearest large city.

With regard to the individual member, Weitz noted that satisfaction of a member with his work group situation may be more a function of a generalized satisfaction with living, home, politics, etc. Most of us are familiar with the chronic griper. For him, most of his interactions with others as well as the task outcomes would be dissatisfying regardless of the objective state of affairs.

Use of the Concepts

Generally, we expect that the influence of task and interaction effectiveness will be the same on leader behavior. Thus, we will develop a series of propositions about group effectiveness and leader behavior and assume that they apply as well (with some qualifications, as needed) to productivity (if relevant) as to satisfaction with the group's activities. This general definition of effectiveness is consistent with the need for personnel psychology to expand its criteria of organizational success. Pointed out elsewhere is the need for psychologists to add to presently accepted criteria of organization efficiency such indices as the value of the organization to its members and the value of the organization to society as a whole. . . .

SOCIAL SETTINGS AND REFERENCE GROUPS
Muzafer Sherif and Carolyn Sherif

Earmarks of a Group and Behavior of Individual Members

The two essential earmarks of adolescent groups, like any other groups, are:

1. Structure or organization of interaction among members, defining the statuses and roles of members in various respects, and thereby defining the proper attitudes of the members toward each other and toward members of other groups.

2. A set of values or group norms shared by group members, over and above the sectors of values they have in common with others in their setting and the society of which they are a part.

The interpersonal expectancies of members and their behaviors within the in-group, and attitude toward and treatment of outsiders, take on a predictable pattern to the extent that the organization of reciprocal positions and roles of members in specific respects is stabilized over a period of time. This property of a group is, therefore, decidedly relevant for behavior of individuals composing it. Corresponding to the degree of stabilization of the patterns of interaction, the individual becomes personally concerned with remaining a part of it, maintaining an unquestioned place in good standing in the group, in proving himself in various respects, in showing that he is not a back number in undertakings (which may be good or bad by outside standards), commensurate with the status and role he has achieved. In fact, the individual's concerns over acceptance or rejection, his experiences of personal achievement or failure, that is, the directive components of his warmly experienced ego, in no small part consist of stuff of this sort.

Individual members in reference groups of this sort have had a hand in shaping the organizational and normative properties of the group. Their own personal attitudes and behaviors, in turn, become more and more shaped by them. This shaping of individual attitude and behavior is proportional to the extent that shared ways emerge and become stabilized for conducting activities toward goals that initially served as common bonds conducive to the members' interaction.

As something they themselves had a hand in shaping, these shared ways of doing things and these rules for conduct are theirs, to be observed without external authority or coercion, even to be cherished. They serve as effective vehicles of solidarity and social control in the group. To the extent that norms of the group's own doing are shared and stabilized, the individual member does *not* experience them as external intrusions demanding arbitrary and functionless conformity. These, their own norms, serve as codified justifications and standards for attitudes and behaviors directed toward more effective handling of problems and plans in pursuit of their common goals—whether for good or evil by other standards.

The group norms that are most binding and most consequential in the members' scheme of concerns are the ones that regulate matters of solidarity among members and that set standards of conduct in the very spheres of motivational promptings that brought them together. These norms define the bounds of what is acceptable and desirable, and the bounds of what is objectionable for personal viewpoint and behavior in matters of consequence to them.

Since members in good standing do share and cherish their own norms, the application of appropriate *sanctions* to behavior that falls outside of their latitude of acceptance in a related sphere is not the sole prerogative of the leader(s) alone. Nor are those of high standing in the group immune from sanctions from others. Correctives become the duly felt business of all group members in varying degree.

To the extent that the individual derives a sense of belongingness and a sense of being somebody to be counted through his membership in the group, the group increasingly becomes the source of his personal security and the context for gauging his personal feelings of success and failure in relevant spheres of activity. Hence, the binding loyalties of the individual, when he has to make a choice, are to his reference group(s). The binding rules, values, or standards for his conduct are those of his reference group(s).

It follows that mere knowledge of rules and standards of society at large and its various agencies does not sensitize the individual, no matter how frequently repeated. When he feels that he does not belong, that he is not wanted, and that his interests are not included in the larger scheme of things, his personal sensitivity is aroused in a context of those who *do* belong to him, who *do* want him, and who *do* take account of his interests. . . .

Motivational Promptings and the Social Setting

Through assessment of influences conducive to the dissolution of ties with adolescent groups, one can point at the motivational promptings that underlie their formation. As reported by a number of investigators with first-hand familiarity with such groups, when members begin to establish themselves in steady jobs, when they marry to establish themselves in ongoing family lives, when they begin to engage in other undertakings that are challenging to them, they are weaned from their adolescent group ties. The adolescent group loses its magic even in the lives of the loyal group members.

When we look at closer range at influences underlying both the formation, functioning, and dissolution of adolescent groups, we start discerning an unmistakable pattern of motivational promptings common both to groups that engage primarily in socially acceptable activities and those that engage in socially objectionable ones. If this be the case, we shall have to cease viewing adolescent groups that engage in socially objectionable activities as the doings of a small number of psychopathic individuals.

The price paid when we view socially objectionable outcomes of group activities as the doings of psychopathic characters is losing sight of the enormity of the problem in its true proportions. In practice, the price paid is resort to measures, such as individual therapy and counseling, which may be appropriate and practical in a relatively small number of cases among the millions who participate in the formation and functioning of groups. There are motivational promptings common to the individuals under the circumstances of their immediate and the larger social setting.

The motivational promptings stem both from biological development of the adolescents and from their setting, but in highly interrelated fashion. Influences stemming from the impulses and urges of a maturing individual and from his setting form a pattern—acting and reacting on one another. Explanations of behavior (whether it is for good or evil) that put the sole weight on the individual's impulses and their vicissitudes, or on the setting alone, have not fared well in either theory or practice.

The gamut of influences shaping behavior composes a system whose parts affect one another. With a changing body reverberating with a dramatic onslaught of the glandular system and its products, the maturing adolescent is throbbing with impulses and desires hard to contain, including sexual urges continually sensitizing the individual for consummation. But even these sexual urges are not one-way affairs. Here too the social setting comes in to define, with sanctions, what he can do and what he cannot do, with all the attendant consequences on the individual (cf. Ford and Beach, 1951).

The same is true of impulses concerned with food to eat, apparel to wear, a dwelling to live in. There are prescriptions, and deprivations as well, the latter owing to constricted family finances, one's station in life relative to others, including the location of the dwelling on this or the other side of the tracks.

It is well known, of course, that the social setting does set limits or bounds within which biological impulses can be carried out, heaping sanctions on the individual who transgresses these bounds. But less seldom is the positive aspect emphasized, using here the term "positive" in a directional sense without judging the efficacy of particular outcomes. The setting provides the adolescent with a framework for a self-picture of the full-fledged male or female in many different and specific respects. This self-picture depicts the characteristics of the approved and the desirable male or female in body proportions, in work and play, as husband or wife, with all the desirable attributes that go with each of these. The setting offers, then, a framework defining the possessions to be attained, the preferable locations in which to live and to aspire to, the particular places and outfits where the individual seeks acceptance as a member in good standing.

In short, for good or bad, the setting depicts affiliations, possessions, social attainments, including *personal* characteristics, that are put at a premium and on a pedestal. These are presented and reinforced through the personal examples of successful men, through books found in drugstores and railway stations, through radio, movies, and television. And, to top it all, one is stimulated by models to get these things *now*—and fast.

But to only a favored few are the instrumentalities for achieving the desired self-picture readily available, and even these are constrained by the very definition of the adolescent period to wait and postpone. It is not a context conducive to a stable identity. Another disruptive influence is an accelerated rate of social change with no recognized alterations in the official prescriptions for the transition. As a consequence, there are varying degrees of cleavage between adult outlook, values, and practices and those seen as necessary, even essential, by the adolescent generation. As noted by various writers, the result is adult-youth conflict. Under the present circumstances, adult-youth conflict in some degree seems to cut across areas of low, middle, and high social rank. The distance between generations is reflected in the not infrequent shift of reference group ties from parents and family to agemates, at least for a period, during the present adolescent generation.

Thus the setting plays its part in bringing adolescents together. All of these motivational promptings impel them toward one another—the deprivations and frustrations of the kinds mentioned above, the self-image to be fulfilled quickly, the state of being caught betwixt and between in a changing world. The informal groups that arise from their interactions are experienced by the individual members as sources of mutual support, vehicles for ventures they would not dare engage in alone, and as secure ground for proving themselves in their strivings to fulfill an identity in the respects depicted by their setting.

To be sure, there are deprivations and frustrations underlying deeds engaged in by individuals in these groups. To be sure, some of these deeds are objectionable. But on the whole, objectionable deeds do not follow directly as a simple consequence of deprivation or frustration. They follow some sort of justification of the deeds provided by the mutual encouragement of other individuals in the same boat. . . .

As noted, every individual involved contributes his bit to the overall picture characterizing a particular neighborhood in this respect. Yet, on the basis of experimental evidence on intergroup conflict, as well as surveys of the literature and the findings in this research, we are forced to conclude that intergroup relations emerge as a set of conditions which continuously affect group properties and member behavior.

The actions of particular groups certainly affect the continuing character of intergroup relations. But primary praise or blame for the character of member attitudes toward out-groups cannot be assigned to strictly individual characteristics of the members, or even to the characteristics of the structure of a single group. On the contrary, some groups and their members maintained friendly relationships with certain groups and hostile relationships with still others. Furthermore, of two groups with friendly relations, one was often friendly with a third, while the other regarded the third as an "enemy."

Thus, our most striking finding is that interpersonal relationships within these informal groups are not insulated from relationships with other groups and adult institutions, or from the character of the setting. Conclusions about them can make sense only when behaviors in give-and-take within a group are considered relative to other groups in the neighborhood, both agemate and adult, including the images fostered so effectively in the larger setting.

Evaluation of Conformity and Deviation in Groups

In this research, we have explored conformity in adolescent groups which was socially acceptable from the adult point of view, and socially objectionable from the adult point of view. In doing so, our aim has been to analyze and understand, not to justify.

Now, certain conclusions will be drawn which have far-reaching implications for theory and action programs. They are based on our data concerning behaviors in spontaneously organized groups, on our experiments on group formation and intergroup relations, and on similar findings in the literature.

One of the strongest promptings of human beings is to establish stable, secure social ties with others, for the following reasons:

1. To have a dependable anchor for a consistent and patterned self-picture, which is essential for personal consistency in experience and behavior, and particularly for a day-to-day continuity of the person's self-identity. Some stability of social ties is a prerequisite condition for the individual to experience himself as the "same person" from day to day, with his characteristic attributes and moorings. There is very considerable evidence that lacking such ties, the individual has great difficulty in establishing a clear self-identity, and that, once developed, the absence of such ties promotes experiences of estrangement and uncertainty, accompanied by erratic and inconsistent behaviors.

2. To provide the individual effective support and vehicles for carrying out the business of living, which requires a shelter and yet a better shelter to live in, food and preferred foods to eat, clothing and better garments to wear, a sex partner and the desirable sex partner, and so on.

The social ties that provide these things for the individual are, as a rule, linked with his membership in groups—in a family, club, church, work group, school group, clique, and so on. These groups are not entities apart from individual members. Lacking individual members, they are consigned, at best, to pages of history books. In view of the still prevailing position that the group and the individuals are entities apart—even dichotomies—it should be reaffirmed that groups exist and continue to exist because of the membership of individuals and because of their active participation in them. In fact, if individuals' existing groups are not functioning as effective vehicles for the business of living and for attaining strongly desired goals, if the groups cease to serve as dependable anchors to center the experience of consistency and continuity as an individual, then individuals do form new groups more effective and more functional in these respects.

On the other hand, to the extent that existing or newly formed groups are stabilized with their organizational systems and norms set, to that extent do individual members experience their place in the scheme of things, their mutual expectancies in interpersonal relations (with regard to the "ins" and "outs") in terms of the prevailing patterns. To that extent, the binding rules for the individuals which they observe with inner conviction are the rules of their groups. The values they uphold and cherish as theirs are the values of the group—thus minimizing the need for punitive sanctions by other members.

Thus, it can and does happen that individuals comply or conform in attitude and behavior to the organizational and normative system of their groups out of requirements of an inner voice (conscience), sense of loyalty, sense of responsibility, even sense of decency relative to follow members. Stepping out of the bounds of propriety defined by his group, thus out of his own role expectancies and self-picture, arouses one's *shame* or *guilt* feelings, and calls for appropriate sanctions from fellow group members. After all, fellow members are important persons in the individual's scheme of things, proportional to the importance of the group in providing support for his personal identity and as an instrumentality for fulfillment of his needs.

These conclusions should not be taken as an apology, justification, or approval of socially objectionable and harmful deeds committed as a function of membership in any group. They are based on study of the outlook and behaviors in actual groups. Realistic analysis of conforming and deviating behavior in groups must look for the standards to which individuals *are* conforming. The weight of the role system and norm set of reference groups in shaping the outlook and behavior of individual members is something one finds. It does not follow, in the least, that the role system, the norms, or the attendant conformity in behavior are something to be glorified and justified.

The role system that enables an individual to contribute his bit to the perpetuation of group formations engaging in antisocial activities, and that provides mutual support for members in these activities, should, as a rule, not exist. Likewise, norms in any group that serve as justifications for personal injury, harm, personal or sexual exploitation with attendant attitude that "the hostile world owes me these things," should not exist and should be eliminated.

This is one thing. But it is another thing to ignore groups as such, to pretend that only "other people" belong to groups. It is another thing to minimize the importance of groups in shaping behavior, as though groups and individuals were distinct entities and behavior was determined only from within the individual. It is another thing to ignore the decisive weight of the norms of groups in shaping the individual's attitudes which become directive attributes of his self-system. It is as though an individual conscience could form in a vacuum, independent of social ties.

Conformity and deviation refer to behavior relative to some standard—no matter what the contemporary connotations of these terms in current literature. It is perfectly feasible to evaluate conforming or deviating behavior in terms of standards of the larger social scene or human well-being. But it is also essential to know what a particular behavior is conforming *to* or deviating *from.* It does not wipe out groups that are antisocial in terms of more encompassing human values to damn groups *as such* or to minimize their influence. Groups are facts of human existence. There are groups which engage in socially laudable and socially obnoxious activities. There will be groups, created by individuals, long after theories and studies that ignore or caricature their properties are in the graveyard of many other artifacts of human history.

Human individuals do live in groups; they form new groups when old groups cease to serve as anchors for their personal experiences, when they become obstacles rather than instrumentalities for pursuing the essentials of living. When a member of a group, an individual does observe the rules as guides of attitude and behavior, including the individual who is the bohemian, the anarchist spurning any government, and including the great majority called "delinquent."

If antisocial groups are to be dealt with effectively, if social norms conducive to debasing, ignobling, and servile conformities are to be dealt with, the first step is to cease condemning groups or conformities *as such,* to stop pretending group organization and their norms are illusory. The basis of human morality is observance of a set of rules or norms—exemplified in such laudable short-cuts as "Thou shalt not kill," "Thou shalt not steal," "Do unto others as you would have others do unto you."

Social isolation, particularly of rejection in a desired setting, is unbearable for the human individual as a permanent state. The state of normlessness is, for the human individual, a state of personal conflict or loss of personal identity. Why, then, denounce groups as such, or norms as such, or conformity as such? Instead, our efforts should be directed toward evaluating particular groups and particular norms in terms of the state of interdependence of human beings in given societies and in terms of enduring, lasting human values in contemporary settings—where what one does relative to others is no longer his own business. What one group does has come to be the business of all groups.

The huge task this implies also entails realistic assessment of the motivational promptings coming from the individual under the particular circumstances and influences impinging on him from his immediate and larger settings. If his group and its values are socially objectionable, it does not profit the knowledge of human action or practical ends to consider him apart from them. Nor are the problems solved simply by isolating him from his objectionable ties if these provide the moorings of his existence. The task is not as simple as erasing his observances and conformities. It is the task of providing group moorings with socially desirable values and goals as integral parts of these moorings. Only in this way can he develop a new sense of self-identity, for observance of values that are not in conflict with the human sense of challenge, that are not in conflict with the enduring and lasting values of his larger setting and other groups in a shrinking world.

THE DISCUSSION GROUP AND DEMOCRATIC BEHAVIOR

Queens College and the Massachusetts Institute of Technology

Milton W. Horowitz and Howard V. Perlmutter

A. Introduction

In the past 15 years there has been a resurgence in interest in the psychology of small groups. This was stimulated by the work in group dynamics, by the growth of sociometry, by group therapeutic procedures, and experiments on group processes. Concomitantly, there has been an interest in democratic and authoritarian procedures, the authoritarian personality, anti-democratic thought, and democratic group functioning. It is worthwhile to examine the relationship between the two, for there is no doubt that there exists some degree of confusion as to the possibilities of the democratic atmosphere.

Psychologists (in part, as private citizens), have been concerned with the problems of democratic and authoritarian group structure and the conditions under which individuals and groups function democratically. But there is great reluctance to consider publicly and seriously the term democracy as a useful psychological concept. Certainly, too, it is difficult to examine a problem without being affected by contemporary values and the cultural pressures that surround us. Nevertheless, the growing interest in group functioning in a country whose government is democratic has posed problems for the social psychologist: "Is the democratic group most efficient?"; "In what sense are voting procedures, or majority decisions, democratic procedures?"; "Why does one group become democratic and another autocratic?" These questions are not necessarily answerable for social psychologists. Certainly we cannot hope to explain the political, economic, and ideological forces that influence a nation in terms of psychological concepts.

It is fruitful to examine the relationship, too, because a kind of lore has sprung up with respect to the discussion group and democracy; a feeling, most usually implicit, that there are great psychological differences between authoritarian and democratic modes of thought; that there is a proper and an improper manner of group performance tied to the given values. Most important, perhaps, is the feeling that although discussion obviously does not in itself make for a democratic procedure or a democratic decision, it is apparently, the only path to that goal.

From, *The Journal of Social Psychology,* 1955, 41, 231-246. Reprinted by permission.

Historically, the development of the concept of democracy has been independent of the development of the concept of the group. And yet it is clear that democracy has no meaning in the context of individual (i.e., general) psychology. The concept of democracy demands a context of two or more people, and of the relationships between or among them, and hence, the relationship to groups. As yet, there has been formulated no explicit, systematic psychology to handle two or more people. There has been, however, considerable work of a more or less systematic nature done on groups. And it is for this reason that this work on the psychology of the discussion group is most pertinent to our discussion of democratic behavior.

We shall be concerned with some anti-democratic tendencies that exist in discussion groups. Most certainly, however, a great many, if not all, of the difficulties that have been raised with respect to democracy stem from two original arguments that have had long currency. It would be well to state these here.

1. *The impossibility of democracy.* This is a point of view that asserts that democracy, while desirable, is impossible, or at least extremely difficult. Therefore, having some body of leadership or some subgroup that controls the discussion is a necessity in order that the group be able to reach some kind of decision or move ahead, or that some kind of gain be obtained from group life. It really becomes a case of getting the right people in power, people of good will, of proper leadership qualities, and with good intent.

2. *The undesirability of democracy.* This is a different point of view that is based upon some of the aristocratic doctrines which imply the incompetence of the average man. It implies that democracy is possible but is really not desirable because only a few "better" people are competent to know what is best. This leadership may be based on intelligence. In a classroom discussion group the teacher becomes the real leader because he is appointed such by the institution to which the students are committed by enrolling. This doctrine often implies that appointed leaders are better, more intelligent, more sensitive, or more perceiving, and that they gravitated naturally to their position of esteem, and that others have a degree of mediocrity that does not allow their expression. This is the concept of the "right" man.

The distinction between these two general categories of anti-democratic thought is clear. One asserts that there are some psychological difficulties to achieving the democratic condition because of the nature of man. The second asserts that, even if it were achievable, democracy is undesirable. Clearly, it is possible to reject both categories of thought. The second category, that democracy is undesirable, is, of course, an assumption with little evidence. Its contrary or contradictory can be assumed with a somewhat greater weight of evidence to back it up. The first category, which questions the possibility of democracy, can be effectively handled by investigating the conditions under which democratic behavior can occur without begging the question.

In this paper we propose to examine in the light of contemporary social psychology and group psychology the concept of the democratic discussion group and some of the conditions under which it may be limited, or achieved.

B. The Discussion as Quasi-Stationary Process

Kurt Lewin(9) introduced the concept of quasi-stationary equilibria in group psychology. In his discussion of this concept he showed that group space can be considered a force field and that the group's behavior can be seen as a resultant of the distribution of forces within that field. The group process is continuously changing, of course, and among other things, the number and quality of the democratic decisions of the group changes also. At any one time, however, we may regard the group as representing a quasi-stationary process, whose resultant behaviors represent a compromise between opposing forces.

We may conceive of the group as having reached a given level at any time in its discussion, and this level will represent an equilibrium of driving and restraining forces.[1] Naturally, the relative strength of the opposing forces, the present level of equilibrium, and other conditions existing in the group space will co-determine the future status of the group process (as well as the group itself).

Logically, any democratic decision is a function then of two opposing forces: (a) forces toward reaching a democratic decision, (b) forces away from reaching a democratic decision. The "democratic forces" may arise from a multitude of factors all having a similar effect: toward increasing, representative, rational participation. Likewise, the "anti-democratic forces" may arise from a multitude of factors whose effect is also similar: toward decreasing, non-representative, non-rational, participation.

---

1. The reader is referred to Lewin, K., "The Conceptual Representation and the Measurement of Psychological Forces," *Contributions to Psychological Theory*, Vol. 1, No. 4, 1938, Duke University Press, for a statement of the logical properties and empirical coordinates of the concept of force.

It is not our purpose, however, to elaborate at this time on Lewin's fruitful theoretical discussion of the group as an example of a quasi-stationary equilibrium. Indeed, before elaboration is possible it is necessary to identify and evaluate the character of the opposing resultant forces. It is our task to examine several of the more important and more subtle of these forces as they occur in the group process. Some of the pertinent empirical work in social and group psychology is presented with this end in mind.

C. Anti-Democratic Forces

1. Interpersonal Factors

Research in social and group psychology has produced indirect evidence that properties of members of a discussion group and relationships between members can affect the quality of a group decision, i.e., will affect "how democratic" the decision will be. We shall consider two of these factors, power and valence, here.

a. Power. Particular individuals in a group possess power. Power may be defined as the partial or total control of the fate of other members of the group and would imply the capacity to reward or punish them. This property is *usually connected with the leader of the group* but exists in other group members to a greater or lesser extent. It obviously makes a difference to group functioning.

For example, both democratic and autocratic leaders possess power, but they tend to use it differently, and the former tends to distribute it (not often with success) and the latter tends to maintain it. Both leaders coerce, help, protect, and restrict but the democratic leader tends to do it benevolently. Both leaders show paths, indicate goals, control reward and punishment, and induce forces for locomotion into certain behavioral or interpersonal regions. Despite this confusion of categories, it will be agreed that some types of leadership can be described as anti-democratic. We shall discuss some of these in this section.

There is some evidence for the general intention of democratic leaders to establish democratic conditions, but there is also considerable evidence of the lack of democratic functioning in the actualities of group behavior. This is, no doubt, partly due to the difficulties of the leader in understanding fully his own motivations and generally, also, because of the nature of the situation in which he finds himself. For example, much of the work done on democratic group decision started out with the idea that a group *had to be changed* to some new way of behaving. By the technique of the "democratic group decision" a group was "convinced" that it needed this change. There is a serious question as to the extent to which the leader induced certain forces for change by relatively autocratic means, because he had the power to do so.

Another misuse of the power of the leader is that he may think of the problem in terms of the *productivity* of the democratic decision rather than in terms of the degree of representation of the group members. Although productivity must remain an important issue, no such pragmatism can be the basis for utilizing what appear to be democratic group conditions. Groups, for example, may be taught to eat beef hearts, kidneys, and other generally undesirable foods by a technique in which the individuals in the group are brought together and asked to discuss how they would convince other groups to buy such kinds of food. The question that must be posed is, in what sense is this democratic? What are the psychological forces that induce these group members to buy beef hearts or kidneys?

One explanation other than that given is that the group establishes some demands and responsibilities upon the members so that once the group commits itself, these group pressures act on an individual to do *contrary* to what he would ordinarily do. This social pressure toward conformity with some group commitment, as a group, is sometimes confused with the establishment of a democratic decision. Making individuals feel guilty if they don't do what they decided as a group, and merely establishing those conditions, cannot strictly be called a democratic procedure. Clearly, leaders must deal with the problem of the "democratic decision" achieved by autocratic means.

Another difficult factor to assess is that of the leader's motivation. It is certainly true that ego needs exist in all of us and must affect our behavior. It is one thing to attempt to be benevolent and attempt to distribute power and another thing to achieve it. Most group leaders have been aware of the tremendous unconscious resistances in group members to functioning democratically. The insecurity of changing to democracy is very real. Not everyone can accept it. Too many are already inured to the experience of catering to the needs of others. While there are tendencies among some group members to say what they feel, the comments made under these conditions of "new freedom" are usually hostile remarks made about the leader or the group in general. Of course this causes resentment in the leader who says rather indignantly, "Why can't these people learn to be democratic?" Leaders frequently experience this conflict based on the paradox that to be democratic a group must express its feelings, but in so doing the group is reducing the ability and tolerance of the leader to further its democracy.

Too much work has been done on leadership that has implied that some kind of training is instilled in the democratic leader, or that he must engage in some kind of activity in order to manipulate his group. It would seem that both autocratic and democratic leaders are trying to create a certain condition in the group and the very fact that they are trying to create it makes it necessary that they have certain powers in order to influence the group to change to whatever new state they want, even when judgments as to what the group really needs are incorrect. Even creating such an "innocuous state" as respect, or love, for the leader means that potential power and influence is available and is being exerted.

b. Valence. Group members also possess another conceptually different property: valence. By the valence of a person is meant his attractiveness and/or prestige value. A member with high valence (often the leader, but perhaps an expert or a personable group member), can exert anti-democratic forces in a direct way.

It is natural to believe that group decisions are entirely rational processes, arrived at by a logical weighing of issues and a mutual respect with give and take until a group approved agreement is concluded. There is pertinent research to indicate that such decisions are both less than and more than this(8). It has been shown that agreements (and disagreements) in purportedly democratic discussion groups are motivated to a large extent by the feeling of the person toward the source of the remark rather than by the intrinsic worth or content of the remark. It is interesting to note, too, that these experiments really confirmed some of the findings that had taken place in other settings.

We knew before, for example, of the halo effect, where a person's performance is judged primarily by feelings of favorable prejudice toward the performer. There is much evidence to show that the perception of, and attitude toward a person's act, depends more upon who says it or does it than what is said or done. The first reaction to this is that these data refer to relatively unsophisticated groups where reason is subordinated to feeling, but that the phenomenon does not occur among the sophisticated or among those of good will. A little reflection on the functioning of halo, prejudice, and the more or less conscious biases that exist in all of us will quickly dispel this belief.

Clearly, attitude is an extremely important variable in a group. We see that a person's contribution to the group process is very often influenced by how other people feel about him. Another way to make the same statement is that contributions to the group process may be rejected simply because of the valence of the person making the contribution. This means, effectively, that a particular person is denied participation in a psychological sense because he is the kind of person with whom one does not agree. It places a greater emphasis upon the desirable person or the leader, the well-liked person whose contributions are received, but rest less upon their merit as contributions and more upon the attractiveness or desirability of the person. The rejected member is not a participant in the group in a real sense because *his right to influence the group process is severely limited,* while others, perhaps more conforming members, are allocated a greater degree of influence, not necessarily commensurate with their skill, knowledge, or ability.

Perhaps of even greater significance is an extension of the principle that agreements and disagreements are tied to the valence of the source. For example, one of the commonest remarks heard in almost every group is the rather plaintive lament, "I said the same thing only five minutes ago and no one paid any attention to me!" Such an experience is common to all of us and yet its importance and meaning in the group process is usually overlooked. It really has a double significance for, on the one hand, the victim is disturbed and unhappy. And on the other hand it indicates that frequent interchanges of opinion in the group are lost—not agreed with, not disagreed with, but simply not listened to. Here exists one of the most subtle, most prevalent, and most insidious of all intra-group processes. For it really signifies that I regard you as so unimportant that I don't need to listen to you; or, I am so little concerned with others or so much concerned with my own thoughts, feelings, and difficulties that I cannot waste psychological energy on others.

We do not wish to suggest that many agreements or disagreements in the group are not necessary or that it is wise, or even possible to listen to everything. Actually, in the group, there are many behaviors which are perhaps only expressive, or allow for catharsis primarily— these are expressions of aggression, hostility, humor, all of which act as tension reducers and, once expressed, the group is able to move on, or the particular individual involved is more able to participate in the group process.

We are referring more to systematic rejection patterns in the group based primarily on valence of the particular person involved, or systematic acceptance patterns on the same basis. This, of course, is the danger in the establishment of sociometric structure, and assuming that this is a good basis for determining how well a group will function or whether a group will function democratically. A sociogram simply tells you the pattern of likes and dislikes. If there are strong patterns of mutual likes it is very possible that groups can proceed in their discussion on a "like" basis rather than on a "content-oriented" basis. That is, there are strong forces to accept another person's opinions because you like him and in this group everybody is liked. These are groups which are very reluctant often to express any kind of disagreement. The tenuous nature of calling such a group democratic is obvious.

No definition of democratic functioning of groups is possible without participatory rights of members, and these rights cannot be granted as in a charter, or a feeling of wholesomeness or benevolence, or through leadership training. There is the right to talk, the right to be heard, the right to be listened to, the right to benefit others, and the right to influence others. Clearly, no *democratic* progress toward action or content goals can occur until interpersonal and other intra-group factors have been resolved.

2. Group Factors

a. Pressures toward conformity. It has long been known that people behave differently as members of a group than they do as individuals although it was early thought that behavioral differences might be quantitative only. For example, a group might induce hesitancy or restraint in one individual and exhilaration in another. The three effects induced by the group which we shall discuss here must be considered as anti-democratic. They appear to operate axiomatically, by virtue of the nature of the group and the group process and the nature of the people.

We know that there exist great forces toward conformity in the group. The experiments on communication(4) and the influence process(5) indicate that communication among parts of the group is often based on a difference of opinion and that there is by implication a great pressure on deviant parts to conform to the group's way of behaving. Subsequent experiments have shown that in cases where the individual continues to deviate from the group process, he is eventually rejected and is not allowed to make a difference in the group process from that point on.

If a democratic decision requires representativeness of individual opinion, it follows that strongly-knit or cohesive groups give rise to anti-democratic forces which make disagreement with the majority undesirable and indeed "dangerous." Groups that feel they must reach decisions frequently use devices and techniques to insure conformity. Sometimes such a technique is used by the leader when he refers to "mystical group wishes." This very often takes the form of "what the group wants right now." In this case the referent is not clear, but the leader, because of his influence, can induce locomotion. Significantly, deviant members are almost always perceived as blockers rather than as symptoms of intra-group jockeying that must equilibrate itself before democratic progress toward action goals can be made.

Group members are aware, in a marginal way, of this induction of forces and of the pressures upon them. There is some awareness, too, that groups develop "desirable characteristics" from group members which exist relatively independently of their meaning to, or their importance for, the group process. This means that in many discussion groups, if a member does not conform to accepted ways of behaving, other areas of activity are affected, and the possibility of his helping make a decision or of changing or clarifying the group process is extremely limited.

a. Security. Cartwright(3) points out that membership in a group itself is a basic source of both security and insecurity for the individual. He defines security in terms of a ratio between the person's perception of his own power *plus* all friendly or supportive power he can count upon from other sources divided by the person's perception of the magnitude of all hostile power that may be mobilized against him (physical, social), where a power is friendly or hostile depending on whether it facilitates or hinders the accomplishment of the individual's goals. If the ratio is low, then security is low and contributions are ego oriented, the potency of success and failure for the person is greater, and he attaches more importance to his contribution and feels a greater need to defend it and have it be acceptable to others.

Obviously, the individual's insecurity can be exaggerated or lessened, both by the dynamics and interpersonal processes of the group itself and the relationship of the group to other groups. It is in the nature of people to regard themselves as positively valent and we may regard this, except in those who are excessively damaged, as a driving force. Concomitantly, other things equal, there is a tendency to perceive the groups in which we have membership as positively valent. It is when the group retains its positive valence for the person and at the same he perceives, correctly or otherwise, that his valence for the group diminishes or becomes negative, that insecurity will arise.

Clearly, feelings of relative security and insecurity will fluctuate with a great many variables, including the stability of the group process, but withal this factor can often be considered as a source of anti-democratic forces.

c. Group growth. As was indicated earlier, from the time of a group's inception its process fluctuates while various intra-group factors are becoming stabilized. At different steps in the group's growth anti-democratic forces are inevitable.

It has been suggested that there are different phases of group development. Early stages are frequently characterized by strong dependency on the leader and group members show unwillingness to contradict him. Subgroups are formed on various interpersonal bases (and ecological factors are important, too). Other phases are characterized by strong needs for harmony and low tolerance for disagreement, or diverging points of view.

In the early life of a group we may expect more and greater fluctuations since forces will be in imbalance. Later, when some stability is achieved, opposing and conflicting forces can appear at relatively high strength and we may expect a higher level of tension in the group.

Depending then on the maturity of the group, and the number and kinds of stresses confronting the group at any one time, democratic functioning may be more difficult, or even impossible to achieve.

3. Personality Factors

a. The authoritarian personality. Since a democratic followership is as vital to democratic group functioning as is democratic leadership, it is pertinent to reflect upon its relationship to personality variables. We have mentioned in passing that certain anti-democratic personalities may exist. Lippitt(10) spoke of such behavior; Adorno, Frenkel-Brunswik, *et al.* (1) wrote of them in detail; therapists and clinicians of all persuasions have known of them. Fromm(6) speaks generally as if a whole population can have some anti-democratic needs, needs to "escape from freedom," as he calls it. Although it is impossible at this time to assess the relative importance of this factor since personality variables are ecological in group psychology, it is certainly a limiting condition to any sort of democratic functioning.

One of the real dilemmas of group psychology is the extent to which personality variables do make a difference to group functioning. All groups have known of, and are disturbed by, deviant group members and, indeed, we have discussed some of the techniques used to keep group members in line. Some of the early work on the discussion group(2, p. 45) attempted to face this difficult problem and discovered empirically that three roles could be distinguished, namely, group task roles, group building and maintenance roles, and individual roles. Individual roles are "bad." As a matter of fact, "A high incidence of 'individual-centered' as opposed to 'group-centered' participation in a group always calls for self-diagnosis of the group. The diagnosis may reveal one or several of a number of conditions—low level of skill training among members, including the group leaders; the prevalence of 'authoritarian' and 'laissez-faire' points of view toward group functioning in the group; a low level of group maturity, discipline and morale; an inappropriately chosen and inadequately defined group task, etc." It is clear that the feeling that some kind of training is necessary to induce people to behave democratically is persistent.

There can be no question, however, that ego needs exist in all of us, now and forever, and, further, they are not to be eliminated. Indeed, it can be shown that it is difficult, and frequently impossible, for a modern parent to submerge, or hold in abeyance, his own needs with respect to his family or his child. It is patently easier to be "individually oriented" where semi-strangers are concerned. But this by no means illustrates the magnitude of the problem for there are many individuals with deep and central needs who are pushed into "anti-democratic" activity. Where behavior is driven by strong needs, compulsive and stereotyped, without spontaneity, and with relatively little influence from outside, it is probable that such a person could not behave "democratically" without considerable therapy.

It is interesting to draw out the implications of this problem. For example, we have seen that some degree of security in the group is a necessity before ego needs can be submerged. The interesting issue, however, concerns the possibility of the elimination of insecurity and here the principles of psychology give us little reason for feeling sanguine. For there are, to a greater or lesser degree, strong and hostile feelings in all of us ready to manifest themselves under the proper psychological conditions. *Group members have valence.* It is simply the fact of psychological life and it will do little good to consider this fact unfortunate. Indeed, it has been shown that the person who is neutral is in even a worse situation. There are strong (and complicated) tendencies to disagree, and also, strong group pressures to agree. There is no moral value to be attached to closure which operates axiomatically in all perception—and yet it leads us to connect people and acts in unit formation. Worse yet, from the dynamics of energy, as well as from empirical studies, we know that simple structure, perceptually, is the rule, and *intolerance of ambiguity* is an easier psychological resolution than its more sophisticated counterpart.

D. Democratic Forces

We have presented evidence to indicate that some types of leadership which are not autocratic in the usual sense must nevertheless be considered as anti-democratic forces. We have also explored some group processes and interpersonal relationships that have the appearance, if not the function, of making the democratic process extremely difficult, and we have shown, in cursory fashion, how personality factors are a limiting condition to any democratic procedure. It is clear that these difficulties are important and serious, and it is certain that if the conditions of democracy in the discussion group exist they must be defined in spite of these factors rather than because of them. We turn now to factors that may be labelled democratic forces.

1. Power and Leadership

We have previously stated that imposed leadership, however benevolently advanced, cannot meet the needs of democratic functioning. It is our belief that the first necessary condition of democracy in the discussion group is the concept of functional leadership.

Actually, the line of thinking that defines democracy (at least initially) in the group by the democratic leader and seeks means to create such a leader, is misguided. There is strong evidence that a democratic followership is equally necessary for a democratic leader and, additionally, the whole conception of the functional leader means that leadership is distributed among the group members— distributed to those members who are most capable at a particular time to sense and mirror the group's needs. It is significant that one of the most noteworthy differences between the democratic and the autocratic group procedures given in the literature is the emphasis that the democratic leader's only function is to act as a mirror for the group, that he should create a permissive atmosphere and he does this by instilling a precedent for free discussion.

The concept of functional leadership stressed by Main and Nyswander(11) is especially appropriate:

> Leadership is not a property of any individual but is a function of the group. Leadership is not necessarily an explicitly declared position but is conferred during group action, sometimes without either the group or the

individual being aware of the process by which this is done. Moreover, leadership varies with the task of the group and may move from one individual to another as the group finds it suitable. It seems to us, then, that leadership is quite different from mere participation by a member who for the moment may hold the attention of the group. Ordinary member contributions are usually listened to with respect and critical evaluation and provoke further contributions in other members. . . Leadership tends to remain with the individual who gives the group the best solution until such times as he can no longer meet its needs.

It is clear that no self-given leader, whether imposed by an institution, by natural ability of one sort or another, or by virtue of the dubious distinction of an election, can square with any realistic concept of democracy or democratic group functioning.[2] In the concept of functional leadership we have a definition of democratic leadership that suggests that *any member may take over the group process at any time and may have some of the administrative and executive powers necessary to move the group, and the group may always have the right to resist these powers.* It is necessary that the powers delegated to any particular person be tentative and that the group does not start with an imposed leader who by his very position in the group must constantly exert forces to maintain this position under the guise of being a benevolent leader.

2. Group Factors

We have stated that imposed leadership, however benevolently advanced, is not likely to meet the demands of democratic functioning, and that the first necessary condition of democracy in the discussion group is the concept of functional spontaneous leadership, in which the leadership function is passed to any group member who can meet the needs of the group at the time. It is more difficult to see how group phenomena and personality variables can be consonant with democratic function. Let us examine each in turn.

a. Feedback. We have seen that there is evidence for the acceptance and rejection of contribution based on personal likes or dislikes and we have here the interesting problem of how a particular anti-democratic interaction can influence the total group process. We see here examples of many kinds of groups whose process is characterized by a number of anti-democratic actions, agreements or disagreements that take place primarily because of the valence of the other person. And yet, counterbalancing processes are set up, either

---

2. The exception here might be an enlightened "imposed leader" who will allow for functional leadership to arise. In this sense he can be a democratic force.

in the form of systematic feedback, or because the group has achieved some democratic norms and is able to reflect upon its own process, re-examine it, and change it from its state of relative autocracy to relative democracy.

The work of the group dynamicists has emphasized the importance of feedback. With the help of an observer-member who is given the task of noting when particular members are being rejected, or when a decision is being pushed through by a "powerful member or leader," the group can constantly evaluate its decisions and increase the number of "democratic forces" in the group discussion.

b. Microscopic autocracy and macroscopic democracy. We have considered the fact that some anti-democratic actions that occur in groups are primarily expressions of cathartic behavior which are required because of the tensions and insecurities that arise in group functioning. By far the great majority of group behavior is not primarily cathartic and these behaviors are most easily explained in terms of valence and unit formation. We have described them as "anti-democratic" interactions also.

If we assume a different perspective in our outlook on these interactions, a new consideration and conceptualization of group decision-making behavior becomes possible. We have a unit of behavior—an interaction, an agreement or disagreement, or a decision—and this can be judged as democratic or anti-democratic. It is our premise that this judgment is not to be made solely in terms of the dynamics of the act or even on the basis of the statistical number of anti-democratic acts that occur, but rather in the context of the entire group process and of the *eventual influence* of these acts in the final decision of the group.

This formulation is, of course, tentative and open to criticism. It attempts to set a larger perspective for acts, which, viewed out of the context of their total influence on the group life, must be judged as irrevocably undemocratic. We have chosen to call the particular interaction that is based on the valence of the person microscopic autocracy; this is to be distinguished from a macroscopic, democratic group decision. The significance of this formulation is clear. Without it, or something like it, *no democratic decisions* in the group are theoretically possible. For, with the possible exception of cathartic responses, the psychology of interpersonal relations tell us that *all* group interactions are at least a partial function of valence, of closure, and unit formation, and of that most "intolerant and biased" process of having each unit maintain the same dynamic character throughout(7, 8). Only in the larger perspective of viewing these interactions in their total final or macroscopic influence is a second condition for democratic functioning possible.

3. The Democratic Personality

The problem of handling the anti-democratic personality is equally difficult. Here, however, the feeling is inescapable that some kind of selection probably has to occur before the democratic group is possible. It is trite but true that we cannot start with a group of psychotic (or even disturbed) individuals and expect them to behave democratically. Consider for example the rigid and inflexible person or those with excessive inhibitions, or strong needs. For some, unquestionably, adjustment to the democratic situation would mean the abandonment of defenses held through life and the "ephemeral" gains that might be won from participating in a democratic discussion group are small recompense for the tremendous price that must be paid.

If we ask what sort of person can be democratic, we can do no better than to utilize Wertheimer's eloquent description(12) of the ideal:

> Sometimes one sees a man, and by the way he goes through life, by his attitudes, by his behavior in dealing with life situations one feels: this is a free man, he lives in an atmosphere of freedom. . . . in the way a man faces counter-arguments, faces new facts! There are men who face them freely, open-mindedly, frankly, dealing honestly with them, taking them duly into account. Others are not able to do so at all: they somehow remain blind, rigid; they stick to their axioms, unable to face the arguments, the facts. They cannot deal with them as free men; they are narrowed and enslaved by their position.

It is difficult to determine exactly where this line of reasoning leads. But even though Wertheimer's description is ideal, the implications of it are clear. In order to have a democratic group you have to have people in it who have strong needs to be democratic. The danger in this assertion is apparent, for with human frailty there is always the possibility of casting away people who have *apparently* strong needs to be autocratic.

Too, research(1) has shown that there are segments of our population who are what might be termed equalitarians. They are able to accept intellectually and emotionally the relative equality of other group members. In our experience we have also found strong needs for complete representation and for allowing one's fellow members their "rights," at least among student groups. Unfortunately, research has tended to emphasize the authoritarian rather than the equalitarian personality.

A further limitation is the fact that so many groups are time-bound and concerned with production. We have to produce results now, in an hour, in three weeks, or a semester. This pressure for accomplishment unquestionably brings to bear many forces and excuses to adopt "more efficient procedures," which in a more realistic sense are simply more autocratic. The important thing here is to consider the growth and development of a group in its democratization, for a group can no more be made or trained into democracy in a few weeks (and without pain) than a culture change can occur soon or painlessly in a society.

It is true that personality variables are, theoretically, independent of the conditions of the social field of which democracy is a function. They are nevertheless, peripheral or limiting conditions of the foreign hull of the group field. It is in this sense that we postulate some level of democratic need or motivation as a third condition of democratic functioning.

E. Summary

We have examined some aspects of the discussion group and the democratic and anti-democratic forces that exist in it. In this paper we have limited our discussion to three main groups of factors; these are interpersonal factors, group phenomena, and personality. All three factors, embodying most of the usual group behaviors, are seen to be anti-democratic. It is shown that in all cases different behaviors are possible and with a different perspective these factors can be viewed as democratic forces.

References

1. Adorno, T.W., Frenkel-Brunswik, E., Levinson, D., & Sanford, R.N. *The Authoritarian Personality*. New York: Harper, 1950. Pp. 989.
2. Benne, K.D., & Sheets, P. Functional roles of group members. *J. Soc. Issues*, 1948, 4, 41-49.
3. Cartwright, D. *Emotional dimensions of group life*. (Read at the Second International Symposium on Feelings and Emotions, Oct. 29, 1948.)
4. Festinger, L. Informal social communication. *Psychol. Rev.*, 1950, 57, 271-282.
5. Festinger, L., Gerard, H.B., Hymovitch, B., Kelly, H.H., & Raven, B. The influence process in the presence of extreme deviates. *Hum. Rel.*, 1952, 5, 327-346.
6. Fromm, E. *Escape From Freedom*. New York: Rinehart, 1941. Pp. 305.
7. Heider, F. Attitudes and cognitive organization. *J. of Psychol.*, 1946, 21, 107-112.
8. Horowitz, M.W., Lyons, J., & Perlmutter, H.V. Induction of forces in discussion groups. *Hum. Rel.*, 1951, 4, 57-76.

9. Lewin, K. Frontiers in Group Dynamics: Concept, Method and Reality in Social Science; Social Equilibria and Social Change. *Hum. Rel.*, 1947, 1, 5-41.

10. Lippitt, R. An experimental study of the effect of democratic and authoritarian group atmospheres. *Univ. Ia. Stud.*, 1940, 16, 43-198.

11. Main, T., & Nyswander, M. *Some observations on the third national training laboratory in group development.* June, 1949. (Author complete.)

12. Wertheimer, M. *A story of three days. In Freedom: Its Meaning.* (Asher, R.N., Ed.) New York: Harcourt Brace, 1940.

chapter 2

Group Facilitation

THE GAMES INDIVIDUALS PLAY IN GROUPS
Eric Berne

Each individual enters a group with the following necessary equipment: (1) biologic needs, (2) psychological needs, (3) drives, (4) patterns of striving, (5) past experience, and (6) adjustive capacities. It is just this equipment which makes it possible for leaders to exploit their members for good or evil, and which hampers the independent flowering of individual personalities. But that is another matter which does not belong in a technical book on group dynamics, any more than a discussion of human morality belongs in a textbook of medicine. After he sees what forces people are up against when they join groups, the reader will be better able to form his own philosophy.

Biologic Needs

The well-known sensory deprivation experiments indicate that a continual flow of changing sensory stimuli is necessary for the mental health of the individual. The study of infants in foundling hospitals, as well as everyday considerations, demonstrates that the preferred form of stimulation is being touched by another human being. In infants, the withholding of caresses and normal human contact, which Rene Spitz calls "emotional deprivation," results directly or indirectly in physical as well as mental deterioration. Among transactional analysts, these findings are summarized in the inexact but handy slogan: "If the infant is not stroked, his spinal cord shrivels up."

As the individual grows up, he learns to accept symbolic forms of stroking instead of the actual touch, until the mere act of recognition serves the purpose. That is why the elements of greeting rituals are called "strokes." What is said is less important than the fact that people are recognizing each other's presence and in that way offering the social contact which is necessary for the preservation of health. Thus, both infants and grown-ups show a need for, or at least an appreciation of, social contact even in its most primitive forms. This can be easily tested by anyone who has the courage to refuse to respond when his friends say "Hello." The desire for "stroking" may also be related to the fact that outside stimulation is necessary to keep certain parts of the brain active in order to maintain a normal waking state. This need to be "recharged," as it were, by stimulation, and especially by social contact, may be regarded as one of the biologic origins of group formation. The fear of loneliness (or of lack of social stimulation) is one reason why people are willing to resign part of their individual proclivities in favor of the group cohesion.

Psychological Needs

Beyond that, human beings find it difficult to face an interval of time which is not allotted to a specific program: an empty period without some sort of structure, especially a long one. This "structure hunger" accounts for the inability of most people simply to sit still and do nothing for any length of time. Structure hunger is well known to parents. The wail of children during summer vacation and of teen-agers on Sunday afternoon—"Mommy, there's nothing to do!"—recurrently taxes their leadership and ingenuity.

Only a relatively small proportion of people are able to structure their time independently. As a class, the most highly paid people in our society are the ones who can offer an entertaining time structure for those whose inner resources are not equal to the task. Television now makes this advantage available in every home. In a group, it is principally the leader who performs the necessary task of structuring time. Capable leaders know that few things are more demoralizing than idleness, and soldiers have said that risking their lives in active combat is preferable to sitting out a "bore war." Psychotherapists see the same thing in a milder degree when their group patients beg them for instructions as to how to proceed and resent it if a program is not forthcoming. One product of structure hunger is "leadership hunger," which quickly emerges if the leader refuses to offer a program or if he is absent from a meeting and there is no adequate substitute. No doubt there are other factors involved here, but the fact remains that a long unexpected silence at any group meeting or on the radio arouses increasing anxiety in most people.

Because a group offers a program for structuring an interval of time, the members are willing to pay a price for their membership.

They are willing to resign still more of their individual proclivities in favor of ensuring the survival of the group and its structure. They also appreciate the fact that the leader is the principal time-structurer, and that is one factor in awakening their devotion.

The reason given by Mrs. Black for playing her games throws some light on why people seek time-structuring. Unless the Adult is kept busy, or the Child's activities are channeled, there is a danger that the Child may run wild, so to speak, in a way the individual is not prepared to handle. The need to avoid this kind of chaos is one of the strongest influences which sends people into groups and disposes them to make the sacrifices and the adjustments necessary to remain in good standing.

The need for social contact and the hunger for time-structure might be called the preventive motives for group formation. One purpose of forming, joining and adjusting to groups is to prevent biologic, psychological and also moral deterioration. Few people are able to "recharge their own batteries," lift themselves up by their own psychological bootstraps, and keep their own morals trimmed without outside assistance.

Drives

On the positive side, the presence of other human beings offers many opportunities for gratification, and everyone intuitively or deliberately acquires a high proficiency in getting as many satisfactions as possible from the people in the groups to which he belongs. These are obtained by means of the options for participation listed in the previous chapter. The surrounding people contribute least to the satisfactions reaped from fantasy and most to those enjoyed in intimacy. Intimacy is threatening for various reasons, partly because it requires independent structuring and personal responsibility; also, as already noted, it is not well suited to public situations. Hence, most people in groups settle for whatever satisfactions they can get from games, and the more timid ones may not go beyond pastimes.

Nevertheless, hidden or open, simple or complicated, a striving for intimacy underlies the most intense and important operations in the group process. This striving, which gives rise to active individual proclivities, may be called the individual anancasm, the inner necessity that drives each man throughout his life to his own special destiny. Four factors lend variety to its expression: (1) the resignations and compromises that are necessary to ensure the survival of the group. This is the individual's contribution to the group cohesion. (2) The disguises resulting from fear of the longed-for intimacy. (3) Individual differences in the meaning of intimacy: to most it means a loving sexual union, to some a one-sided penetration into the being of another through torture; it may involve self-glorification or self-abasement. There are differences in the kind of stroking received or given. Most want a partner of the opposite sex, some want one of the same sex, in love or in torment. All of these elements are influenced by the individual's past experiences in dealing with or being dealt with by other human beings. From the very day of birth, each person is subjected to a different kind of handling: rough and harsh or soft and gentle or any combination or variation of these may signify to him the nature of intimacy. (4) Differences in the method of operation, the patterns of behavior learned and used in transacting emotional business with other people.

Patterns of Striving

Each person has an unconscious life plan, formulated in his earliest years, which he takes every opportunity to further as much as he dares in a given situation. This plan calls for other people to respond in a desired way and is generally divided, on a long-term basis, into distinct sections and subsections, very much like the script of a play. In fact, it may be said that the theatre is an outgrowth of such unconscious life plans or scripts. The original set of experiences which forms the pattern for the plan is called the protocol. The Oedipus complex of Sigmund Freud is an example. In transactional analysis the Oedipus complex is not regarded as a mere set of attitudes, but as an ongoing drama, divided, as are Sophocles's *Oedipus Rex, Electra, Antigone,* and other dramas, into natural scenes and acts calling for other people to play definite roles.

Partly because of the advantages of being an infant, even under bad conditions, every human being is left with some nostalgia for his infancy and often for his childhood as well; therefore, in later years he strives to bring about as close as possible a reproduction of the original protocol situation, either to live it through again if it was enjoyable, or to try to re-experience it in a more benevolent form if it was unpleasant. In fact, many people are so nostalgic and confused that they try to relive the original experience as it was even if it was very unpleasant—hence the peculiar behavior of some individuals who are willing to subject themselves to all sorts of pain and humiliation, repeating the same situation again and again. In any case, this nostalgia is the basis for the individual anancasm. This is something like what Freud calls the "repetition compulsion," except that a single re-enactment may take a whole lifetime, so that there may be no actual repetition but only one grand re-experiencing of the whole protocol.

Since the script calls for the manipulation of other people, it is first necessary to choose an appropriate cast. This is what takes place in the course of pastimes. Stereotyped as they are, they nevertheless give some opportunity for individual variations which are revealing of the underlying personalities of the participants. Such indications help each player to select the people he would like to know better, with the object of involving suitable ones in his favorite games. From among those who are willing and able to play his games, he then selects candidates who show promise of playing the roles called for in his script; this is an important factor in the choice of a spouse (the chief supporting role). Of course, if things are to progress, this process of selection must be mutual and complementary.

Because of its complexity, it is fortunate that it is not necessary to consider the script as a whole in order to understand what is going on in most group situations. It is usually enough to be aware of the favorite games of the people concerned.

The Provisional Group Imago

There are various forces which determine group membership, and the individual is not necessarily attracted mainly by the activity of a group. If it is the kind of group in which he will meet other members face to face, his more personal desires become important. As soon as his membership is impending, he begins to form a provisional group imago, an image of what the group is going to be like for him and what he may hope to get out of it. In most cases, this provisional group imago will not long remain unchanged under the impact of reality; but, as already noted, the internal group process is based on the desire of each member to make the actual, real group correspond as closely as possible to his provisional group imago. For example, a man may join a country club because that will offer him an opportunity to engage in his favorite pastimes. If the club is not equipped for one of them, he may try to introduce it. Membership in any group that includes unmarried people is nearly always influenced by the hope of finding a mate, and this may give rise to a very lively and colorful provisional group imago.

Psychotherapists often have to deal with provisional group imagoes when they suggest that a patient join a therapy group. The patient questions the therapist either to adjust an imago he has already formed from reading or gossip or to start forming one so that he will know what to expect. If the picture offered by the therapist does not meet his desires, the patient will not be favorably inclined and may join only to please the doctor rather than with the hope that "the group" will be of value to him.

While the script and the games that go along with it and set it in action come from older levels of the individual's history, his provisional group imago is based on more recent experiences: partly first-hand, from groups he has been a member of, and partly second-hand, from descriptions of groups similar to the one he desires or expects to join. One branch of the advertising and procurement professions is particularly concerned with favorably influencing provisional group imagoes.

It should be clear now that each member first enters the group equipped with: (1) a biologic need for stimulation; (2) a psychological need for time-structuring; (3) a social need for intimacy; (4) a nostalgic need for patterning transactions; and (5) a provisional set of expectations based on past experience. His task is then to adjust these needs and expectations to the reality that confronts him.

Adjustment

Each new member of a group can be judged according to his ability to adjust. This involves two different capacities: adaptability and flexibility.

Adaptability is a matter of Adult technics. It depends on the carefulness and the accuracy with which he appraises the situation. Some individuals make prudent estimates of the kinds of people they are dealing with before they make their moves. They are tactful, diplomatic, shrewd or patient in their operations, without swerving from their purposes. The adaptable person continually adjusts his group imago in accordance with his experiences and observations in the group, with the practical goal of eventually getting the greatest satisfaction for the needs of his script. If his script calls for him to be president, he picks his way carefully and with forethought through the hazards of political groups.

On the other hand, the arbitrary person proceeds blindly on the basis of his provisional group imago. This is typical of a certain type of impulsive woman, who will launch a sexually seductive game immediately on entering a group, hardly glancing around the room to see what company she has to reckon with. Occasionally her crude, unadapted maneuvers may be successful, and she will get the responses her script calls for: advances from the men and jealousy from the women. However, if the other members are not so easily manipulated, she may be ignored or rebuffed by both sexes. Then she is faced with the alternatives of either adjusting or withdrawing; otherwise, she may be extruded by the other members.

The second variable, flexibility, depends on the individual's ability and willingness to modify or sacrifice elements of his script. He may decide that he cannot obtain a certain type of satisfaction from a group and may settle for other satisfactions which are more readily available. Or he may settle for a lesser degree of satisfaction than he originally hoped for. The rigid person is unable or unwilling to do either of these things.

Adaptability, then, concerns chiefly the Adult, whose task it is to arrange satisfactions for the Child. The adaptable person may keep his script intact by modifying his group imago in a realistic way. Flexibility becomes the concern of the Child, who must modify his script to accord with the possibilities presented by the group imago. From this it can be seen that adaptability and flexibility often overlap, but they may also be independent of each other, as consideration of four extreme cases will demonstrate.

The adaptable, flexible individual will carry out his operations smoothly and with patience and will settle for what is expedient. ("Politics is the science of the possible.") He is the rather uninspiring "socially adjusted" person that some school systems take as their ideal, the "common-ground finder" who sacrifices principle to convenience in a "socially acceptable" way. In certain professions, such capacities may be desirable or profitable and may be deliberately cultivated.

The adaptable, inflexible member will carry on patiently and diplomatically but will not yield on any of the goals he is striving for. In this class are many successful business men who do things their own way. The arbitrary, flexible person will shift from one goal to another, showing little skill or patience, and will settle for what he can get without changing his tactics. The arbitrary, inflexible person is the dictator: ready to accomplish his aims without regard to the needs of others and inflexible in his demands. The others play it his way, and he gets and gives what he wants to.

The above descriptions are transactional and refer to the individual's behavior in a group situation, but they resemble character types described from other points of view.

It should be noted that it is the group process and not the group activity that leads to adjustment. For example, a certain type of bookkeeper may never adjust himself to the office group; he may concentrate on his work and do it well while remaining an isolate year in and year out except for participating in greeting rituals.

The Group Imago

The complete process of adjustment of the group imago involves four different stages. The provisional group imago of a candidate for membership, the first stage, is a blend of Child fantasy and Adult expectations based on previous experience. This is modified into an adapted group imago, the second stage, by rather superficial Adult appraisals of the other people, usually made by observing them during rituals and activities. At this point, the member is ready to participate in pastimes, but if he is careful and not arbitrary, he will not yet start any games of his own, although he may become passively involved in the games of others. Before he begins his own games, his adapted imago must be changed into an operative one, which is the third stage. This transformation works on the following principle: the imago of a member does not become operative until he thinks he knows his own place in the leader's group imago, and this operative group imago remains shaky unless it has repeated existential reinforcement. To become operative, an imago must have a high degree of the differentiation mentioned in Chapter 5.

Grim examples may be found in the memoirs of officers of secret police forces. Many of these officers felt uncertain of their positions in the hierarchy until they thought they knew how they rated with their superiors, whom they were continually trying to impress in the course of their work. Once they felt that their positions were established, they were then able to differentiate themselves and their colleagues more clearly in their own group imagoes, whereupon they felt free to unleash the full force of their individual proclivities. They grew more and more confident in their atrocious actions and in their relationships with other party members as the approval of their leaders was reinforced.

A more commonplace example of operative adjustment is the case of the inhibited boy in kindergarten. He may find it difficult to associate with the other children until he feels sure that he knows how he stands with the teacher. Of course, this principle is intuitively known to all capable teachers, and they act accordingly. If they are successful, they will then note that "this boy has improved his adjustment and has now made some friends," i.e., he has differentiated some of the other children in a meaningful way. Similarly, in a psychotherapy group, an adaptable member will not begin to play his games until he thinks he knows how he stands with the leader. If he is arbitrary and not adaptable (e.g., the impulsive type of woman mentioned in the previous section), he may act prematurely and pay the penalty.

The operative principle may sound complicated, but it is really very simple. After a new child is born into a family, the other children treat him cautiously until they think they know how they stand in relation to the baby in the group imagoes of their parents, which they find out by testing. If a father is replaced by a stepfather, the wise child walks softly with the other children until he finds out how he and they stand with the new parent.

The operative principle is what makes it advisable to draw an authority diagram in considering an ailing group. The imago of each person on such a diagram operates according to how he thinks he stands with his superiors, and what he thinks they expect from him; this determines how he will behave in his role in the organizational structure. The primal leader, or the leader who is on his own, has to raise his imago by its own bootstraps, as it were. But even here the operative principle may come into play. An independent leader, such as a group therapist in private practice, may feel responsible to his own Parent, and his group imago becomes operative on that basis. Thus it may be said that the true leader of some psychotherapy groups is the therapist's father. The leadership slot in such an imago is occupied by a phantom, and the therapist operates as the executive of his father's canon. (Incidentally, a phantom is also left whenever a well-differentiated member leaves a group, and it persists until the mourning process is completed, if it ever is. Since only autistic transactions are possible with phantoms, they give rise to many interesting and complex events.)

The fourth phase of the group imago is secondary adjustment. At this stage the member begins to give up his own games in favor of playing it the group's way, conforming to its culture. If this occurs in a small group or subgroup, it may prepare the way for game-free intimacy. However, activity may be carried on effectively regardless of the state of an individual's group imago.

The four stages of adjustment of the group imago and their suitability for structuring time are: (1) the provisional imago for rituals; (2) the adapted imago for pastimes; (3) the operative imago for games; and (4) the secondarily adjusted imago for intimacy.

Knowledge of this progression makes it possible to define with some exactness four popular terms which are usually used carelessly and even interchangeably: participation, involvement, engagement and belonging.

An individual who gives any transactional stimuli or transactional responses, in words or otherwise, is to that extent participating. Thus, participation is the opposite of withdrawal. It may occur at any stage of adjustment. A member may participate in activities, rituals, pastimes or games, depending on how far his provisional group imago has been adjusted.

A person who plays a passive role in the game of another member, without taking the initiative, is involved. Involvement may occur with an adapted group imago which is not yet operative.

A member who takes the initiative in starting one of his own games, or who actively tries to influence the course of someone else's game to his own advantage, is engaged. This occurs only after his group imago becomes operative. As already noted, this may happen prematurely and inappropriately in arbitrary individuals.

Belonging is more complicated. A member belongs when he has met three conditions: eligibility, adjustment and acceptance. Eligibility means that he can meet the requirements for membership. Adjustment means that he is willing to resign his own games in favor of playing it the group's way. Such a resignation results from secondary adjustment of an operative group imago. Those who are "born to belong" are taught very early certain rituals, pastimes and games which are acceptable to their class; their secondary adjustment takes place during their early training. Acceptance means that the other members recognize that he has given up some of his individual proclivities in favor of the group cohesion, and that he will abide by the group canon. If he fails to do so, acceptance may be withdrawn. The sign of belonging is assurance, and the sign of acceptance is that the members give the responses required by the canon. If they break the social contract and show rudeness, the member loses his assurance. All this is well illustrated in the process of naturalization. The foreigner must first be eligible to cross the external boundary by immigration. Then he is required to study the canon of his adopted country. The better he adjusts his group imago, the more he is accepted and the more he belongs.

The Script

The script is the most important item and, at the same time, the most difficult to investigate of all the items of equipment which the individual brings with him when he enters a group. For example, in choosing a new president from among the vice-presidents of a corporation, a psychologist can test the capacities of the various candidates for the job, but the script will determine what use each individual will make of his capacities, and the script cannot be reliably brought to light by any form of testing. Its unmasking requires a long period of psychiatric investigation by a skilled script analyst. Fortunately, however, the intuition of the member's associates or superiors, especially those who have known him a long time and have seen him react to a variety of pressures, is sometimes fairly reliable in this respect. There are outstanding vice-presidents whose scripts call for them to excel the deceased president in effectiveness, and there are equally capable vice-presidents who may give no indication to an untrained observer that their scripts call for them to destroy what the deceased president has built up and also destroy themselves in the process.

The adjustment of a script is similar to the adjustment of a group imago, but the preparatory stages occur before the individual enters the group.

The original drama, the protocol, is usually completed in the early years of childhood, often by the age of 5, occasionally earlier. This drama may be played out again in more elaborate form, in accordance with the growing child's changing abilities, needs and social situation, in the next few years. Such a later version is called a palimpsest. A protocol or palimpsest is of such a crude nature that it is quite unsuitable as a program for grown-up relationships. It becomes largely forgotten (unconscious) and is replaced by a more civilized version, the script proper: a plan of which the individual is not actively aware (preconscious), but which can be brought into consciousness by appropriate procedures. The script proper is closely related to the provisional group imago and can be found along with it among the fantasies of a candidate about to enter a group. Once he becomes a member, the script goes through the same processes of adjustment as the provisional group imago, depending on the individual's flexibility. In a clear-cut case there is an adapted script, called the adaptation, then an operative script and finally a secondary adjustment. The similarity to the development of theatrical and movie scripts is evident, and sometimes it is remarkable.

Since some scripts may take years or even a whole lifetime to play out, they are not easily studied in experimental situations or in groups of short duration. They are most efficiently unmasked by a careful review of the life history or in long term psychotherapy groups, which are much better than individual therapy for this purpose. But in some measure, the script influences a large percentage of the individual's transactions in any group meeting in which he participates actively.

One of the easiest scripts to observe in action is that of the man whose individual anancasm tragically drives him to failure. He can be followed through his expulsion from college to his discharge from one job after another, and the acute observer can soon spot the decisive moments in each of these performances which set the stage for the final outcome and can see the same drama being played over and over again with a different cast.

The adjustment of a script can be illustrated by a more constructive example. A therapist whose protocol had to do with "curing lots of people" (siblings) had a palimpsest by the age of 5 where he would invite his neighborhood contemporaries en masse to his house to play doctor. The protocol was based on a beloved family physician and much illness in the family. The palimpsest was necessary because Davy's siblings, being of various ages up to adolescence, were not readily available for his performances, so that he had to fill his cast with extras off the street. The script proper was active for a while during his grade-school years when he would invite various clubs to "meet at my house," hoping in this way to become a leader. The adaptation occurred years later when he was able to become a group therapist, which was a socially acceptable way of trying to "cure a lot of people, who meet at my house." During the period of the adaptation, his efforts were tentative and not very successful. During the phase of his operative script when he took more initiative in structuring his therapy groups, he was more efficient but became heavily involved ("identified") with his patients. Finally, his script underwent a secondary adjustment, in which his therapeutic efforts were better controlled, involved fewer games, and were still more successful. He still had "lots of sick people meeting at my house" but was flexible enough to give up the magical satisfactions of "curing" them, acting in accordance with Ambroise Pare's dictum "I treated them, but God cured them." This "meeting at my house" was the first act of a long script which led to a satisfactory professional career when it was properly adjusted.

Summary

We have now studied the individual's course from infancy until the time he belongs to a group, the kinds of transactions he may participate in and the manner in which he sets up and becomes engaged in chains of transactions. This is sufficient information to understand the operations of any individual in any group in terms of social dynamics and complements the study of the structure and the dynamics of groups as a whole.

The most important hypotheses on which this discussion of the adjustment of the individual to the group is based are as follows:

1. Social contact and time-structuring are necessary for psychological survival and probably for biologic survival as well.

2. Therefore, the problem of the healthy individual is primarily to find a suitable group for structuring his time. Secondarily, he strives to attain the maximum possible satisfactions from the facilities available.

3. The secondary considerations lead to the emergence of a provisional group imago before entering the group.

4. The individual then adjusts his operations in the group according to his adaptability and flexibility.

5. His participation is programmed by a mental picture of the group, its social customs, certain idiosyncratic patterns of manipulation and specific predetermined long-term goals, or, more concisely, his group imago, the group culture, his games and his script.

6. He will not take the initiative in the group process until he thinks he knows his place in the leader's group imago, although he may be premature in his inferences.

7. The group imago and the script go through well-defined phases of adjustment.

THE PRESENTATION OF SELF IN GROUPS
Erving Goffman

Individuals may be bound together formally or informally into an action group in order to further like or collective ends by any means available to them. In so far as they co-operate in maintaining a given impression, using this device as a means of achieving their ends, they constitute what has here been called a team. But it should be made quite clear that there are many means by which an action group can achieve ends other than by dramaturgical co-operation. Other means to ends, such as force or bargaining power, may be increased or decreased by strategic manipulation of impressions, but the exercise of force or bargaining power gives to a set of individuals a source of group formation unconnected with the fact that on certain occasions the group thus formed is likely to act, dramaturgically speaking, as a team. (Similarly, an individual who is in a position of power or leadership may increase or decrease his strength by the degree to which his appearance and manner are appropriate and convincing, but it is not claimed that the dramaturgical qualities of his action necessarily or even commonly constitute the fundamental basis of his position.)

If we are to employ the concept of team as a fundamental point of reference, it will be convenient to retrace earlier steps and redefine our framework of terms in order to adjust for the use of team, rather than individual performer, as the basic unit.

It has been suggested that the object of a performer is to sustain a particular definition of the situation, this representing, as it were, his claim as to what reality is. As a one-man team, with no teammates to inform of his decision, he can quickly decide which of the available stands on a matter to take and then wholeheartedly act as if his choice were the only one he could possibly have taken. And his choice of position may be nicely adjusted to his own particular situation and interests.

When we turn from a one-man team to a larger one, the character of the reality that is espoused by the team changes. Instead of a rich definition of the situation, reality may become reduced to a thin party line, for one may expect the line to be unequally congenial to the members of the team. We may expect ironic remarks by which a teammate jokingly rejects the line while seriously accepting it. On

---

the other hand, there will be the new factor of loyalty to one's team and one's teammates to provide support for the team's line.

It seems to be generally felt that public disagreement among the members of the team not only incapacitates them for united action but also embarrasses the reality sponsored by the team. To protect this impression of reality, members of the team may be required to postpone taking public stands until the position of the team has been settled; and once the team's stand has been taken, all members may be obliged to follow it. . . .

However, unanimity is often not the sole requirement of the team's projection. There seems to be a general feeling that the most real and solid things in life are ones whose description individuals independently agree upon. We tend to feel that if two participants in an event decide to be as honest as they can in recounting it, then the stands they take will be acceptably similar even though they do not consult one another prior to their presentation. Intention to tell the truth presumably makes such prior consultation unnecessary. And we also tend to feel that if the two individuals wish to tell a lie or to slant the version of the event which they offer, then not only will it be necessary for them to consult with one another in order, as we say, "to get their story straight," but it will also be necessary to conceal the fact that an opportunity for such prior consultation was available to them. In other words, in staging a definition of the situation, it may be necessary for the several members of the team to be unanimous in the positions they take and secretive about the fact that these positions were not independently arrived at. (Incidentally, if the members of the team are also engaged in maintaining a show of self-respect before one another, it may be necessary for the members of the team to learn what the line is to be, and take it, without admitting to themselves and to one another the extent to which their position is not independently arrived at, but such problems carry us somewhat beyond the team-performance as the basic point of reference.)

It should be noted that just as a teammate ought to wait for the official word before taking his stand, so the official word ought to be made available to him so that he can play his part on the team and feel a part of it. For example, in commenting on how some Chinese merchants set the price of their goods according to the appearance of the customer, one writer goes on to say:

> One particular result of this study of a customer is seen in the fact that if a person enters a store in China, and, after examining several articles, asks the price of any one of them, unless it is positively known that he has

spoken to but one clerk, no answer will be made by him to whom the question is put until every other clerk has been asked if he has named a price for the article in question to the gentleman. If, as very rarely happens, this important precaution is neglected, the sum named by different clerks will almost invariably be unlike, thus showing that they fail to agree in their estimates of the customer.[1]

To withhold from a teammate information about the stand his team is taking is in fact to withhold his character from him, for without knowing what stand he will be taking he may not be able to assert a self to the audience. Thus, if a surgeon is to operate on a patient referred to him by another doctor, common courtesy may oblige the surgeon to tell the referring doctor when the operation will be and, if the referring doctor does not appear at the operation, to telephone him the result of the operation. By thus being "filled in," the referring doctor can, more effectively than otherwise, present himself to the patient's kinfolk as someone who is participating in the medical action.[2]

I would like to add a further general fact about maintaining the line during a performance. When a member of the team makes a mistake in the presence of the audience, the other team members often must suppress their immediate desire to punish and instruct the offender until, that is, the audience is no longer present. After all, immediate corrective sanctioning would often only disturb the interaction further and, as previously suggested, make the audience privy to a view that ought to be reserved for teammates. Thus, in authoritarian organizations, where a team of superordinates maintains a show of being right every time and of possessing a united front, there is often a strict rule that one superordinate must now show hostility or disrespect toward any other superordinate while in the presence of a member of the subordinate team. Army officers show consensus when before enlisted men, parents when before children,[3] managers when before workers, nurses when before patients,[4] and the like. Of course, when the subordinates are absent, open, violent criticism may

---

1. Chester Holcombe, *The Real Chinaman* (New York: Dodd, Mead, 1895), p. 293.
2. Solomon, *op. cit.,* p. 75.
3. An interesting dramaturgical difficulty in the family is that sex and lineal solidarity, which crosscut conjugal solidarity, make it difficult for husband and wife to "back each other up" in a show of authority before children or a show of either distance or familiarity with extended kin. As previously suggested, such crosscutting lines of affiliation prevent the widening of structural cleavages.
4. Taxel, *op. cit.,* pp. 53-54.

and does occur. For example, in a recent study of the teaching profession, it was found that teachers felt that if they are to sustain an impression of professional competence and institutional authority, they must make sure that when angry parents come to the school with complaints, the principal will support the position of his staff, at least until the parents have left.[5] Similarly, teachers feel strongly that their fellow teachers ought not to disagree with or contradict them in front of students. "Just let another teacher raise her eyebrow funny, just so they [the children] know, and they don't miss a thing, and their respect for you goes right away."[6] Similarly, we learn that the medical profession has a strict code of etiquette whereby a consultant in the presence of the patient and his doctor is careful never to say anything which would embarrass the impression of competence that the patient's doctor is attempting to maintain. As Hughes suggests, "The [professional] *etiquette* is a body of ritual which grows up informally to preserve, before the clients, the common front of the profession."[7] And, of course, this kind of solidarity in the presence of subordinates also occurs when performers are in the presence of superordinates. For example, in a recent study of the police we learn that a patrolling team of two policemen, who witness each other's illegal and semi-illegal acts and who are in an excellent position to discredit each other's show of legality before the judge, possess heroic solidarity and will stick by each other's story no matter what atrocity it covers up or how little chance there is of anyone believing it.[8]

It is apparent that if performers are concerned with maintaining a line they will select as teammates those who can be trusted to perform properly. Thus children of the house are often excluded from performances given for guests of a domestic establishment because often children cannot be trusted to "behave" themselves, i.e., to refrain from acting in a way inconsistent with the impression that is being fostered.[9] Similarly, those who are known to become intoxi-

---

5. Howard S. Becker, "The Teacher in the Authority System of the Public School," *Journal of Educational Sociology*, XXVII, p. 134.

6. *Ibid.*, from an interview, p. 139.

7. E.C. Hughes, "Institutions," *New Outline of the Principles of Sociology*, ed. Alfred M. Lee (New York: Barnes and Noble, 1946), p. 273.

8. William Westley, "The Police" (unpublished Ph.D. dissertation, Department of Sociology, University of Chicago, 1952), pp. 187-96.

9. In so far as children are defined as "non-persons" they have some license to commit gauche acts without requiring the audience to take the expressive implications of these acts too seriously. However, whether treated as non-persons or not, children are in a position to disclose crucial secrets.

cated when drink is available and who become verbose or "difficult" when his occurs constitute a performance risk, as do those who are sober but foolishly indiscreet, and those who refuse to "enter into the spirit" of the occasion and help sustain the impression that guests tacitly unite in maintaining to the host. . . .

A team, then, may be defined as a set of individuals whose intimate co-operation is required if a given projected definition of the situation is to be maintained. A team is a grouping, but it is a grouping not in relation to a social structure or social organization but rather in relation to an interaction or series of interactions in which the relevant definition of the situation is maintained.

We have seen, and will see further, that if a performance is to be effective it will be likely that the extent and character of the co-operation that makes this possible will be concealed and kept secret. A team, then, has something of the character of a secret society. The audience may appreciate, of course, that all the members of the team are held together by a bond no member of the audience shares. Thus, for example, when customers enter a service establishment, they clearly appreciate that all employees are different from customers by virtue of this official role. However, the individuals who are on the staff of an establishment are not members of a team by virtue of staff status, but only by virtue of the co-operation which they maintain in order to sustain a given definition of the situation. No effort may be made in many cases to conceal who is on the staff; but they form a secret society, a team, in so far as a secret is kept as to how they are co-operating together to maintain a particular definition of the situation. Teams may be created by individuals to aid the group they are members of, but in aiding themselves and their group in this dramaturgical way, they are acting as a team, not a group. Thus a team, as used herein, is the kind of secret society whose members may be known by non-members to constitute a society, even an exclusive one, but the society these individuals are known to constitute is not the one they constitute by virtue of acting as a team.

Since we all participate on teams we must all carry within ourselves something of the sweet guilt of conspirators. And since each team is engaged in maintaining the stability of some definitions of the situation, concealing or playing down certain facts in order to do this, we can expect the performer to live out his conspiratorial career in some furtiveness.

SYMBIOSIS AND CONSENSUS AS INTEGRATIVE FACTORS IN SMALL GROUPS

Edward Gross

The subject of small group integration or cohesiveness has attracted interest among researchers ever since Simmel speculated on the differential structural characteristics of dyads and triads. It has been a subject of theoretical interest[1] as well as a research focus[2] since it attempts to grapple with a question that lies close to if not at the center of sociological problems: What is the nature of the social bond? What holds people together in groups?

The present study is a segment of a larger inquiry into the significance of symbiosis and consensus as integrative forces in small groups. The concepts of symbiosis and consensus were first given wide currency in sociology by Robert E. Park who utilized them in the study of the community.[3] By a symbiotic tie, we understand a relationship of interdependence, which may be illustrated by the division of labor. Two people may cohere as a group if each has something needed to offer the other. A consensual tie, on the other hand, signifies a relationship in which persons are held together by agreement, by common subscription to a set of values or culture. Such groups are characterized by like characteristics among their membership.

From *American Sociological Review*, April, 1956, Vol. 21, No. 2. Reprinted by permission of the author and the American Sociological Association.

1. See, for example, N. Gross and W.E. Martin, "On Group Cohesiveness," *American Journal of Sociology*, 57 (May, 1952), pp. 546-554, and R.S. Albert, "Comments on the Scientific Function of the Concept of Cohesiveness," *American Journal of Sociology*, 59 (November, 1953), pp. 231-234.

2. See F.L. Strodtbeck and A.P. Hare, "Bibliography of Small Group Research," *Sociometry*, 17 (May, 1954), pp. 107-178. A large proportion of the items in that bibliography have been annotated and brought up to date in A.P. Hare, E.F. Borgatta and R.F. Bales, *Small Groups: Studies in Social Interaction*, New York: Alfred A. Knopf, 1955, pp. 579-661. For useful summaries of research trends and illustrations see D. Cartwright and A.F. Zander (editors), *Group Dynamics: Research and Theory*, Evanston: Row, Peterson and Co., 1954; Special Issue on Small Group Research, *American Sociological Review*, 19 (December, 1954), pp. 651-781, and H.W. Riecken and G.C. Homans, "Psychological Aspects of Social Structure," in G. Lindzey (editor), *Handbook of Social Psychology*, Cambridge, Mass.: Addison-Wesley Publ. Co., 1954, Vol. 2, pp. 786-832. Particularly useful is the well-chosen selection in Hare, Borgatta, and Bales, *op. cit.*

3. See his "The Urban Community as a Spacial Pattern and a Moral Order," in E.W. Burgess (editor), *The Urban Community*, Chicago: University of Chicago Press, 1926, pp. 3-18; "Reflections on Communication and Culture," *American Journal of Sociology*, 44 (September, 1938), pp. 187-205; "Human Ecology," *American Journal of Sociology*, 42 (July, 1936), pp. 1-15; and (with E.W. Burgess) *Introduction to the Science of Sociology*, Chicago: University of Chicago Press, 1921, pp. 165-166, 505-511.

The research reported here was carried out on an air force population in the Air Defense Command.[4] Data were gathered at one air site on group participation in six informal activities—eating lunch, drinking coffee, get-togethers (bull sessions) in living quarters, informal activity on the job (horseplay and joking), leaving the air site and spending time off the air site (dates and other recreational activities). These had been found, by prior observation, to be the major activities in which small groups formed or were observable.

The first procedure followed was to observe group interaction directly and to record that interaction. This proved to be extremely difficult, particularly since the air site population was expanded to several times its original size shortly after observation had begun, and the task of direct observation became wholly unwieldy. Men left the site continually and returned at random periods several hours later. Bull-sessions in the barracks went on to late hours and took place simultaneously in many rooms. It became necessary to devise an alternative procedure, which took the following form.

A questionnaire was constructed in which each man was asked to *recall* whom he was with at very recent, specified lunch periods, coffee periods, etc. Each man then listed those whom he recalled. Each questionnaire was identified. Questionnaires were then compared and the original groups were reconstructed. For example, in answer to the question: "Whom did you spend time with off the site last night?" four men—Joe, Frank, Tom, and Bill—gave the following names:

Joe	Frank	Tom	Bill
Frank	Joe	Joe	Tom
Tom	Tom	Frank	Joe
Harry	Bill	Bill	Jack
		George	

The criterion was adopted that men would constitute a group if they confirmed each other's presence (in the case of dyads) or if two men who mentioned each other both agreed on a third of fourth. In the above case, Joe mentioned Frank and Frank mentioned Joe. Therefore, they confirmed each other's presence. But Joe and Frank both mentioned Tom. Therefore all three were present. Finally, Frank and Tom, who we have already decided were present, agree that Bill was also present. Consequently, it was decided that these

4. The writer was assisted by three graduate students, Herman J. Loether, Duane N. Strinden, and L. Wes Wager.

four were present.[5] By means of this technique, a total of 182 groups, varying in size from two to four,[6] were obtained for analysis.

A measure of group cohesion was next devised in the following manner. After the respondent had listed names of group members, he was asked to draw a circle around those he most enjoyed being with, and to underline the names of those he "would rather not have had around." Each member's circlings and underlinings were given a score, and this was added to the score the rater received from other members of the group. On this basis, a score was obtained for each person expressing the degree to which he accepted others in the group and how others accepted him. These scores were averaged to give a single score for the group, which was called its Index of Integration.[7]

Each group was next analyzed according to its composition with reference to seventeen variables.[8] Each variable was dichotomized. Thus, with reference to age, the distribution was split at the median and all those above it were called "old" and all those below, "young." A dyad, for example, might thus be of three, and only three, types: both members "old," both members "young," and one member "old" and one "young." For discrete variables, categories were meaningfully combined. . .

A second analysis, which was possible with dyads only, made possible a refinement in the research. It was thought worth inquiring whether any types of groups might be found which would be neither high nor low in integration, but would exhibit only moderate integration. . .

---

5. This approach of which limitations of space prevent further description, offers a number of unique features. A reconstruction of a group is possible without direct observation and without even a full report from each man. In the hypothetical case cited, Bill's report was actually not required. Thus if he had been away, or refused to fill out a questionnaire, the results would not be affected. It was also possible to secure data on normally secret or private activities that could not be observed directly. The validity of the technique was subjected to rigorous testing, the results of which form the subject of a forthcoming paper. This testing involved a comparison of reconstructed groups with a time sample of actually observed groups.

6. Actually some of larger size were discovered, but their numbers were too few to admit of precise statistical treatment.

7. For further description of this measure, see E. Gross, "Primary Functions of the Small Group," *American Journal of Sociology*, 60 (July, 1954), pp. 24-29.

8. These variables were: age, marital status, siblings, nativity of parents, education, religion, enlistment career intention, months in service, months in other branches of service, overseas service, time in present specialty, technical training in the service, other source of income, pre-service occupation, and work section, time in present specialty, and present career intent.

The findings were next subjected to conceptual synthesis in terms of social organization theory. Observation and interviewing had led to the conclusion that groups could be roughly classified into two great categories: those in which members were interdependent because each satisfied some important need of his fellow—the symbiotic group—and those in which the members shared a value or goal or viewpoint—the consensual group.

Symbiotic groups tended to be composed of men of dissimilar or contrasting characteristics. This was found to be especially likely if the characteristics were related to adjustment to the job or to living or recreational conditions on the air site.[9] An illustration is provided by groups of mixed marital status, for example, a group composed of one single and one married man. At the air site under study, married men lived with their families off the site, while single men lived in barracks on the site. It was found that groups of mixed marital status could and did meet off the site in the married man's home and the single man was a friend of the family as well. In such situations, the married man tended to function as a link with home and family life for the single man. He was a resource to whom the single man, away from home, could and did turn. The married man enjoyed the role of father-substitute, and he offered the single man such help and guidance as he could. Typically this situation could fairly be called a symbiotic one. A similar situation was found to prevail for the other groups of unlike characteristics.

On the other hand, it was discovered that consensual groups tended to be composed of men of like characteristics. The formation of consensual groups was especially likely when the characteristics were related to adjustment to the Air Force as a whole and to its group goals.[10] This was found to be the case for the groups of like characteristics.

The explanation for this contrast between groups of unlike and like characteristics seemed to be the following: When men became upset about their jobs or air site living conditions, they needed and sought *help* from others. The persons sought out were likely to be men who had solved those problems or could help the men in trouble solve the problems (e.g., the single men seeking out the married man), and as such, were likely to be men *unlike* those who were seeking help. By contrast, men find the Air Force and its goals touch more significant matters of values and long-range plans. On these

---

9. The data in support of this generalization are presented in E. Gross, *op. cit.*
10. *Ibid.*

matters, they do not seek help—they are not "gripe" or problem areas which can be handled by going to a buddy. Instead dissatisfaction or concern in these areas was handled by individual decision: the individual sought out his superior or commanding officer and secured conclusive action of some kind. On these matters then, men were likely to find congenial others who had made similar decisions reflecting values similar to those held by themselves, and these were usually persons of similar background and personality characteristics to themselves. The neophyte who can scarcely wait to conclude his four-year "hitch" does not find the company of the old-soldier congenial.

These statements, however, do not imply that persons of unlike characteristics form symbiotic groups and persons of like characteristics form consensual groups. The relationship may be stated in the following form: *if* a group is symbiotic, then it tends to be made up of men of unlike characteristics, and *if* a group is consensual, then it tends to be made up of men of like characteristics. The reverse of either proposition does not necessarily follow. Indeed, the inability to make any direct inferences from a mere inspection of group make-up is brought out in Table 1. In this table are presented the findings with reference to groups that were found to be reliably *low* in integration. Thus, a group composed of two single men was likely to be significantly *poorly* integrated. The other findings may be read in a similar manner.

An inspection of Table 1 might lead one to conclude that three of the groups are consensual and three are symbiotic, and, since all these groups are poorly integrated, that symbiosis and consensus may act, not as cohesive ties, but as divisive or disintegrative forces. But the point is that closer observation revealed that none of these groups was in fact symbiotic *or* consensual. Thus, in the case of the two single men, their common marital status was the *only* thing (of seventeen possibilities) that they had in common (reliably, at the 5 per cent level). The group was of low integration because there were divisive forces present in it, and the common marital status of the members was not in itself a strong enough cohesive tie to offset the divisive forces. A similar reasoning applies to the other groups composed of men of like characteristics. Similarity of birthplace of parents and the fact that both men do not have an outside source of income are not in themselves enough to bind the men together to any degree. In the case of groups made up of men of contrasting characteristics, the point is well brought out for the variable of technical training. In Table 1 if a triad is composed of two men with such

training and one without, then the group is highly integrated. But if
the situation is reversed and two of the men do not have such training and one does, then the group is poorly integrated. Now, the point
is that the former type of triad was found to be symbiotic: the men
with the training were able to help the man without it. But in the
case of the latter type of triad, the common situation was one in
which the one man who had secured technical training had oriented
himself to an Air Force career whereas the other two had not. The
group was thus split by a difference in point of view. A similar
situation seemed to prevail in the case of the tetrad composed of
three men who did not plan a career in the Air Force and one who
did. The final tetrad type was split equally on religion and is suggestive of a coalition type of situation, but such groups were not observed with any degree of intensity, and no explanation can at present be ventured. But it did not perform symbiotic functions for its
members so far as was observable.

Table 1
Group Types Significantly Low in Degree of Integration

Variable	Group Size	Group Composition
Marital status	2	2 single
Birthplace of parents	2	2 American
Outside source of income	2	2 without outside source
Technical training in Air Force	3	2 without, 1 with
Enlistment with Air Force career intent	4	3 no, 1 yes
Religion	4	2 Catholic, 2 non-Catholic

From this point of view an examination of the findings suggests
the following. Of our *highly* integrated groups, four of the five rela-

tionships found to be significant involved symbiotic groups. These were groups made up of men of dissimilar marital status, technical training in the Air Force, and religion. By contrast, out of the *moderately* integrated groups, four of the five relationships involved consensual groups.[11] They were found to be characterized by similarity of career intent, service background, and education. We are led to the conclusion, then, that both symbiosis and consensus may operate as cohesive ties in small groups, but that symbiosis seems to be a more powerful tie than does consensus. One further point may be made. It will be recalled that our integration measure involved the expression of mutual dislikes and likes. Another way of stating the conclusion, then, is that in small groups men get along with each other better if they are united symbiotically than they do if they are united by consensus. So stated, implications for sociometric analysis of group composition would follow. It is often assumed in small group research, that work teams, for example, will have higher morale or productivity if the members prefer each other than otherwise.[12] The research described here suggests that such preference may be made more likely through putting together people of *complementary* characteristics, rather than persons of similar background or viewpoint.[13]

The most important question raised by these conclusions has to do with their generality. Although the analysis is based on a number of groups considerably larger than is usual in small group studies, these groups were all drawn from one unit of a military organization in Western culture. One would wish for replicated studies in many different types of organizations, and it is unfortunate that limitations of resources have so far prevented that kind of approach. Yet there is an important line of thought in sociology which suggests that *theoretical* generalization, at least, is possible.

---

11. It is difficult to assess the statistical probability of this number of relationships. If one thinks of them as being drawn from a universe of possible relationships, then the findings are distinctly better than chance would lead us to expect. For a given variable, 12 tests were employed. At the 5 per cent level of significance, we would expect .6, or less than one, of these tests to produce a chance finding.

12. See, for example, J.H. Jacobs, "The Application of Sociometry to Industry," *Sociometry*, 8 (May, 1945), pp. 181-198; Maria Rogers, "Problems of Human Relations Within Industry," *Sociometry*, 9 (November, 1946), pp. 350-371; and L.D. Zeleny, "Selection of Compatible Flying Partners," *American Journal of Sociology*, 52 (March, 1947), pp. 424-431.

13. It is no accident that Durkheim makes similar remarks with reference to the division of labor in marriage. (See *The Division of Labor in Society*, Glencoe, Ill.: The Free Press, 1947, pp. 56 ff.). As pointed out above, the division of labor is a major form of expression of symbiosis.

The concepts of symbiosis and consensus are, after all, special facets of a typological analysis of social organization which has been central to the thinking of a number of the major figures in the history of sociological theory. The distinction was recognized, at least implicitly, by Ibn Khaldoun[14] in the contrast he drew between the nomadic life and the sedentary life; by Henry Sumner Maine[15] in his recognition of law based on status as opposed to law based on contract; by Ferdinand Tonnies[16] in the distinction between *Gemeinschaft* and *Gesellschaft;* by Emile Durkheim[17] in the striking contrast between the two types of solidarity, *solidarite mechanique* and *solidarite organique;* by William Graham Sumner[18] in the distinction between mores and law; by Charles Horton Cooley[19] when he contrasted the concept of the primary group with the concept of the institution; and recently, by Robert Redfield[20] in the distinction between folk and urban cultures. It is not meant, of course, that these distinctions are equivalent. All that is being maintained is that, in spite of diverse interests and foci, an important group of scholars has recognized that a fundamental distinction may be made in terms of whether people meet as segmented personalities or whether they meet as total personalities. And this distinction is central to the distinction between, respectively, symbiosis and consensus. These are, of course, ideal types, and one should think in terms of a continuum between polar types with actual relationships falling somewhere in between.

In these theoretical terms, one may speculate on the differential cohesive strengths of symbiosis and consensus. In terms of the family of concepts of which they are members, symbiosis is probably generally stronger than consensus. What distinguishes symbiosis most clearly is that it implies a segmented relation and is least dependent for its operation on positive feelings. The relation between the shoemaker and the customer is symbiotic: each has something that the other needs—services, on the one hand, and money, on the other. As

---

14. See H.E. Barnes and H. Becker, *Social Thought from Lore to Science,* Boston: D.C. Heath and Co., 1938, Vol. 1, pp. 270 ff.
15. See his *Ancient Law,* New York: Henry Holt and Co., 1873, pp. 164-165.
16. See his *Fundamental Concepts of Society,* (Translated by C.P. Loomis) New York: American Book Co., 1940, *passim.*
17. See *The Division of Labor in Society, op. cit.,* Chaps. 2 through 7.
18. See *Folkways,* Boston: Ginn and Co., 1906, Chaps. 1 and 2.
19. See his *Social Organization,* New York: Chas. Scribner's Sons, 1909, Chaps. 3 and 4.
20. See his article, "The Folk Society," *American Journal of Sociology,* 52 (January, 1947), pp. 293-308.

long as those needs persist, and as long as each has no easy alternative way of satisfying those needs, then the two will be linked. This does not mean that they will necessarily like each other; it does mean that they will remain united *whether they like each other or not.* And therein lies the strength of the symbiotic tie. Consensus, by contrast, depends wholly on the strength of positive feelings. Anything therefore, which produces disharmony or a conflict of views is likely to break up a consensual group. It is, potentially, more unstable. These theoretical considerations do not, of course, prove or disprove any hypothesis. They do suggest, however, that the analysis of cohesiveness in small groups in terms of symbiosis and consensus should be more generally fruitful and theoretically rewarding.

COMPONENTS OF GROUP RISK TAKING[1]

Allan I. Teger and Dean G. Pruitt

Since Stoner (1961) first demonstrated that groups have a tendency to take greater risks than individuals, many studies have shown similar results over many tasks and conditions (Bem, Wallach, and Kogan, 1965; Marquis, 1962; Wallach and Kogan, 1965; Wallach, Kogan, and Bem, 1962; Wallach, Kogan, and Bem, 1964). The standard method for studying this effect consists of two steps. The subjects are first asked to make individual decisions on a series of problems in which it is possible to take greater or lesser risk. They are then placed in a group situation and required to discuss and make a group decision on the same problems. The difference between the mean level of risk taken initially by the individuals and the mean of their later group decisions is termed a "shift." If there is change toward greater risk, it is termed a "risky shift." A risky shift is almost always found.

Various theories have been put forward to explain this risky shift, and evidence has been brought to bear on some of them. The hypothesis that a value of risk in male society produces the shift was ruled out when Wallach *et al.* (1962) found a risky shift among women. Bem *et al.* (1965) demonstrated that the effect is not due to an expectation of sympathy from others in the event of failure, since those who expected others to be present during possible failure took less risk rather than more risk.

Wallach and Kogan (Wallach *et al.,* 1962; Wallach and Kogan, 1965) have theorized that the risky shift is due to a spread of responsibility. According to these authors, the fact that others are present to share the responsibility if failure occurs allows each group member to feel less personal blame for a possible failure. With less fear of failure, the group members feel free to take greater risk. While this theory has not been tested directly, Wallach and Kogan (1965) have developed evidence which they consider relevant to the conditions under which a risky shift occurs and hence the conditions underlying diffusion of responsibility (since they consider this to be the immediate antecedent of the risky shift). These authors found no difference

From *Journal of Experimental Social Psychology* 3, 1967.

1. This research was performed at the University of Delaware and was supported by Contract Nonr-2285(02) from the Office of Naval Research. This report is based, in large part, on a master's thesis submitted by the same title by the first author to the University of Delaware in June, 1966. The authors wish to thank Dr. John McLaughlin and Dr. George Hauty for their many helpful suggestions and Miss Bette Anne Lanning for her assistance in the statistical analyses.

in risky shift between groups that had to reach a consensus and groups that only had to engage in a discussion. Hence, they conclude that the risky shift results from some element of group discussion. They also found that simple acquaintance with the prior decisions made by other group members, without a group discussion, produced no risky shift. Hence, they conclude that the risky shift is due to some element of group discussion other than the exchange of information about preferences. They suggest that the "affective bonds formed in discussion" facilitate a diffusion of responsibility onto other group members and, hence, encourage a shift toward risk. As will be shown later, there are problems with the finding upon which this conclusion is based.

Brown's (1965) "value theory" is the major alternative to that advanced by Wallach and Kogan. According to this theory, cultural norms cause people initially to label most decision problems of the kind used in this research as warranting either a "risky" or a "cautious" approach. Such problems are said by Brown to generate a "value of risk" or a "value of caution." The implications of these labels are differently interpreted, so that in the actual initial decision, some people take more risk than others on an item. The risky shift occurs only with items that generate a value of risk. It is due, in part, to an exchange of information about initial decision during the group discussion. As a result of this exchange, most group members discover that the other members of their group have taken as much or more risk than themselves on a problem. Consequently, they begin to wonder whether their behavior is actually in line with the value of risk that they have adopted. While they thought that they were being quite risky in their initial decision, comparison with others suggests that they were taking only an average level of risk (or less). Hence, they become more risky on the second decision, in an effort to conform to the value of risk as newly interpreted.

The risky shift also results in part from persuasive communication. If most members of the group agree that risk is the correct value for the problem under consideration, then most of the reasons and justifications brought out in the discussion will favor risk. The subjects will then hear additional reasons why risk is correct, moving them further toward the value of risk, and causing them to take even greater risk.

According to Brown, the same two mechanisms should produce a shift away from risk on problems that generate a value of caution.

Brown's theory is supported tangentially by two lines of evidence: (1) Hinds (1962) has found that subjects typically believe that they are taking more risk than the average man in their initial decision. This supports the assumption that people are trying to be risky in these decisions. (2) Two of the decision problems that have been used in most of the studies in this area consistently show a shift *away from risk,* and Nordhoy (1962) has developed other items that produce a similar "cautious shift."[2] This evidence suggests the need for a theory which, like Brown's, accounts for shifts away from risk as well as risky shifts.

Kogan and Wallach (1967) have criticized Brown's theory as being inconsistent with one of their research findings cited above: that simple acquaintance with the views of other group members, in the absence of discussion, produced no risky shift. Brown's theory is vulnerable to this criticism, since he assumes that exchange of information about initial decisions causes people to revise their interpretation of the value of risk and, therefore, to shift toward greater risk. However, the validity of this research finding is in doubt, as will now be shown.

This finding (Wallach and Kogan, 1965) was based on an experimental condition in which the subjects silently exchanged information on their answers to the decision problems. The problems were dealt with one by one as follows: Each group member made a tentative decision, which was posted by the experimenter for everyone to see. Another round of choices was then made and posted, and this procedure was continued until consensus was achieved. No risky shift was found.

The validity of this result is in question, because the method employed appears to encourage group convergence on the mean of the initial decisions in two ways: (a) The groups were required to reach consensus. Under normal conditions, such a requirement would cause many members to stand fast and argue for their own viewpoints in an effort to sway the others in their direction. But in this case, the subjects were not permitted to communicate. Hence, the only strategy for achieving consensus that may have seemed available to many subjects was to move toward the other group members, i.e., toward the group average. (b) The subjects were told that their recommendations "should consist of what you think the group *can* agree on and what you think the group should agree on." Given these instructions, it is not surprising that a risky shift failed to materialize, since the initial mean is the most obvious point on which the group "can" agree.

---

2. However, the consistency of the cautious shift on Nordhoy's items is somewhat in doubt, according to a personal communication from Donald Marquis.

Not only is the finding based on this questionable method relevant to the adequacy of Brown's theory; it is also, as was mentioned earlier, the basis for Wallach and Kogan's conclusion that affective bonds formed in the discussion underlie the risky shift. Hence, this finding is of considerable theoretical importance and deserves replication with a more adequate methodology. Such replication was one of the major purposes of the present study.

This study was also designed to determine whether discussion will produce a greater risky shift than simple information exchange.[3] The earlier study by Wallach and Kogan also examined this issue, but it deserves to be looked at again in light of the criticism just given of their method. Wallach and Kogan would undoubtedly predict that discussion will produce more risky shift than information exchange, since discussion should permit the development of affective bonds that facilitate a diffusion of responsibility. Brown would probably also make the same prediction, since discussion provides everything that information exchange provides *plus* an opportunity for the presentation of reasons and justifications for taking risk, which may move people further toward the value of risk.

A third purpose of the study was to examine the relationship between the initial level of risk taken on a decision problem and the risky shift on that problem. One interpretation of Brown's theory would lead to the prediction of a positive correlation between these variables. This follows from the assumption that the value of risk or caution elicited by a problem will affect the initial decision on that problem as well as the subsequent shift. Problems that elicit a value of risk should show a risky initial decision and a shift toward risk; problems that elicit a value of caution should show a conservative initial decision and a shift away from risk. Hence, the prediction of a correlation between these variables. Wallach and Kogan's theory does not yield a prediction about this issue, since it does not deal with differences between decision problems.

The final aim of the study was to examine the relationship between group size and the extent of the risky shift. Both theories would probably agree that a larger discussion group should produce a greater risky shift. Wallach and Kogan might argue that this is due to the increased ability to shift responsibility in a larger group, while Brown might hold that more information is brought out in a larger group to support the initial value produced by the problem.

---

3. This and the prior statement of purpose are worded in a way that assumes we are dealing with problems that elicit a value of risk. This is because of a history of risky shift in most of the problems used in the study. Problems that elicit a value of caution should show some cautious shift under information exchange and a greater cautious shift under discussion.

Method

Subjects

A total of 165 male undergraduates at the University of Delaware took part in the experiment. All were volunteers for experiments on decision making and were paid for their time. They were assigned at random to the various conditions and participated in groups of from 3 to 5 students.

Measure of Risk Taking

The decision task was the choice dilemma questionnaire devised by Wallach and Kogan (1959, 1961) and used in many of their studies. It consists of twelve items, each of which requires the subject to give advice to a hypothetical person who is faced with a difficult decision. The subject must decide whether to advise the person to take a risky or a nonrisky alternative. If the risky alternative is chosen, he must also decide the minimum odds of success which should be demanded before choosing that alternative. In all items, the risky alternative involves a better outcome than the nonrisky alternative *if it is successful.* If the risky alternative is not successful, then the nonrisky alternative would be preferable. A preference for higher risk is indicated by choice of the risky alternative with lower odds of success. The lowest risk would be indicated by a choice of the nonrisky alternative.

All of the items are sufficiently ambiguous that the subject is forced to make some assumptions. This prevents an obvious solution for optimal gain. The questions cover a wide range of topics, with the stakes varying from money, to life, to a victory in a chess game. . . .

The results. . .reveal a significant risky shift for the larger (four- and five-man) discussion groups. This is in line with the findings of Stoner (1961), Wallach *et al.* (1962), Wallach and Kogan (1965), and others. On the other hand, . . .the smaller (three-man) discussion groups failed to show a significant risky shift. . . .

There was a significant risky shift in condition III, where the groups were able to compare notes regarding their decisions but were not allowed to discuss the items or decisions. This result is contrary to that of Wallach and Kogan (1965), and is presumably due to the fact that the present subjects were not instructed to try to reach consensus as were those in the Wallach and Kogan study. . . .

The results. . .are compatible with Brown's theory, which would attribute such positive correlations to the operation of a third common factor: the value of risk or conservatism elicited by each item.

Such a value presumably determines both the initial level of risk and the extent of risky shift. However, another possible way of explaining these results would be to assume that the two variables being correlated are causally related, i.e., that the initial level of risk taken by any person on any item somehow determines the extent of his subsequent risky shift. If this were true, then one would expect to find positive correlations between these two variables *across groups* within each item[4] . . .

It appears that there is no relationship between the initial risk taken by a person and the extent of his risky shift. Therefore, the most appropriate interpretation. . .would appear to be that initial risk and risky shift are both greatly affected by the nature of the item, as implied by Brown's theory. . .

Convergence Shift

The extent to which the members of a group agree on the answer to a problem can be called "convergence." The variance estimate calculated over the members of a group for a given problem can be used as an inverse measure of convergence. This has the advantage of being unaffected by group size, which was of course a variable in this experiment. The difference between the convergence on the initial decision and the convergence on the second can be termed "convergence shift." As a measure of this variable, we used the variance estimate on the initial decision minus the variance estimate on the second. This reflects the extent to which a group moves toward agreement on an item. . . .

Discussion

Exchange of Information

The results of this study appear to confirm the criticism that was made of the Wallach and Kogan (1965) study. With an improved methodology, a risky shift was found in groups that were not permitted to engage in a discussion but whose members could only exchange minimal information about their prior decisions. This finding is evidence against the assertion by Wallach and Kogan that group discussion is the "necessary and sufficient condition" for occurrence of the shift toward risk, and against their associated viewpoint that the risky shift grows exclusively out of the affective bonds that develop among the members of a group in the give and take of

---

4. If individuals who take greater initial risk show greater risky shift, then groups whose members take greater initial risk should show greater risky shift.

discussion. This finding is compatible with one part of Brown's (1965) value theory. Brown asserts that acquaintance with the decisions of others leads many group members to conclude that they are not sufficiently adhering to the value of risk, which causes them to become more risky in their subsequent decisions.

Discussion

A greater risky shift was found in the discussion condition than in the information exchange condition. This finding is in line with the thinking of Wallach and Kogan as well as with that of Brown, but for different reasons. The former authors would probably attribute it to the opportunity afforded by a discussion for the development of affective bonds, while the latter would probably point out that discussion provides a better opportunity for group members to acquaint one another with the arguments in favor of the value of risk. Since the discussion condition is compared with an information exchange condition that does not encourage a convergence on the prior group mean but does demonstrate a risky shift, the present test of the discussion variable is stronger than that in the Wallach and Kogan (1965) study.

Differences between Decision Problems

As in other studies, a shift away from risk was observed in most conditions for problems Nos. 5 and 12, though statistical significance could not be demonstrated for this shift when these 2 items were examined separately. The importance of considering individual decision problems is, however, clearly shown by the high correlations that were found between initial risk and risky shift, across items.

These correlations are compatible with Brown's value theory. One would expect an item that elicits an initial value of risk to produce relatively risky initial decisions and an item that elicits an initial value of caution to produce relatively cautious initial decisions. Since, according to Brown, the former kind of item also produces a risky shift and the latter a conservative shift, a positive correlation is insured. That positive correlations were found across the ten risk items as well as the full 12 items suggests the need for a slight modification of Brown's theory. Presumably all ten of the risk items elicit a value of risk. Hence, the variance reflected in these correlations must be attributed to differences in the strength of or adherence to the value of risk. In other words, in some sense, the value of risk or caution may be a *continuous variable*, ranging from strong risk to strong caution[5] . . . .

Though a high positive correlation between these variables is found in three studies, it does not necessarily follow that the decision problems produce the same initial level of risk and risky shift in all three studies. Indeed, problem No. 5, which produced a cautious shift in the Wallach and Kogan studies and under most conditions of the present study, produced a relatively high initial risk and a risky shift in the Stoner study. A possible explanation for this discrepancy may lie in the relationship between the subject matter of this problem and the background of Stoner's subjects. Stoner's subjects were students in a school of industrial management and presumably accustomed to dealing with risk in business ventures. Problem No. 5 concerns a businessman who must decide whether to build a factory in a country that may nationalize all foreign investments. It is not surprising that such subjects would attach a value of risk to such an item, although ordinary college students appear to attach to it a value of caution.

The line of reasoning just presented suggests that Brown's theory should be expanded so that the background of the subject as well as the nature of the problem is seen as determining the value given to a problem.

Group Size

The present study contains strong evidence that group size is positively related to the extent of the risky shift. A minimal risky shift was found in groups of size three, a moderate shift in groups of size four, and a large shift in groups of size five. This finding is compatible with the two major theories in this field: Brown can accommodate this finding by assuming that more arguments favoring the initial value of risk are brought out in a larger group; Wallach and Kogan, by assuming that a larger group permits greater spread of responsibility. The latter interpretation might be called into question by our failure to find any differences between larger and smaller groups in the amount of responsibility felt for the group decision. However, this evidence is somewhat weak because the validity of our responsibility measure has not been established, and it is quite possible that such a self-description is highly affected by social desirability considerations.

---

5. This notion is really implicit in Brown's second mechanism, that the presentation of arguments favoring the value of risk moves people *toward* this value.

Though a statistically significant risky shift was not found for groups of three (condition II), it would probably be a mistake to assume that no shifts were taking place, because high (and in one case significant) positive correlations were found for this condition between initial risk and risky shift, just as in the other conditions. The nature of the effect in this condition is somewhat mystifying.

Theories of the Risky Shift

Taking an overview of the findings reported in this study. Brown's theory seems to come off better than that of Wallach and Kogan. The case made by the latter authors for the exclusive importance of emotional bonds generated in discussion seems clearly mistaken. While the importance which they give to diffusion of responsibility is not directly examined in this study, the irrelevance of this hypothesis to the findings about differences between decision problems is damaging. In particular, the diffusion-of-responsibility hypothesis suffers by having no apparent relevance to the strong correlations that we found between initial risk and risk shift. On the other hand, Brown's value-of-risk theory clearly implies all of the findings in this study.

References

Bem, D.J., Wallach, M.A., and Kogan, N. Group decision making under risk of aversive consequences. *Journal of Personality and Social Psychology*, 1965, 1, 453-460.

Brown, R. *Social psychology*. New York: The Free Press, 1965.

Hinds, W.C. *Individual and group decisions in gambling situations.* Unpublished master's thesis, Massachusetts Institute of Technology, School of Industrial Management, 1962.

Kogan, N., and Wallach, M.A. *Risk taking: a study in cognition and personality.* New York: Holt, Rinehart, and Winston, 1964.

Kogan, N., and Wallach, M.A. Risk taking as a function of the situation, the person, and the group. In *New directions in psychology III*. New York: Holt, Rinehart, and Winston, 1967.

Marquis, D.G. Individual responsibility and group decisions involving risk. *Industrial Management Review*, 1962, 3, 8-23.

Nordhoy, F. *Group interaction in decision-making under risk.* Unpublished master's thesis, Massachusetts Institute of Technology, School of Industrial Management, 1962.

Stoner, J.A.F. *Comparison of individual and group decisions involving risk.* Unpublished master's thesis, Massachusetts Institute of Technology, School of Industrial Management, 1961.

Wallach, M.A., and Kogan, N. Sex differences and judgment processses. *Journal of Personality*, 1959, 27, 555-564.

Wallach, M.A., and Kogan, N. Aspects of judgment and decision making: interrelationships and changes with age. *Behavioral Science*, 1961, 6, 23-26.

Wallach, M.A., and Kogan, N. The roles of information, discussion, and consensus in group risk taking. *Journal of Experimental Social Psychology*, 1965, 1, 1-19.

Wallach, M.A., Kogan, N., and Bem, D.J. Group influence on individual risk taking. *Journal of Abnormal and Social Psychology*, 1962, 65, 75-86.

Wallach, M.A., Kogan, N., and Bem, D.J. Diffusion of responsibility and level of risk taking in groups. *Journal of Abnormal and Social Psychology*, 1964, 68, 263-274.

COOPERATION CONTRASTED WITH INTRA-GROUP AND INTER-GROUP COMPETITION*

James W. Julian and Franklyn A. Perry

Competition and cooperation have been in danger of becoming catchall labels for any research making comparisons among the performances of individuals and/or groups. Despite early recognition of a need for clarification in the area,[1] little progress has been made since Deutsch's classic papers.[2] A persisting ambiguity in the interpretation of much work comparing cooperation and competition results from the usual confounding of cooperation among individual group members and competition among groups.[3] Comparisons are actually made between two conditions both of which involve an important element of competition.[4] Hence, particular effects attributed to cooperation may well have been due to the competitive inter-group relations rather than the cooperative relations which existed among the members of the group. The present investigation examines the differential effects of purely cooperative conditions and the competitive and cooperative conditions more typically employed in studies following the Deutsch paradigm.

From *Sociometry*, Vol. 30, No. 1, March, 1967. Reprinted by permission of the authors and The American Sociological Association.

*Portions of this paper were presented at the Midwestern Psychological Association Convention, Chicago, 1965. The study was supported in part by a National Science Foundation Institutional Grant GU-908 to the senior author. The authors are particularly indebted to William N. Hayes and Jean Rickwood for their cooperation in the use of the experimental psychology laboratory classes and to Stephen C. Jones and Edwin P. Hollander for critical reviews of an earlier draft of the paper.

1. M.A. May and L.W. Doob, "Cooperation and Competition: An Experimental Study in Motivation," *Social Science Research Council Bulletin*, No. 25 (1937).

2. M. Deutsch, "A Theory of Cooperation and Competition," *Human Relations*, 2 (April, 1949a), pp. 129-152; M. Deutsch, "An Experimental Study of the Effects of Cooperation and Competition upon Group Process," *Human Relations*, 2 (July, 1949b), pp. 199-231.

3. An important contribution to the clarification of ambiguity in this area is L.K. Miller and R.L. Hamblin's "Interdependence, Differential Rewarding, and Productivity," *American Sociological Review*, 28 (October, 1963), pp. 768-778.

4. See, for example, E. Gottheil, "Changes in Social Perceptions Contingent upon Competing or Cooperating," *Sociometry*, 18 (May, 1955), pp. 132-137; M. Grossack, "Some Effects of Cooperation and Competition upon Small Group Behavior," *Journal of Abnormal and Social Psychology*, 49 (July, 1954), pp. 341-348; S.C. Jones and V.H. Vroom, "Division of Labor and Performance under Cooperative and Competitive Conditions," *Journal of Abnormal and Social Psychology*, 68 (March, 1964), pp. 313-320; B.H. Raven and H.T. Eachus, "Cooperation and Competition in Means-Interdependent Triads," *Journal of Abnormal and Social Psychology*, 67 (October, 1963), pp. 307-316; A.J. Smith, H.E. Madden, and R. Sobol, "Productivity and Recall in Cooperative and Competitive Discussion Groups," *Journal of Psychology*, 43 (April, 1957), pp. 193-204; E.J. Thomas, "Effects of Facilitative Role Interdependence on Group Functioning," *Human Relations*, 10 (November, 1957), pp. 347-366.

Some of the earliest experimental research in social psychology[5] found that competition on simple tasks induced high levels of motivation and greatly facilitated the speed or quantity of individual task performance. Deutsch,[6] however, failed to find such differences in motivation and involvement in his intensive study of cooperation and competition in the classroom. He explained his result by noting ". . . the co-operative groups were in a position of inter-group competition, thus possibly eliminating differential ego-involvement."[7] The potential significance of this inclusion of inter-group competition as a feature of "cooperation" has more recently been emphasized by writers such as Phillips and DeVault,[8] Shaw,[9] and Hammond and Goldman.[10] Consistent with their view, the present study contrasts a purely cooperative setting with the usual conditions involving group competition.

Three experimental conditions were created from the two factors of *individual* cooperation or competition and *group* competition or non-competition. Thus, the experimental design was an incomplete 2 X 2 matrix, including the following conditions: (a) individual group members competing but groups not competing (Ind Comp); (b) individual group members cooperating with groups competing (Group Comp); and (c) individual group members co-operating with groups not competing (Pure Coop). It was condition *c*, Pure Coop, which differed from earlier investigations.[11]

Although the recent literature has recognized the enhancement of individual motivation under competitive conditions,[12] no attempt

5. See, for example, N. Triplett, "The Dynamogenic Factors in Pace-Making and Competition," *American Journal of Psychology,* 9 (July, 1898), pp. 507-533; J.B. Maller, "Cooperation and Competition: An Experimental Study in Motivation," *Teachers College, Columbia University Contributions to Education,* No. 384 (1929); I.C. Whittemore, "The Influence of Competition on Performance: An Experimental Study," *Journal of Abnormal and Social Psychology,* 19 (October, 1924), pp. 236-253.

6. Deutsch, 1949a, *op. cit.*

7. *Ibid.,* p. 143.

8. B.N. Phillips and M.V. DeVault, "Evaluation of Research on Cooperation and Competition," *Psychological Reports,* 3 (June, 1957), pp. 289-292.

9. M.E. Shaw, "Some Motivational Factors in Cooperation and Competition," *Journal of Personality,* 26 (June, 1958), pp. 155-169.

10. L.K. Hammond and M. Goldman, "Competition and Non-Competition and Its Relationship to Individual and Group Productivity." *Sociometry,* 24 (March, 1961), pp. 46-60.

11. The missing cell of the design, individual group members competing with groups also competing, had to be excluded because of the limited number of laboratory teams available for the study.

12. Such effects were more recently proposed by L. Berkowitz, "Effects of Perceived Dependency Relationship upon Conformity to Group Expectations," *Journal of Abnormal and Social Psychology,* 55 (November, 1957), pp. 350-354; E. Gottheil, *op. cit.;* Shaw, *op. cit.;* Raven and Eachus, *op. cit.*

has been made to differentiate systematically the effects of individual and group competition from pure cooperation. Expectations with regard to differentiating the effects of the cooperative condition were here guided by the consideration that competition induces greater motivation and involvement. If we assume with Deutsch,[13] that individual and group competition result in similar motivational levels, then we can propose that competitive conditions will differ from non-competitive, cooperative conditions in the level of member task motivation, with the competitive conditions inducing higher motivation. Shaw[14] has indicated that although competition engenders a higher level of motivation, it leads to a decrement in the *quality* of performance when compared with cooperative conditions. Therefore, in the present instance, using a relatively complex task, we hypothesized that both individual and group competitive conditions would yield higher motivation and a greater quantity of performance than a purely cooperative case, but that the quality of performance would be highest under inter-group competitive conditions, where members could capitalize on both the higher motivation and the potential benefits of shared resources. Purely cooperative conditions would thus be distinguished by relatively high quality performance but a lower quantity of performance.

We further hypothesized that cooperative conditions, which included competition among groups, would induce more positive relations among group members. Inter-group competition appears to enhance group morale and cohesiveness by posing an external threat to the group.[15] It was anticipated that although purely cooperative conditions would not induce high levels of task motivation, they would also not produce the interpersonal antagonisms which arise under individually competitive conditions. Therefore, purely cooperative conditions were also expected to yield relatively positive relations among the members of each group. . . .

---

13. Deutsch, 1949a, *op. cit.*

14. Shaw, *op. cit.*

15. This rationale is well developed in the classic writings of Georg Simmel (see L.A. Coser, *The Functions of Social Conflict*, Glencoe: The Free Press, 1956) and receives support from the recent findings of A.E. Myers, "Team Competition, Success, and Adjustment of Group Members," *Journal of Abnormal and Social Psychology*, 65 (November, 1962), pp. 325-332; J.W. Julian, D.W. Bishop, and F.E. Fiedler, "The Quasi-Therapeutic Effects of Squad Competition," *Journal of Personality and Social Psychology*, 3 (March, 1966), pp. 321-327.

Method

Subjects and Procedure

One hundred fifty-seven undergraduate psychology majors at the State University of New York at Buffalo served as subjects. They participated at a regular meeting of the two-hour laboratory session of a course in experimental psychology. All students were in their sophomore or junior years.

When students met for class, they were randomly assigned to four-person teams.[16] Team members were instructed to work out the laboratory exercise together and were assigned to their own room. This procedure differed from the more usual classroom routine only in the number of persons working together (four rather than two) and the controlled assignment of persons to teams, rather than allowing students to choose their own lab partners. At the conclusion of these laboratory meetings the members of each team were asked to complete a brief questionnaire, ostensibly evaluating the conduct of the class.

Experimental Manipulation

The study took place during the first week of the semester when no formal organization for the laboratory meetings had yet been set up. Laboratory sessions are normally conducted by graduate teaching assistants and procedures have varied from semester to semester and from section to section. Therefore, the situation during this first week was fluid and ambiguous. This permitted the introduction of different experimental instructions to different sections without arousing undue suspicion. The entire study was conducted under the guise of trying out a different organization for the lab to see how well it worked. Thus, although the situation was experimental, it was quite relevant to the interests of the student participants.

The induction of cooperative or competitive relations took the form of instructions to the students as to how their laboratory exercises were to be graded. Three instructional sets were used: (a) grades will be assigned on an individual basis with the best papers receiving an "A," the next best papers "B," etc., regardless of whom the individuals worked with as partners (Ind Comp, i.e., individuals competing, groups not competing); (b) grades will be assigned on a curve, where each member of the team which turns in the best exercise will

---

16. When necessary, five-person teams were formed instead of four. In all, nine such teams were needed to accommodate all students.

get an "A," the next best team "B," etc. (Group Comp, i.e., individual members cooperating, groups competing); and (c) grades will be
assigned on the basis of number of points the team earns, where each
member of those teams which get 90 per cent of the possible points
will get an "A," 80 per cent a "B," etc. (Pure Coop, i.e., individual
team members cooperating, groups not competing). Conditions differed systematically only in terms of these instructions. Thirteen
teams were formed for the Pure Coop and Group Comp conditions,
and eleven teams were formed for the Ind Comp condition. . . .

Results

Performance of Laboratory Groups

Performance levels for the three experimental conditions were
hypothesized to differ in terms of both quantity and quality. . . .

These results strongly confirm the hypothesis that competition leads
to greater productivity. Both the Ind Comp and the Group Comp
conditions were significantly more productive than the Pure Coop
condition. Under the Pure Coop condition team members wrote significantly less for both items of the exercise, and in addition, they
offered far fewer explanations for the observed data. . . .

As noted above, two dimensions of group process were rated both
by the student participants and by an observer. These two clusters
were labeled social-emotional tone and task orientation and are presented in Table 2. In terms of the participants' reports, the least
productive condition (Pure Coop) was also the most positive in its
emotional tone. Members described their groups as warmer, happier,
and more active. These ratings were thus inversely related to productivity. For the mean observer rating of emotional tone, we find that
the Pure Coop and Group Comp conditions were more positive, with
the Group Comp condition judged most positively.

Turning to the ratings of task orientation, an opposite picture
emerges. The Ind Comp condition was here characterized as highest
in task orientation, though not significantly so for either the participant or observer ratings. The only significant comparison for the task
orientation cluster was the interaction between condition and time
of rating by the observer. Inferring process changes as the basis of the
direction of differences in these scores for the conditions, we may
say that team members in the Ind Comp condition became less cooperative, efficient, and relaxed, while Group Comp groups and the
Pure Coop groups increased in their task orientation over time.

Table 2
Mean Ratings of Group Process

Ratings	Ind Comp	Group Comp	Pure Coop	F	P
Students:					
Social-emotional tone	13.4	14.2	15.2	4.31	<.05
Task orientation	9.6	8.5	8.8	<1.0	N.S.
Observer:					
Social-emotional tone	9.5	12.0	11.3	79.55	<.01
Time 1	10.0	11.1	11.0		
Time 2	9.1	13.0	11.6	<1.0[a]	N.S.
Task orientation	12.3	10.7	11.7	1.63	N.S.
Time 1	13.1	9.7	11.4		
Time 2	11.6	11.7	12.0	<1.0[a]	N.S.

Note: The interaction of condition X time on observer ratings of task orientation was significant, P (F $\geqslant$ 5.07) <.05, for 2 and 34 degrees of freedom.

[a]F-ratio for comparison of time 1 and time 2 rating.

Participant Reactions

The participant reactions reported in the post-session questionnaire further specify an impression of the teams operating under these cooperative and competitive conditions (see Table 3). The items have been grouped in terms of a rough ordering of the means. Items one through five show that under the Pure Coop condition team members were more willing to work together again, felt greater responsibility for the quality of team performance, saw others as contributing more to team performance, described the group as more cooperative, and perceived one another in relatively more positive terms. Although some of these comparisons did not reach significance, they showed that in terms of the participants' reactions, the conditions involving cooperative relations developed consistently more favorable interpersonal relations among team members.

The additional mean levels of response shown in Table 3 were not as discriminating in terms of significant relationships. However, responses to items six through ten tended to show that the members of the Ind Comp teams had greater difficulty in communicating, saw others as more disruptive, initiated more structure, and described one another as more task oriented.

We note further that item ten, perceived task orientation of group members, included a judgment of the motivation of team members. Although analysis of the cluster scores failed to reach significance, a comparison of the mean levels of perceived motivation only was significant (P [F≥4.80]<.05). The respective means were 2.51, 2.06, and 1.95, supporting our original proposition that greater productivity under competitive conditions was mediated by higher task motivation.

Table 3
Mean Participant Reactions to Each Experimental Condition

Items	Ind Comp	Group Comp	Pure Coop	F	P
1. Degree to which you would like to work with team again	2.70	2.99	3.33	4.41	<.05
2. Degree of responsibility for quality of performance	2.88	3.35	3.54	11.45	<.01
3. Extent of others' contributions to task	3.98	4.04	4.51	4.81	<.05
4. Amount of cooperation among team members	3.80	4.15	4.17	1.49	N.S.
5. Interpersonal esteem	4.61	4.76	4.90	1.57	N.S.
6. Extent of communication difficulties	3.20	2.77	3.11	3.73	<.05
7. Degree of own satisfaction with grading procedure	2.74	2.56	2.71	<1.0	N.S.
8. Degree to which others initiated organization	3.11	2.80	2.70	1.38	N.S.
9. Extent to which others were disruptive	3.01	2.87	2.79	<1.0	N.S.
10. Perceived task orientation of group members	2.35	2.08	2.03	1.91	N.S.

Discussion

It was hypothesized that group members are more highly motivated and more productive under both individually and group competitive conditions than under purely cooperative conditions. This hypothesis was clearly substantiated. Team members wrote more, produced more ideas, and offered more explanations for their data in the Ind Comp and Group Comp conditions. In addition, team members working under these competitive conditions described one another as more highly motivated than did those under purely cooperative conditions. However, it was also hypothesized that on a relatively complex task, the *quality* of performance, evaluated in terms of ideas presented and their coherence, would be highest under the Group Comp condition and lowest under the Ind Comp condition. Contrary to hypothesis, in the present study both the quality and quantity of team performance consistently favored the competitive conditions with the Ind Comp condition being best.

Exploring determinants of this unexpected result led to the speculation that differences in the level of ability for the three experimental conditions might account for differences in quality of performance. Such differences in ability, however, would no doubt have produced average differences in the number of psychological terms used correctly. This was not the case. Apparently, sophistication in psychology did not differ for the three samples.

Although the focus here was the purely cooperative condition, the group and individually competitive conditions were also expected to yield differential productivity. It was argued that Group Comp conditions would be characterized by greater productivity as a function both of high motivation and the relative advantages of cooperative effort in the pooling of resources, distribution of sub-tasks, etc. Gains that would have presumably accrued here may have been offset by increased efforts to solve problems of communication, coordination and the pooling of task relevant information. Such difficulties could also account for the relatively poorer performance under the purely cooperative condition. This interpretation, however, was not consistent with the ratings provided by the observer or by the student participants. For example, the ratings of social-emotional tone revealed both the Group Comp and the Pure Coop conditions to be relatively warmer, more comfortable, and relaxed; and the participants further reported relatively fewer communication difficulties under Group Comp. Therefore, it does not appear that communication difficulties or frustrations in getting organized characterized either the team competition or the purely cooperative conditions. Indeed, under these conditions there appeared to be less task pressure.

The possibility remains that these differences in performance result from differences in the subjective probability of earning high grades under the respective conditions. Such an alternative, though not ruled out, was not consistent with the roughly equal levels of satisfaction with the grading procedure under the three conditions (item seven, Table 3).

The additional hypothesis which predicted the development of more positive interpersonal relations among team members in Group Comp conditions was supported only for the observer's ratings of social-emotional tone. Participant ratings were generally more favorable under the Pure Coop condition. Of course, participant ratings typically bear the combined effects of task success and interpersonal variables, as was the case for the Deutsch[17] and Myers[18] studies. In the present data, however, task success and positive interpersonal relations were not positively correlated; hence, post-session ratings were not simply a function of higher task success.

Deutsch[19] studied what we have here called individual and group competitive conditions. He found that group performance was higher under Group Comp conditions, and in addition, that Group Comp team members developed more positive interpersonal relations. Present results also tended to show the Group Comp teams to have better interpersonal relations; however, it was the Ind Comp teams which were more productive. Although the present classroom study differs in a number of important ways from Deutsch's classic investigation, we may speculate as to determinants of this discrepant result.

A close examination of the parameters of the respective individually competitive conditions suggests a critical difference between the studies. In Deutsch's case, each group was required to submit a common product which represented the collective efforts of group members, whereas the conditions of the study here reported required each individual group member to submit his own completed exercise. Deutsch *imposed* a relatively higher degree of means-control interdependence, as well as the goal interdependence represented in both studies. Hence, the important distinction between means-control and goal interdependence contributed by Thomas[20] and Raven and Eachus[21] may offer a key to explaining our discrepant results. In the present study, group members presumably generated means-control interdependence only as it was seen to facilitate individual goal attainment.

Within the limitations of the present experiment, we can now consider a number of important qualifications of the effects of cooperation. Present results clearly imply that cooperation does engender more positive interpersonal relations among group members, replicating many earlier findings in this area. The more positive, re-

17. Deutsch, 1949b, *op. cit.*
18. Myers, *op. cit.*
19. Deutsch, 1949b, *op. cit.*
20. Thomas, *op. cit.*
21. Raven and Eachus, *op. cit.*

laxed atmosphere characteristic of the cooperative teams was not a response to higher group productivity, nor did it reflect a greater satisfaction with the grading procedure which formed the basis for the experimental manipulation. Rather, under the purely cooperative condition there appeared a greater sharing of responsibility for task performance, less individual task involvement, and lower task motivation. In sum, cooperation among group members without the pressure of inter-group comparisons may be a pleasant circumstance in which to work, but it does not necessarily foster high productivity. We note, however, that the observer ratings of task orientation implied that under different time constraints, the cooperative groups might yet have improved their performance.

BIBLIOGRAPHY
Part I

Asch, S.E. "Effects of Group Pressure Upon the Modification and Distortion of Judgments," *Group Dynamics*, ed. A. Cartwright and D. Zander, Evanston, Ill., (1953), 153.

Back, Kurt W. "Influence Through Social Communication," *The Journal of Abnormal and Social Psychology*, 46, 1 (January, 1951), 9-23.

Bales, Robert. *Interaction Process Analysis*, Cambridge: Addison-Wesley Press, Inc., 1951.

Baxter, Bernice and Rosiland Cassidy. *Group Experience: The Democratic Way*, New York: Harper and Brothers, 1943.

Bennis, W.G. et al. (eds.). *Interpersonal Dynamics: Essays and Readings on Human Interaction*, Homewood, Ill.: Dorsey Press, 1964.

Berg, Irwin A. and Bernard M. Bass. *Conformity and Deviation*, New York: Harper and Brothers, 1961.

Berkowitz, L. "Effects of Perceived Dependency Relationships Upon Conformity to Group Expectations," *Journal of Abnormal and Social Psychology*, 55 (November, 1957), 350-354.

Berne, Eric. *The Structure and Dynamics of Organization and Groups*, Philadelphia: Lippincott, 1963.

Blatz, William E. "The Individual and the Group," *The American Journal of Sociology*, 44 (May, 1939), 829-838.

Bonner, Hubert. *Group Dynamics*, New York: The Ronald Press Co., 1959.

Borgatta, Edgar F. *Social Interaction Process*, Chicago: Rand McNally and Co., 1955.

Borgatta, Edgar F. and Betty Crowther. *A Workbook for the Study of Interaction Processes: Direct Observation Procedures in the Study of the Group and Individual*, Chicago: Rand McNally, 1965.

Cartwright, Dorwin and Alvin Zander (eds.). *Group Dynamics*, Evanston, Ill.: Row, Peterson and Co., 1953.

Coser, L.A. *The Functions of Social Conflict*, Glencoe: The Free Press, 1956.

Coyle, Grace Longwell. *Social Process in Organized Groups*, New York: Richard R. Smith, Inc., 1930.

Criswell, Joan, Herbert Solomon and Patric Suppes. *Mathematical Methods in Small Group Processes*, Stanford, Cal.: Stanford University Press, 1962.

Dentler, Robert A. and Kai Erikson. "The Function of Deviance in Groups, *Social Problems*, 7, 1 (Summer, 1959).

Deutsch, M. "An Experimental Study of the Effects of Cooperation and Competition Upon Group Process," *Human Relations*, 2 (July, 1949), 100-231.

Deutsch, M. "A Theory of Cooperation and Competition," *Human Relations*, 2 (April, 1949) 129-152.

Emerson, A.E. "The Biological Basis of Cooperation," *Illinois Academy of Science Transactions*, 39 (1946).

Festinger, Leon, Stanley Schachter and Kurt Black. *Social Pressures in Informal Groups*, Stanford, Cal.: Stanford University Press, 1950.

Festinger, L. et al. *Theory and Experiment in Social Communication*, Ann Arbor: Research Center for Group Dynamics, University of Michigan, 1950.

Goffman, Erving. *The Presentation of Self in Everyday Life*, New York: Doubleday, 1959.

Golembieski, Robert T. *The Small Group: An Analysis of Research Concepts and Operation*, Chicago: The University of Chicago Press, 1962.

Gross, Edward. "Primary Functions of the Small Group," *American Journal of Sociology*, 60 (July, 1954), 24-29.

Hall, Darl M. *Dynamics of Group Action*, 2nd ed., Danville, Ill.: Interstate, 1960.

Hammond, L.K. and Morton Goldman. "Competition and Non-Competition and its Relationship to Individual and Group Productivity," *Sociometry*, V, 24 (1961).

Hare, Paul A. *Handbook of Small Group Research*, New York: The Free Press, 1962.

Hare, Paul A., Edgar F. Borgatta and Robert F. Bales (eds.). *Small Groups: Studies in Social Interaction*, New York: Alfred A. Knopf, 1955.

Hawthorne, William. "The Influence of Individual Members on the Characteristics of Small Groups," *Journal of Abnormal and Social Psychology*, 48 (April, 1953), 276-284.

Heinichke, Christoph and Robert F. Bales. "Developmental Trends in the Structure of Small Groups," *Sociometry*, 16 (February, 1953).

Homans, George C. "A Conceptual Scheme for the Study of Social Organization," *American Sociological Review*, 12 (February, 1947), 13-26.

———. *The Human Group*, New York: Harcourt, Brace and Co., Inc., 1950.

Hopkins, Terence K. *The Exercise of Influence in Small Groups*, Ottowa, New Jersey: The Bedminster Press, 1964.

Israel, Joachim. *Self-Evaluation and Rejection in Groups*, Stockholm: Almquist & Wiksell, 1956.

James, J. "A Preliminary Study of the Size Determinants in Small Group Interaction," *American Sociological Review*, 16 (1951).

Jennings, Helen H. "Sociometry and Social Theory," *American Sociological Review*, (August, 1941), 512-522.

Julian, James W. and Franklyn A. Perry. "Cooperation Contrasted with Intra-Group Competition," *Sociometry*, 30, 1 (March, 1967).

Keltner, John W. "Communication in Discussion and Group Process: Some Research Trends of the Decade 1950-1959," *Journal of Communication*, X (December, 1960), 195-204; XI (March, 1961), 27-33.

Klein, Alan F. *Society—Democracy—and the Group*, New York: William Morrow and Co., 1953.

Klein, Josephine. *The Study of Groups*. London: Routledge & Kegan Paul Ltd., 1956.

Knowles, Malcom and Hulda Knowles. *Introduction to Group Dynamics*, New York: The Association Press, 1959.

Laing, R.D. *Interpersonal Perception: A Theory and Method of Research*, Springer Publishing Co., Inc., 1966.

Lambert, William W. and E. Wallace Lambert. *Social Psychology*, Prentice Hall, Inc., 1964.

Lasswell, Harold and Daniel Lerner, (eds.). *The Policy Sciences: Recent Development in Scope and Method*, Stanford: University of Stanford Press, 1951.

Leake, C. "Ethicogenisis," *Proceedings of the Philosophical Society of Texas*, 10 (1944), 7-34.

Levin, Gilbert. *The Operant Conditioning of Social Response*, Boston University, 1935.

Lewin, Kurt. *Resolving Social Conflict*, New York: Harper and Brothers, 1948.

Lewin, K. "The Conceptual Representation and the Measurement of Psychological Forces," *Contributions to Psychological Theory*, 1, 4 (1938).

Lippett, Ronald. "An Experimental Study of Authoritarian and Democratic Group Atmospheres," *Studies in Topological and Vector Psychology*, University of Iowa Press, 1940.

Lippett, Ronald and others. *The Dynamics of Planned Change*, New York: Harcourt, Brace and World, Inc., 1958.

May, M.A. and L.W. Doob. "Cooperation and Competition: An Experimental Study in Motivation," *Social Science Research Council Bulletin*, 25 (1937).

Montagu, Ashley. *On Being Human*, New York: Henry, Shuman, 1959.

————. *The Humanization of Man*, New York: The World Publishing Co., 1962.

Moreno, Jacob L. and Helen H. Jennings. "Sociometric Methods of Grouping and Re-Grouping," *Sociometry*, 7 (November, 1944), 397-414.

Myers, A.E. "Team Competition, Success, and Adjustment of Group Members," *Journal of Abnormal and Social Psychology*, 65 (November, 1962).

Olmstead, Michael S. *The Small Group*, New York: Random House, 1959.

Paulson, Stanley F. "Pressures Toward Conformity in Group Discussion," *Quarterly Journal of Speech*, XLIV, 1 (February, 1958).

Phillips, Beeman N. "Effects of Cooperation and Competition on the Cohesiveness of Small Face-to-Face Groups," *Journal of Educational Psychology*, 47 (February, 1956), 65-70.

Phillips, Gerald M. *Communication and the Small Group*, New York: The Bobbs-Merrill Co., Inc., 1966.

Riesman, David, Nathan Glazer and Revel Denney. *The Lonely Crowd*, New York: Doubleday, Anchor Series, 1956.

Ruitenbeck, Hendrik. *The Individual and the Crowd*, New York: Mentor Book, 1965.

Sampson, Edward E. and Arlene C. Brandon. "The Effects of Role and Opinion Deviation on Small Group Behavior," *Sociometry*, 27, 3 (September, 1964), 261-281.

Schachter, S. "Deviation, Rejection, and Communication," *Journal of Abnormal Psychology*, XLVI (1951), 190-207.

Schachter, Stanley et al. "Cross-Cultural Experiments on Threat and Rejection." *Human Relations*, 8, 4 (1954), 403-439.

Schien, E.H. and W.G. Bennis. *Personal and Organizational Change Through Group Methods: The Laboratory Approach*, New York: Wiley and Sons, 1965.

Schneirla, T.C. "Problems in the Biopsychology of Social Organization," *Journal of Abnormal and Social Psychology*, 41 (1946), 385-402.

Shaw, Marjorie E. "A Comparison of Individuals and Small Groups in the Rational Solution of Complex Problems," *Readings in Social Psychology*, (Society for the Psychological Study of Social Issues), New York: Henry Holt and Co., 1952.

Sherif, Muzafer. "Integrating Field Work and Laboratory in Small Group Research," *American Sociological Review*, 19, 6 (December, 1954), 759-771.

Sherif, M. *The Psychology of Social Norms*, New York: Harper, 1936.

Sherif, M. and Carolyn Sherif. *Groups in Harmony and Tension*, New York: Harpers, 1953.

Sherif, Muzafer and Carolyn Muzafer. *Reference Groups*, New York: Harper and Row, 1964.

Sherif, Muzafer and M.O. Wilson (eds.). *Group Relations at the Crossroads*, New York: Harper and Brothers, 1953.

Sherif, M. et al. "Intergroup Conflict and Cooperation: The Robbers Cave Experiment," *University of Oklahoma Institute of Group Relations*, Norman, Oklahoma, 1961.

Stock, Dorothy and Herbert A. Thelen. *Emotional Dynamics and Group Culture*, New York: New York University Press, 1958.

Stogdill, Ralph M. *Individual Behavior and Group Achievement: A Theory, The Evidence*, New York: Oxford University Press, 1959.

Strodbeck, Fred L. "The Case for the Study of Small Groups, *American Sociological Review*, 19, 6 (December, 1954), 651-657.

Taylor, D.W. and W.L. Faust. "Efficiency in Problem-Solving as a Function of Group Size," *The Journal of Experimental Psychology*, 44 (1952).

Teger, Allan I. and Dean G. Pruitt. "Components of Group Risk Taking," *Journal of Experimental Social Psychology*, 3 (1967).

Theodorson, George A. "Elements in the Progressive Development of Small Groups," *Social Forces*, 31 (May, 1953), 311-320.

Thelen, Herbert A. *Dynamics of Groups at Work*, Chicago: University of Chicago Press, 1954.

Thelen, Herbert A. and Dorothy Stock. "The Mature and Effective Group," *NEA*, 44 (February, 1955), 105-106.

Thelen, Helen and Watson Dickerman. "Stereotypes and the Growth of Groups," *Educational Leadership*, 6 (February, 1949), 309-316.

Thibaut, John W. and Harold H. Kelley. *The Social Psychology of Groups*, New York: John Wiley & Sons, Inc., 1959.

Thorndike, R.L. "The Effect of Discussion Upon the Correctness of Group Decisions," *Journal of Social Psychology*, 9 (1938).

Walker, E.L. and R.W. Heyns. *An Anatomy for Conformity*, Englewood Cliffs, New Jersey: Prentice-Hall, 1962.

White, Ralph K. and Ronald Lippot. *Autocracy and Democracy: An Experimental Inquiry*, New York: Harper, 1960.

Whyte, William H. Jr. "Groupthink," *Fortune*, (March, 1952), 114-115.

———. *The Organization Man*, New York: Simon and Schuster, 1956.

Wirth, Louis. "Social Interaction: The Problem of the Individual and the Group," *American Journal of Sociology*, 44 (May, 1939), 965-979.

PART II

INDIVIDUAL AND GROUP OPERATIONS

The history of man is replete with examples of his concern for his personal problems. Man's need to locate shelter, find food and fulfill his bodily wants characterized much of his early development. As man found ways to satisfy basic needs he continued to use his energies to pursue personal goals. He now became concerned with his pleasures as well as his needs. Just as a new dimension was added to his existence once survival was mastered, so too man had to search for new areas once he placed his comforts in a definable perspective.

With the same vitality that typified his earlier desires to endure and to be comfortable, man now started to ask questions. It was not enough to accept notions and schemes, but man began to wonder "why." He not only became concerned with the realization that he behaved in certain ways, but more importantly he asked questions relevant to the motivation and stimulus behind this behavior.

This questioning of human behavior has in recent times turned to our actions and operations not just as individuals but also in groups. It has long been accepted that we, as social beings, divide our time and allegiance among a wide assortment of groups, all of which make rival membership claims on us. The mere admission of this view is no longer enough for us—we now want to know not only how we function, but also what forces alter and manipulate both us and the group as we engage in the countless group activities we face each day.

In Part I we noted that the study of groups, how they function and operate, is a comparatively new discipline, comprising only the last three decades.[1] The relative newness of this study has contributed to the fact that there is not a large body of agreed upon univer-

---

1. Dorwin Cartwright and Alvin Zander, eds., *Group Dynamics: Research and Theory*, 2nd ed., New York: Harper and Row, 1968, p. vii.

sal precepts and theories. Yet there are some observations and conclusions that do seem apparent, one of which is clearly stated by
McGrath and Altman:

> Historically one of the main arguments for the study of groups has been
> that groups are not mere summations of individuals but a different system
> level, with properties arising from the patterns of member characteristics
> in interaction with the situation.[2]

Any study of groups, as the above quotation points out, must by
necessity, examine both individuals and groups. It is therefore the
purpose of this section to deal with questions related to both how
the individual and the group operate—how groups and individuals
function in their desire to solve problems and accomplish their goals.
It is our contention that group and individual operations must be
examined together. It is the operations and functions of the individual that directly relates to the processes carried out by the group; the
group, in turn, influences the actions, reactions, and activities of its
individuals. This interdependence is made clear when we realize that
the individual and the group function in tandem. It is this relationship that forms the basis of this chapter.

This chapter is divided into three interconnected sections. The
first section attempts to set forth a model of group discussion. The
model enables us to re-create a structure that possesses the characteristics of the system.[3] An examination and analysis of the model (in
this case a model of group discussion) offers us a device by which we
can isolate, in both time and space, a phenomenon that in reality is
active and dynamic. Admittedly, we must keep in mind the fact that
we have stopped, and made static, a dynamic process, but even with
this limitation the model does make it possible to better predict how
the model (and subsequently the "thing" it represents in reality) will
react if one or more of the elements are submitted to certain modifications.[4]

The second section of this chapter looks at how the individual
operates *within* the group. In the first chapter we attempted to present some selections that dealt with how the individual confronts the
group on a philosophical and theoretical level. Our main purpose in

---

2. Joseph E. McGrath and Irwin Altman, *Small Group Research,* (New York: Holt, Rinehart
and Winston, Inc., 1966), p. 60.
3. For a further explanation of the advantages and disadvantages of models see: Irwin D.J.
Bross, "Models," *Dimensions in Communications: Readings,* James H. Campbell and Hal W.
Heiler, eds., (Belmont, California: Wadsworth Publishing Company, 1965), p. 17-22.
4. Claude Levi-Strause, "Social Structure," *Anthropology Today: Selections,* Sol Tax ed.,
(Chicago: The University of Chicago Press, 1962), p. 322.

this section is to offer some selections that are much more pragmatic. Selections that both describe and propose how the individual might operate in the group, and how he might act out his role as a participant. Most of the standard textbooks in group discussion contain lists and enumerations of do's and don'ts for successful participation. It is, therefore, our intent not to duplicate these rosters, but instead to present some selections that offer an original or unique outlook on the issue of individual operations.

The third portion of this chapter is called "Group Operations." The main intent of this section is to present some writings and studies that both depict and prescribe how groups operate. Since groups engage in a variety of processes, procedures, and operations as they attempt to solve problems, accomplish goals and perform tasks, this section offers a view of some of the ways groups carry out these functions. Our purpose is not to advocate any one procedure or operation over another, but rather to offer varying viewpoints as to how and why groups operate in the patterns and styles that they do.

The eleven selections that follow represent some of the current thinking in this area of individual and group operations. These viewpoints are by no means exhaustive or definitive. Instead, they attempt to present but one level of the total spectrum of thought on this important topic of group and individual operations. The reader is reminded that a subject as broad as individual and group operations is indeed limitless—subject to changes and refinements from *each* individual and group. In short, there may well be as many operations and processes as there are individuals and groups.

In the first selection Martin Andersen offers a Model of group discussion. The value of the model as a means of understanding and defining an area of investigation has of late developed into a prevalent educational device. It offers a method in the establishing of boundary lines for the discipline as well as a tool for examining basic components of that particular discipline. The need for such examination seems crucial and vital in the case of group discussion. For as Andersen notes, ". . .currently there are evidences that, while widely used, the discussion process is not always understood and is frequently misused or abused."

One does not have to be exposed to the literature of group discussion for long before he becomes aware of the fact that much of the thinking and teaching in this field has its roots in the theories and philosophies of John Dewey. In the selection "How We Think," Dewey attempts to define and explain thought and thinking. His definitions serve as a basis for his subsequent account of what he refers to as "reflective thinking." For Dewey it is this technique of reflective thinking that we should try to develop as part of our individual operations. This will, in time, help our functioning in group operations. For Dewey, "reflective thinking was the active, persistent and careful consideration of any belief or supposed form of knowledge in the light of the grounds that support it, and the conclusions to which it tends."

Clovis Shepherd, as a sociologist, is concerned with the relationship existing between our individual operations and how we operate in groups. He maintains that in order to understand, work with, and utilize the small group an individual must begin by gaining some insight into his personal attitude toward everyday life. What Shepherd is appealing for is a scientific attitude in our daily lives that will carry over into our small group activities. For him the scientific attitude is characterized by a general perspective, a posture of doubt, and typifications.

The selection by Benne and Sheats deals with how the individual operates not in isolation, but rather how he functions *as part* of the group process. In their article, "Functional Roles of Group Members," they attempt to identify and explain the various roles individuals play during group activity. It is their thesis that if one is going to operate effectively in a group he must be able to locate, identify and analyze member roles that are actually enacted in group process. In their point of view, Benne and Sheats classify member-roles into three broad groupings (1) Group task roles, (2) Group building and maintenance roles, and (3) Individual roles.

John Petelle faces still another issue in the area of individual operation. His concern is for the person who operates as a source of conflict for the group. Petelle's approach, based mainly on the work of Simmel and Cooley, is that deviation of thought (conflict), if used correctly, serves as a positive force in aiding us to achieve a greater and more comprehensive understanding of what group discussion should be. For him, conflict in discussion tends to encourage inquiry, to promote objectivity, and to sharpen analysis. In addition, Petelle maintains that conflict may also act as a cohesive agent.

As we noted earlier, not only do individuals function and operate *within* the group, but the group *itself* can be characterized as having certain functions and processes. When one considers the values of individual operations versus group operations there is always the question of which of the two is the most effective method of solving problems. Kelley and Thibout look at this problem as they review and discuss a variety of experimental studies that center on some of

35213

the reasons why there are differences in group versus individual solutions. They hold to the view, not without some reservations, that in most instances group products are superior to individual solutions.

Although the steps of reflective thinking are the most common of all group operational patterns, it is by no means the only format with which groups attempt to accomplish their goals. One recent form, which has been widely misunderstood and misused, is what Arthur Coon refers to as "Brainstorming." In Coon's analysis of Brainstorming it is viewed as a technique for stimulating the generation of ideas and facilitating their expression. To this end, he adds, it may well contribute to a climate that is conducive to effective problem-solving.

Many groups and organizations discover that their main emphasis is not in solving the problem, but rather how does the solution become operational once the program has been decided upon. Most books, in both management and discussion, have offered very little in this important area of implementation. PERT (a quasi-mathematical procedure) is an operation that attempts to offer a framework for planning as well as a methodology for implementation. Gerald M. Phillips, as one of the chief spokesmen for PERT, offers a rationale for PERT as well as an outline of the steps of PERT as they fit into the standard discussion agenda.

In the introduction to this section it was noted that there might well be as many individual and group operations as there are groups and individuals. The list and index of discussion processes is limitless (as a review of discussion textbooks will reveal). Writers have long been concerned with the issue of which of these discussion patterns has the most beneficial effect. Ovid Bayless attempted to answer this question by means of an experimental study that examined the effect of three different patterns upon the outcome of problem-solving discussion. His results are of significance for those who must, at one time or another, select a discussion pattern and a method of operation for their group.

In recent years the intensive group experience has become part of our modern life. News magazines tell us about the countless variations we find in sensitivity groups. Local P.T.A.'s, church groups, college courses, business organizations and the like have all been caught up in the excitement and perhaps the novelty of intensive group experience. This group activity has been called the T-group (for training group), lab-group, sensitivity training, group encounters, synanon "games," and even "nude therapy." Perhaps of all group situations the intensive group experience is the one that is most often misconstrued and maltreated. Carl Rogers, who is in the *avant-garde* of this technique, attempts to describe the intensive groups' goals and objectives. In his essay, "The Process of the Basic Encounter Group," Rogers explains the workings of this type of group, while indicating what the intensive group *is* and what it *is not*. He maintains that in an atmosphere of much freedom and little structure, the individual will gradually feel safe enough to drop some of his defenses and facades. One of his premises is that the correct use of this group process can aid an individual in both understanding himself and his relationships with others.

One of the unresolved issues that faces both scholars and students of discussion deals with the question of which is the most effective methodology to employ in both the teaching and learning of this highly complex activity. Barnlund and Haiman attempt to manage this very problem. They present a brief review of some of the methods of learning and then offer an analysis of some of the ways group discussion can be taught.

chapter 3

A Model

A MODEL OF GROUP DISCUSSION
Martin P. Andersen [*]

Historical antecedent and current practice attest to the widespread use and practical value of group discussion as a tool for decision-making and learning, a training method, and a technique for therapy and research. The situation is well stated in these words:

> Executives hold conferences at all levels in an organization; scientists work in teams; educators serve on committees; church workers hold conferences; parents serve on action groups; teachers educate by the use of participation methods; phychologists and psychiatrists practice group therapy; and teen-agers hold meetings. [1]

Currently there are evidences that, while widely used, the discussion process is not always understood and is frequently misused or abused. One author has noted that there is a "dilemma as to just what principles and concepts make up the rhetoric of discussion and how they should be presented." [2] An earlier article pointed out that at times certain characteristics of discussion are idealized (emphasized) to the exclusion of others. [3] This disparity in focus is seen in the different approaches of persons who employ discussion in research. At one extreme discussion appears to be viewed as a form of stimulus-response activity, a unidimensional variable mediating relatively simple, predetermined goals and outcomes. At the other extreme discussion is seen as a complex form of goal-seeking behavior,

Reprinted from *Southern Speech Journal*, XXX, No. 4 (Summer, 1965), pp. 279-293. Reprinted with the permission of the author. This is a slightly abridged version of the original article.

*Mr. Andersen (Ph.D., University of Wisconsin, 1957) is Professor of Speech at California State College, Fullerton, California.

1. Norman R.F. Maier, *Problem-Solving Discussions and Conferences* (New York: McGraw-Hill Book Company, Inc., 1963), v.

2. Harold P. Zelko, *The Quarterly Journal of Speech*, L (April, 1964), 202.

3. Dean C. Barnlund, "Our Concept of Discussion: Static or Dynamic," *The Speech Teacher*, III (January, 1954), 8.

a multidimensional variable mediating the life space[4] of the group and the need-value-skill systems of its members.

Differences in the understanding of discussion are also revealed by its practice. A few persons deliberately hide authoritarian decision-making and advocacy under the cloak of discussion.[5] Others seem to believe that an "unstructured situation" and a "permissive atmosphere" are the essential components of a successful discussion. Apparently there is a need to attempt to answer the question, "What constitutes the principles and concepts of discussion?" We need periodically to formulate an integrated statement of the rhetoric of discussion.[6]

The purpose of this paper is to present a broad conceptual model of discussion, including its essential components, their interrelationships, and the cognitive-perceptual processes involved. The model is descriptive. It ties together a variety of observed characteristics of discussion and portrays the ways in which people act as participants. The model is normative. It indicates the ways in which people should behave, and the characteristics of the output when productivity in discussion is maximized. The model is tentative. Refinements and modifications can and should be made. Finally, the model is incomplete and necessarily oversimplified. For example, one element of discussion is oral communication, a process which in itself has been the object of a large number of model representations.[7] The values of the model are that it seeks to establish boundary lines for the discipline of discussion, focus on integral socio-psychological constructs and their interrelationships, and provides an operational guide for practice and prediction in discussion.[8]

In this paper discussion is viewed as a system of communicative and adaptive behavior growing out of imbalances in the need-value systems of the participants, both individually and collectively, and dynamically interrelated to specified properties of the "field subre-

4. See Kurt Lewin, *Field Theory in Social Science* (New York: Harper & Row, Publishers, 1951), xi.

5. See the description of "pseudo-discussion" in William S. Howell and Donald K. Smith, *Discussion* (New York: The Macmillian Company, 1956), 7-9.

6. See Daniel Fogarty, *Roots for a New Rhetoric* (New York: Bureau of Publications, Teachers College, Columbia University, 1959), 132-140, for a preliminary exploration of the rhetoric of discussion.

7. F. Craig Johnson and George R. Klare, "General Models of Communication Research: A Survey of the Developments of a Decade," *Journal of Communication,* XI (March, 1961), 13-33.

8. See Irwin D.J. Bross, *Design for Decision* (New York: The Macmillian Company, 1953), 161-182, for a statement of types, criteria, and values of models.

gion"[9] in which the discussion occurs. A model of such behavior is concerned with the components of the system itself (structure), the sociological, psychological, and physical forces which determine the type, intensity, and direction of the interaction within the system (movement) and the outcomes as they relate to the subregion in which the interaction takes place (productivity). In other words, the model should describe input into a system, interactive processes within the system, and output. The components and processes must be considered as functionally and dynamically interrelated at all times, even though we may consider them separately in our analysis.

Bases for the Model Construction

Numerous sources have contributed to the construction of the model. Empirical data covering a large number and variety of group discussions have been examined. A survey of approximately sixty currently-used discussion and communication textbooks revealed considerable unanimity as to the essential elements of group discussion.[10] An analysis of books on small group process directed attention to socio-psychological conceptualizations relative to human communicative and adaptive behavior. Pertinent research studies in discussion and related disciplines provided two types of helpful findings: (1) reconfirmation of conclusions based on the sources listed above, and (2) a set of tested hypotheses which verified certain of the theoretical assumptions incorporated in the model. Finally, critical evaluation by graduate students and colleagues resulted in several revisions of the model.

We now turn to a detailed description of our discussion model, which is diagrammed in Figure 1.

---

9. An illustration will make the meaning of this expression clear. The decisions made by a group research team in a local branch (sub-region) of a national organization constructing a missile component (region) are affected by the current needs and plans of the National Aeronautics and Space Administration (field).

10. The reader may be interested in checking on the following sampling: Harold A. Brack and Kenneth G. Hance, *Public Speaking and Discussion for Religious Leaders* (Englewood Cliffs, N.J.: Prentice-Hall, Inc., 1961), 153-254; Laura Crowell, *Discussion: Method of Democracy* (Chicago: Scott, Foresman and Company, 1963), 7; Jon Eisenson, J. Jeffery Auer, and John V. Irwin, *The Psychology of Communication* (New York: Appleton-Century-Crofts, 1963), 253-268; Giles Wilkeson Gray and Waldo W. Braden, *Public Speaking: Principles and Practice*, 2nd ed. (New York: Harper & Row, Publishers, 1963), 416; and Halbert E. Gulley, *Discussion, Conference, and Group Process* (New York: Henry Holt and Company, 1960), 4-5.

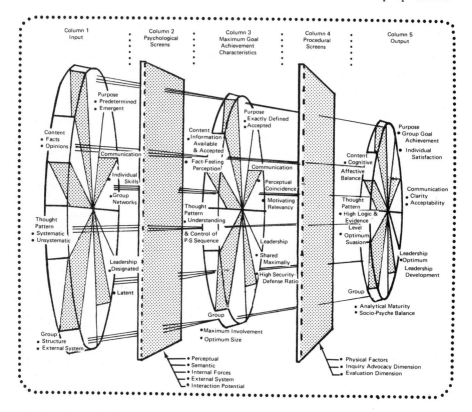

Figure 1. Model of group discussion.

Essential Components of Group Discussion

The solids in Column 1 represent the six essential components of the discussion process: *purpose, thought pattern, content, the group, leadership,* and *communication.* Each is considered as one-sixth of the total. The descriptive terms near each solid designate the pre-discussion characteristics of that component as it forms a part of the input. These characteristics are manifested through the group members, both individually and collectively.

1. One essential component is purpose. Discussion is not an end in itself; it is a means to some group goal which individuals cannot achieve alone. Discussion usually has one of three purposes: to solve a problem, to aid in learning, and to secure commitment to later action. Depending on circumstances before a discussion, its purpose may be *predetermined* or *emergent.*

2. Every discussion starts with a varying quantity and quality of meaningful content: reliable *facts* and *considered opinion* which are related to the discussion purpose. This content is brought to the discussion by the group members. At one extreme the essential information is available or accessible; at the other it is partially lacking or unavailable. In every instance the facts and opinions which each individual brings with him are set in the perceptual field of that individual.[11]

3. The third component of discussion is the thought pattern. Facts and opinions alone are not enough; they must be dealt with in a way which will contribute to the purpose. Almost without exception authorities say that discussion is a process of reflective thinking. Its success depends on the way a topic is developed systematically, moving from the location and definition of the problem through a consideration of possible solutions to the selection of the one preferred. Obviously, the quality of group thinking is a function of the members' skills in inquiry. Some persons are objective, thorough, logical, and have the ability to suspend judgment; others are at the opposite pole. Therefore, the thought pattern input in discussion, as it applies both to individuals and the group, may be described as *systematic* or *unsystematic*.

4. A fourth component of any discussion is the group in which it occurs. This may be a small face-to-face, informal group or a large, more formal, co-acting group. The pre-discussion characteristics of any group are *structure* and its *external system*. Some discussion groups meet only once. In this case there is little prior structure, or differentiations among the members and their relationships, which together determine the flow of information, the flow of work,[12] and power relationships. When a group has stability (has continued over time) some hierarchical structure may have developed.[13] In every case a discussion group also functions within the matrix of some external system, by which we mean the configuration of interlocking individual and group frames of reference impinging on the movement within the group. Thus, decisions made by a local chapter of the

---

11. The implications of this statement and a definition of "perceptual field" are found in Arthur W. Combs and Donald Snygg, *Individual Behavior: A Perceptual Approach to Behavior,* rev. ed. (New York: Harper & Row, Publishers, 1959), 16-36.

12. See Dorwin Cartwright and Alvin Zander, *Group Dynamics: Research and Theory,* 2nd ed. (Evanston: Row, Peterson and Company, 1960), 648-649.

13. A meaningful statement of the dimensions of the group structure is found in John K. Hemphill and Charles N. Westie, "The Measurement of Group Dimensions," *Journal of Psychology,* XIX (April, 1950), 325-342.

Congress of Parents and Teachers are affected by the state and national policies of that body as well as by the school system with which the local PTA is associated and the community in which the school is located.

5. The leadership pattern is a fifth component of discussion. This element is conceived of as being of two possible conditions before discussion: *designated* or *latent*. There are two situations in which we have designated leadership: (1) where there is a single leader (moderator, chairman, president, etc.) who is named in advance, and (2) where leadership is shared among several who know their responsibilities in advance. In contrast leadership may be latent. Then the potential lies within the group members who—once discussion has started—exercise initiative in carrying out whatever leadership functions are needed.

6. The sixth component in discussion is communication, which is manifested in input in *individual skills* and *group networks*. Each group member brings with him varying skills in the use of verbal and nonverbal symbols, the media of communication. Also, each member has a potential for listening. When a group has met over a period of time it may have developed some dominant pattern of communication which is a function of both the dimensions of the group structure and the potency of the external system. This network of communication gives intensity and direction to the interaction. When a discussion group meets for the first time the potential communication networks are latent; then there can only be a predisposition to interact in a certain way.

Socio-Psychological Screens in Discussion

In the diagram of our model, the horizontal lines connecting Columns 1 and 2 represent different group members, who function unilaterally until the start of the discussion. When the discussion begins a number of socio-psychological processes becomes immediately operative in interpersonal and intrapersonal interaction. These processes function in both speakers and listeners as screens which filter all contributions. Every individual has a uniquely different filtering mechanism so that how a contribution is structured by a speaker or perceived by a listener is always a function of the filtering mechanism operating within that person. Five of these screens are of special significance: the *perceptual, semantic, internal forces, external system,* and *interaction potential.* While considered separately here, they are in reality closely interrelated; each affects and is affected by the others.

The first screen is that created by each member's *perceptual* field, which is defined as "the entire universe, including himself, as it is experienced by the individual at the instant of action."[14] All behavior of an individual is completely determined by his perceptual field which, in fact, is the only reality he can accept. He sees another's perceptual field as containing much error and illusion.[15] It becomes important in discussion, therefore, to establish a "common ground" of content and deal with that content objectively and impersonally.

A second screen, stemming from the first, is a *semantic* one. This screen filters the word meanings; it determines whether the signification of a symbol-stimulus is denotative or connotative. Even when this differentation is perceived, it is still essential that sender and receiver understand the frame of reference in which a word is used. For example, an "extremist" might be understood to be "a person who holds extreme, or advanced views," but there might be a misunderstanding in discussion because two different frames of reference were used, one being "to the left" and the other "to the right." One writer says that content "must be susceptible to similar structurizations by both communicator and interpreter."[16]

The third screen is designated as that of *internal forces,* of both the individual and the group. Each individual in discussion seeks some combination of overt or covert personal or group goals. This goal-seeking behavior stems from and is shaped by the perceived instabilities in the members' beliefs, attitudes, statuses, values, desires, and needs as these are related to the discussion topic. Forces within the group also filter the discussion content. These forces might be any of the group's dimensions: norms, cohesiveness, extent of cooperation or competition, hedonic tone, permeability, and stability, to mention only a few.[17] Research has shown beyond any doubt that these and other group dimensions have significant impact on the behavior of the group members.

---

14. Combs and Snygg, *op. cit.,* 20.

15. *Ibid.,* 21.

16. Franklin Fearing, "Toward a Psychological Theory of Human Communication," *Journal of Personality,* XXII (Sept., 1953), 73. This article provides an excellent theoretical statement of the conceptual framework within which communication occurs.

17. See Edgar F. Borgatta, Leonard S. Cottrell, and Henry J. Meyer, "On the Dimensions of Group Behavior," *Sociometry,* XIX (Dec., 1956), 223-240; Raymond B. Cattell, "New Concepts for Measuring Leadership, In Terms of Group Syntality," *Human Relations,* IV (1951), 161-184; Hemphill and Westie, *op. cit.;* George C. Homans, *The Human Group* (New York: Hancourt, Brace and Company, 1950); and George A. Theodorson, "Elements in the Progressive Development of Small Groups," *Social Forces,* XXXI (May, 1953), 311-320. These articles present different approaches to the analysis of group dimensions.

The nature of the third screen just described is partially determined by a fourth, the *external system,* which includes the total physical, technical, and social environment in which the discussion occurs: its "field." Sometimes the external system has the characteristics of a primary group, as when discussion occurs in a family, a peer group, or a play group. In other situations the external system takes on the character of secondary groups, such as the nation, political party, church, union, industry, or social movement. Frequently, the external system combines the characteristics of both, as when the frames of reference of a discussant include his family, the union of which he is a member, the company for which he works, and the political party in which he is registered. The filtering effect on discussion content of each of these types of external systems will vary in directness, intensity, frequency, duration, and formality.

A final screen in discussion is the group's *interaction potential.* This is defined by one author as "the tendency of a given pair of members of a group to interact."[18] This concept has been expanded to apply to all possible combinations of group members and to include the "freedom" as well as the "tendency" to interact. It is generally accepted that productivity in discussion is a function of the extent to which this potential is maximized, how well the group's resources are used. One of the theoretical assumptions underlying the use of such techniques as brainstorming, T-Group training, role-playing, buzz groups, and the audience interaction panel is that optimum participation improves the quantity and quality of the outcomes and the members' satisfactions. Research also supports the conclusion that full involvement improves productivity.[19] It becomes apparent, then, that when interaction is kept at a low level because of status barriers, personal differences, semantic problems, group size, or variance in discussion skills, productivity will be directly affected.

These screens act as a unified filter on all six components of discussion. They are always present and are partial determinants of the discussion outcomes. They are operative at the start and during the discussion and hence we place them immediately after input in our model.

---

18. Bernard M. Bass, *Leadership, Psychology and Organizational Behavior* (New York: Harper & Row, Publishers, 1960), 342.
19. See Ralph K. White and Ronald Lippitt, *Autocracy and Democracy: An Experimental Inquiry* (New York: Harper & Row, Publishers, 1960), 282-285.

Conditions Essential for Maximum Goal Achievement

As indicated earlier, the separate horizontal lines between Columns 1 and 2 suggest that prior to discussion each individual functions unilaterally. Once the process starts, it may be assumed that there is some concern for goal achievement. This is indicated by the convergence of lines between Columns 2 and 3.

One value of a model is its use in prediction. To know the conditions under which the discussion process functions at its best, the characteristics of each component which are essential for maximum goal achievement must be considered.

1. The two essential characteristics for the first component are that the purpose must be *exactly defined* and *accepted*. Problem location and definition is the first step in the reflective thinking process and is equally important when understanding or commitment are the goals. In a summary of the characteristics of productive groups, one author states: "The most productive groups. . .are found to be those which can best carry out the steps in the problem-solving process."[20] A second condition under which purpose contributes maximally to goal achievement is when the defined goal is accepted by the group members. While it is impossible to suppress completely the hidden agendas of some group members, the publicly stated goal must take precedence. Membership in any discussion group is predicated on the assumption that goal achievement is desired.

2. The second component in discussion is content. Maximum productivity should occur under two conditions: (1) when needed *facts and opinions are optimally available and accepted,* and (2) when their *fact-feeling* (cognitive-affective) *qualities are perceived.* Discussion cannot take place in a vacuum, in a situation in which facts and opinions are not available.[21] When this extreme situation exists, the discussion should be postponed or not held. Then, too, these facts and opinions, when properly tested, must be accepted. A second essential characteristic of content is that its cognitive-affective (fact-feeling) qualities be perceived by the group members. A person who cannot differentiate between the objective meaning of a contribution and the subjective feelings of the contributor is apt to focus on personalities rather than issues.

---

20. A. Paul Hare, *Handbook of Small Group Research,* (New York: The Free Press of Glencoe, 1962), 375.
21. See Maier, *op. cit.,* 138-139, 211-238, for a statement of methods of decision-making when all desired facts are not available.

3. The characteristics of the thought pattern which are essential for maximum productivity are that the members *understand the problem-solving sequence* and *exercise control* over its progress. Persons who do not understand the reflective thought process are apt to perceive discussion as advocacy, indoctrination, compromise, or as an unsystematic approach toward goals. However, understanding what constitutes sould thinking is not enough. The members must be free to make procedural decisions in discussion; they must be aware of the progress being made; and they must be courageous in their insistence that the best thinking procedures be followed.

4. As far as the group itself is concerned, productivity is dependent on *maximum involvement* of the members and *optimum size*. People become members of a discussion group because they have a contribution to make or an interest in the topic. To the extent that group members are not maximally involved the end product suffers. A second essential is that the group be of optimum size for the achievement of its task and social needs. The group must be large enough to accomplish its goal and small enough to insure member satisfaction through participation. This is related to Thelen's "principle of individual challenge in the least-sized group," which he describes in these words:

> The central assumption of this principle is that the quality of performance depends on how one is motivated to perform, and that it is possible to compose groups in such a way that motivation is high. Such groups are the *"smallest groups in which it is possible to have represented at a functional level all the social and achievement skills required for the particular required activity."*[22]

In large discussion groups, as the panel-forum, special techniques may be employed to increase participation.

5. The leadership component characteristics which are essential for highest productivity are that leadership tasks be *shared maximally* and that there be a *high security-defense ratio*. In practice the division of leadership functions in discussion varies greatly. There is considerable support, however, for the belief that "the experience of group discussion will be more satisfying psychologically when the leader shares this responsibility with qualified members, or when they exercise initiative in undertaking these tasks themselves."[23] The second essential of the leadership component concerns the leader-

---

22. Herbert A. Thelen, *Dynamics of Groups at Work* (Chicago: The University of Chicago Press, 1954), 187.

23. Eisenson, Auer, and Irwin, *op. cit.,* 262.

member relationships. To participate effectively in discussion the members must feel secure in the feeling that their contributions will be understood and accepted. At the same time there must be a minimum of feelings of defensiveness, of always having to "fight" for or against ideas presented.

6. Finally, for maximum achievement communication in discussion must be characterized by maximum *perceptual coincidence* and *motivating relevancy*. The first characteristic refers to the need for establishing "common ground" in the discussion. What is said must be similarly structured (perceived) by both speaker and listeners. Group members must be able to differentiate between the affective and cognitive aspects of discussion content. The second characteristic means that what is said must be relevant to the goal of the group and the need-value systems of the participants. It also means that member contributions must be presented with the forcefulness sufficient to insure their thorough examination.

Procedural Screens in Discussion

In the diagram Columns 3 and 4 are connected by three parallel lines to suggest that the interaction of the members, through which the dynamic interrelationships among the six components are manifested, is primarily goal and group centered. This interaction is also filtered through a second set of screens shown in Column 4. These three screens are placed together because they seem to lend themselves to more direct control by the group members than the screens in Column 2.

The first screen encompasses all the *physical factors* of the situation in which the discussion occurs. For example, the acoustics of the meeting room, its size and shape, the availability and comfort of tables and chairs, the heating and lighting, the timing, outside noises and disturbances, and the availability of presentation aids such as projection equipment and blackboards are factors which affect both the quantity and quality of the discussion. Consideration must be given to these factors in preplanning.

A second procedural screen may be designated as the *inquiry-advocacy dimension*. As already stated, discussion is characterized by reflective thinking, in which the best or correct answer to some problem is sought. In contrast, intentional thinking, which characterizes debate, is that in which support for some predetermined answer is sought. In any given situation, an appropriate balance between inquiry and considered support of ideas must be maintained.

A third procedural screen in discussion is its *evaluation dimension.* This refers to the extent and nature of the "assessment of progress" made during and after a discussion. The implication is that there should be a balance in discussion between content and process. Too infrequently are discussion group members concerned with such questions as "How well are we doing?" and "How can we improve?" Too frequently there is little concern about standards for effectiveness.

Output Characteristics for Maximum Productivity

Obviously, the outcome of any discussion ought to represent the highest possible achievement. Column 5 presents the essential characteristics of each component under conditions of maximum output productivity. Columns 4 and 5 are connected by a wide (three strand) horizontal line suggesting that under conditions of highest achievement the group interaction is unitary. The size of the solids in Column 5 are smaller than in Columns 1 or 3 to suggest that the output in discussion is less inclusive, more refined, more focused than the input.

1. The purpose of every discussion is twofold: (1) to insure *group goal achievement* and, (2) to provide some *member satisfaction.* The first is of primary importance but the second cannot be overlooked.

2. Under conditions of maximum productivity the component of content should be characterized by a *cognitive-affective-balance.* Denotative meanings must be understood. Connotative meanings must be understood and accepted.

3. The output characteristics of the thought pattern are that the decisions and understandings reached should be based on the *highest level of logic and evidence* and *optimum suasion.* This again suggests a balance: sound reasoning, well-supported facts and opinions, a proper inquiry-advocacy relationship, and sufficient motivating relevancy to insure that decisions made will be supported.

4. Two qualities should characterize the group under conditions of maximum productivity. The first is *analytical maturity.* That is, the group must have reached a point where it can and does assess its own progress critically. At the point of maximum productivity the group must also have achieved a *socio-psyche balance.* It should be able to satisfy ego-needs while working effectively toward goals.

5. When a discussion group is functioning at its peak, there should be optimum *opportunity for leadership development.* Leadership tasks should be shared when possible; members should have opportunities to practice different leadership roles.

6. Finally, at its best the communication component should be characterized by *clarity* and *acceptability*. What is said must be mutually understood by the members; what is said must also contribute to behavioral or attitudinal change.

Summary

This paper presents a theoretical-operational model of group discussion. The paper describes the basic and essential components of discussion at three sequential points: (1) at the time of input, (2) during discussion under conditions of maximum goal achievement, and (3) at the time of output under conditions of maximum productivity. Brief descriptions are also given of two sets of screens, one composed of socio-psychological and the other of procedural factors, which filter the discussion interaction. The model proposes that group discussion is a form of communicative-adaptive, goal-seeking behavior having structure, movement, and productivity, which acts as a multidimensional variable mediating the field subregion in which the discussion occurs and the need-value systems of the group members. Specific relationships among the elements of input, process filters, and output are hypothesized. The model is not definitive. It attempts to describe a set of relationships which are sufficiently general to account for and enable predictions to be made about the phenomena of discussion.

chapter 4

Individual Operations

HOW WE THINK
John Dewey

What Is Thought?

Varied Senses of the Term

No words are oftener on our lips than *thinking* and *thought.* So profuse and varied, indeed, is our use of these words that it is not easy to define just what we mean by them. The aim of this chapter is to find a single consistent meaning. Assistance may be had by considering some typical ways in which the terms are employed. In the first place *thought* is used broadly, not to say loosely. Everything that comes to mind, that "goes through our heads," is called a thought. To think of a thing is just to be conscious of it in any way whatsoever. Second, the term is restricted by excluding whatever is directly presented; we think (or think of) only such things as we do not directly see, hear, smell, or taste. Then, third, the meaning is further limited to beliefs that rest upon some kind of evidence or testimony. Of this third type, two kinds—or, rather, two degrees—must be discriminated. In some cases, a belief is accepted with slight or almost no attempt to state the grounds that support it. In other cases, the ground or basis for a belief is deliberately sought and its adequacy to support the belief examined. This process is called reflective thought; it alone is truly educative in value, and it forms, accordingly, the principal subject of this volume. We shall now briefly describe each of the four senses.

I. In its loosest sense, thinking signifies everything that, as we say, is "in our heads" or that "goes through our minds." He who offers "a penny for your thoughts" does not expect to drive any great bargain. In calling the objects of his demand *thoughts,* he does not intend to ascribe to them dignity, consecutiveness, or truth. Any idle fancy, trivial recollection, or flitting impression will satisfy his de-

This is an abridged version of the original chapter that appeared in *How We Think,* by John Dewey, Copyright 1910 by Heath, D.C., & Company.

mand. Daydreaming, building of castles in the air, that loose flux of casual and disconnected material that floats through our minds in relaxed moments are, in this random sense, *thinking*. More of our waking life than we should care to admit, even to ourselves, is likely to be whiled away in this inconsequential trifling with idle fancy and unsubstantial hope. . . .

Now reflective thought is like this random coursing of things through the mind in that it consists of a succession of things thought of; but it is unlike, in that the mere chance occurrence of any chance "something or other" in an irregular sequence does not suffice. Reflection involves not simply a sequence of ideas, but a *consequence*— a consecutive ordering in such a way that each determines the next as its proper outcome, while each in turn leans back on its predecessors. The successive portions of the reflective thought grow out of one another and support one another; they do not come and go in a medley. Each phase is a step from something to something— technically speaking, it is a term of thought. Each term leaves a deposit which is utilized in the next term. The stream or flow becomes a train, chain, or thread.

II. Even when thinking is used in a broad sense, it is usually restricted to matters not directly perceived: to what we do not see, smell, hear, or touch. We ask the man telling a story if he saw a certain incident happen, and his reply may be, "No, I only thought of it." A note of invention, as distinct from faithful record of observation, is present. Most important in this class are successions of imaginative incidents and episodes which, having a certain coherence, hanging together on a continuous thread, lie between kaleidoscopic flights of fancy and considerations deliberately employed to establish a conclusion. The imaginative stories poured forth by children possess all degrees of internal congruity; some are disjointed, some are articulated. When connected, they simulate reflective thought; indeed, they usually occur in minds of logical capacity. These imaginative enterprises often precede thinking of the close-knit type and prepare the way for it. But *they do not aim at knowledge, at belief about facts or in truths;* and thereby they are marked off from reflective thought even when they most resemble it. Those who express such thoughts do not expect credence, but rather credit for a well-constructed plot or a well-arranged climax. They produce good stories, not—unless by chance—knowledge. Such thoughts are an efflorescence of feeling; the enhancement of a mood or sentiment is their aim; congruity of emotion, their binding tie.

III. In its next sense, thought denotes belief resting upon some basis, that is, real or supposed knowledge going beyond what is directly present. It is marked by *acceptance or rejection of something as reasonably probable or improbable.* This phase of thought, however, includes two such distinct types of belief that, even though their difference is strictly one of degree, not of kind, it becomes practically important to consider them separately. Some beliefs are accepted when their grounds have not themselves been considered, others are accepted because their grounds have been examined.

When we say, "Men used to think the world was flat," or, "I thought you went by the house," we express belief: something is accepted, held to, acquiesced in, or affirmed. But such thoughts may mean a supposition accepted without reference to its real grounds. These may be adequate, they may not; but their value with reference to the support they afford the belief has not been considered.

Such thoughts grow up unconsciously and without reference to the attainment of correct belief. They are picked up—we know not how. From obscure sources and by unnoticed channels they insinuate themselves into acceptance and become unconsciously a part of our mental furniture. Tradition, instruction, imitation—all of which depend upon authority in some form, or appeal to our own advantage, or fall in with a strong passion—are responsible for them. Such thoughts are prejudices, that is, prejudgments, not judgments proper that rest upon a survey of evidence.

IV. Thoughts that result in belief have an importance attached to them which leads to reflective thought, to conscious inquiry into the nature, conditions, and bearings of the belief. To *think* of whales and camels in the clouds is to entertain ourselves with fancies, terminable at our pleasure, which do not lead to any belief in particular. But to think of the world as flat is to ascribe a quality to a real thing as its real property. This conclusion denotes a connection among things and hence is not, like imaginative thought, plastic to our mood. Belief in the world's flatness commits him who holds it to thinking in certain specific ways of other objects, such as the heavenly bodies, antipodes, the possibility of navigation. It prescribes to him actions in accordance with his conception of these objects.

The consequences of a belief upon other beliefs and upon behavior may be so important, then, that men are forced to consider the grounds or reasons of their belief and its logical consequences. This means reflective thought—thought in its eulogistic and emphatic sense. . . .

Active, persistent, and careful consideration of any belief or sup-posed form of knowledge in the light of the grounds that support it, and the further conclusions to which it tends, constitutes reflective thought. Any one of the first three kinds of thought may elicit this type; but once begun, it is a conscious and voluntary effort to estab-lish belief upon a firm basis of reasons. . . .

The Central Factor in Thinking

The function by which one thing signifies or indicates another, and thereby leads us to consider how far one may be regarded as warrant for belief in the other, is, then, the central factor in all reflective or distinctively intellectual thinking. By calling up various situations to which such terms as *signifies* and *indicates* apply, the student will best realize for himself the actual facts denoted by the words *reflective thought.* Synonyms for these terms are: points to, tells of, betokens, prognosticates, represents, stands for, implies.[1] We also say one thing portends another; is ominous of another, or a symptom of it, or a key to it, or (if the connection is quite obscure) that it gives a hint, clue, or intimation.

Reflection thus implies that something is believed in (or disbe-lieved in), not on its own direct account, but through something else which stands as witness, evidence, proof, voucher, warrant; that is, as *ground of belief.* At one time, rain is actually felt or directly experi-enced; at another time, we infer that it has rained from the looks of the grass and trees, or that it is going to rain because of the condition of the air or the state of the barometer. At one time, we see a man (or suppose we do) without any intermediary fact; at another time, we are not quite sure what we see, and hunt for accompanying facts that will serve as signs, indications, tokens of what is to be believed.

Thinking, for the purposes of this inquiry, is defined accordingly as *that operation in which present facts suggest other facts (or truths) in such a way as to induce belief in the latter upon the ground or warrant of the former.* We do not put beliefs that rest simply on inference on the surest level of assurance. To say "I think so" implies that I do not as yet *know* so. The inferential belief may later be confirmed and come to stand as sure, but in itself it always has a certain element of supposition.

---

1. *Implies* is more often used when a principle or general truth brings about belief in some other truth; the other phrases are more frequently used to denote the cases in which one fact or event leads us to believe in something else.

Elements in Reflective Thinking

So much for the description of the more external and obvious aspects of the fact called *thinking*. Further consideration at once reveals certain subprocesses which are involved in every reflective operation. These are: (*a*) a state of perplexity, hesitation, doubt; and (*b*) an act of search or investigation directed toward bringing to light further facts which serve to corroborate or to nullify the suggested belief.

(*a*) In our illustration, the shock of coolness generated confusion and suspended belief, at least momentarily. Because it was unexpected, it was a shock or an interruption needing to be accounted for, identified, or placed. To say that the abrupt occurrence of the change of temperature constitutes a problem may sound forced and artificial; but if we are willing to extend the meaning of the word *problem* to whatever—no matter how slight and commonplace in character—perplexes and challenges the mind so that it makes belief at all uncertain, there is a genuine problem or question involved in this experience of sudden change.

(*b*) The turning of the head, the lifting of the eyes, the scanning of the heavens, are activities adapted to bring to recognition facts that will answer the question presented by the sudden coolness. The facts as they first presented themselves were perplexing; they suggested, however, clouds. The act of looking was an act to discover if this suggested explanation held good. It may again seem forced to speak of this looking, almost automatic, as an act of research or inquiry. But once more, if we are willing to generalize our conceptions of our mental operations to include the trivial and ordinary as well as the technical and recondite, there is no good reason for refusing to give such a title to the act of looking. The purport of this act of inquiry is to confirm or to refute the suggested belief. New facts are brought to perception, which either corroborate the idea that a change of weather is imminent, or negate it. . . .

Thinking begins in what may fairly enough be called a *forked-road* situation, a situation which is ambiguous, which presents a dilemma, which proposes alternatives. As long as our activity glides smoothly along from one thing to another, or as long as we permit our imagination to entertain fancies at pleasure, there is no call for reflection. Difficulty or obstruction in the way of reaching a belief brings us, however, to a pause. In the suspense of uncertainty, we metaphorically climb a tree; we try to find some standpoint from which we may survey additional facts and, getting a more commanding view of the situation, may decide how the facts stand related to one another.

Demand for the solution of a perplexity is the steadying and guiding factor in the entire process of reflection. Where there is no question of a problem to be solved or a difficulty to be surmounted, the course of suggestions flows on at random; we have the first type of thought described. If the stream of suggestions is controlled simply by their emotional congruity, their fitting agreeably into a single picture or story, we have the second type. But a question to be answered, an ambiguity to be resolved, sets up an end and holds the current of ideas to a definite channel. Every suggested conclusion is tested by its reference to this regulating end, by its pertinence to the problem in hand. This need of straightening out a perplexity also controls the kind of inquiry undertaken. . . . *The problem fixes the end of thought* and *the end controls the process of thinking.*

Summary

We may recapitulate by saying that the origin of thinking is some perplexity, confusion, or doubt. Thinking is not a case of spontaneous combustion; it does not occur just on "general principles." There is something specific which occasions and evokes it. General appeals to a child (or to a grown-up) to think, irrespective of the existence in his own experience of some difficulty that troubles him and disturbs his equilibrium, are as futile as advice to lift himself by his bootstraps.

Given a difficulty, the next step is suggestion of some way out—the formation of some tentative plan or project, the entertaining of some theory which will account for the peculiarities in question, the consideration of some solution for the problem. The data at hand cannot supply the solution; they can only suggest it. What, then, are the sources of the suggestion? Clearly past experience and prior knowledge. If the person has had some acquaintance with similar situations, if he has dealt with material of the same sort before, suggestions more or less apt and helpful are likely to arise. But unless there has been experience in some degree analogous, which may now be represented in imagination, confusion remains mere confusion. There is nothing upon which to draw in order to clarify it. Even when a child (or a grown-up) has a problem, to urge him to think when he has no prior experiences involving some of the same conditions, is wholly futile.

If the suggestion that occurs is at once accepted, we have uncritical thinking, the minimum of reflection. To turn the thing over in mind, to reflect, means to hunt for additional evidence, for new data, that will develop the suggestion, and will either, as we say, bear it out or else make obvious its absurdity and irrelevance. Given a genuine difficulty and a reasonable amount of analogous experience to draw upon, the difference, *par excellence,* between good and bad thinking is found at this point. The easiest way is to accept any suggestion that seems plausible and thereby bring to an end the condition of mental uneasiness. Reflective thinking is always more or less troublesome because it involves overcoming the inertia that inclines one to accept suggestions at their face value; it involves willingness to endure a condition of mental unrest and disturbance. Reflective thinking, in short, means judgment suspended during further inquiry; and suspense is likely to be somewhat painful. As we shall see later, the most important factor in the training of good mental habits consists in acquiring the attitude of suspended conclusion, and in mastering the various methods of searching for new materials to corroborate or to refute the first suggestions that occur. To maintain the state of doubt and to carry on systematic and protracted inquiry—these are the essentials of thinking.

THE SCIENTIFIC ATTITUDE
Clovis R. Shepherd

The Attitude of Everyday Life[1]

The attitude of daily life refers to the perspective which people employ in their day-to-day activities. It provides people a background for understanding events, interpreting behavior, and predicting the course of affairs. This perspective may be described in a few propositions which capture some of the major aspects of it and sift out much of the disorderly or idiosyncratic. One of the major assumptions of the scientific approach to everyday life is that behavior is orderly or can be made to appear orderly, and this orderliness should be capable of being characterized in a few propositions.

The attitude of everyday life may be said to be characterized by at least three major propositions. First, that a person views the world about him from his *personal perspective,* not from a general perspective. Second, that a person is constrained to *routinize* the world about him. Third, that a person is engaged in a process of *typification,* a process of forming generalized judgments about the world about him.

Personal Perspective

In everyday life a person adopts a personal perspective and tends to feel that the world revolves around him, that he is the center of the universe. This egocentric attitude is modified by the ability to be perceptive of and sensitive to others.[2] Perceptiveness and sensitivity are limited by the personal perspective, for a person tends to see

---

From *Small Groups; Some Sociological Persepectives,* by Clovis R. Shepard, published by Chandler Publishing Company, San Francisco. Copyright 1964 by Chandler Publishing Company. Reprinted by permission.

1. The following discussions of the attitude of daily life and the scientific attitude are based primarily on the writings of Alfred Schutz and Harold Garfinkel. See Garfinkel, "The Rational Properties of Scientific and Common Sense Activities," *Behavioral Science,* 5, 1960, pp. 72-83; Schutz, "Common-Sense and Scientific Interpretation of Human Action," *Philosophy and Phenomenological Research,* 14, 1953, pp. 1-38; _____, "On Multiple Realities," *Philosophy and Phenomenological Research,* 5, 1945, pp. 533-575; _____, "Choosing Among Projects of Action," *Philosophy and Phenomenological Research,* 12, 1951, pp. 161-184; _____, "Making Music Together," *Social Research,* 18, 1951, pp. 76-97; _____, "The Social World and the Theory of Social Action," *Social Research,* 27, 1960, pp. 203-221.

2. Tamotsu Shibutani, "Reference Groups as Perspectives," *American Journal of Sociology,* 60, 1955, pp. 562-569; _____, *Society and Personality* (Englewood Cliffs, N.J.: Prentice-Hall 1961), pp. 250-260; Renato Tagiuri and Luigi Petrullo (eds.), *Person Perception and Interpersonal Behavior* (Stanford: Stanford University Press, 1958).

things which fit the world as he sees it—he can imaginatively put himself in others' shoes, but he still knows which shoes belong to him. This process of perceiving and interpreting events in terms of one's individualized perspective leads a person to see what he expects to see, to interpret events in familiar terms, and to reconstruct events as he now (after the event) thinks they must have been.

The personal perspective is a product of the interplay between the individual and social life. A person's perspective reflects the shared perspective of members of one or more groups or social relations in which he is or has been involved, or into which he hopes to enter.[3] His perspective may also reflect the perspective of historical individuals who have left a written record of their experiences and ideas (such as St. Thomas Aquinas, Confucius, or Aristotle) or of historical groups (such as the ancient Greeks, the Mayans, or the Cretans). Some of these sources of a person's perspective may be called *reference groups*,[4] to indicate those groups which the individual uses as a point of reference for his own perspective. Reference groups may be *membership groups* (a person's family, his bowling team, his professional association, his colleagues at work, his lodge, or his church) or *nonmembership groups* (the ancient Greeks, the Apostles of Jesus, the bowling team of which he hopes to become a member). Nonmembership reference groups may be groups in which a person could not possibly become a member or they may be groups in which he hopes to become a member. In any case, the idea is that a person's perspective is a product partly of his own inclinations and partly of his accepting what he takes to be the ideas and sentiments of others, whether these others be specific persons with whom he has a relationship, members of groups in which he is also a member or hopes to become a member, or persons or groups with whom he is unlikely to have any personal contact but with whose ideas and sentiments he is familiar.

The personal perspective is one of the major characteristics of the attitude of everyday life. The fact that a person can imaginatively put himself in another's place to some degree and feel that others can see his position and in some degree understand his feelings makes social life possible. But no one can fully appreciate another person's perspective, just as no one can really believe that someone else can truly understand his perspective.[5]

---

3. See Shibutani, "Reference Groups as Perspectives," *op. cit.* in note 2.
4. Ralph H. Turner, "Role-Taking, Role Standpoint, and Reference-Group Behavior," *American Journal of Sociology,* 61, 1956, pp. 316-328.
5. See Shibutani, *op. cit.* in note 3; Schutz, "Common-Sense and Scientific Interpretation of Human Action," *op. cit.* in note 1.

Routinization

The second characteristic of the attitude of everyday life is the inevitability of routinization. People reduce to routine many of the numerous decisions they are confronted with daily in order to increase that part of their daily lives which they can take for granted, which they can assume to be predictable. It is necessary to keep in mind that predictability in everyday life is assumed and not scientifically proved, for it is based on plausibility. It is plausible at best because people often encounter something only once before they enmesh it in their routine daily life—they are not concerned about gathering evidence regarding its existence or its nature. Having encountered it once in common circumstances they take it for granted that they will encounter it again in very much the same form.

The process of routinization is necessary for the existence of social life. It would be impossible to adopt a doubtful posture regarding everything encountered, for were people to do so they would be able to accomplish little more than the care of their basic physical needs.[6] Try an experiment, some day, of adopting a questioning posture— from the time you arise, try to take nothing for granted, including the existence of water in the pipes, the proper functioning of the faucet, the presence of your toothbrush where you last left it, the adequate functioning of your car, and all other things you encounter during the day. If you do so you will find that it takes much more time to process your daily routine and you will be so engaged in the immediate situation that you will not anticipate future events to any degree. . . .

Of course, routinization can be carried too far. In its extreme form it can become a deadening influence, a rigidity and compulsiveness which not only reduce effectiveness by limiting flexibility and adaptiveness but also reduce enjoyment by eliminating surprise. Most people balance routinization with a taste of surprise—they occasionally purposefully break up their routines, they are attracted to the unusual and to the unanticipated, and they sometimes actively search for surprise. Most people cherish the surprises they encounter—not too much surprise, however, for too much surprise pushes a person too far toward the other extreme. Too much surprise with too little routine leads to chaos and the disruption of daily life. . . .

---

6. For example, the struggle for food and shelter among primitive peoples living in niggardly geographical environments, such as deserts and snow-covered areas.

Typifications

The third characteristic of daily life is the development of typifications. Obviously people cannot maintain a complete depiction of what they encounter, nor can they interact meaningfully with others unless they develop a generalized conception of what others are like and how they are likely to behave.[7] The typifications used by strangers are apt to be wrong, at times, because they use stereotypes and judgments about categories of people. The typifications used by friends are more apt to be accurate, because friends have more personal acquaintance with each other than strangers and are less likely to view each other as representatives of categories. Friends may err, though, because of the self-sustaining nature of typifications. People know their friends well enough to think they know what their friends intended to say and sometimes they are right. But a person may overlook the weaknesses and magnify the strengths of a friend, just as he may overlook the strengths and magnify the weaknesses of a stranger or an opponent.[8]

The typifications in daily life are not developed in order to test hypotheses in a scientific manner, but rather to serve people by helping to maintain their personal perspectives and their routines. Stereotypes (a major kind of typification) persist because they work, not always but often enough to satisfy most people within their attitudes of daily life. If a person were to think that his typifications were wrong, he would have to reorganize a good deal of his symbolic world and to question some of what he had taken for granted.[9]

These characteristics of the attitude of daily life serve the purposes of individuals who are confronted with an ongoing round of life and who must invest it with meaning consistent with expectations. People can have firsthand knowledge, at best, of only a small portion of what affects them—this portion they see from their own perspective. Much that is seen and done must be reduced to routine both to conserve energy and to satisfy others. Finally, much of what affects people can only be known from a distance—this portion must be

---

7. Shibutani, *Society and Personality, op. cit.* in note 2, pp. 111-118; Harold J. Leavitt, *Managerial Psychology* (Chicago: University of Chicago Press, 1958) pp. 65-80, for a discussion of storage capacity and the necessity for successive levels of generalized conceptions in dealing with complex situations.

8. Shibutani, *Society and Personality, op. cit.* in note 2, pp. 228-239; David Krech, Richard S. Crutchfield, and Egerton L. Ballachey, *Individual in Society* (New York: McGraw-Hill, 1962), pp. 51-65.

9. Leon Festinger, *A Theory of Cognitive Dissonance* (Evanston, Ill.: Row, Peterson, 1957); Krech, Crutchfield, and Ballachey, *op. cit.* in note 8; Schutz, "Common-Sense," *op. cit.* in note 1; Shibutani, *Society and Personality, op. cit.* in note 2, Chapter 16 and 17.

typified as well as those things which are experienced directly. The total of these characteristics leads to multiple realities[10] —to a succession of multiple worlds in which people must move and pretend to be knowledgeable; they must also take at face value much of what is presented to them, just as their associates must honor them by taking much of what they present to others at face value. To do otherwise is to court disaster—people cannot afford to question all the motivations of others, much less of themselves. The sociologist interpreting daily life might well subscribe to a sociological paraphrasing of Occam's razor: First seek the explanation of events in observed, manifest behavior; probe the underlying dynamics only if the explanations are inadequate.

The Scientific Attitude

The attitude of daily life cannot by itself lead to the development of scientific principles of human behavior, and any understanding sought in this attitude may not lead people far beyond colloquial knowledge. In order to develop scientific knowledge it is necessary to adopt a *scientific attitude* and, armed with this perspective, to approach the study of daily life. The attitude which the social scientist seeks to develop is characterized by a *general perspective,* a posture of *doubt,* and *typifications.*

General Perspective

The scientist seeks to develop a general perspective which will enable him to escape from the limitations of the personal perspective. He is interested in things common to all people or to groups of people. He seeks to abstract from the personal perspectives those elements which are common and to discard those elements which are idiosyncratic. In adopting a general perspective the scientist confronts two methodological problems. First, he must control his own personal perspective by removing himself from the behavior he is studying.[11] By not being a participant in the group he is better able to control his personal biases and identifications and better able to understand the diverse personal perspectives of the participants. When he finds it necessary to be a participant, he seeks to adopt a neutral role to avoid involvement in the politics of the group.

---

10. Schutz, "On Multiple Realities," *op. cit.* in note 1.
11. Ralph Ross, *Symbols and Civilization* (New York: Harcourt, 1962), and Peter L. Berger, *Invitation to Sociology: A Humanist Perspective* (Garden City, N.Y.: Doubleday, 1963) provide good introductions to the problem of the observer removing himself from what he studies.

Second, he must control the nature of the abstractions he makes from the personal perspectives of the participants by using standardized procedures (such as observer forms, questionnaires, and the like) and associates.[12] The standardized procedures help him avoid missing relevant things, and the associates help him check on the reliability of his observations and abstractions.

The Posture of Doubt

The scientist must also reverse the routinization of daily life—he can afford to take nothing for granted except the basic assumptions of science.[13] In daily life the individual is led to question something he has taken for granted only after he encounters trouble, but in scientific research the scientist must question everything. Even when observations and abstractions are supported by a great deal of evidence, the scientist must still consider them open to disproof.[14] In everyday life people can hold on to their attitudes and beliefs in the face of overwhelming contrary evidence[15]—after all, it is a person's right and privilege to be stubborn or stupid, and he is likely to find someone who agrees with him. As long as someone else feels the same way, this support can go a long way in helping him maintain his position.

But a scientist who maintains a position in the face of overwhelming contrary evidence is due to be ridden out of the professional fraternity. To be sure, the matter isn't quite this simple—what constitutes "overwhelming contrary evidence" may be a controversial matter. Raise the question of the existence of extrasensory perception (ESP) in a gathering of psychologists or sociologists and the fur is apt to fly. A few will defend its existence staunchly, a few more will admit there is probably something there to be explained, but most will question the existence of unexplained phenomena. However, the one statement that they are all likely to accept, even though grudgingly, is that the existence of ESP is not a closed matter and it would

---

12. Herbert Hyman, *Survey Design and Analysis* (Glencoe, Ill.: Free Press, 1955), and Claire Selltiz, Marie Jahoda, Morton Deutsch, and Stuart W. Cook, *Research Methods in Social Relations* (revised one-volume edition; New York: Holt, 1959) provide good introductions to the use of standardized procedures and associates in improving reliability of observations.

13. See Ross, *op. cit.* in note 11; Berger, *op. cit.* in note 11; Schutz, "Common-Sense and Scientific Interpretation of Human Action," *op. cit.* in note 1.

14. See Ross, *op. cit.* in note 11; Berger, *op. cit.* in note 11; Hans Reichenbach, *The Rise of Scientific Philosophy* (Berkeley and Los Angeles: University of California Press, 1951).

15. Leon Festinger, Henry W. Riecken, Jr., and Stanley Schachter, *When Prophecy Fails* (Minneapolis: University of Minnesota Press, 1956). In this book the authors show how members of a religious sect maintain their faith and their belief in the prophetic wisdom of their leader in the face of a series of disconfirming evidences of the leader's prophecies.

be foolish, scientifically, to ignore it without taking a close look at the evidence.[16]

The posture of doubt leads social scientists to question things which people take for granted in everyday life, and to insist on evidential proof of even the most rudimentary aspects of human behavior. It is no longer necessary to caution many people that some of the things they take for granted are culturally determined and vary from one culture to another (examples: forms of greeting, foods, marriage customs, or the distance people maintain between themselves when conducting business or having a private talk[17]). It is more difficult, though, to convince people that they should be wary of accepting the wisdom of proverbs, sayings, or folk knowledge. Proverbs provide a basis for predicting the future and explaining the past, and almost any behavior can be predicted or explained by one or another proverb. Of a couple anticipating a separation of several months, one may console himself by thinking "absence makes the heart grow fonder," while the other is fearful because of thinking "out of sight, out of mind." Careful research will probably show that both of these sayings are right under some conditions and wrong under other conditions.

The goal of the scientist is to achieve the maximum possible accuracy in prediction—but prediction based on theory and research, not on one's personal preferences. The maximum possible accuracy in prediction is achieved by substituting scientific evidence for assumption and by testing the adequacy of explanation by the accuracy of prediction. For example, the assumption that absence makes the heart grow fonder would be questioned and data gathered to indicate whether, when people separate for a length of time, the separation leads to greater, lesser, or the same fondness for each other. Gathering data would become complex because the researcher would have to decide what is meant by fondness, what kinds of relations are involved (one would not equate lovers with friends or acquaintances), what kinds of separation exist, and other details. The researcher would also have to decide what other kind of information might make the answer to the question conditional. If both persons in a given case believe "out of sight, out of mind," this agreement might lead to a different result than would follow if both persons believe "absence makes the heart grow fonder." Once the researcher

---

16. See, for example, Gardner Murphy, "Trends in the Study of Extrasensory Perception," *American Psychologist,* 13, 1958, pp. 69-76.
17. See Clyde Kluckhohn, *Mirror For Man* (New York: McGraw-Hill, 1949).

feels he has some evidence to justify the idea that, under some conditions, absence makes the heart grow fonder, he then must gather new data and predict this result in order to test the adequacy of his explanation.[18]

Typifications

The scientist is engaged in developing typifications, but the typifications he develops differ from those in daily life in two major ways. First, they are typifications of typifications.[19] The raw data of the social scientist are the ideas and feelings of people in everyday life. What is perceived, thought, or felt by people is the reality of the social scientist's subject matter—if a person believes in ghosts and this belief affects his behavior, then the social scientist accepts "belief in ghosts" as reality. The scientist is more concerned with how this belief influences a person's behavior than whether ghosts exist or not. He suspects that if a person believes in ghosts he is not likely to change this belief very easily because within the attitude of daily life this belief may be desirable, meaningful, or necessary in order to maintain acceptance in a social group or to sustain a person's conception of himself or the world about him.

Second, the scientist's typifications are developed in order to serve a common goal with other social scientists, rather than to serve his own personal ends. He must follow certain rules in developing typifications in order for them to gain acceptance—otherwise, the typifications are suspect of being only his own personal preferences. The typifications must be consistent with what is taken to be the abstract nature of that part of human behavior comprised in his field, with what other people have found in research, and with the measuring instruments which are in use. . . .

Conclusion

The scientific attitude differs in many respects from the attitude of everyday life. Some of these differences are obvious, but many more are subtle and difficult to portray in a few sentences. A person within the attitude of daily life may function well or poorly in small groups but he cannot develop tested and testable propositions about

18. The distinction between *ex post facto* and predictive studies is very important. See Selltiz, *et. al., op. cit.* in note 12; Hyman, *op. cit.* in note 12.

19. See Schutz, "Common Sense and Scientific Interpretation of Human Action," *op. cit.* in note 1, on the notion of typifications of typifications, especially on this point as an important distinction between social and physical science.

behavior in small groups. If he desires to understand and be able to utilize the work of social scientists on small groups he will have to cultivate the scientific attitude. . . .

Selected Bibliography

Articles

Abraham Kaplan, "Sociology Learns the Language of Mathematics," in James R. Newman (ed.), *The World of Mathematics, Volume Two* (New York: Simon and Schuster, 1956), pp. 1294-1313. A discussion of promising leads and disappointing results in attempts to apply mathematical models to social behavior.

Alfred Schutz, especially "Common-Sense and Scientific Interpretation of Human Action," *Philosophy and Phenomenological Research*, 5, 1945, pp. 533-575; and "Choosing Among Projects of Action," *Philosophy and Phenomenological Research*, 12, 1951, pp. 161-184; see also footnote 1, this chapter. The work of Alfred Schutz follows in the phenomenological heritage of German philosophers and bears a close resemblance in many ways to the American tradition in sociology and social psychology stemming from the works of George H. Mead and Charles H. Cooley.

Books

Peter Berger, *Invitation to Sociology: A Humanist Perspective* (Garden City, N.Y.: Doubleday, 1963). A readable and knowledgeable introduction to the sociological perspective.

Abraham Kaplan, *The Conduct of Inquiry* (San Francisco: Chandler, 1964). A penetrating and wide-ranging analysis of methodological problems in behavioral science.

Ralph Ross, *Symbols and Civilization* (New York: Harcourt, 1962). A discussion of the role of symbols in thought, logical analysis, science, and society.

FUNCTIONAL ROLES OF GROUP MEMBERS
Kenneth D. Benne and Paul Sheats

The Relative Neglect of Member Roles in Group Training

Efforts to improve group functioning through training have traditionally emphasized the training of group leadership. And frequently this training has been directed toward the improvement of the skills of the leader in transmitting information and in manipulating groups. Little direct attention seems to have been given to the training of group members in the membership roles required for effective group growth and production. The present discussion is based on the conviction that both effective group training and adequate research into the effectiveness of group training methods must give attention to the identification, analysis, and practice of leader *and* member roles, seen as co-relative aspects of over-all group growth and production.

Certain assumptions have undergirded the tendency to isolate the leadership role from membership roles and to neglect the latter in processes of group training. (1) "Leadership" has been identified with traits and qualities inherent within the "leader" personality. Such traits and qualities can be developed, it is assumed, in isolation from the functioning of members in a group setting. The present treatment sees the leadership role in terms of functions to be performed within a group in helping that group to grow and to work productively. No sharp distinction can be made between leadership and membership functions, between leader and member roles. Groups may operate with various degrees of diffusion of "leadership" functions among group members or of concentration of such functions in one member or a few members. Ideally, of course, the concept of leadership emphasized here is that of a multilaterally shared responsibility. In any event, effectiveness in the leader role is a matter of leader-member relationship. Any one side of a relationship cannot be effectively trained in isolation from the retraining of the other side of that relationship. (2) It has been assumed that the "leader" is uniquely responsible for the quality and amount of production by the group. The "leader" must see to it that the "right" group goals are set, that the group jobs get done, that members are "motivated" to participate. On this view, membership roles are of secondary importance. "Membership" is tacitly identified with "followership." The present discussion assumes that the quality and

Reprinted with permission from *Journal of Social Issues*, Vol. IV, No. 2 (Spring, 1948), pp. 41-49.

amount of group production is the "responsibility" of the group. The setting of goals and the marshalling of resources to move toward these goals is a group responsibility in which all members of a mature group come variously to share. The functions to be performed both in building and maintaining group-centered activity and in effective production by the group are primarily member roles. Leadership functions can be defined in terms of facilitating identification, acceptance, development and allocation of these group-required roles by the group. (3) There has frequently been a confusion between the roles which members enact within a group and the individual personalities of the group members. That there are relationships between the personality structures and needs of group members and the range and quality of group membership roles which members can learn to perform is not denied. On the contrary, the importance of studies designed to describe and explain and to increase our control of these relationships is affirmed. But, at the level of group functioning, member roles, relevant to group growth and accomplishment, must be clearly distinguished from the use of the group environment by individuals to satisfy individual and group-irrelevant needs, if clear diagnosis of member-roles required by the group and adequate training of members to perform group-required roles are to be advanced. Neglect of this distinction has been associated traditionally with the neglect of the analysis of member roles in group growth and production.

A Classification of Member Roles

The following analysis of functional member roles was developed in connection with the First National Training Laboratory in Group Development, 1947. It follows closely the analysis of participation functions used in coding the content of group records for research purposes. A similar analysis operated in faculty efforts to train group members in their functional roles during the course of the laboratory.[1]

The member-roles identified in this analysis are classified into three broad groupings.

1. Group task roles. Participant roles here are related to the task which the group is deciding to undertake or has undertaken. Their purpose is to facilitate and coordinate group effort in the selection

---

1. A somewhat different analysis of member-participations, in terms of categories used by interaction-observers in observation of group processes in the First National Training Laboratory, is described in the *Preliminary Report* of the laboratory, pages 122-132. The number of categories used by interaction observers was "directed primarily by limitations of observer load."

and definition of a common problem and in the solution of that problem.

2. Group building and maintenance roles. The roles in this category are oriented toward the functioning of the group as a group. They are designed to alter or maintain the group way of working, to strengthen, regulate and perpetuate the group as a group.

3. Individual roles. This category does not classify member-roles as such, since the "participations" denoted here are directed toward the satisfaction of the "participant's" individual needs. Their purpose is some individual goal which is not relevant either to the group task or to the functioning of the group as a group. Such participations are, of course, highly relevant to the problem of group training, insofar as such training is directed toward improving group maturity or group task efficiency.

Group Task Roles

The following analysis assumes that the task of the discussion group is to select, define and solve common problems. The roles are identified in relation to functions of facilitation and coordination of group problem-solving activities. Each member may of course enact more than one role in any given unit of participation and a wide range of roles in successive participations. Any or all of these roles may be played at times by the group "leader" as well as by various members.

a. The *initiator-contributor* suggests or proposes to the group new ideas or a changed way of regarding the group problem or goal. The novelty proposed may take the form of suggestions of a new group goal or a new definition of the problem. It may take the form of a suggested solution or some way of handling a difficulty that the group has encountered. Or it may take the form of a proposed new procedure for the group, a new way of organizing the group for the task ahead.

b. The *information seeker* asks for clarification of suggestions made in terms of their factual adequacy, for authoritative information and facts pertinent to the problem being discussed.

c. The *opinion seeker* asks not primarily for the facts of the case but for a clarification of the values pertinent to what the group is undertaking or of values involved in a suggestion made or in alternative suggestions.

d. The *information giver* offers facts or generalizations which are "authoritative" or relates his own experience pertinently to the group problem.

e. The *opinion giver* states his belief or opinion pertinently to a suggestion made or to alternative suggestions. The emphasis is on his proposal of what should become the group's view of pertinent values, not primarily upon relevant facts or information.

f. The *elaborator* spells out suggestions in terms of examples or developed meanings, offers a rationale for suggestions previously made and tries to deduce how an idea or suggestion would work out if adopted by the group.

g. The *coordinator* shows or clarifies the relationships among various ideas and suggestions, tries to pull ideas and suggestions together or tries to coordinate the activities of various members or sub-groups.

h. The *orienter* defines the position of the group with respect to its goals by summarizing what has occurred, points to departures from agreed upon directions or goals, or raises questions about the direction which the group discussion is taking.

i. The *evaluator-critic* subjects the accomplishment of the group to some standard or set of standards of group-functioning in the context of the group task. Thus, he may evaluate or question the "practicality," the "logic," the "facts" or the "procedure" of a suggestion or of some unit of group discussion.

j. The *energizer* prods the group to action or decision, attempts to stimulate or arouse the group to "greater" or "higher quality" activity.

k. The *procedural technician* expedites group movement by doing things for the group—performing routine tasks, e.g., distributing materials, or manipulating objects for the group, e.g., rearranging the seating or running the recording machine, etc.

l. The *recorder* writes down suggestions, makes a record of group decisions, or writes down the product of discussion. The recorder role is the "group memory."

Group Building and Maintenance Roles

Here the analysis of member-functions is oriented to those participations which have for their purpose the building of group-centered attitudes and orientation among the members of a group or the maintenance and perpetuation of such group-centered behavior. A given contribution may involve several roles and a member or the "leader" may perform various roles in successive contributions.

a. The *encourager* praises, agrees with and accepts the contribution of others. He indicates warmth and solidarity in his attitude toward other group members, offers commendation and praise and in various ways indicates understanding and acceptance of other points of view, ideas and suggestions.

b. The *harmonizer* mediates the differences between other members, attempts to reconcile disagreements, relieves tension in conflict situations through jesting or pouring oil on the troubled waters, etc.

c. The *compromiser* operates from within a conflict in which his idea or position is involved. He may offer compromise by yielding status, admitting his error, by disciplining himself to maintain group harmony, or by "coming half-way" in moving along with the group.

d. The *gate-keeper and expediter* attempts to keep communication channels open by encouraging or facilitating the participation of others ("we haven't got the ideas of Mr. X yet," etc.) or by proposing regulation of the flow of communication ("why don't we limit the length of our contributions so that everyone will have a chance to contribute?", etc.).

e. The *standard setter* or *ego ideal* expresses standards for the group to attempt to achieve in its functioning or applies standards in evaluating the quality of group processes.

f. The *group-observer* and *commentator* keeps records of various aspects of group process and feeds such data with proposed interpretations into the group's evaluation of its own procedures.

g. The *follower* goes along with the movement of the group, more or less passively accepting the ideas of others, serving as an audience in group discussion and decision.

"Individual" Roles

Attempts by "members" of a group to satisfy individual needs which are irrelevant to the group task and which are non-oriented or negatively oriented to group building and maintenance set problems of group and member training. A high incidence of "individual-centered" as opposed to "group-centered" participation in a group always calls for self-diagnosis of the group. The diagnosis may reveal one or several of a number of conditions—low level of skill-training among members, including the group leader; the prevalence of "authoritarian" and "laissez faire" points of view toward group functioning in the group; a low level of group maturity, discipline and morale; an inappropriately chosen and inadequately defined group task, etc. Whatever the diagnosis, it is in this setting that the training needs of the group are to be discovered and group training efforts to meet these needs are to be defined. The outright "suppression" of "individual roles" will deprive the group of data needed for really adequate self-diagnosis and therapy.

a. The *aggressor* may work in many ways—deflating the status of others, expressing disapproval of the values, acts or feelings of others, attacking the group or the problem it is working on, joking aggressively, showing envy toward another's contribution by trying to take credit for it, etc.

b. The *blocker* tends to be negativistic and stubbornly resistant, disagreeing and opposing without or beyond "reason" and attempting to maintain or bring back an issue after the group has rejected or by-passed it.

c. The *recognition-seeker* works in various ways to call attention to himself, whether through boasting, reporting on personal achievements, acting in unusual ways, struggling to prevent his being placed in an "inferior" position, etc.

d. The *self-confessor* uses the audience opportunity which the group setting provides to express personal, non-group oriented, "feeling," "insight," "ideology," etc.

e. The *playboy* makes a display of his lack of involvement in the group's processes. This may take the form of cynicism, nonchalance, horseplay and other more or less studied forms of "out of field" behavior.

f. The *dominator* tries to assert authority or superiority in manipulating the group or certain members of the group. This domination may take the form of flattery, of asserting a superior status or right to attention, giving directions authoritatively, interrupting the contributions of others, etc.

g. The *help-seeker* attempts to call forth "sympathy" response from other group members or from the whole group, whether through expressions of insecurity, personal confusion or depreciation of himself beyond "reason."

h. The *special interest pleader* speaks for the "small business man," the "grass roots" community, the "housewife," "labor," etc., usually cloaking his own prejudices or biases in the stereotype which best fits his individual need.

The Problem of Member Role Requiredness

Identification of group task roles and of group building and maintenance roles which do actually function in processes of group discussion raises but does not answer the further question of what roles are required for "optimum" group growth and productivity. Certainly the discovery and validation of answers to this question have a high priority in any advancing science of group training and development. No attempt will be made here to review the bearing of the analyzed data from the First National Training Laboratory in Group Development on this point.

It may be useful in this discussion, however, to comment on two conditions which effective work on the problem of role-requiredness must meet. First, an answer to the problem of optimum task role requirements must be projected against a scheme of the process of group production. Groups in different stages of an act of problem selection and solution will have different role requirements. For example, a group early in the stages of problem selection which is attempting to lay out a range of possible problems to be worked on, will probably have relatively less need for the roles of "evaluator-critic," "energizer" and "coordinator" than a group which has selected and discussed its problem and is shaping to decision. The combination and balance of task role requirements is a function of the group's stage of progress with respect to its task. Second, the group building role requirements of a group are a function of its stage of development—its level of group maturity. For example, a "young" group will probably require less of the role of the "standard setter" than a more mature group. Too high a level of aspiration may frustrate a "young" group where a more mature group will be able to take the same level of aspiration in its stride. Again the role of "group observer and commentator" must be carefully adapted to the level of maturity of the group. Probably the distinction between "group" and "individual" roles can be drawn much more sharply in a relatively mature than in a "young" group.

Meanwhile, group trainers cannot wait for a fully developed science of group training before they undertake to diagnose the role requirements of the groups with which they work and help these groups to share in such diagnosis. Each group which is attempting to improve the quality of its functioning as a group must be helped to diagnose its role requirements and must attempt to train members to fill the required roles effectively. This describes one of the principal objectives of training of group members.

The Problem of Role Flexibility

The previous group experience of members, where this experience has included little conscious attention to the variety of roles involved in effective group production and development, has frequently stereotyped the member into a limited range of roles. These he plays in all group discussions whether or not the group situation requires them.

Some members see themselves primarily as "evaluator-critics" and play this role in and out of season. Others may play the roles of "encourager" or of "energizer" or of "information giver" with only small sensitivity to the role requirements of a given group situation. The development of skill and insight in diagnosing role requirements has already been mentioned as an objective of group member training. An equally important objective is the development of role flexibility, of skill and security in a wide range of member roles, on the part of all group members. . . .

Methods of Group Member Training

The objectives in training group members have been identified. Some of the kinds of resistances encountered in training group members to diagnose the role requirements of a group situation and to acquire skill in a variety of member roles have been suggested. Before analyzing briefly the methods used for group member training in the First National Training Laboratory, a few additional comments on resistances to member training may be useful. The problem of group training is actually a problem of re-training. Members of a training group have had other group experiences. They bring to the training experience attitudes toward group work, more or less conscious skills for dealing with leaders and other members, and a more or less highly developed rationale of group processes. These may or may not support processes of democratic operation in the training group. Where they do not, they function as resistances to retraining. Again, trainees are inclined to make little or no distinction between the roles they perform in a group and their personalities. Criticism of the role a group member plays is perceived as criticism of "himself." Methods must be found to reduce ego-defensiveness toward criticism of member roles. Finally, training groups must be helped to make a distinction between group feeling and group productivity. Groups which attain a state of good group feeling often perceive attempts to diagnose and criticize their level of productivity as threats to this feeling of group warmth and solidarity.

1. Each Basic Skill Training group in the Laboratory used self-observation and diagnosis of its own growth and development as a primary means of member training.

a. Sensitization to the variety of roles involved in and required by group functioning began during the introduction of members to the group. In one BST group, this early sensitization to member role variety and role requiredness began with the "leader's" summarizing, as part of his introduction of himself to the group, certain of the member roles in which he was usually cast by groups and other roles which he found it difficult to play, even when needed by the group. He asked the group's help in criticizing and improving his skill in those roles where he felt weakest. Other members followed suit. Various members showed widely different degrees of sensitivity to the operation of member roles in groups and to the degree of their own proficiency in different roles. This introduction procedure gave the group a partial listing of member roles for later use and supplementation, initial self-assessments of member strengths and weaknesses and diagnostic material concerning the degree of group self-sophistication among the members. The training job had come to be seen by most members as a re-training job.

b. A description of the use of training observers in group self-evaluation sessions is given in the next paper in this issue. At this point, only the central importance which self-evaluation sessions played in member training needs to be stressed. Research observers fed observational data concerning group functioning into periodic discussions by the group of its strengths and weaknesses as a group. Much of these data concerned role requirements for the job the group had been attempting, which roles had been present, which roles had probably been needed. "Individual" roles were identified and interpreted in an objective and non-blaming manner. Out of these discussions, group members came to identify various kinds of member roles, to relate role requiredness to stages in group production and in group growth and to assess the range of roles each was able to play well when required. Out of these discussions came group decisions concerning the supplying of needed roles in the next session. Member commitments concerning behavior in future sessions also came out of these evaluations. These took the form both of silent commitments and of public commitments in which the help of the group was requested.

c. Recordings of segments of the group's discussion were used by most Basic Skill Training groups. Groups listened to themselves, diagnosed the member and leader functions involved and assessed the adequacy of these.

2. Role-played sessions in each group, although they were pointed content-wise to the skills of the change-agent, offered important material for the diagnosis of member roles and of role-requiredness. These sessions offered an important supplement to group self-diagnosis and evaluation. It is easier for members to get perspective on their participation in a role-played episode of group process than it is

on their own participation in a "real" group. The former is not perceived as "real." The role is more easily disengaged for purposes of analysis and evaluation from the person playing the role. Ego-defensiveness toward the role as enacted is reduced. Role-playing sessions also provided practice opportunity to members in a variety of roles.

3. Practice by group members of the role of *observer-commentator* is especially valuable in developing skill in diagnosing member roles and in assessing the role requirements of a group situation. In several groups, each member in turn served as observer, supplementing the work of the research observers in evaluation sessions. Such members worked more or less closely with the anecdotal observer for the group on skill-problems encountered. Practice opportunity in the *observer-commentator* role was also provided in clinic group meetings in the afternoon.

Summary

Training in group membership roles requires the identification and analysis of various member roles actually enacted in group processes. It involves further the analysis of group situations in terms of roles required in relation both to a schema of group production and to a conception of group growth and development. A group's self-observation and self-evaluation of its own processes provides useful content and practice opportunity in member training. Practice in enacting a wider range of required roles and in role flexibility can come out of member commitment to such practice with help from the group in evaluating and improving the required skills. Member training is typically re-training and resistances to re-training can be reduced by creating a non-blaming and objective atmosphere in group self-evaluation and by using role-playing of group processes for diagnosis and practice. The training objectives of developing skill in the diagnosis of group role requirements and developing role flexibility among members also indicate important research areas for a science of group training.

THE ROLE OF CONFLICT IN DISCUSSION

John L. Petelle*

The place of cooperation in group discussion has long been stressed by those persons interested in the discussion process. Definitions of discussion such as ". . . the conversation that results when members of a group gather to share their information and opinions on a topic, or to think through a common problem . . ."[1] indicate the cooperative effort. Statements regarding the importance of "cooperative investigation"[2] and concepts such as discussion is primarily a "cooperation-enlisting"[3] process, illustrate the role of cooperation in discussion. At the same time, however, the majority of persons describing discussion also admit the need for conflict. Howell and Smith, for example, point out that "Good discussion is born in conflict and thrives on conflict. But the conflict must be one of ideas rather than personalities."[4] Ewbank and Auer maintain that there ". . . is a need for differences of opinion."[5] Harnack and Fest acknowledge that:

> Cooperative groups are obviously preferable to competitive groups, yet cooperation does not mean absence of conflict, as some believe. It does mean absence of conflict to *block individuals* and the vigorous presence of conflict intended to explore ideas.[6]

Although many persons agree that conflict as well as cooperation is needed in the discussion process, little attention has been given to the role of conflict. It is my position that the presence of conflict may be a positive force in intercommunication.

While most of us in the field of speech agree upon the importance of understanding the process of communication in small groups probably few of us would embark upon identical or perhaps even similar courses of action in carrying out such an objective. I would submit

---

Reprinted with permission from *Speaker and Gavel,* Vol. 2, No. 1 (November, 1964), pp. 24-28.

*Professor of Speech, University of Nebraska (Ph.D., University of Minnesota, 1962).

1. Henry L. Ewbank and J. Jeffery Auer, *Discussion & Debate,* New York: F.S. Crofts & Co., 1946, p. 289.
2. *Ibid.,* p. 300.
3. Laura Crowell, *Discussion: Method of Democracy,* Chicago: Scott, Foresman, & Co., 1963, p. 10.
4. William S. Howell and Donald K. Smith, *Discussion,* New York: The Macmillan Co., 1956, p. 256.
5. Ewbank and Auer, *op. cit.,* p. 295.
6. Victor Harnack and Thorrel B. Fest, *Group Discussion, Theory and Teachnique,* New York: Appleton-Century-Crofts, 1964, p. 176.

that such deviation of thought, conflict, if you will, serves as a positive force in aiding us to achieve a greater and more comprehensive understanding of what this process is. It is not, however, the purpose of this article to examine what this course of action might be. Rather, it is my intention to examine conflict as a common operating force in society, to determine what, if any positive functions it may have, and then to determine the role of conflict in the discussion process.

The presence of conflict in today's society is quite apparent. A scanning of the headlines, a twist of the radio dial, a flick of the TV switch brings to us only all too readily, the element of conflict. Types of conflict and situations where conflict occurs are so numerous it would be impossible to consider them all within the scope of this article. Broadly speaking, we may cite two general categories of conflict; conflict of force and conflict of ideas. Although admittedly the two may, and indeed often do, occur together, and while one is often the cause of the other, let us limit ourselves to that category of conflict which manifests itself most commonly in small group communication; the conflict of ideas.

I believe we may accept as our initial premise, that conflict is a common element in society. As we consider conflict I would like to think of it as being a continuum, ranging from a deviant thought to overt physical force. In this context we can see that conflict must, at some point on the continuum, always exist whenever people interact. Thus, as the German sociologist, Georg Simmel pointed out, conflict must be considered as a form of socialization.[7] Granting then, that conflict is a common operating force in society, our immediate concern is whether this force may ever exist in a positive nature.

Since the beginning of civilization, conflict has been a vital force in the progress of man. From the conflict of force which drove the piltdown man toward the creation of new weapons for survival, to the twentieth century's conflict of multi-ideologies, conflict has operated not only as a destructive element which has separated men, but also as a positive force which has stimulated advancement. Edward A. Ross in *Principles of Sociology,* pointed out that "The good side of opposition is that it stimulates."[8] And indeed, there have been few, if any, forward steps in man's progress which did not have their origin in point and counterpoint.

---

7. Georg Simmel, *Conflict,* trans. by Kurt H. Wolff, Illinois: The Free Press, 1955, p. 13.
8. Edward A. Ross, *The Principles of Sociology,* New York: The Century Co., 1920, p. 167.

Perhaps one of the most advanced as well as thorough theories of conflict is the product of Georg Simmel. In his treatise, *Conflict,* Simmel outlines his philosophy of the nature of conflict. In examining this work one can hardly help but observe that Simmel accords a number of positive functions to conflict. In considering what I believe to be some of the major positive functions of conflict as they relate to the small group communicative process, I am heavily indebted to Simmel's theories.

According to Simmel, one of the positive functions of conflict, as it relates to the group is that conflict tends to create order within the group.[9] That is, as a result of conflict either from within the group or from an outside origin, the group begins to structure itself into some form of an organized hierarchy. This does not mean to imply that structure is dependent upon conflict but rather that conflict often aids the ordering process.

Another positive function of conflict, according to Simmel, is that it acts as a cohesive agent upon the group. A state of conflict tends to ". . . pull the members so tightly together and subject them to such a uniform impulse that they either must completely get along with or completely repel one another."[10] In addition to this, conflict not only acts as a cohesive force in uniting the group but it may also be the prime agent which brings groups or individuals together. Thus, conflict may establish communication where before there was none. Again turning to Simmel, he remarks:

> Conflict may not only heighten the concentration of an existing unit, radically eliminating all elements which might blur the distinctness of its boundaries against the enemy; it may also bring persons and groups together which have otherwise nothing to do with each other.[11]

Finally, Simmel contends that conflict is an indication of group stability.[12] That is, the more intimate and secure the group, the more intense the conflict and the greater its frequency. Our individual experiences bear out, I believe, this particular aspect of Simmel's theory inasmuch as each of us tends to be less patient, more direct, more openly hostile in situations we feel confident in and in groups we know. Much more tact and reserve, for example, is often accorded a stranger than is given a wife, a brother, or even a close friend.

---

9. Simmel, *op. cit.,* pp. 87-91.
10. *Ibid.,* pp. 92-93.
11. *Ibid.,* pp. 98-99.
12. *Ibid.,* pp. 43-49.

In relating these concepts of conflict to small group communication, or anything else for that matter, I feel no matter how obvious it would seem, that a note of caution should be injected. That is, one cannot conclude from these propositions that such will always be the case. As long as we deal with human behavior we must ever keep in mind the element of probability.

Thus far we have determined that conflict is a common force in our society and that it does possess certain positive functions. At this point then, let us try to correlate the positive elements of conflict with the role of conflict in small group communication.

The discussion or small group communicative situation is obviously in its very essence, a social function. Inasmuch as conflict is an inherent element in almost all social interactions we might expect to find conflict present in group discussions. As has been pointed out by any number of discussion textbooks, the basic purpose of discussion is a problem-solving activity and as such has as its main objective to serve as a testing ground whereby through cooperational effort ideas and information may be exchanged and evaluated. Now as was pointed out earlier, while discussion textbooks deal with the element of cooperation as requisite to a successful group discussion, little seems to have been done regarding the necessity for the presence of conflict, or in fact, what one may tell about the group after observing group conflict in operation.[13] It is my contention that the presence of conflict in group discussion may be just as requisite and valuable as cooperation. Indeed, I would argue, as did Cooley, that "The more one thinks of it the more he will see that conflict and cooperation are not separable things, but phases of one process which always involves something of both."[14] Granted then, the presence of conflict in discussion, let us return to our definition of conflict. That is, a continuum ranging from deviant thought to overt force. Considering discussion as a problem-solving activity in which there is an exchange and evaluation of ideas we must recognize that to some extent conflict must be present in this communicative interaction. It would be difficult to imagine any "exchange and evaluation" without some disagreement. In fact, one might very well question the effectiveness of a problem-solving activity devoid of different ideas and thinking. If the group were unanimous in ideas and action little, in most cases, would be achieved toward the solution of a problem. And if a solution were reached through unani-

---

13. Although not elaborated upon in great detail, categories 10 and 12 of Bales' interaction chart in his *Process Analysis* at least recognizes the possibility of utilizing conflict in this manner.

14. Charles H. Cooley, *Social Process*, New York: Charles Seribner's Sons, 1918, p. 39.

mous thought and action the progress and success of the group interaction could at best be representative of the weaker elements of the
group.

If the real aim of discussion is to make progress in a problem area
then perhaps we should recognize and encourage the presence of
conflict as a stimulant to group interaction. Naturally, however, we
do not want conflict merely for the sake of conflict. Nor do we want
just any kind of conflict. Lewis A. Coser in *The Functions of Social
Conflict*[15] identifies two kinds of conflict; realistic and non-realistic.[16] Realistic conflict, according to Coser, is that conflict which is
the result of frustration in attempting to achieve a goal. It is a means
toward a specific result and in such conflict, one may find functional
alternatives as to the desired means. Non-realistic conflict, on the
other hand, is conflict which is a result of a lack of a release of
tension and in such conflict there exists only functional alternatives
as to objects. Groups, of any type, form for a variety of reasons.
Certainly one of the reasons for the formation of a discussion group
is the recognition of a common problem or goal. The need for the
interaction of ideas would imply that among individuals there exists
a frustration of how to reach a goal or solve a problem. Once such a
problem or goal is recognized a means is required by which to
achieve or solve it. It would seem then, that realistic conflict, the
conflict arising from frustration or inability to select the proper
means, is one conflict which may have been the result of a dialectical
intracommunicative process which might be observed and indeed encouraged in the group's interaction, for out of the expression of such
frustrations, real forward progress may be made.

The presence of conflict in discussion, then, is perhaps requisite to
group progress. Using this conflict, however, as a tool in furthering
the group requires caution and knowledge; caution in exercising control of it, in that it must be allowed to flourish but not dominate,
and knowledge in being able to recognize it in its form and when
possible, its origin and purpose.

It would seem that the proper role or function of conflict in
discussion is to encourage inquiry, to promote objectivity, and to
sharpen analysis. From this we might contend that conflict exists as a
positive functioning element in the dialectical interchange between
and among individuals.

---

15. Lewis A. Coser, *The Functions of Social Conflict,* Illinois: The Free Press, 1956, pp.
49-50.
16. *Ibid.*

But internal conflict in a discussion group is more than just a force to encourage inquiry. It is also a criteria by which we may make certain value judgments concerning both individuals and the group. To begin with, we may observe that a group which experiences a conflict of ideas is one in which overt interest and concern is being manifested. Keeping Simmel's theories of conflict in mind, we may relate the presence of conflict to group structure and hierarchal order. From this we may also consider the relationship of conflict to lines of communication. We might also relate the presence of conflict with the emergence of ingroups and outgroups within the primary group. Another way in which conflict might be used as a group measurement is to relate it to group cohesiveness and stability. And finally, we might relate the presence of conflict as a stimulus to group productivity and success in reaching desired ends.

The presence of conflict in society may be stated with certainty. The positive force of conflict may be stated with almost equal certainty. The role or function of conflict in discussion, or the use of conflict as a criterion in the measurement and evaluation of discussion, however, is quite something else. As a point of departure in analyzing the role of conflict or in utilizing conflict as a measuring device of small group communication we might begin with certain of Simmel, Ross, and Cooley's postulates. We may observe conflict as a stimulus in discussion and observe certain responses and reactions to it; we may even observe arising in the presence of conflict, the same pattern of behavior mentioned by Simmel, Ross, and Cooley. But to establish the causal relationship between group conflict and group communicative behavior, we need more investigation, more study, more experimentation. It has not been my intention in this article to argue at this time that conflict is a "must" in effective group discussion, or that it "is" a useful criterion in measuring small group communication. Rather, I am suggesting a point of view that it is quite possible that conflict could become a valuable criterion to help us further evaluate the process of group discussion. It would seem that such a force, operational in practically all social interaction, is worthy of more experimentation by those interested in understanding and evaluating small group communication.

chapter 5

Group Processes

THEORETICAL ANALYSIS OF INDIVIDUAL AND GROUP SOLUTIONS

Harold H. Kelley and John W. Thibout

The foregoing studies have compared pooled individual solutions (judgments, opinions) with group solutions arrived at by some process of discussion and group decision or vote. It is apparent that the group solutions differ from the pooled individual solutions. In most of the instances reviewed above, this divergence is in the direction of superiority of the group products. It is clear, however, that group solutions are not always superior. Furthermore, as careful analyses of products are made, it seems likely that qualitative discrepancies will appear which are not capable of being described on a simple dimension of "goodness" of solution.

The question now arises as to what accounts for the unique properties of group solutions as compared with pooled individual solutions. There are two logical possibilities, not mutually exclusive, either or both of which can account for this uniqueness. As a result of the group problem-solving situation and the interaction process involved, (1) *the individual solutions available for pooling or combination differ from the individual solutions derived under conditions of independent problem solving,* and/or (2) *the individual solutions are combined or assembled in a manner not reproducible by simple averaging, use of majority vote, or similar methods.*

In the present section we shall speculate a bit about the social processes and psychological phenomena which these two logical possibilities suggest. The subsequent parts of the chapter will be devoted largely to the concrete research evidence bearing upon the factors and relationships which we shall postulate here.

From Harold H. Kelley and John W. Thibout, "Experimental Studies of Group Problem Solving and Process," Chapter 21 in Gardner Lindzey, *Handbook of Social Psychology,* Vol. 2, 1954. Addison-Wesley, Reading, Massachusetts. Pp. 741-747, 782-785. Reprinted with the permission of the publisher.

The Social Modification of Individual Solutions

Here we wish to explore the possibility that the individual products available for incorporation into the group product are modified by the problem-solving situation and process.

Modifications Produced by Direct Social Influence

Perhaps the most obvious as well as the most important way in which individual solutions are modified is through the direct social influence exerted in the course of the group discussion. An example of change in individual opinions as a result of discussion is provided by Timmons'[1] investigation, described earlier. As a result of the group discussion of the parole problem, the subjects in the experimental groups were significantly more accurate in their subsequent individual rankings than were the control subjects, who had merely restudied the parole problem. It was also found that the subsequent rankings made by individuals who had participated in the discussion groups correlated fairly highly with the rankings agreed upon by their respective groups (i.e., the rankings constituting the group solutions to the problem). Thus it is clear that not only did individual judgments change, but they changed in the direction of the group consensus. The importance of this phenomenon for understanding group solutions is obvious: If persons change their opinions as a result of interaction, then the individual solutions available for combination into the group solution will differ from what they would have been if there had been no interaction.

As to the process by which such opinion changes are mediated, several generalizations can be made. To begin with, the views held by a given person will be influential only if they are communicated, either by him or by someone else, to others within the group. In other words, shifts of opinion need be analyzed only with respect to those ideas and views which are expressed in some manner. This immediately suggests that an analysis of the influence process must start with an investigation of the factors which act to facilitate or inhibit communication. In the terms used by Festinger,[2] what are the forces to communicate and what are the restraining forces against communication?

---

1. W.M. Timmons, "Decisions and Attitudes as Outcomes of the Discussion of a Social Problem," in *Contrib. Educ.*, No. 777 (New York: Bureau of Publications, Teachers College, Columbia University, 1939).

2. L. Festinger, "Informal Social Communication,'" *Psychological Review*, LVII (1950), 271-282.

Once a person communicates his point of view, his effectiveness in producing covert changes in other persons' opinions depends upon a variety of factors. In the analysis of influence transmitted through mass media, it has been emphasized that for a communication to be successful the recipient must attend to it, comprehend and learn its contents, and accept them. ... Although the attainment of these stages of influence may present somewhat different practical problems in direct interpersonal influence, they seem to be as essential here as in mass communications.

To simplify the discussion, consider member A communicating his solution or judgment to member B. Since it is essential that B attend to A, influence will be facilitated if B has some tendency to orient himself toward A or if A has abilities, mannerisms, or striking characteristics which elicit attention. Likewise, at the comprehension stage, influence will be facilitated by A's skill at expressing clearly his ideas, and/or by B's verbal and intellectual ability.

Assuming the attention and comprehension requirements are fulfilled, the extremely complex problem of acceptance is encountered. In some instances, acceptance will depend largely upon the intrinsic properties of A's solution and the arguments with which he supports it. For example, the solution may interact with and fit into B's prior cognitive structure so as to produce a new structure more tenable and satisfactory than the old one. The new cognitive structure may take account of more factors, be simpler, or more aesthetic, etc. In other instances, B may be able to test or prove the suggested solution by logical processes. These possibilities suggest that the individual may sometimes change his opinion after simply hearing other opinions, regardless of their source. It has been held that if the person is aware of the great variety of solutions or judgments possible in any given situation, he will be better able to reach a correct judgment.[3] If this is true, the simple fact of making public the opinions held by various members would provide the basis for an improvement in the average quality of their contributions. Relevant to this process would be any factor such as group size or permissiveness which affected the number and range of ideas made public within the group.

When the problem at issue requires opinions and judgments which cannot be validated by logic or by empirical tests, people tend to seek support for their opinions through agreement with their associates. There appear to be at least two general types of relationship

---

3. J. F. Dashiell, "Experimental Studies of the Influence of Social Situations on the Behavior of Individual Human Adults," in C. Murchison (ed.), *Handbook of Social Psychology* (Worcester, Mass.: Clark University Press, 1935), pp. 1097-1158.

between the initiator and the recipient of a suggestion that can function to determine the degree to which the recipient agrees with and accepts the suggestion. In certain instances, the initiator may be viewed instrumentally as a "mediator of fact" by virtue of his perceived expertness, credibility, and trustworthiness. In other instances, the recipient may be motivated to agree with the initiator without regard for his "correctness"; agreement may become an independent motive. The strength of this motive seems to depend partly on the strength of positive attachment to and affection for the initiator. Thus, A can produce a change in B's opinion if he is liked by B or provides the means whereby B satisfies important drives. When the group member has a strong positive attachment to his group and its members, he will tend to conform to the modal opinion expressed in the group. In such instances, the opinion change resulting from discussion may produce a convergence upon the opinion initially held by the majority, as noted by Thorndike.[4] (Majority opinion may also be effective in the absence of positive feelings for the group. Where no expert opinion is available, the opinion held by most persons may be perceived as the "safest bet.")

Another relationship which may be relevant to the acceptance of the initiator's opinion is that in which the recipient's real or apparent acceptance is motivated by a desire to avoid punishment or unpleasantness in general. A is able to deliver punishment to B even though B has no positive feelings toward him. Thus, a powerless B may be physically or socially constrained to the relationship with a punitive A. In the case of group membership, B may be physically unable to leave the group or may maintain membership merely to avoid dangers that exist outside the group. Festinger[5] proposes the hypothesis that such relationships can produce overt compliance to social influence but do not lead to covert acceptance of it. Other theories and evidence suggest that certain of these situations, where pressure can be exerted on a person to express an opinion different from the one he privately affirms, do tend to produce covert opinion change.[6]

---

4. R. L. Thorndike, "The Effect of Discussion Upon the Correctness of Group Decisions, When the Factor of Majority Influence Is Allowed For," *Journal of Social Psychology* IX (1938), 343-362.

5. L. Festinger, "An Analysis of Compliant Behavior," in M. Sherif and M.O. Wilson (eds.), *Group Relations at the Crossroads* (New York: Harper & Brothers, 1953), pp. 232-255.

6. Cf. H.C. Kelman, "Attitude Change as a Function of Response Restriction," *Human Relations,* VI (1953), 185-214; I.L. Janis and B.T. King, "The Influence of Role Playing on Opinion Change," *Journal of Abnormal and Social Psychology,* XLIX (1954), 211-218; and C.I. Hovland, I.L. Janis, and H.H. Kelley, *Communication and Persuasion: Psychological Studies of Opinion Change* (New Haven: Yale University Press, 1953), Chapter 7.

However, in the following discussion, we shall consider these con-
formity-producing pressures primarily from the point of view of the
behavioral changes they produce.

Finally, no discussion of the factors affecting opinion change
would be complete without mention of those determining the degree
to which change is resisted. Broadly speaking, resistance stems from
the strength of initial opinions; the basis they have in fact, experience, or logic, the person's "anchorage" through loyalty to other
groups; and possibly the fact of overt commitment to a given point
of view. The amount of change produced in any case may be considered to be a resultant of the strength of influence exerted minus the
strength of the resistance to change.

Modifications Produced by the Social Context
of Individual Problem Solving

Even in the absence of direct social influence, the group member's
problem-solving activity may differ from what it would be if he were
working as an independent individual, by himself and for himself.
Thus, his motivation and thought processes may be modified by the
social context in which he works—by his group membership, the
social situation in which the task is presented or decided upon, the
presence of others who may be working on the same problem, the
eventuality of communicating his product to others, their anticipated
social reactions, etc.

Of great importance in determining an individual's effort and concentration on a task is the strength of his motivation to complete it.
This can be quite different when working for oneself than when
working for a group, depending upon such factors as the degree of
identification with the group, the amount of responsibility felt for
the outcome of the problem-solving process, and the kinds of rewards given for successful task completion.

Also of relevance here are the investigations of social facilitation,
which we shall discuss more fully in the next section. These indicate
that working in the presence of others who have the same task (or
even working with the belief that other persons have the same task)
produces variations in accuracy, speed, and quality of output.

A related notion is contained in the suggestion by Bos[7] that the
very act of formulating an opinion or idea for communication to the
group leads to a sharpening and refining of the idea. Thorndike[8] also

7. Maria C. Bos, "Experimental Study of Productive Collaboration," *Acta Psychologica*, III
(1937), 315-426.
8. *Op. cit.*

comments that in a problem-solving group, individuals appear to think about an issue more carefully and more cautiously before announcing an opinion to the group. Of course, the latter suggests the existence of restraints in the communication process, which might seriously modify the assembly of individual solutions. However, Bos and Thorndike appear to agree that even prior to communication the group member's covert opinion undergoes some change toward greater sharpening and clarity.

A series of experiments by Bos[9] may be taken as illustrating the effects of a hypothesized process of sharpening and clarifying, not because her research provides a test of the hypothesis but because she interprets much of her results in these terms. In her first experiment Bos studied sixty-eight children eleven to thirteen years old. One group of subjects worked first individually and then after "some weeks" repeated the same tasks in pairs. A second group began as individuals and was retested individually. The third group began work in pairs and later worked as individuals. The tasks set for the children involved the identification, from sets of reproductions, of paintings done by the same painter. Children working in pairs were encouraged to talk freely. The experimenter observed informally.

In her second experiment, Bos studied forty-three younger children (ages six to nine), this time eliminating from her design the treatment in which pairs preceded individuals. The tasks were to arrange five sets of pictures in such a way that each series conveyed a sensible story. Again paired children were encouraged to interact and the process was observed. In both experiments children in pairs were substantially more accurate than as individuals. Part of this superiority Bos credits to the resistance offered to vague ideas by the demands of communication. She also observes, however, that this process occasionally has a negative effect, as when a person attains a correct insight based on a general intuition which he finds difficult to communicate in a rational, persuasive way.

The Combination or Weighting of Individual Solutions

The second possible way of accounting for the unique properties of group solutions as compared with individual solutions is that the latter are combined and weighted in a complicated way in arriving at the group product. The focus here is upon the processes of proposal, compliance, concession, compromise, and rejection whereby some sort of group decision is reached. These processes affect the outcome

---

9. *Op. cit.*

only if the discussion preceding the decision fails to produce covert agreement among the various members as to the most appropriate solution. If the discussion produces complete consensus at the covert level, the decision process usually can have only one outcome, however it proceeds. (An exception to this generalization is the state of "pluralistic ignorance," where the covert consensus so sharply violates some cultural norm that group members will neither express their covert opinions nor even expect one another to hold them.) We shall consider, then, instances where at the time of deciding upon a group solution there are differences among the members with respect to what they privately believe to be the best solution.

To arrive at a group solution, there must be a presentation of alternatives and a process of decision in which one alternative is selected as the group's response to the problem under consideration. Under the conditions specified in most experimental studies, this decision involves the achievement of some sort of agreement which is mediated by the proposal of solutions and formal or informal voting upon them. In this decision, the *overt* proposal and the *overt* vote are crucial. The unexpressed and unsupported covert opinion, no matter how strongly held, is not recorded in the outcome. Furthermore, only if there are discrepancies between overt votes and covert opinions does this aspect of the total problem-solving process contribute to the unique properties of group solutions. If all members vote and if they vote in accordance with their private opinions, the group vote can be determined simply by summarizing their individual private solutions. However, if persons with one opinion support a different one or fail to vote *or* if persons without an opinion take a definite stand, then the group product is not related in any simple way to individual covert opinions. In other words, during the decision process persons who fail to act in accordance with their private opinions (by withholding their vote when they have some opinion, voting when they have none, or voting for an alternative other than the one they privately think best) give extra weight to others' opinions at the expense of their own.

To understand this process of weighting it is necessary to examine factors which make for discrepancies between covert and expressed opinion. Sometimes these discrepancies are to be traced to external social pressures; on other occasions, they are due to self-imposed restraints which we shall refer to as "self-weightings." In particular instances, it may be difficult to locate the cause of a given discrepancy, but in principle it seems desirable to distinguish between externally initiated weighting (direct social pressure) and internally initiated (self) weighting.

Weighting Produced by Direct Social Pressure

One of the obvious situations in which expressed opinions diverge from covert ones is when external social pressures are brought to bear upon behavior. Festinger[10] has analyzed the relations between a group and its members which lead on the one hand to covert acceptance of the group's norms and, on the other, to mere overt compliance with them. He suggests that overt compliance without covert acceptance occurs when (a) the member is constrained to membership in a group by physical or social restrictions or by external dangers, but (b) the group does *not* provide positive satisfactions or mediate positive goals for him. Thus, the group or its representative is able to produce behavioral conformity through punishment or threats of punishment, but the recipient has no basis for positive feelings toward the group and no desire to be like its model members.

Members who stand in this relation to a group can be expected on occasion to support solutions or judgments which they do not privately accept. They will support what they believe to be the opinions held by the majority of the members or by the most powerful members, i.e., those who are most influential in setting the group standards and in applying group sanctions. In general, the discrepancies between private opinion and public vote will be maximal in groups where membership results from restraints and external threats and minimal in groups where membership is characterized by positive satisfactions. In the latter groups, a high degree of covert consensus will develop in the course of the discussion and, as noted before, the group decision will be a relatively simple reflection of this consensus. In the former groups, the greater the power differential among members, the greater will be the tendency toward differential weighting of their private opinions in arriving at the group solution.

The process by which compliance occurs need not involve explicit threat or pressure. On the basis of prior experiences of pressure, a person may express opinions he expects more powerful members to hold. But frequently the less powerful member waits for others to express their opinions or follows closely the social reactions to others' contributions and to his own trial balloons.

---

10. *Op. cit.* (1953).

Social reactions to various proposals—reactions of rejection, approval, or toleration—can play an important role in the success of a problem-solving group. The high quality of group products has been attributed to the "corrective" responses made by the group to various contributions and proposals.[11] In this process the group is reported to reject, modify, and correct at least some of the ill-conceived and erroneous conceptions of its members. Obviously, this process, in part, results in changing the initiator's or other persons' opinions or solutions. At the same time, however, such social reactions may cause a person either to withhold his opinion (without necessarily changing his mind about it) or to publicize it even more strenuously. In either case, the social reactions may modify markedly the weight his individual opinion carries in the final group decision. Whatever the nature of this process, as long as the social response is cued to the contribution and not to the contributor (his status, friendliness, etc.), its result seems to be a reduction of errors in the final group product.

Self-Weighting

On certain occasions, a member may voluntarily withhold his vote or support a position not his own. Gurnee's investigations suggest that this may be due to the degree of confidence a person feels in his private opinion. Consider first his study of maze learning by individuals as compared with groups. At the end of the learning series, the groups performed much better than their individual members. Therefore, the superiority of the groups cannot be accounted for by improvement in individual solutions as a result of the group problem-solving situation or discussion. Rather, the superiority of the groups seems attributable either to a cancelling out of individual errors or to the voting process. The acclamation method of voting constituted the means by which individuals' ideas were combined into the group decision at each choice point in the maze. This method provides the opportunity for people who are most confident to carry greater weight in the group vote than those who are less confident. In his second study, Gurnee explicitly attributed the superiority of his groups to the process of voting. He observed that correct subjects were apt to respond more quickly and hence carry more weight than the more doubtful subjects. Thorndike also found that higher confidence on the part of those subjects initially holding the correct views

---

11. M.E. Shaw, "A Comparison of Individuals and Small Groups in the Rational Solution of Complex Problems," *American Journal of Psychology*, XLIV (1932), 491-504.

accounted for part of the discussion-mediated shift toward more correct answers.

These results suggest a *self-weighting* process whereby individuals contribute or withhold their suggestions according to the degree of certainty they feel about them. (We may not, of course, always find a positive relationship between confidence and correctness, such as apparently existed in the foregoing studies.) It may be hypothesized that this tendency toward differential self-weighting would be most marked in groups where there is great heterogeneity among the members in their ability or expertness on the problem at hand.

A variety of other factors may also affect the weight a person gives his private opinion in voting for the group decision. There may be personality predispositions related to self-confidence which lead certain individuals consistently to place great or little weight upon their own opinions. The perception that others will be more affected by the decision than himself might be expected to heighten an individual's tendency to permit their opinions to carry the decision. For example, if a particular member has a very great stake in the quality of the decision (e.g., he must act upon it; it determines his future success), other members may defer in their voting to his opinions. Other self-imposed restraints against expressing one's private opinion may arise out of desire to avoid hurting the feelings of a friend who holds an opposite opinion. Similarly, if a high premium is placed on group unity or if schism within the group would place its existence in peril, members may suppress their private feelings and at the behavioral level present a united front.

Finally, it should be noted that the process of voting can be formalized to minimize differential weighting tendencies, whether self-imposed or due to external pressures. Everyone in the group may be required to vote simultaneously, privately, and anonymously, with all votes being given equal weight in the decision. Even this type of procedure, however, may fail to eliminate all sources of differential self-weighting. "Game" considerations, as described by von Neumann and Morgenstern[12] may frequently lead to distortion of covert preferences, as for example in the common practice of supporters of a minor party who actually vote for a major party candidate rather than "throw away their votes."

---

12. J. von Neumann and O. Morgenstern, *Theory of Games and Economic Behavior,* Second Edition (Princeton, N.J.: Princeton University Press, 1947).

Summary

In brief, it appears that a variety of factors may affect the group product and account for its unique character as compared with a simple pooling of individual products. These factors can be analyzed in terms of whether they affect (1) the individual solutions, judgments, opinions, etc., which are available to be combined into the group product, and/or (2) the actual combination or voting process in which individual contributions are "weighted" in some way to determine the final group outcome. With regard to the first, modifications in individual solutions can be traced to (a) the operation of direct social influence or (b) the social context in which the individual works on the problem. With regard to the second, the differential weights given individual solutions are reflected in discrepancies between private opinions and public votes and these discrepancies are attributable to (a) the operation of external social pressures or (b) self-imposed restraints in voting behavior.

Observation of the problem-solving process in natural informal groups reveals that all of the above aspects of the process frequently proceed simultaneously. Often, members are considering the problem for the first time even as the discussion goes forward. The "voting" process usually goes on implicitly during the discussion—persons indicate their position and make it clear how they will vote. After a thorough airing of opinions, a formal vote is often unnecessary. However, this typical collapsing and overlapping of the various aspects of the process does not mean that factors shown to affect the total outcome need remain unanalyzed as to their more specific effects. . . .

BRAINSTORMING—A CREATIVE PROBLEM-SOLVING TECHNIQUE

Arthur M. Coon *

Simply put, brainstorming is a technique for stimulating the generation of ideas and facilitating their expression. To define further: brainstorming is an application of methods suggested by Alex F. Osborn for explicit stimulation of the imagination in the production of ideas. It usually involves cooperative thinking by groups and is usually directed to the solution of specific problems.

The technique has been so bandied about by Babbitts, so juggled by journalists, so pawed and promoted and perverted by proselytes that the above definition may come as a surprise to many. Such distortions are to be expected when some new process or attitude catches the fancy of the public. First the press celebrates it with awe, and its disciples and converts cannot say enough in its praise. Then a new crop of journalists have to write new stories. Since praise has been exhausted, they go to the other extreme (ironically using a device of brainstorming itself!) and condemn. Meanwhile rival "innovators" spring up to claim the new process is not so novel as theirs, or that it is not new at all, or that their model is a vast improvement over the original.

If the process or attitude has real merit, it will survive these superficial gusts and squalls. The almost universal testimony of those who have tried brainstorming, according to the suggestions of its inventor, is that it does have real merit. It stands the pragmatic test. It works.

Not that it is a cure-all, nor the only way to do creative thinking. But the results so far indicate that through its employment individuals produce more ideas than they would otherwise; in some cases two or three times as many as when they do their celebrating solo. Further, they tend to retain this greater fluency of ideation. They also experience side- or after-effects which perhaps are even more important. (These will be referred to later.) Therefore, brainstorming—with whatever refinements and improvements are suggested by research and experiment—will probably be around for some time.

I should like to conclude these prefatory remarks with the reminder that brainstorming is by no means all there is to Osborn's theory of creative thinking. It is simply one of a number of advo-

Reprinted with permission from *Journal of Communication*, Vol. VII, No. 3, (Autumn, 1957), pp. 111-118.

*Arthur M. Coon, Ph.D.—Associate Director, Creative Education Foundation, Rand Building, Buffalo, New York. (Since writing this article, Dr. Coon has joined the faculty of Communication Skills at Michigan State University.)

cated techniques which happens to have caught the public fancy. As a result it has been ballyhooed out of all proportion in the public press. Those wishing to understand its relative and full significance are referred to Osborn's books which I shall shortly mention. . . .

In the course of his work [as a successful advertising man] Osborn found himself constantly confronted with the necessity of producing, or creating, new ideas that would help sell the products of his clients. In other words, he was in the business of using his imagination. He also found it incumbent upon him—to a small degree at first, more and more later—to supervise the similar creation of ideas in his assistants, and teach them, too, to be more creative.

At this point, for some reason difficult to explain, Osborn began to become interested in the processes of imagination: perhaps because he was more analytical than others, perhaps just because it was a way of getting a job done better. At any rate, he found that some things helped him think up ideas, and that others hindered or inhibited the process. He began to experiment—to try to find more things that helped, and things that helped more; at the same time trying to identify and avoid things that wery inhibitive: times, places, attitudes, what-not. . . .

As usually practiced, brainstorming is engaged in by a group. The group may range from as many as several hundred to as few as three or four. But the optimum number averages ten or twelve. The group does not meet to *settle* a problem, but to get ideas on how to settle it, or at the very least (if the problem is intricate, or highly difficult or technical) to evolve fresh approaches to the problem. But here again Osborn frequently points out that a specific problem is not absolutely essential.

Therefore, it is not strictly correct to call brainstorming either a group technique or a problem-solving technique, although in practice it is usually both. Neither, though it involves discussion, is it exactly a discussion technique. It is best to think and speak of it simply as a device for stimulating the production of ideas.

With the above matters clarified, we come to the four "Brainstorming Rules" with which practitioners of the Osborn technique always preface their sessions, and which they constantly emphasize. These are of great importance, as they are the heart of the method:

1. Adverse criticism is taboo.
2. "Free-wheeling" is welcomed.
3. Quantity of ideas is desired.
4. Combination and improvement of ideas are sought.

It is difficult to say that one of these rules is more important than another. But if one had to be so designated, it would be the first. It is probably also the most misunderstood. Osborn observed that nothing had so inhibiting an effect on his production of ideas as concurrent criticism.

What causes some people to underrate the magnitude of Osborn's contribution to creative thinking is that most of us have observed the same thing. We have all been excited over some new idea, and are full of further thoughts upon it, only to have someone nip our enthusiasm in the bud by saying, "That won't work," or "It's too expensive," or "We tried that in 1943 and it was no good." The result was that we never expressed the further ideas.

But Osborn had the originality to do something about the fact that he and others had observed. He suggested that adverse criticism be held back for the time being. Therefore, at all Osbornian brainstorms there is a wielder of a bell, empowered and instructed to sound it at any manifestation of adverse judgment of ideas—even a derisive laugh.

Almost everyone is surprised at how freely ideas flow forth, once the critical attitude is suspended. Please note the word "suspended"—not "abandoned." This point is one that results in a good deal of misunderstanding, and it is often mistakenly said that Osborn underrates the importance of criticism. This is not the case. He only advocates postponing operations of the critical faculty until the creative faculty has had a chance to function. "Don't try to drive with your brakes on," is how he puts it. "Evaluation is important, essential, but it can and should come later."[1]

By "free-wheeling is welcomed" Osborn means to encourage the wild, implausible, even impossible flights of fancy without which the wings of imagination cannot be fledged. No one knows how the imagination works, but it certainly cannot soar if "cabined, cribb'd, confined."

A third objective in brainstorm sessions is to get as many ideas as possible, the theory being that if the number is great, the laws of probability will work in favor of the proportion of good ideas being larger than otherwise.

Finally, Osborn advocates building and improving upon ideas already expressed. This, indeed, is a key point, since everyone's experience is different, and that of one person in a group may well reinforce and supplement that of another. In practice, Osbornian

---

1. Cf. the similar doctrine of Wordsworth and Coleridge, that colored the whole Romantic Movement in English Literature: "the willing suspension of disbelief."

Brainstormers use here what is called the "hitch-hike" technique. A person who thinks of an addition to an idea already expressed snaps his fingers to get attention. The moderator or leader of the session then recognizes him ahead of the person with the completely new idea.

Some observations may be offered here as to various other mechanical aspects of brainstorming. The moderator just referred to has the duty of recognizing participants with ideas. He announces the subject or problem, and gives necessary background information upon it, answering questions if necessary. He may offer a few suggestive ideas or solutions, as pump-primers, at the beginning. He should also keep the ideation moving, with an occasional priming suggestion if needed, such as, "Who else could help?" "How could color be used?" or "Can this be combined with that in some way?" It is important that he recognize speakers only when they raise their hands. Otherwise the less self-assured are left out, or some ideas lost.

To another person will also usually be assigned the function of writing the ideas down, reportorially. Such a person should be quick-witted to catch them all rapidly, and it is best that he write the ideas where all can see them, as on a large flip-chart or blackboard. In practice with actual problems, it has been found productive of best results to announce the subject to participants some little time in advance—several days, perhaps—so they can be thinking about it.

The statement of the problem also demands considerable thought. Time spent on getting it exact, specific, and clear is usually rewarded by a more productive brainstorm. A good beginning for a Brainstorm question is, "How many ways can we think of to. . .?"

A relaxed yet alert attitude in participants produces the best results, and Osborn employs various techniques to secure this attitude. Brainstorm sessions in Batten, Barton, Durstine, and Osborn usually take place after a luncheon. Often it is found best to break large questions into smaller ones so that about half an hour can be spent on each.

Sometimes the best ideas emerge after the participants have been going for some time, and are even slightly weary. Osborn theorizes that at the beginning they are skimming the familiar and superficial ideas off the surfaces of their minds, and that only after these are gone do the brains really get busy and begin to think creatively.

At least two operations follow the actual brainstorm session. These are of great importance.

One is the evaluation of ideas. Here the critical faculty, suspended before, comes into its own. The evaluation is usually done by others than the brainstormers, though the moderator often participates, if only to interpret some of the ideas.

Before the ideas can be evaluated, they often have to be categorized. Here the discovery of a new or missing category often leads to further ideas.

Still further ideas may also occur to one or more of the participants after the brainstorm session. These ideas are often as good as or better than the original ones. For this reason Osborn places great emphasis on this part of the "follow-up." Sometimes, also, a new brainstorm session may be held after the follow-up, categorization, and evaluation.

It will be observed that each of these rules embodies the "horse sense" of which Osborn speaks, no doubt because each is the result of trial and error, selection, elimination, and all that this implies—in other words, is based upon successful pragmatic experience.

Many other aspects of Osborn's techniques deserve comment. For instance, one realizes after some experience with brainstorming that many of the reasons ideas are never born, or—once born—quickly stifled, have nothing to do with the value of the ideas themselves. A cartoon which showed a conference leader addressing his group well illustrated an aspect of this. The leader says "Those opposed will signify by clearing out their desks, putting on their hats, and saying: 'I resign.' "

Osborn observed in the advertising business what is equally true elsewhere, that fear, jealousy, pride, timidity, and other emotions and attitudes discourage the conception of ideas.

One result of this understanding is that the person with the problem is almost never invited to sit in on its brainstorming. He already knows too many ways in which the thing cannot be done, and is likely to inhibit the ideas of others by word, gesture, or even silence, and at best to contribute little to the discussion. In Osborn's method, the person closest to the problem presents it as clearly and specifically as he can to the brainstorm group: then leaves the room before brainstorming actually starts.

Connected is the fact that many of us spend most of our entire days critically evaluating ideas and saying "no." Such ingrained habits and attitudes are very difficult to shake off, and are apt to carry over into brainstorming. For this reason executives and others whose critical judgment is their stock in trade may have the most difficulty using the Brainstorm technique, and sometimes succeed only imperfectly even after training and practice.

It will be observed also that Osborn's technique sets up what the psychiatrists call a "permissive situation." In psychiatry, the patient is encouraged to feel that he need fear no punishment—of which critical and especially adverse judgment is of course a type—no matter what he says.

In this way he is encouraged to discharge all his troubles, just as by similar means the brainstormer is encouraged to pour out all his ideas—good, bad, or indifferent. I believe that this element of what Aristotle would call *katharsis* is an important aspect of the satisfaction people find in brainstorming, and in its consequent success.

One may also observe a parallel with education, in which many a successful teacher finds—by experience or through instruction—that the best way to encourage success and happiness in students is to create in the classroom this permissive situation. Probably it is not necessary here again to refer to the derivation of the word "education."

In fact, many feel that the importance of brainstorming for business, where it originated, or for any problem-solving situation, will be less than its importance for education generally. Some who have tried it in business, perhaps with a good deal of skepticism, report, "There are many worthwhile by-products of brainstorming beyond new solutions arrived at. We were amazed at the new attitudes encouraged among our employees. Many of them have gained self confidence at having their ideas listened to with respect for the first time. They are more willing to advance new ideas. And those to whom the new ideas are advanced seem to have a more receptive and tolerant attitude not only toward the ideas, but toward those who submit them."

I submit that if by practice with this technique educators can stimulate in students more creative and original thought along with a greater sympathy and tolerance for the ideas of others, they will have achieved something of major importance—whether or not the students reach any final conclusive solutions in their Brainstorm sessions.

I might conclude with the probably obvious observation that Osborn's technique is still too new for all its implications to be realized. I have suggested a few. But the whole technique deserves a great deal of further study, experiment, and research. . . .

"PERT" AS A LOGICAL ADJUNCT TO THE
DISCUSSION PROCESS

Gerald M. Phillips *

The traditional method of teaching group discussion in departments of speech is based on John Dewey's "Five Phases of Reflective Thought," modified somewhat by the findings of specialists in group dynamics. Elaboration of the five phases of reflective thought into "agendas" is characteristic of the treatment in most major textbooks. Virtually all authorities (4, 6, 9, 11, 15, 17) include some combination of the following major steps as agendas for the discussion process:

1. Making a precise statement of the nature and scope of the problem.
2. Finding information about the problem.
3. Determining causes of the problem.
4. Specifying the goal to be achieved in the solution.
5. Stipulating limitations on the group's problem-solving and implementation ability.
6. Proposing a variety of possible solutions.
7. Testing the solutions against goals and limitations.
8. Accepting a final solution.
9. Putting the solution into operation.

Little practical information is offered by these books about methods and procedures for moving through the recommended steps on the agenda.(4) Rather, theoretical information is offered, as well as some practical suggestions for examining evidence and procedures for preparing discussion outlines. This may be perfectly defensible in terms of the academic goals of discussion instruction. However, it may not be useful to the student who will confront discussion as it occurs in problem solving in business and industry.

Writers in the area of business and management recognize somewhat the same steps on the discussion agenda. Dill, for example, specifies a five-point agenda.(7)

1. Agenda building—defining goals and tasks.
2. Search for alternative courses of action and information useful for evaluation.
3. Commitment—testing proposals and choosing one.

Reprinted with permission from *Journal of Communication,* Vol. XV, No. 2, (June, 1965), pp. 89-99. The material in this article has been expanded and detailed in a chapter in *Communication and the Small Group* published by Bobbs-Merrill in 1966.

*Dr. Gerald M. Phillips is Professor of Speech at the Pennsylvania State University.

4. Implementation of the program.

5. Evaluation of effects of the program.

Banfield(2) covers essentially the same group with four major points:

1. Analysis of the situation.

2. End reduction and elaboration.

3. Design of courses of action.

4. Evaluation of consequences of choices.

In each of these cases, considerable emphasis seems to be on the empirical process of implementation. Problem-solving discussion is not regarded by management as an end in itself, but rather as a means of working toward a program-end, which can be evaluated in terms of how closely it approximated the desired goals. The worth and merit of the discussion can be found only by evaluating the worth and merit of the program, whereas in academic discussion, worth can be estimated in terms of adherence to recommended pattern and procedures. Academic discussion could be thus compared to a procedure of determining who won the football game by comparing the number of first downs rather than total points scored, important in football theory, but meaningless in win-loss records.

Most business and government groups are not concerned with their ability to follow through the steps of a prescribed discussion procedure. Their success or failure is dependent on the effectiveness of their solution *after* it has been placed into operation. Their main problem is to prepare plans for implementation or operationalization of programs they propose.(3) Even where business and government groups are concerned with policy making, they are often charged with the responsibility of presenting implementation plans along with their policy proposals.(7)

Textbooks on management offer little information about the stages of discussion that most concern the discussion teacher, i.e., those steps that precede the acceptance of a program solution.(5) Textbooks in academic discussion offer little material on implementation.[1] A synthesis of information from the two sources would be useful to groups whose responsibility includes both stipulating goals and devising the means of operationalizing solutions to meet the goals. The Western Branch of the American Public Health Association, for example, held a series of seminars for their member agencies

---

1. Barnlund and Hairman's [4] plan ends at evaluation. Others offer no implementation step though they refer to "action" with no methodology presented. Zelko [17] gives the leader responsibility for carrying out the plan (p. 100). Crowell [6] calls for an outline for operationalization but states, "... your outline ... will likely be relatively short." (p. 149).

in which emphasis was on *both* developing program goals (academic) and planning operationalizing procedures (practical).

The quasi-mathematical procedure called PERT offers a synthesis point, for PERT offers a framework for planning as well as a methodology for implementation. The procedures are eventually formalized into a statistical cast which tends to push group members away from interpersonal conflict as they contend, instead, against the odds of accomplishing the program goal.(16)

   I. Define problem source
      A.   Group feeling
      B.   Group assigned to problem
      C.   Group accepts problem as part of routine
  II. Leader states problem
      A.   Terms and phrases are defined until group agrees they understand problem
 III. Factual statement offered
      A.   Factual statement classified and tested
          1.   Statement should not be opinion or evaluation
          2.   Statement must meet test for facts
          3.   Statement must be pertinent to problem
      B.   Group agrees fact list complete
  IV. Leader restates problem in the light of the facts
      A.   Terms and phrases redefined until group agrees they understand problem
   V. Causal statement offered
      A.   Cause must relate to observable phenomena
      B.   Cause must relate to controllable elements
      C.   Cause must be pertinent to problem
      D.   Group agrees cause list complete
  VI. Group authority and limitations defined
      A.   Group determines power, scope of authority, time, money, and personnel available
      B.   Group establishes legal, moral, and practical limits on activity
 VII. Goal statement offered
      A.   Goal must be pertinent to redefined problem
      B.   Goal must fit within authority and limitations
      C.   Group agrees list of goals complete
VIII. Group determines extent to which goals are realized or in process of realization through ongoing programs
  IX. Solution proposed
      A.   Solution must be goal-directed
      B.   Solution must be feasible
      C.   Solution must fit within authority and limitations

Figure 3. Continued.

X. PERT plan developed for program
- A.   Event list established
- B.   Event list ordered
- C.   Necessary precedence determined
- D.   Network drawn and tested
- E.   Activities listed
- F.   Time (t.) estimates calculated
- G.   Variances calculated
- H.   Expected times calculated
- J.   Scheduled completion time set
- K.   Latest completion times calculated
- L.   Slack time determined
- M.   Critical path set
- N.   Probability of completion calculated
- P.   Network revised as necessary

XI. Program actuated and completed

XII. Program evaluated against goals
- A.   If goals not satisfied, group attempts new solution
- B.   If goals satisfactorily met, group may receive new problem

Figure 3. Formalized Procedure for Problem-Solving Discussion.

PERT (Program Evaluation and Review Technique) was introduced by the U.S. Navy in 1958 as a response to some of the problems arising in coordinating activities involved in the Polaris Missile program.(1) It was later adopted by the Air Force and numerous other government units and private industrial concerns for it was well suited to program planning and management control. PERT procedure consists in the group working together to plot a network of the activities that necessarily precede a specific desired outcome or goal. The completed network serves to define and coordinate what must be done to accomplish the desired goal, as well as revealing weaknesses in the implementation plan.(8) CPM (Critical Path Method) was introduced about the same time by DuPont and is a similar method of outlining in time sequence the steps that must be taken to achieve an objective.(12)

Both methods are designed to coordinate with systems analysis through the use of the computer, and offer the advantage of enabling a planning group to spot impending bottlenecks, to allocate personnel appropriately, to estimate times for operations, to determine starting points for procedures, as well as to test the total logic of a plan of procedure. Based on the concept of probabilities, the logical structure of a proposed program plan can be tested in advance and illogical or unfeasible steps revised or eliminated.(10)

A simplified adaptation of these techniques is useful to agencies, boards, and smaller industrial divisions. The technique provides a visual estimate of program needs, details how long it will take to accomplish and what kinds of activities are to be carried out, by whom and when. The computer is not necessary in the simpler model, for all of the statistical procedure can be done by hand. Use of such models, however, aids in involving personnel in program planning and facilitates clear and rapid communication between persons, divisions, or departments of the same organization by clarifying the role of each person, division, or department in the total process of the program.(14)

In order to fit the steps on the standard discussion agenda, the PERT model can be applied to standard discussion procedure to clarify for participants and leader alike their obligations in the problem-solving phase of discussion. Figure 1 shows how a formalization of standard discussion procedure can serve as a simplified guide to active participation and leadership. Figure 4 shows the steps of the PERT process.

The steps in the PERT procedure(8) are simple and clearcut:[2]

1. Stipulate a final "event" or occurrence which will mark the completion of the program. The word "event" is defined as an occurrence that takes no time, but marks the start or end of a process.

2. List events that must happen before the final event can happen. The events need not be listed in order. Care should be taken to evaluate each item listed to make sure it conforms to the definition of "event" and does not name a process. The entire resources of the planning group must be mobilized so that no major element of implementation is left out in listing the events.

3. Events are ordered in sequence of occurrence if possible. (See Figure 5) Sometimes this procedure leads to the discovery that events can occur simultaneously, i.e., are not dependent on each other, and sometimes events are discovered that depend on the completion of more than one precedent event. The ordering procedure consists in laying out a table as follows:

| | | Necessarily |
| Event No. | Name of Event | Preceded by |

The group then determines which events *must* occur immediately before each named event. This is not a matter of preference, but of logic. If it makes no difference whether one event precedes another, it cannot be listed as precedent. Only if an event is absolutely dependent on another event is it listed in the third column. Figure 5

---

2 For a list of publications detailing with the PERT process, see [13].

shows this ordering of events in an agency plan for a proposed television documentary.

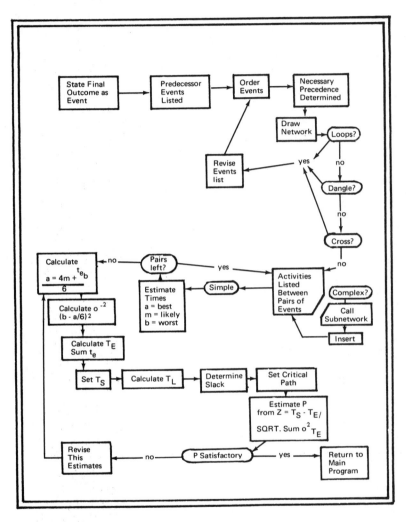

Figure 4. Steps in the pert process.

Note that event numbers do not have to follow in order. Event numbers are not sequential, they are, rather, names of locations on the PERT diagram.

Agency: City Engineer's Office
Goal: Community Education Drive on Air Pollution
Program: Television Documentary

Event No.	Event	Necessarily preceded by
1	Campaign planning meeting adjourns	0
5	Film ordered	4
4	Film selected	3
6	Film received	5
3	Approval letter from superviser received	2
2	Campaign proposal presented to superviser	1
7	Meeting with TV station manager	4
10	Publicity items mailed to newspaper	9
8	TV schedule confirmed	7
15	Spot announcements played	14
14	Spot announcement drafts complete	4, 13
16	Film delivered to TV studio	6
17	Film discussants arrive at studio	13
11	Film discussants selected	4
13	Film discussants accept invitation	12
12	Film discussants invited	11
9	Publicity items written	8, 13
18	FINAL EVENT. Televised documentary film off air.	15, 16, 17, 10

Figure 5. Sequencing of events.

4. The next step is to fit the event chart together into a PERT diagram. Figure 6 shows such a diagram.

The PERT diagram is a representation of a skeleton of the whole program. It can be examined visually for errors in logic. If two lines cross, for example, it would mean that two activities would interfere with each other. If lines looped, it would reveal an endless activity, carried on for no reason. If some lines did not connect, it would indicate either an error in planning or scheduling of an unnecessary activity.

5. After the group is satisfied with the logic of its PERT diagram, it proceeds to the planning of the activities that must take place. It also estimates the time that the activities require and records the estimated time (t_e) on the track between each event. In order to calculate estimated time, group members make three time estimates:

an optimistic estimate (a), a pessimistic estimate (b), and an estimate of the most likely time (m). Estimate time is calculated from a weighted average:

$$t_e = \frac{a + 4m + b}{6}$$

As each estimated time is calculated, the group also calculates a variance (σ^2) for each combination of events:

$$\sigma^2 = \left(\frac{b\text{-}a}{6}\right)^2$$

The estimated times and variances are recorded in a summary table for use in further calculations.

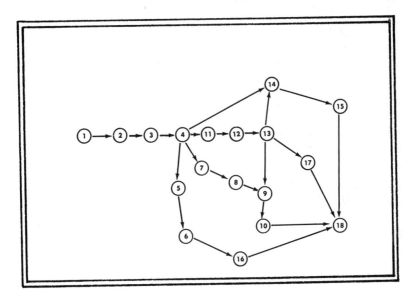

Figure 6. Pert diagram for TV show—in blank.

6. The group then proceeds to the statistical analysis. First they determine how long it will take to accomplish each event (T_E). Then the latest time each event will be completed (T_L) is calculated by working backward from the starting date for the project (T_S). Using these calculations the group can fill in the blanks on their network and determine a "critical path," i.e., a path to the final outcome which has the least slack time (Slack Time $= T_L \text{-} T_E$). The path with

Be-tween events	Activities	(Time in days)				
		a	m	b	t_e	σ^2
1 & 2	Committee appointed to write report Report draft written Report approval obtained Reported delivered to supervisor	7	14	28	15.2	11.25
2 & 3	Superviser reads report Approval granted					
3 & 4	Committee appointed and meets Screening and acceptance of films Previewing films Approval letter received Film selected	7 21	10 42	14 56	10.2 40.8	1.44 33.99
4 & 5	Letter written Check obtained Order mailed and received	7	10	14	10.2	1.44
4 & 7	Meetings held with TV director	7	10	14	10.2	1.44
4 & 14	Copywriter hired Drafts written and approved	21	28	35	28.0	5.29
5 & 6	Film shipped and received	21	28	35	28.0	5.29
6 & 16	Film inspected, packaged, delivered	0.25	1	2	1.0	0.08
16 & 18	Film played	0.25	0.27	0.50	0.3	0.004
7 & 8	Schedule prepared and approved	7	14	21	14.0	1.37
8 & 9	Drafts written and approved	21	28	35	28.0	5.29
9 & 10	Releases mimeographed and mailed	1	2	3	2.0	0.11
10 & 18	Releases received and run 5 times	5	6	8	6.2	0.25
4 & 11	List of possible dicussants made Discussants and alternates selected	14	21	28	21.0	5.44
11 & 12	Phone calls made	1	2	3	2.0	0.11
12 & 13	Details given discussants Alternates contacted if necessary Final confirmation of discussants	7	14	21	14.0	1.37
13 & 14	Notification sent	0.1	0.1	0.1	0.1	0
14 & 15	Announcements delivered Run for one week	8	12	15	11.8	1.35
15 & 18	Interval to program	0.25	0.25	0.25	0.25	0
13 & 17	Instructions given discussants Discussants preview film Discussion rehersal	14	21	28	21.0	5.44
17 & 18	Warm up discussion	0.12	0.20	0.25	0.2	0.04
13 & 9	Biographies and background obtained	7	10	12	9.9	0.69

Figure 7. Activity chart calculation of t_e and σ^2.

the least slack time is the critical path in the program. Estimates about the probable success of the program depends on the critical path. The estimate is made by calculating Z from:

$$Z = \frac{T_S - T_E}{\sqrt{\Sigma \sigma^2 T_E}}$$

Z is then checked on a table of the normal curve for an estimate of *P*, or the probability that the program will be completed on time. The network can also be examined for areas of extra heavy slack time, for these represent overcommitment of facilities and personnel. Figure 7 shows the completed activity chart, and Figure 8 shows the PERT diagram and calculation of *P* for the event considered above.

7. Often agencies and groups will find it necessary to have subsections PERT their own assignments. These sub-PERTs can then be fitted into the main diagram so that once the program is activated, the supervisor will have control over all operations and be kept posted with necessary progress reports.

The PERT procedure, based on computer logic, has a decided advantage in blocking interpersonal conflict and forcing groups to concentrate on necessity rather than whim or desire in formulating

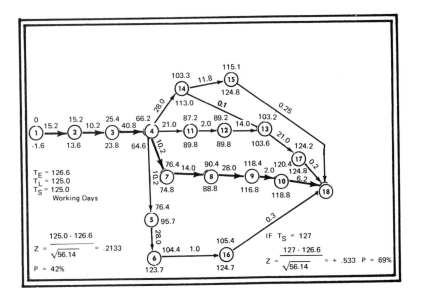

Figure 8. Completed pert network showing t_e, T_E & T_L thick arrow is critical path (least slack)

aims and goals as well as in devising solutions in the form of programs. Desirability does not influence the outcome of the PERT process. After preferences and consensus have played their part in developing a proposal, PERT applies a final empirical test by evaluating the solution for its probability of success. Government and business are only interested in successful solutions. To the extent that it is rational to prepare employees to perform according to expectancies, PERT can play an important role in conference training.

References

1. Avots, Ivars. The management side of PERT. *California Management Review* 4 (1962) 16.
2. Banfield, Edward C. Ends and means in planning. *Concepts and Issues in Administrative Behavior* ed. Sidney Mailick and Edward Van Ness. Englewood Cliffs: Prentice-Hall, 1962, pp. 72-73.
3. Barnard, Chester L. *The Function of the Executive.* Cambridge: Harvard University Press, 1938, p. 158.
4. Barnlund, Dean and Franklyn Haiman. *The Dynamics of Discussion.* Boston: Houghton, Mifflin Co., 1960, p. 72.
5. Boulanger, David G. Program evaluation and review technique. *Advanced Management* 26 (1961) 8.
6. Crowell, Laura. *Discussion: Method of Democracy.* Chicago: Scott, Foresman Co., 1963, pp. 131-149.
7. Dill, William R. Administrative decision making. *Concepts and Issues in Administrative Behavior* ed. Sidney Mailick and Edward Van Ness. Englewood Cliffs, N.J.: Prentice-Hall, 1962, p. 32.
8. Federal Electric Corporation. *A Programmed Introduction to PERT.* New York: John Wiley and Sons, Inc., 1963, p. 1.
9. Harnack, Victor and Thorrell Fest. *Group Discussion: Theory and Techniques.* New York: Appleton-Century-Crofts, 1964, pp. 64-68.
10. MacCrimmon, K.R. and C.A. Ryavec. *An Analytical Study of the PERT Assumptions.* Santa Monica: RAND Corporation, 1962.
11. McBurney, James and Kenneth Hance. *Discussion in Human Affairs:* New York: Harper & Brothers, 1950, p. 17.
12. Miller, Robert W. How to Plan and Control with PERT. *Harvard Business Review* 40 (1962) 94.
13. PERT Orientation and Training Center. *Bibliography, PERT and Other Management Systems and Techniques.* Bolling Air Force Base: 1963.
14. Phillips, Gerald, Eugene Erickson, and Mary B. Arnold. Problem solving and implementation of programs through PERT. *Bulletin,* Western Branch, American Health Association, 1964.
15. Utterback, William. *Group Thinking and Conference Leadership.* New York: Rinehart & Co., 1964, pp. 31-36.
16. Van Slyke, Richard. *Uses of Monte Carlo in Part.* Santa Monica: RAND Corporation, 1963, p. 1.
17. Zelko, Harold P. *Successful Conference and Discussion Technique.* New York: McGraw-Hill Book Co., 1957, pp. 56-57.

AN ALTERNATE PATTERN FOR
PROBLEM-SOLVING DISCUSSION
Ovid L. Bayless

In the first discussion text McBurney and Hance(6) modified Dewey's(4) five steps of reflective thinking and advocated these steps as a pattern for problem-solving discussion. Though there is little empirical evidence to support the reflective thinking pattern as an effective device in a group's problem-solving endeavor, it is still widely prescribed by discussion textbook writers.[1] Many of these authors[2] recommend that consideration of criteria precede ideation. Others however, notably Osborn(8) and Parnes(9), contend that ideation should come before consideration of any criteria.

In an effort to determine the relative effects of patterns upon the outcome of discussion, Brilhart and Jochem(3) compared three different patterns: ideas-criteria (brainstorming), criteria-ideas (a form of reflective thinking), and problem-solution (based on Bales'(2) phase movements). They found that groups using the ideas-criteria pattern tended to produce both significantly more and "better" possible solutions than did groups using other patterns. The authors concluded that a criteria-ideas pattern is "dubious at best and harmful at worst."

Earlier studies by Parnes and Meadow(10), and Meadow, Parnes, and Reese(7) established the potential superiority of an ideas-criteria pattern over another type of pattern in terms of total production of ideas and total "good" ideas. Both of these studies revealed that significantly more "good quality" ideas were generated when Ss received deferred-judgment (brainstorming) instructions than when they followed concurrent-judgment (a form of reflective thinking) instructions.

Reprinted with permission from *Journal of Communication*, Vol. XVII, No. 3., (September, 1967), pp. 188-197.

1. After reviewing eleven books Byron and Sharp [12] noted that "an examination of currently used college discussion texts reveals that, although the authors have added bits and pieces to Dewey's basic definition it remains in all cases very close to the original." Hastings [5] remarked that discussion "textbook prescriptions have not advanced much beyond the steps [Dewey's reflective thinking steps] presented by McBurney and Hance."

2. For example Laura Crowell, *Discussion: Method of Democracy* (Chicago: Scott, Foresman, 1963); H.E. Gulley, *Discussion, Conference, and Group Process* (New york: Holt, Rinehart & Winston, 1961); J.W. Keltner, *Group Discussion Processes* (New York: Longmans-Green, 1957); R.H. Wagner and C.C. Arnold, *Handbook of Group Discussion* (Boston: Houghton Mifflin, 1950); and W.E. Utterback, *Group Thinking and Conference Leadership* (New York: Holt, Rinehart & Winston, 1964).

It should be noted that the conclusions in each of these studies were based primarily on productivity of groups (or individuals in the case of the Parnes, Meadow and Reese research) during what may be termed the middle part of their discussions rather than upon any "final" products. Hence it is possible that these findings do not provide insight into the relative overall merits of the ideas-criteria and the criteria-ideas patterns.

Besides the inclusiveness of present research, other important questions remain unanswered. The most essential it would seem is, does the pattern followed have a significant affect upon the *final* product of the group discussion? Furthermore, would separating ideation and criteria spatially, as well sequentially alter significantly the effects of the group discussion? Additionally, would asking certain members of a group to specialize on a particular aspect of a problem have a significant bearing upon the outcome of the discussion?

This study sought to do two things: (1) construct a problem-solving pattern which separated ideation, criteria, and causality, both spatially and sequentially, and (2) compare this pattern with two others, ideation-criteria and criteria-ideation. The null hypothesis was that there would be no significant difference in the effects of these various patterns on the outcomes of problem-solving discussion.

The pattern formulated for this study was adapted largely from PERT,[3] a management system devised to measure progress toward project objectives, to evaluate current and potential project problems, and to reduce the project completion date to the shortest time possible. Three embellishments of this system were used: (1) working back from the "end event," (2) subdividing project activities, and (3) balancing available resources. A flow chart of this pattern is illustrated in Figure 9. Note how this pattern differs from the continuous line approach of other patterns, *i.e.,* three of the steps are attacked simultaneously.

The directions for this pattern are presented under the heading "Experimental Procedure." Despite the fact that this pattern was not a "pure" PERT application, it was nevertheless identified as a "PERT" pattern.[4]

---

3. PERT is an acronym for Program Evaluation and Review Technique and is a management device for the planning and control of work force activities in business and industrial operations. For a more complete description see Harry F. Evarts, *Introduction to Pert* (Boston: Allyn and Bacon, 1964).

4. For a more orthodox application of PERT in a discussion situation see Phillips [11].

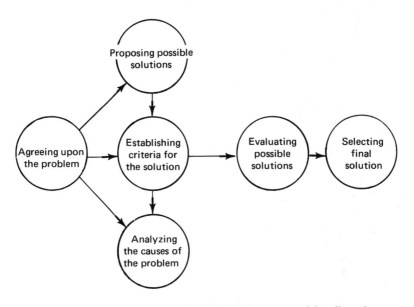

Figure 9. Procedural movement in the PERT program solving discussion pattern.

Method

Subjects

The Ss (N = 192) were members of an elementary speech course at the University of Denver. At the time of this experiment Ss had received no formal training in discussion techniques.

The six discussion group Ls (leaders) were graduate students; each had completed an advanced discussion course as well as a class in group dynamics. The Ls were given three hours of instruction and special training for the experiment. One hour was devoted to either participation in or observation of a pilot experiment related to this study.

Problems

The two discussion problems used in this investigation were taken from Brilhart and Jochem(3). Though both were policy problems, one dealt with a local affair in which Ss had firsthand knowledge; the other was more national in character, and it presented circumstances in which Ss had little or no immediate and direct involvement.

Library Problem. This problem dealt with a situation familiar to the Ss:

The Mary Reed Library has been plagued with books' and magazines' being mutilated, articles cut out, pages ripped away, and materials' being stolen. What might be done to alleviate this problem?

Teacher Problem. Most, if not all Ss had recently been students in the public schools and were to some degree aware of this problem. Even so, few if any of the students had an intimate knowledge of it:

Because of the rapidly increasing birthrate beginning in the 1940s, it is now clear that by 1970 public school enrollment will be very much greater than it is today. In fact, it has been estimated that if the student-teacher ratio were to be maintained at what it is today, 50 percent of all individuals graduating from college would have to be induced to enter teaching. What different steps might be taken to insure that schools will continue to provide instruction at least equal in effectiveness to that now provided?

Experimental Procedure

Twenty-four small groups were used in this experiment. Eight groups employed each of the three patterns in their discussion. Half the groups in each pattern (four) discussed the library problem and half the teacher problem. Though the 24 small groups ranged in size from 6 to 11, the procedure did provide a minimum of 30 Ss in each of the 6 conditions. To avoid potential bias Ls were counter balanced in 18 groups and randomly assigned in the remaining 6.

During the first five minutes each L introduced himself, stated that his role was to guide the group and not to participate actively, that no right or wrong answer existed, and that the group would have 35 minutes to seek a solution. Each L then read a brief outline of the pattern the group would follow and answered any pertinent questions. He then read the problem.

The Ls utilizing the PERT pattern read the following instructions: to facilitate understanding of the problem he began by asking these questions:

1. What exactly is the problem? What has been happening? Why? How serious is this? (To L: limit to five minutes.)
2. Now we're going to split into smaller groups and attack various aspects of this problem. You three people get together and think up every possible solution to this problem, the more the better. Don't worry about anything except thinking up solutions and don't criticize no matter how "far out" an idea might seem; just keep thinking up new ideas to solve the problem. Come up with as many ideas as you can. One of you act as recorder and jot down everything you come up with.

You three people get together and think up every possible standard which the solution will have to meet. This means the requirements the solution must have in order to be feasible and workable. In other words, you set the standards for the final solution. One of you act as recorder.

You three people are to work on the causal analysis aspects of this problem. Be sure you take into account the psychological and economic considerations of all parties involved. Your task is to consider every possible cause which might have a bearing on this problem. One of you act as recorder. (To *L*: limit to ten minutes; if the group runs dry ask the members questions.)

3. Now, let's get back together and see what we've got. Since you've been working on different aspects of the problem we want to evaluate what each of you has to contribute. The recorder for the "solution" group will read off the possible solutions and we'll see how they measure up to the standards of the criteria group and also whether there are any causal considerations that might have a bearing, and should be resolved in the solution we select. You decide whether to rate the solutions E for excellent, G for good, F for fair, or P for poor. (To *L*: limit to 15 minutes.)

4. Now that we've evaluated the possibilities what will we report as the best solution for the problem? (To *L*: this may have been decided, but in no case should you allow more than five minutes for selecting the final solution.)

Instructions for reflective thinking and brainstorming were identical to those used in Brilhart and Jochem(3). The reflective thinking pattern included a separate criteria step prior to the discovery step. Instructions for brainstorming groups were identical to reflective thinking instructions with the exception that criteria and ideation were reversed. In varying degrees all three patterns incorporated the "rules" of brainstorming: no criticism, wild ideas, quantity, and combination building for improvement.

Measurement

Immediately following the discussion Ss completed a 12-item questionnaire.[5] It was designed to assess the success of the experimental manipulation and to ascertain how Ss perceived their experience in the group.

The Ss' ratings were made by placing a check mark on a 3-inch line just below each question. Printed under the line-scale from left to right were the numbers 7 . . . 1. Below number 7 was a phrase identifying a positive reaction and below number 1 a phrase indicating the opposite. For example, the question "How satisfied are you with your contribution?" was identified by "very satisfied" on the positive end and by "very unsatisfied" on the negative end.

---

5. Eight of the questions were taken from a study by Anderson and Fiedler [1].

Results

Effectiveness of Experimental Procedure

The last item on the questionnaire attempted to determine the extent to which Ss perceived that Ls had followed instructions in leading the discussion. Each S marked the box on the questionnaire opposite the discussion outline which best described the procedure used in his group. A chi square comparison of Ss' responses revealed significant differences ($p < .001$) in the three conditions, providing evidence that the experimental variables were effectively manipulated.

Products of Discussion

Final Solutions. Four experts graded the 24 "final" solutions on a scale between 0 and 100. The Director of Circulation of the university library and a professor in the School of Librarianship evaluated the 12 library solutions. The coefficient of correlation between the two grades assigned by the raters was r = + .47. Two professors in the School of Education scored the 12 answers to the teacher problem. The coefficient of correlation was r = + .81. An analysis of variance comparing the "final" evaluations failed to reveal any significant differences in the solutions. (F, pattern = 1.877; F, problem = .002; F, interaction = 2.142.)

Number of Ideas. A significant relationship existed between the pattern a group used, problem discussed, and total number of possible solutions. Groups utilizing brainstorming composed a significantly greater number of potential ideas for the library problem. However, the reflective thinking groups originated significantly more ideas for the teacher problem. These data were significant ($p < .001$) when analyzed by a chi square test of association which compared the actual number of ideas with the expected frequency of ideas. (χ^2 = 28.82, df = 2)

Number of Good Ideas. The total number of solution ideas was placed in random order and the "good" ideas identified by two qualified graders; a third expert was called in to resolve disagreements. The ratio of "good" ideas to total number of ideas remained relatively constant. For example, brainstorming groups produced approximately twice as many possible solutions for the library problem as groups using reflective thinking; brainstorming groups also had roughly double the number of "good" ideas. A chi square analysis, comparing actual frequency of "good" ideas with expected frequency of "good" ideas, revealed the outcome was significant at the five percent level. (χ^2 = 6.91, df = 2)

Questionnaire Results

The Ss' replies to the questionnaire revealed significant differences on five questions; the significance was related to task rather than pattern on four of the items. Those Ss who discussed the library problem indicated that they were more satisfied with their group's decisions; interaction was also significant. (F, problem = 10.23, $p < .01$: F, interaction = 4.11, $p < .05$.) They also revealed that their group members communicated better with each other. (F, problem = 5.61, $p < .05$.) These Ss indicated that the discussion procedure used by their group helped them in reaching a solution. (F, problem = 9.95, $p < .01$.) And they disclosed that a problem-solving pattern aided the group in its tasks. (F, problem = 4.51, $p < .05$.) Only those groups which used the reflective-thinking pattern revealed that the L was effective in directing the groups activity. (F, pattern = 4.11, $p < .05$.)

No significant differences were found in Ss' response to six items: how Ss enjoyed being a member of a group; how much Ss influenced a group's decision; how relaxed and comfortable Ss felt in a group; how satisfied Ss were with their contribution; whether Ss felt anxious or tense in a group; or whether they would follow the procedure used in their group if they were the L in a problem-solving discussion group.

Discussion

This study provided no evidence that the pattern followed by a group in its problem-solving discussion has a significant effect upon the quality of the "final" group product. This suggests that the pattern *per se* may be a relatively unimportant variable for groups engaged in problem-solving endeavors.

The present study, like the investigation by Brilhart and Jochem,(3) failed to reveal any significant relationships between the number of "good" ideas a group proposed and the quality of its "final" solution. Even though the findings of the present study, as well as research by Parnes and Meadow(10) and Meadow, Parnes, and Reese(7), does support the notion that the number of "quality" ideas is increased consistently as quantity of ideas is multiplied, there seems to be no relationship between a greater number of "good" ideas and the quality of the "final" solution.

Separating the ideation and criteria steps spatially and asking certain members of the group to specialize on particular steps apparently hindered the PERT groups from producing a higher volume of possible solutions. This can probably be attributed to the fewer number of people actually engaged in producing ideas (usually 3 compared with 9 in the other groups). However, since it did not affect the quality of the "final" solution and since it may allow a group to conclude its problem-solving discussion sooner because of the distributed workload, it may be that this type of approach has practical value in terms of manhour savings.

The present study revealed a significant relationship between the type of problem discussed by a group and that group's effectiveness as measured by the quantity and quality of possible solutions it produces during the middle stages of the discussion. This finding tends to support the idea that the effectiveness of a problem-solving pattern *during the middle part of the discussion* is somewhat dependent upon situational variables, one of which seems to be the problem facing the group.

The Ss' reaction to experimental conditions lends additional importance to the group task. Group members who worked on the library problem tended to perceive their experience in a more positive manner than did those Ss who encountered the teacher problem. Familiarity of Ss with the library problem probably provided a more "secure" environment. Insufficient information may have made Ss who discussed the teacher problem feel somewhat inadequate to their task. Their inability may have caused feelings of frustration which left them unsatisfied with their group's decision, and may have inhibited their ability to communicate with one another.

The Ss' ability, or perceived ability, to deal with the library problem may have had a positive carryover effect upon their reaction to the problem-solving pattern as an effective tool. It apparently led Ss to feel that the procedure was extremely helpful.

That members of the reflective thinking groups perceived their Ls as more effective than other groups is an interesting finding. Since the criteria-ideation procedure tends to be somewhat more restrictive than the other two patterns, the L who follows this procedure may be acting in a manner which more nearly approximates Ss' preconceived notion of leadership. Brainstorming, with its increased emphasis on "free-wheeling," and PERT, with its system of delegated responsibility, are perhaps too permissive to fit an undergraduate's conception of "effective" leadership.

Summary

This study examined the effect of three different patterns upon the outcome of problem-solving discussions. Twenty-four small groups, representing a total of 192 Ss discussed two policy problems, one more familiar, the other less familiar to the Ss. The results indicated that the pattern followed by the group had no significant relationship to the quality of the groups' "final" product. Significantly more ideas and more "good" ideas were produced during the middle stage of the discussion for the more familiar problem by groups utilizing an ideation-criteria (brainstorming) pattern, while groups following a criteria-ideation (reflective thinking) pattern produced significantly more ideas and more "good" ideas for the less familiar problem. The Ss who discussed the more familiar problem indicated they were significantly more satisfied with their groups' decisions, revealed they communicated significantly better with other members of their groups, felt the procedure used by their groups had a significant bearing in assisting their groups in reaching a solution, and indicated that the pattern employed would be a significant aid for any group in accomplishing its tasks. Members of groups which used a criteria-ideation (reflective thinking) pattern felt the leadership in their groups was significantly more effective than did the Ss in other groups.

References

1. Anderson, L.R. and F.E. Fiedler. Effects of Participatory and Supervisory Leadership on Group Creativity. *Journal of Applied Psychology* 48 (1964) 227-236.
2. Bales, R.F. *Interaction Process Analysis.* Cambridge: Addison-Wesley, 1950.
3. Brilhart, J.K. and L.M. Jochem. Effects of Different Patterns on Outcomes of Problem Solving Discussion. *Journal of Applied Psychology* 48 (1964) 175-179.
4. Dewey, J. *How We Think.* Boston: Heath. 1910.
5. Hastings, A. Twenty-five Years of Discussion Textbooks. *Journal of the American Forensic Association* 1 (1964) 120-122.
6. McBurney, J.H. and K.G. Hance. *The Principles and Methods of Discussion.* New York: Harper, 1939.
7. Meadow, A., S.J. Parnes, and H. Reese. Influence of Brainstorming Instructions and Problem Sequence on a Creative Problem Solving Test. *Journal of Applied Psychology* 43 (1959) 413-416.
8. Osborn, A. *Applied Imagination.* New York: Scribners, 1957.
9. Parnes, S.J. "The Creative Problem Solving Course and Institute at the University of Buffalo." *In* S.J. Parnes and H.F. Harding (Eds.), *A Source Book for Creative Thinking.* New York: Scribner's Sons, 1962.

10. Parnes, S.J. and A. Meadow. Effects of 'Brainstorming' Instructions on Creative Problem Solving by Trained and Untrained Subjects. *Journal of Educational Psychology* 50 (1959) 171-176.
11. Phillips, G.M. 'PERT' as a Logical Adjunct to the Discussion Process. *Journal of Communication* 15 (1965) 89-99.
12. Pyron, H.C. and H. Sharp, Jr. A Quantitative Study of Reflective Thinking and Performance in Problem Solving Discussion. *Journal of Communication* 13 (1963) 46-53.

THE PROCESS OF THE BASIC ENCOUNTER GROUP
Carl R. Rogers

I would like to share with you some of my thinking and puzzlement regarding a potent new cultural development—the intensive group experience.[1] It has, in my judgment, significant implications for our society. It has come very suddenly over our cultural horizon, since in anything like its present form it is less than two decades old.

I should like briefly to describe the many different forms and different labels under which the intensive group experience has become a part of our modern life. It has involved different kinds of individuals, and it has spawned various theories to account for its effects.

As to labels, the intensive group experience has at times been called the *T-group* or *lab group,* "T" standing for training laboratory in group dynamics. It has been termed *sensitivity training* in human relationships. The experience has sometimes been called a *basic encounter group* or a *workshop*—a workshop in human relationships, in leadership, in counseling, in education, in research, in psychotherapy. In dealing with one particular type of person—the drug addict—it has been called a *synanon.*

The intensive group experience has functioned in various settings. It has operated in industries, in universities, in church groups, and in resort settings which provide a retreat from everyday life. It has functioned in various educational institutions and in penitentiaries.

An astonishing range of individuals have been involved in these intensive group experiences. There have been groups for presidents of large corporations. There have been groups for delinquent and predelinquent adolescents. There have been groups composed of college students and faculty members, of counselors and psychotherapists, of school dropouts, of married couples, of confirmed drug addicts, of criminals serving sentences, of nurses preparing for hospital service, and of educators, principals, and teachers.

In their outward pattern these group experiences also show a great deal of diversity. There are T-groups and workshops which have ex-

From *Challenges of Humanistic Psychology*, by James F.T. Bugental. Copyright © 1967 by McGraw-Hill, Inc. Used by permission of McGraw-Hill Book Company.

1. In the preparation of this paper I am deeply indebted to two people, experienced in work with groups, for their help: Jacques Hochmann, M.D., psychiatrist of Lyon, France, who has been working at WBSI on a U.S.P.H.S. International Post-doctoral Fellowship, and Ann Dreyfuss, M.A., my research assistant. I am grateful for their ideas, for their patient analysis of recorded group sessions, and for the opportunity to interact with two original and inquiring minds.

tended over three to four weeks, meeting six to eight hours each day. There are some that have lasted only 2½ days, crowding twenty or more hours of group sessions into this time. A recent innovation is the "marathon" weekend, which begins on Friday afternoon and ends on Sunday evening, with only a few hours out for sleep and snacks.

As to the conceptual underpinnings of this whole movement, one may almost select the theoretical flavor he prefers. Lewinian and client-centered theories have been most prominent, but gestalt therapy and various brands of psychoanalysis have all played contributing parts. The experience within the group may focus on specific training in human relations sills. It may be closely similar to group therapy, with much exploration of past experience and the dynamics of personal development. It may focus on creative expression through painting or expressive movement. It may be focused primarily upon a basic encounter and relationship between individuals.

Simply to describe the diversity which exists in this field raises very properly the question of why these various developments should be considered to belong together. Are there any threads of commonality which pervade all these widely divergent activities? To me it seems that they do belong together and can all be classed as focusing on the intensive group experience. They all have certain similar external characteristics. The group in almost every case is small (from eight to eighteen members), is relatively unstructured, and chooses its own goals and personal directions. The group experience usually, though not always, includes some cognitive input, some content material which is presented to the group. In almost all instances the leader's responsibility is primarily the facilitation of the expression of both feelings and thoughts on the part of the group members. Both in the leader and in the group members there is some focus on the process and the dynamics of the immediate personal interaction. These are, I think, some of the identifying characteristics which are rather easily recognized.

There are also certain practical hypotheses which tend to be held in common by all these groups. My own summary of these would be as follows: In an intensive group, with much freedom and little structure, the individual will gradually feel safe enough to drop some of his defenses and facades; he will relate more directly on a feeling basis (come into a basic encounter) with other members of the group; he will come to understand himself and his relationship to others more accurately; he will change in his personal attitudes and behavior; and he will subsequently relate more effectively to others in his everyday life situation. There are other hypotheses related more to the group than to the individual. One is that in this situation of minimal structure, the group will move from confusions, fractionation, and discontinuity to a climate of greater trust and coherence. These are some of the characteristics and hypotheses which, in my judgment, bind together this enormous cluster of activities which I wish to talk about as constituting the intensive group experience. . . .

The Group Process

As I consider the terribly complex interactions which arise during twenty, forty, sixty, or more hours of intensive sessions, I believe that I see some threads which weave in and out of the pattern. Some of these trends or tendencies are likely to appear early and some later in the group sessions, but there is no clear-cut sequence in which one ends and another begins. The interaction is best thought of, I believe, as a varied tapestry, differing from group to group, yet with certain kinds of trends evident in most of these intensive encounters and with certain patterns tending to precede and others to follow. Here are some of the process patterns which I see developing, briefly described in simple terms, illustrated from tape recordings and personal reports, and presented in roughly sequential order. I am not aiming at a high-level theory of group process but rather at a naturalistic observation out of which, I hope, true theory can be built.[2]

Milling Around

As the leader or facilitator makes clear at the outset that this is a group with unusual freedom, that it is not one for which he will take directional responsibility, there tends to develop a period of initial confusion, awkward silence, polite surface interaction, "cocktail-party talk," frustration, and great lack of continuity. The individuals come face-to-face with the fact that "there is no structure here except what we provide. We do not know our purposes; we do not even know one another, and we are committed to remain together over a considerable period of time." In this situation, confusion and frustra-

---

2 Jack and Lorraine Gibb have long been working on an analysis of trust development as the essential theory of group process. Others who have contributed significantly to the theory of group process are Chris Argyris. Kenneth Benne, Warren Bennis, Dorwin Cartwright, Matthew Miles, and Robert Blake. Samples of the thinking of all these and others may be found in three recent books: Bradford, Gibb, & Benne (1964): Bennis, Benne, & Chin (1961): and Bennis, Schein, Berlew & Steele (1964). Thus, there are many promising leads for theory construction involving a considerable degree of abstraction. This chapter has a more elementary aim—a naturalistic descriptive account of the process.

tion are natural. Particularly striking to the observer is the lack of continuity between personal expressions. Individual A will present some proposal or concern, clearly looking for a response from the group. Individual B has obviously been waiting for his turn and starts off on some completely different tangent as though he had never heard. A. One member makes a simple suggestion such as, "I think we should introduce ourselves," and this may lead to several hours of highly involved discussion in which the underlying issues appear to be, "Who is the leader?" "Who is responsible for us?" "Who is a member of the group?" "What is the purpose of the group?"

Resistance to Personal Expression or Exploration

During the milling period, some individuals are likely to reveal some rather personal attitudes. This tends to foster a very ambivalent reaction among other members of the group. One member, writing of his experience, says:

> There is a self which I present to the world and another one which I know more intimately. With others I try to appear able, knowing, unruffled, problem-free. To substantiate this image I will act in a way which at the time or later seems false or artificial or "not the real me." Or I will keep to myself thoughts which if expressed would reveal an imperfect me.
> My inner self, by contrast with the image I present to the world, is characterized by many doubts. The worth I attach to this inner self is subject to much fluctuation and is very dependent on how others are reacting to me. At times this private self can feel worthless.

It is the public self which members tend to reveal to one another, and only gradually, fearfully, and ambivalently do they take steps to reveal something of their inner world.

Early in one intensive workshop, the members were asked to write anonymously a statement of some feeling or feelings which they had which they were not willing to tell in the group. One man wrote:

> I don't relate easily to people. I have an almost impenetrable facade. Nothing gets in to hurt me, but nothing gets out. I have repressed so many emotions that I am close to emotional sterility. This situation doesn't make me happy, but I don't know what to do about it.

This individual is clearly living inside a private dungeon, but he does not even dare, except in this disguised fashion, to send out a call for help. . . .

Description of Past Feelings

In spite of ambivalence about the trustworthiness of the group and the risk of exposing oneself, expression of feelings does begin to assume a larger proportion of the discussion. The executive tells how frustrated he feels by certain situations in his industry, or the housewife relates problems she has experienced with her children. A tape-recorded exchange involving a Roman Catholic nun occurs early in a one-week workshop, when the discussion has turned to a rather intellectualized consideration of anger:

Bill: What happens when you get mad, Sister, or don't you?

Sister: Yes, I do—yes I do. And I find when I get mad, I, I almost get, well, the kind of person that antagonizes me is the person who seems so unfeeling toward people—now I take our dean as a person in point because she is a very aggressive woman and has certain ideas about what the various rules in a college should be; and this woman can just send me into a high "G"; in an angry mood. *I mean this.* But then I find, I. . . .

Facil.:[3] But what, what do you do?

Sister: I find that when I'm in a situation like this, that I strike out in a very sharp, uh, *tone,* or else I just refuse to respond—"All right, this happens to be her way"—I don't think I've ever gone into a tantrum.

Joe: You just withdraw—no use to fight it.

Facil.: You say you use a sharp tone. To *her,* or to other people you're dealing with?

Sister: Oh, no. To *her.*

This is a typical example of a *description* of feelings which are obviously current in her in a sense but which she is placing in the past and which she describes as being outside the group in time and place. It is an example of feelings existing "there and then."

Expression of Negative Feelings

Curiously enough, the first expression of genuinely significant "here-and-now" feeling is apt to come out in negative attitudes toward other group members or toward the group leader. In one group in which members introduced themselves at some length, one woman refused, saying that she preferred to be known for what she was in the group and not in terms of her status outside. Very shortly after this, one of the men in the group attacked her vigorously and angrily for this stand, accusing her of failing to cooperate, of keeping herself aloof from the group, and so forth. It was the first *personal current feeling* which had been brought into the open in the group.

Frequently the leader is attacked for his failure to give proper guidance to the group. One vivid example of this comes from a

---

3. The term "facilitator" will be used throughout this paper, although sometimes he is referred to as "leader" or "trainer."

recorded account of an early session with a group of delinquents, where one member shouts at the leader (Gordon, 1955, p. 214):

> You will be licked if you don't control us right at the start. You have to keep order here because you are older than us. That's what a teacher is supposed to do. If he doesn't do it we will cause a lot of trouble and won't get anything done. [Then, referring to two boys in the group who were scuffling, he continues.] Throw 'em out, throw 'em out! You've just *got* to make us behave! . . .

Why are negatively toned expressions the first current feelings to be expressed? Some speculative answers might be the following: This is one of the best ways to test the freedom and trustworthiness of the group. "Is it really a place where I can be and express myself positively and negatively? Is this really a safe place, or will I be punished?" Another quite different reason is that deeply positive feelings are much more difficult and dangerous to express than negative ones. "If I say, 'I love you,' I am vulnerable and open to the most awful rejection. If I say, 'I hate you,' I am at best liable to attack, against which I can defend." Whatever the reasons, such negatively toned feelings tend to be the first here-and-now material to appear.

Expression and Exploration of Personally Meaningful Material

It may seem puzzling that following such negative experiences as the initial confusion, the resistance to personal expression, the focus on outside events, and the voicing of critical or angry feelings, the event most likely to occur next is for an individual to reveal himself to the group in a significant way. The reason for this no doubt is that the individual member has come to realize that this is in part *his* group. He can help to make of it what he wishes. He has also experienced the fact that negative feelings have been expressed and have usually been accepted or assimilated without any catastrophic results. He realizes there is freedom here, albeit a risky freedom. A climate of trust is beginning to develop. So he begins to take the chance and gamble of letting the group know some deeper facet of himself. One man tells of the trap in which he finds himself, feeling that communication between himself and his wife is hopeless. A priest tells of the anger which he has bottled up because of unreasonable treatment by one of his superiors. What should he have done? What might he do now? A scientist at the head of a large research department finds the courage to speak of his painful isolation, to tell the group that he has never had a single friend in his life. By the time he finishes telling of his situation, he is letting loose some of the tears of sorrow for himself which I am sure he has held in for many years. A psychiatrist tells of the guilt he feels because of the suicide of one of his patients. A woman of forty tells of her absolute inability to free herself from the grip of her controlling mother. A process which one workshop member has called a "journey to the center of self," often a very painful process, has begun. . . .

The Expression of Immediate Interpersonal Feelings in the Group

Entering into the process sometimes earlier, sometimes later, is the explicit bringing into the open of the feelings experienced in the immediate moment by one member about another. These are sometimes positive and sometimes negative. Examples would be: "I feel threatened by your silence." "You remind me of my mother, with whom I had a tough time." "I took an instant dislike to you the first moment I saw you." "To me you're like a breath of fresh air in the group." "I like your warmth and your smile." "I dislike you more every time you speak up." Each of these attitudes can be, and usually is, explored in the increasing climate of trust.

The Development of a Healing Capacity in the Group

One of the most fascinating aspects of any intensive group experience is the manner in which a number of the group members show a natural and spontaneous capacity for dealing in a helpful, facilitative, and therapeutic fashion with the pain and suffering of others. As one rather extreme example of this, I think of a man in charge of maintenance in a large plant who was one of the low-status members of an industrial executive group. As he informed us, he had not been "contaminated by education." In the initial phases the group tended to look down on him. As members delved more deeply into themselves and began to express their own attitudes more fully, this man came forth as, without doubt, the most sensitive member of the group. He knew intuitively how to be understanding and acceptant. He was alert to things which had not yet been expressed but which were just below the surface. When the rest of us were paying attention to a member who was speaking, he would frequently spot another individual who was suffering silently and in need of help. He had a deeply perceptive and facilitating attitude. This kind of ability shows up so commonly in groups that it has led me to feel that the ability to be healing or therapeutic is far more common in human life than we might suppose. Often it needs only the permission granted by a freely flowing group experience to become evident. . . .

Self-acceptance and the Beginning of Change

Many people feel that self-acceptance must stand in the way of change. Actually, in these group experiences, as in psychotherapy, it is the *beginning* of change. Some examples of the kind of attitudes expressed would be these: "I *am* a dominating person who likes to control others. I do want to mold these individuals into the proper shape." Another person says, "I really have a hurt and overburdened little boy inside of me who feels very sorry for himself. I *am* that little boy, in addition to being a competent and responsible manager." . . .

In another group one man kept a diary of his reactions. Here is his account of an experience in which he came really to accept his almost abject desire for love, a self-acceptance which marked the beginning of a very significant experience of change. He says (Hall, 1965):

> During the break between the third and fourth sessions, I felt very droopy and tired. I had it in mind to take a nap, but instead I was almost compulsively going around to people starting a conversation. I had a begging kind of a feeling, like a very cowed little puppy hoping that he'll be patted but half afraid he'll be kicked. Finally, back in my room I lay down and began to know that I was sad. Several times I found myself wishing my roommate would come in and talk to me. Or, whenever someone walked by the door, I would come to attention in side, the way a dog pricks up his ears; and I would feel an immediate wish for that person to come in and talk to me. I realized my raw wish to receive kindness.

Another recorded excerpt, from an adolescent group, shows a combination of self-acceptance and self-exploration. Art had been talking about his "shell," and here he is beginning to work with the problem of accepting himself, and also the facade he ordinarily exhibits:

> *Art:* I'm so darn used to living with the shell; it doesn't even bother me. I don't even know the real me. I think I've uh, well, I've pushed the shell more away here. When I'm out of my shell—only twice—once just a few minutes ago—I'm really me, I guess. But then I just sort of pull in the [latch] cord after me when I'm in my shell, and that's almost all the time. And I leave the [false] front standing outside when I'm back in the shell.
> *Facil.:* And nobody's back in there with you?
> *Art (crying):* Nobody else is in there with me, just me. I just pull everything into the shell and roll the shell up and shove it in my pocket. I take the shell, and the real me, and put it in my pocket where it's safe. I

> guess that's really the way I do it—I go into my shell and turn off the
> real world. And here: that's what I want to do here in this group, ya
> know, come out of my shell and actually throw it away.
>
> *Lois:* You're making progress already. At least you can talk about it.
>
> *Facil.:* Yeah. The thing that's going to be hardest is to stay out of the
> shell.
>
> *Art (still crying):* Well, yeah, if I can keep talking about it, I can come out
> and stay out, but I'm gonna have to, ya know, protect me. It hurts: it's
> actually hurting to talk about it.

Still another person reporting shortly after his workshop experience said "I came away from the workshop feeling much more deeply that 'It is all right to be me with all my strengths and weaknesses.' My wife has told me that I appear to be more authentic, more real, more genuine."

This feeling of greater realness and authenticity is a very common experience. It would appear that the individual is learning to accept and to *be* himself, and this is laying the foundation for change. He is closer to his own feelings, and hence they are no longer so rigidly organized and are more open to change.

The Cracking of Facades

As the sessions continue, so many things tend to occur together that it is difficult to know which to describe first. It should again be stressed that these different threads and stages interweave and overlap. One of these threads is the increasing impatience with defenses. As time goes on, the group finds it unbearable that any member should live behind a mask or a front. The polite words, the intellectual understanding of one another and of relationships, the smooth coin of tack and cover-up—amply satisfactory for interactions outside—are just not good enough. The expression of self by some members of the group has made it very clear that a deeper and more basic encounter is *possible,* and the group appears to strive, intuitively and unconsciously, toward this goal. Gently at times, almost savagely at others, the group *demands* that the individual be himself, that his current feelings not be hidden, that he remove the mask of ordinary social intercourse. In one group there was a highly intelligent and quite academic man who had been rather perceptive in his understanding of others but who had not revealed himself at all. The attitude of the group was finally expressed sharply by one member when he said, "Come out from behind that lectern, Doc. Stop giving us speeches. Take off your dark glasses. We want to know *you*."...

If I am indicating that the group at times is quite violent in tearing down a facade or a defense, this would be accurate. On the other hand, it can also be sensitive and gentle. The man who was accused of hiding behind a lectern was deeply hurt by this attack, and over the lunch hour looked very troubled, as though he might break into tears at any moment. When the group reconvened, the members sensed this and treated him very gently, enabling him to tell us his own tragic personal story, which accounted for his aloofness and his intellectual and academic approach to life.

The Individual Receives Feedback

In the process of this freely expressive interaction, the individual rapidly acquires a great deal of data as to how he appears to others. The "hail-fellow-well-met" discovers that others resent his exaggerated friendliness. The executive who weighs his words carefully and speaks with heavy precision may find that others regard him as stuffy. A woman who shows a somewhat excessive desire to be of help to others is told in no uncertain terms that some group members do not want her for a mother. All this can be decidedly upsetting, but as long as these various bits of information are fed back in the context of caring which is developing in the group, they seem highly constructive.

Feedback can at times be very warm and positive as the following recorded excerpt indicates:

> *Leo* (very softly and gently): I've been struck with this ever since she talked about her waking in the night, that she has a very delicate sensitivity. *(Turning to Mary and speaking almost caressingly.)* And somehow I perceive—even looking at you or in your eyes—a very— almost like a gentle touch and from this gentle touch you can tell many—things—you sense in—this manner.
>
> *Fred:* Leo, when you said that, that she has this kind of delicate sensitivity, I just felt, *Lord yes!* Look at her eyes.
>
> *Leo:* M-hm.

A much more extended instance of negative and positive feedback, triggering a significant new experience of self-understanding and encounter with the group, is taken from the diary of the young man mentioned before. He had been telling the group that he had no feeling for them, and felt they had no feeling for him (Hall, 1965):

> Then, a girl lost patience with me and said she didn't feel she could give any more. She said I looked like a bottomless well, and she wondered how many times I had to be told that I *was* cared for. By this time I was feeling panicky, and I was saying to myself, "My God, can it be true that I can't be satisfied and that I'm somehow compelled to pester people for attention until I drive them away!"
>
> At this point while I was really worried, a nun in the group spoke up. She said that I had not alienated her with some negative things I had said to

her. She said she liked me, and she couldn't understand why I couldn't see that. She said she felt concerned for me and wanted to help me. With that, something began to really dawn on me, and I voiced it somewhat like the following. "You mean you are all sitting there, feeling for me what I say I want you to feel, and that somewhere down inside me I'm stopping it from touching me?" I relaxed appreciably and began really to wonder why I had shut their caring out so much. I couldn't find the answer, and one woman said: "It looks like you are trying to stay continuously as deep in your feelings as you were this afternoon. It would make sense to me for you to draw back and assimilate it. Maybe if you don't push so hard, you can rest awhile and then move back into your feelings more naturally."

Her making the last suggestion really took effect. I saw the sense in it, and almost immediately I settled back very relaxed with something of a feeling of a bright, warm day dawning inside me. In addition to taking the pressure off of myself, however, I was for the first time really warmed by the friendly feelings which I felt they had for me. It is difficult to say why I felt liked only just then, but as opposed to the earlier sessions, I really *believed* they cared for me. I never have fully understood why I stood their affection off for so long, but at that point I almost abruptly began to trust that they did care. The measure of the effectiveness of this change lies in what I said next. I said, "Well, that really takes care of me. I'm really ready to listen to someone else now." I *meant* that, too.

Confrontation

There are times when the term "feedback" is far too mild to describe the interactions which take place, when it is better said that one individual *confronts* another, directly "leveling" with him. Such confrontations can be positive, but frequently they are decidedly negative, as the following example will make abundantly clear. In one of the last sessions of a group, Alice had made some quite vulgar and contemptuous remarks to John, who was entering religious work. The next morning, Norma, who had been a very quiet person in the group, took the floor:

Norma (loud sigh): Well, I don't have *any* respect for you, Alice. *None!* *(Pause.)* There's about a hundred things going through my mind I want to say to you, and by God I hope I get through 'em all! First of all, if you wanted us to respect you, then why couldn't you respect *John's* feelings last night? Why have you been on him today? Hmm? Last night—couldn't you—couldn't you accept—*couldn't you* comprehend in any way at all that—that *he felt* his unworthiness in the service of God? Couldn't you accept this, or did you have to dig into it today to find something *else there?* And his respect for womanhood—he *loves* women—yes, he does, because he's a real person, but you—you're not a real woman—to me—and thank God, you're not my mother!!! I want to come over and beat the hell out of you!!! I want to slap you across the mouth so hard and—oh, and you're so, you're many years above me—and I respect age, and I respect people who are older than me, *but I*

> *don't respect you, Alice. At all!* And I was so *hurt* and *confused* be-
> cause you were making someone else feel *hurt* and *confused....*

It may relieve the reader to know that these two women came to accept each other, not completely, but much more understandingly, before the end of the session. But this *was* a confrontation!

The Helping Relationship outside the Group Sessions

No account of the group process would, in my experience, be adequate if it did not make mention of the many ways in which group members of assistance to one another. Not infrequently, one member of a group will spend hours listening and talking to another member who is undergoing a painful new perception of himself. . . .

Let me give an example of the healing effect of the attitudes of group members both outside and inside the group meetings. This is taken from a letter written by a workshop member to the group one month after the group sessions. He speaks of the difficulties and depressing circumstances he has encountered during that month and adds:

> I have come to the conclusion that my experiences with you have pro-
> foundly affected me. I am truly grateful. This is different than personal
> therapy. None of you *had* to care about me. None of you had to seek me
> out and let me know of things you thought would help me. None of you
> had to let me know I was of help to you. Yet you did, and as a result it has
> far more meaning than anything I have so far experienced. When I feel the
> need to hold back and not live spontaneously, for whatever reasons, I
> remember that twelve persons, just like those before me now, said to let go
> and be congruent, to be myself, and, of all unbelievable things, they even
> loved me more for it. This has given me the *courage* to come out of myself
> many times since then. Often it seems my very doing of this helps the
> others to experience similar freedom.

The Basic Encounter

Running through some of the trends I have just been describing is the fact that individuals come into much closer and more direct contact with one another than is customary in ordinary life. This appears to be one of the most central, intense, and change-producing aspects of such a group experience. To illustrate what I mean, I would like to draw an example from a recent workshop group. A man tells, through his tears, of the very tragic loss of his child, a grief which he is experiencing *fully,* for the first time, not holding back his feelings in any way. Another says to him, also with tears in his eyes, "I've never felt so close to another human being. I've never before felt a real physical hurt in me from the pain of another. I feel *completely* with you." This is a basic encounter.

One member, trying to sort out his experiences immediately after a workshop, speaks of the "commitment to relationship" which often developed on the part of two individuals, not necessarily individuals who had liked each other initially. He goes on to say:

> The incredible fact experienced over and over by members of the group was that when a negative feeling was fully expressed to another, the relationship grew and the negative feeling was replaced by a deep acceptance for the other. . . . Thus real change seemed to occur when feelings were experienced and expressed in the context of the relationship. "I can't *stand* the way you talk!" turned into a real understanding and affection for you the *way* you talk.

This statement seems to capture some of the more complex meanings of the term "basic encounter."

The Expression of Positive Feelings and Closeness

As indicated in the last section, an inevitable part of the group process seems to be that when feelings are expressed and can be accepted in a relationship, a great deal of closeness and positive feelings result. Thus as the sessions proceed, there is an increasing feeling of warmth and group spirit and trust built, not out of positive attitudes only, but out of a realness which includes both positive and negative feeling. One member tried to capture this in writing very shortly after the workshop by saying that if he were trying to sum it up, ". . .it would have to do with what I call confirmation—a kind of confirmation of myself, of the uniqueness and universal qualities of men, a confirmation that when we can be human together something positive can emerge." . . .

Behavior Changes in the Group

It would seem from observation that many changes in behavior occur in the group itself. Gestures change. The tone of voice changes, becoming sometimes stronger, sometimes softer, usually more spontaneous, less artificial, more feelingful. Individuals show an astonishing amount of thoughtfulness and helpfulness toward one another.

Our major concern, however, is with the behavior changes which occur following the group experience. It is this which constitutes the most significant question and on which we need much more study and research. One person gives a catalog of the changes which he sees in himself which may seem too "pat" but which is echoed in many other statements:

I am more open, spontaneous. I express myself more freely. I am more sympathetic, empathic, and tolerant. I am more confident. I am more religious in my own way. My relations with my family, friends, and co-workers are more honest, and I express my likes and dislikes and true feelings more openly. I admit ignorance more readily. I am more cheerful. I want to help others more.

Another says:

Since the workshop there has been a new relationship with my parents. It has been trying and hard. However, I have found a greater freedom in talking with them, especially my father. Steps have been made toward being closer to my mother than I have ever been in the last five years. . . .

Sometimes the changes which are described are very subtle. "The primary change is the more positive view of my ability to allow myself to *hear,* and to become involved with someone else's 'silent scream.' " . . .

Disadvantages and Risks

Thus far one might think that every aspect of the group process was positive. As far as the evidence at hand indicates, it appears that it nearly always is a positive process for a majority of the participants. There are, nevertheless, failures which result. Let me try to describe briefly some of the negative aspects of the group process as they sometimes occur.

The most obvious deficiency of the intensive group experience is that frequently the behavior changes, if any, which occur, are not lasting. This is often recognized by the participants. One says, "I wish I had the ability to hold permanently the 'openness' I left the conference with." Another says, "I experienced a lot of acceptance, warmth, and love at the workshop. I find it hard to carry the ability to share this in the same way with people outside the workshop. I find it easier to slip back into my old unemotional role than to do the work necessary to open relationships." . . .

Some Data on Outcomes

What is the extent of this "slippage"? In the past year, I have administered follow-up questionnaires to 481 individuals who have been in groups I have organized or conducted. The information has been obtained from two to twelve months following the group experience, but the greatest number were followed up after a three- to six-month period.[4] Of these individuals, two (i.e., less than one-half

---

4. The 481 respondents constituted 82 percent of those to whom the questionnaire had been sent.

of 1 percent) felt it had changed their behavior in ways they did not like. Fourteen percent felt the experience had made no perceptible change in their behavior. Another fourteen percent felt that it had changed their behavior but that this change had disappeared or left only a small residual positive effect. Fifty-seven percent felt it had made a continuing positive difference in their behavior, a few feeling that it had made some negative changes along with the positive.

A second potential risk involved in the intensive group experience and one which is often mentioned in public discussion is the risk that the individual may become deeply involved in revealing himself and then be left with problems which are not worked through. There have been a number of reports of people who have felt, following an intensive group experience, that they must go to a therapist to work through the feelings which were opened up in the intensive experience of the workshop and which were left unresolved. It is obvious that, without knowing more about each individual situation, it is difficult to say whether there was a negative outcome or a partially or entirely positive one. There are also very occasional accounts, and I can testify to two in my own experience, where an individual has had a psychotic episode during or immediately following an intensive group experience. On the other side of the picture is the fact that individuals have also lived through what were clearly psychotic episodes, and lived through them very constructively, in the context of a basic encounter group. My own tentative clinical judgment would be that the more positively the group process has been proceeding, the less likely it is that any individual would be psychologically damaged through membership in the group. It is obvious, however, that this is a serious issue and that much more needs to be known. . . .

Out of the 481 participants followed up by questionnaires, two felt that the overall impact of their intensive group experience was "mostly damaging." Six more said that it had been "more unhelpful than helpful." Twenty-one, or 4 percent, stated that it had been "mostly frustrating, annoying, or confusing." Three and one-half percent said that it had been neutral in its impact. Nineteen percent checked that it had been "more helpful than unhelpful," indicating some degree of ambivalence. But 30 percent saw it as "constructive in its results," and 45 percent checked it as a "deeply meaningful, positive experience."[5] Thus for three-fourths of the group, it was *very* helpful. These figures should help to set the problem in perspec-

---

5. These figures add up to more than 100 percent since quite a number of the respondents checked more than one answer.

tive. It is obviously a very serious matter if an intensive group experience is psychologically damaging to *anyone*. It seems clear, however, that such damage occurs only rarely, if we are to judge by the reaction of the participants.

Other Hazards of the Group Experience

There is another risk or deficiency in the basic encounter group. Until very recent years it has been unusual for a workshop to include both husband and wife. This can be a real problem if significant change has taken place in one spouse during or as a result of the workshop experience. One individual felt this risk clearly after attending a workshop. He said, "I think there is a great danger to a marriage when one spouse attends a group. It is too hard for the other spouse to compete with the group individually and collectively." One of the frequent aftereffects of the intensive group experience is that it brings out into the open for discussion marital tensions which have been kept under cover.

Another risk which has sometimes been a cause of real concern in mixed intensive workshops is that very positive, warm, and loving feelings can develop between members of the encounter group, as has been evident from some of the preceding examples. Inevitably some of these feelings have a sexual component, and this can be a matter of great concern to the participants and a profound threat to their spouses if these feelings are not worked through satisfactorily in the workshop. Also the close and loving feelings which develop may become a source of threat and marital difficulty when a wife, for example, has not been present, but projects many fears about the loss of her spouse—whether well founded or not—onto the workshop experience. . . .

It is of interest in this connection that there has been increasing experimentation in recent years with "couples workshops" and with workshops for industrial executives and their spouses.

Still another negative potential growing out of these groups has become evident in recent years. Some individuals who have participated in previous encounter groups may exert a stultifying influence on new workshops which they attend. They sometimes exhibit what I think of as the "old pro" phenomenon. They feel they have learned the "rules of the game," and they subtly or openly try to impose these rules on newcomers. Thus, instead of promoting true expressiveness and spontaneity, they endeavor to substitute new rules for old—to make members feel guilty if they are not expressing feelings, are reluctant to voice criticism or hostility, are talking about situations outside the group relationship, or are fearful of revealing themselves. These old pros seem to be attempting to substitute a new tyranny in interpersonal relationships in the place of older, conventional restrictions. To me this is a perversion of the true group process. We need to ask ourselves how this travesty on spontaneity comes about.

Implications

I have tried to describe both the positive and the negative aspects of this burgeoning new cultural development. I would like now to touch on its implications for our society.

In the first place, it is a highly potent experience and hence clearly deserving of scientific study. As a phenomenon it has been both praised and critized, but few people who have participated would doubt that *something* significant happens in these groups. People do not react in a neutral fashion toward the intensive group experience. They regard it as either strikingly worthwhile or deeply questionable. All would agree, however, that it is *potent*. This fact makes it of particular interest to the behavioral sciences since science is usually advanced by studying potent and dynamic phenomena. This is one of the reasons why I personally am devoting more and more of my time to this whole enterprise. I feel that we can learn much about the ways in which constructive personality change comes about as we study this group process more deeply.

In a different dimension, the intensive group experience appears to be one cultural attempt to meet the isolation of comtemporary life. The person who has experienced an I-Thou relationship, who has entered into the basic encounter, is no longer an isolated individual. One workship member stated this in a deeply expressive way:

> Workshops seem to be at least a partial answer to the loneliness of modern man and his search for new meanings for his life. In short, workshops seem very quickly to allow the individual to become that person he wants to be. The first few steps are taken there, in uncertainty, in fear, and in anxiety. We may or may not continue the journey. It is a gutsy way to live. You trade many, many loose ends for one big knot in the middle of your stomach. It sure as hell isn't easy, but it is a *life* at least—not a hollow imitation of life. It has fear as well as hope, sorrow as well as joy, but I daily offer it to more people in the hope that they will join me. . . . Out from a no-man's land of *fog* into the more violent atmosphere of extremes of thunder, hail, rain, and sunshine. It is worth the trip.

Another implication which is partially expressed in the foregoing statement is that it is an avenue to fulfillment. In a day when more income, a larger car, and a better washing machine seem scarcely to be satisfying the deepest needs of man, individuals are turning to the psychological world, groping for a greater degree of authenticity and fulfillment. One workshop member expressed this extremely vividly:

> [It] has revealed a completely new dimension of life and has opened an infinite number of possibilities for me in my relationship to myself and to everyone dear to me. I feel truly alive and so grateful and joyful and hopeful and healthy and giddy and sparkly. I feel as though my eyes and ears and heart and guts have been opened to see and hear and love and feel more deeply, more widely, more intensely—this glorious, mixed-up, fabulous existence of ours. My whole body and each of its systems seems freer and healthier. I want to feel hot and cold, tired and rested, soft and hard, energetic and lazy. With persons everywhere, but especially my family, I have found a new freedom to explore and communicate. I know the change in me automatically brings a change in them. A whole new exciting relationship has started for me with my husband and with each of my children—a freedom to speak and to hear them speak.

Though one may wish to discount the enthusiasm of this statement, it describes an enrichment of life for which many are seeking.

Rehumanizing Human Relationships

This whole development seems to have special significance in a culture which appears to be bent upon dehumanizing the individual and dehumanizing our human relationships. Here is an important force in the opposite direction, working toward making relationships more meaningful and more personal, in the family, in education, in government, in administrative agencies, in industry.

An intensive group experience has an even more general philosophical implication. It is one expression of the existential point of view which is making itself so pervasively evident in art and literature and modern life. The implicit goal of the group process seems to be to live life fully in the here and now of the relationship. The parallel with an existential point of view is clear cut. I believe this has been amply evident in the illustrative material.

There is one final issue which is raised by this whole phenomenon: What is our view of the optimal person? What is the goal of personality development? Different ages and different cultures have given different answers to this question. It seems evident from our review of the group process that in a climate of freedom, group members move toward becoming more spontaneous, flexible, closely related to their feelings, open to their experience, and closer and more expressively intimate in their interpersonal relationships. If we value this type of person and this type of behavior, then clearly the group process is a valuable process. If, on the other hand, we place a value on the individual who is effective in suppressing his feelings, who operates from a firm set of principles, who does not trust his own reactions and experience but relies on authority, and who remains aloof in his interpersonal relationships, then we would regard the group process, as I have tried to describe it, as a dangerous force. Clearly there is room for a difference of opinion on this value question, and not everyone in our culture would give the same answer.

Conclusion

I have tried to give a naturalistic, observational picture of one of the most significant modern social inventions, the so-called intensive group experience, or basic encounter group. I have tried to indicate some of the common elements of the process which occur in the climate of freedom that is present in such a group. I have pointed out some of the risks and shortcomings of the group experience. I have tried to indicate some of the reasons why it deserves serious consideration, not only from a personal point of view, but also from a scientific and philosophical point of view. I also hope I have made it clear that this is an area in which an enormous amount of deeply perceptive study and research is needed.

References

Bennis, W.G., Benne, K.D., & Chin, R. (Eds.) *The planning of change.* New York: Holt, Rinehart and Winston, 1961.

Bennis, W.G., Schein, E.H., Berlew, D.E., & Steele, F.I. (Eds.) *Interpersonal dynamics.* Homewood, Ill.: Dorsey, 1964.

Bradford, L., Gibb, J.R., & Benne, K.D. (Eds.) *T-group theory and laboratory method.* New York: Wiley, 1964.

Casriel, D. *So fair a house.* Englewood Cliffs, N.J.: Prentice-Hall, 1963.

Gibb, J.R. Climate for trust formation. In L. Bradford, J.R. Gibb, & K.D. Benne (Eds.), *T-group theory and laboratory method.* New York: Wiley, 1964.

Gordon, T. *Group-centered leadership.* Boston: Houghton Mifflin, 1955.

Hall, G.F. A participant's experience in a basic encounter group. (Mimeographed) Western Behavioral Sciences Institute, 1965.

A PHILOSOPHY AND METHOD OF CHANGE

Dean C. Barnlund and Franklyn S. Haiman

How does one go about teaching or learning the art of group discussion? Is it enough for a student to read a book such as this one, perhaps pass an examination on it, and then store it on the library shelf? Will this improve his understanding and skills of group participation and group leadership? Or would he be better off forgetting about the books and getting as much practice as he can in actual discussion? To answer questions such as these we must first recognize that there are several possible kinds of learning that an individual can experience, and that the methods for achieving each type are quite different. All learning is essentially change, but one can change in many ways.

Intellectual Learning

The first, and perhaps most commonly accepted interpretation of the word "learning," can be described as *change in the amount of information or knowledge that the learner possesses.* In other words, it is learning *about* things and people in the world around us. This is the kind of change that usually is associated with studying a subject in school, reading books, listening to others talk, and observing our environment. It is a predominantly intellectual process, and that is why formal education is so often thought of as the "cultivation of the mind." Intellectual learning involves, in large measure, the acquisition of a broader vocabulary, since new concepts or ideas are most easily assimilated when we have names for them. Thus we can say that intellectual learning is basically a verbal process, it requires exposure to and acquisition of new terms as well as new ideas. . . .

Skills Learning

A second kind of learning has to do with *change in the learner's skills*—that is, in his ability to perform certain acts, be it bowling, cooking, driving a car, painting a picture, or exerting leadership in a discussion. Learning, in this sense, has to do with the development of the student's motor skills or of his techniques of manipulating tools, words, or even people. The process through which change of this kind is brought about is often called training rather than education (though some people use the words synonymously), since it usually involves considerable practice, and can also be a relatively "blind" sort of learning. That is to say, behavioral skills can be developed without much involvement of one's conscious thought processes, since it is often simply a matter of mastering new habit patterns. . . .

To be sure, many complex human skills such as operating the controls of an automated factory, analyzing an argument, or summarizing a discussion require more than blind training. Intellectual learning must also take place if the activity is to be carried out successfully. Yet the fact that one can gain proficiency in so many skills without much accompanying mental activity is what has led the proponents of the so-called "liberal arts" in education to scorn the "mere training" offered in vocational, professional, or skills courses, and to suggest that this work is not worthy of academic credit. Too often these critics fail to see the distinction between a course in basket-weaving, typing, penmanship, or voice and diction, on the one hand, and surgery, English composition, teaching, or discussion and debate, on the other. All involve the performance of skills, but only those at the first extreme can be accomplished simply through imitation and practice. At the latter extreme the learner must understand the whys and wherefores behind what he is "trained" to do, or he will develop only stereotyped patterns of behavior which are too inflexible to be adapted to the variety of unique situations which he must be prepared to confront.

Emotional Learning

A third type of learning is that which involves *change in the student's attitudes, feelings, or values.* Some of us like to refer to this inelegantly, but expressively, as "gut learning." Although the general semanticist shies away from making a separation between "mind" and "emotion" and reminds us, quite properly, that there can be no "mental" activity without "emotional" activity, and vice versa, nevertheless one can make a rough distinction between learning which is *predominantly* verbal in nature, and that which affects the entire nervous system. Anyone who has worked with people who have emotional problems knows that it is one thing to help an individual gain intellectual insight to the point where he can talk about himself rather perceptively, and quite another thing to help him *feel* different. Many people have experienced this distinction in the realm of race relations, where they may understand, "intellectually," that prejudice is foolish, and yet they still *feel* prejudiced. In other words, they have learned, at the verbal level, that racial prejudice makes no sense, but they have not learned it in their "bones."

By the same token, it is quite possible for emotional learning to take place with relatively little conscious awareness of what is happening on the part of the learner. Traumatic experiences which are repressed in the unconscious, but which nevertheless profoundly affect a person's attitudes, are one kind of illustration. Courses in which a common student reaction is, "I know I've learned a lot, but I can't tell you what it is" are another. In short, the change which takes place comes about primarily through direct experience, and to the extent that the learning has not been intellectualized, hence verbalized, it is incommunicable. As Louis Armstrong is reported to have said of the appreciation of jazz, "If you have to ask, you'll never find out."

The debate in educational circles over intellectual versus emotional learning is at least as vehement, if not more so, as that between intellectual and skills learning. There are those, for example, who heatedly condemn the extent to which our public schools have "gone soft" by moving in the direction of teaching for "life adjustment" rather than for "discipline of the mind." Likewise, at the level of higher education, there are those who argue that it is not the business of a college or university to change people's values, but only to expose them to information. On the other hand, there are teachers who feel that there is not much point in a course in race relations, political philosophy, economic policy, or group discussion which affects nobody's attitudes. The first school of thought charges the second with indoctrination. The second charges the first with sterility. Both charges are in most cases probably unfounded, since we suspect that it is only poor courses which deserve these labels, and we are confident that a good teacher, regardless of which school of thought he leans toward, is one who will provide some degree of balance for his students.

Learning at All Three Levels

Having explored the various kinds of learning to which a student can be exposed we return again to the question: How should one learn to discuss? And, like typical integrationists, the authors reply, "we like all three ways." We believe that for education in group discussion to be effective the intellect, the feelings, and the actual behavior of the student must become involved in the process. None of the three kinds of learning alone, nor any two of them in combination, are sufficient to produce the results we regard as most ideal.

To emphasize intellectual learning at the expense of the others, we feel, is to run the risk of leaving the student with only a change in his vocabulary, plus perhaps an increased ability to observe discussions analytically. Although we would not want to deprecate the latter achievement, it has obvious limitations. Without any increase in the learner's emotional sensitivity to people or any new behavior patterns to accompany his greater intellectual understanding, he has become neither a better participant nor a more effective leader. Even his analyses may be warped by virtue of his missing some of the subtle interactions which cannot be detected from a position of emotional detachment.

A strong emphasis on skills training, though appropriate for learning to operate a drill press, is grossly inadequate when it comes to the complex interactions of human relationships. There are too many people who think that effective communication with others can be reduced to a set of simple formulae or bag of tricks. We have seen the sad effects of this kind of training in discussion—the participant who launches forth on an eloquent summary when no summary is needed or wanted by the group, or the leader who graciously asks all the members for their opinions when it is painfully obvious that he is not the least bit interested in them or their opinions. True skill in discussion, although it does take practice, can occur only when one has learned to think his way through each new situation in creative and adaptive ways. It requires intellectual understanding and emotional sensitivity as well as verbal skills. It cannot come about through the learning of stereotyped patterns of behavior. . . .

Emotional change, by itself, is also a limited kind of experience. We have already seen that the individual whose learning is too heavily weighted in this direction is unable to communicate his understanding to others, except perhaps by his own example. Operating by hunch, he is also less able than the "intellectual" person to engage in self-analysis and self-correction, because he lacks the mental tools with which to do so. Finally, it is frequently possible for a person to have the "right" attitudes about a situation and still not be able to act effectively due to lack of practice. We conclude, therefore, that the most successful kind of learning for the student of discussion is that which takes place at all three levels of change which we have described. . . .

The next question is how to achieve such a combination. It cannot come simply from reading about discussion or listening to lectures on the subject, for these are primarily, though not exclusively, intellectual experiences. Nor can it result from practicing the skills of discussion in exercises which are arranged, guided, and evaluated solely by an instructor, for this makes insufficient allowance for the development of the student's own creative standards. It comes too close to "mere training." On the other hand, participation alone, even if it be in a multitude of discussion groups and even though it provide a wealth of satisfying emotional experiences, does not constitute the most effective kind of learning *unless* some provision is made for the analysis of those experiences. A combination of the three levels *can* be achieved in a learning situation wherein teacher and student, working together, create opportunities for the practice of discussion skills, and where these experiences are collaboratively analyzed and evaluated, using whatever useful concepts have been derived from readings or other authoritative presentations. . . .

Methods for Learning to Discuss

Having outlined in broad terms the philosophy we feel should underlie any process of learning to discuss, we now turn to some of the specific methods by which these goals may be achieved. We shall cite four possible patterns which are representative of some of the best current practices, and which may be employed separately or in various combinations. There may be other worthy alternatives now in use or yet to be developed, but these four are ones which our own experience recommends.

Lecture-Discussion Method

This pattern for teaching and learning discussion is the one most widely employed in college and university courses. The instructor presents occasional lectures on topics such as those which have been dealt with in the various chapters of this book. The remainder of class time is devoted to practice discussions among the students on subjects of current political, economic, or social affairs, followed by critical analysis and evaluation utilizing some of the tools for that purpose which are described in Appendix B. In the lecture-discussion method, the teacher plays essentially two roles. As occasional lecturer he provides the students with theoretical (or verbal) tools which may be used to analyze and better understand group interaction. As an observer of the practice sessions he provides group members with feedback which they can use in evaluating their discussions. He also helps to stimulate analysis with leading questions. Sometimes the instructor participates in discussions, and frequently students take over the responsibilities of observing and of instigating evaluation.

The subject matter for discussion is usually selected by the participants, with or without guidance from the teacher. Topics are such that they make some intellectual demands upon the student in the way of preparatory research. (See Appendix C for some of the forms this preparation may take.) Ideally the topics should also be such that the learner can become emotionally involved in them. It may be that both of these objectives cannot be obtained with one topic—in which case a variety of subjects, some doing the first job and others the second, is advisable. A sequence of subjects such as, "What should be our foreign policy with regard to Communist China?" "Should we discourage interracial dating?" and "What can be done to improve student government on our campus?" would provide such a balance. . . .

Role-Playing

Although the use of role-playing is becoming increasingly popular in the formal classroom, it has had its greatest application in various kinds of short courses for adults. Under this method of learning, students participate in spontaneous, simulated discussions in which each member acts out the role of some individual whom he has chosen or been assigned to represent. The group may pretend that it is the local Board of Education, the executive committee of a civic organization, or the staff of a business concern. Individual participants may attempt to portray the behavior of apathetic or overaggressive people; they may enact the role of mediators; or they may create and try to deal with hidden agenda, autocratic leadership, highly emotional conflict, or decision-making under deadline conditions.

Role-playing may be employed for two somewhat different purposes. First, as a demonstration, the instructor may set up a scene by briefing each of the members in such a way that some procedural or interpersonal problem is illustrated which is common to discussion groups. This is a vivid and emotionally involving way of calling the attention of students to an important issue, such as group disorganization; having them experience it, at least vicariously; and providing a concrete episode which all have observed and can analyze together. Here, the evaluative discussion which follows the demonstration is more important than the role-playing itself, which can be done rather ineptly and still provide a useful springboard for analysis

The other use of role-playing is for the purpose of providing the learner with an opportunity to practice certain discussion skills. For instance, if it is desired to develop ability to resolve differences, an imaginary conflict situation can be set up, and the student asked to do his best to help the parties to the dispute to find an agreement. Or, if initiating discussion and stimulating thinking are the skills in need of practice, an apathetic group setting can be enacted in which the student attempts to arouse interest. As in the case of role-playing for demonstration purposes, this kind of scene is also analyzed and evaluated. But, in contrast to demonstrations, the hope here is that learning will come about not only from the post-role-playing discussion, but that also the scene itself will be enacted realistically enough that effective skills practice can be achieved.

It is at this point that some of the critics of role-playing raise objections. They feel it is impossible to derive useful practice from mock sessions which, no matter how well acted, are bound to be somewhat artificial. Although it is often true that role-playing exercises do fail for this reason (and the teacher cannot always predict or control this), we have also found them to be exceedingly helpful. In the first place, the same kind of objection that is raised against role-playing can also be leveled against any educational program, because no two situations are ever exactly alike and there is always the problem of transfer of learning from one setting to another. If students are made aware of this, and seek to discover basic principles of operation rather than specific patterns of behavior which they can literally transfer *in toto,* then the artificiality of role-playing is no more of a handicap than any other off-the-job educational program. Also, the student must be sufficiently flexible and imaginative to overlook minor flaws of amateur acting and focus his attention on the elements of reality that are present. These there will always be, inasmuch as the participants in role-playing are never able completely to divorce themselves from the parts they are playing. They become somewhat identified with their roles and, as a result, bits of real human interaction emerge out of the scene. . . .

Case Method

The case method is often used in conjunction with the lecture-discussion approach, and actually adds only one new element. The practice discussions in which students participate center around a concrete case rather than a generally phrased topical question. Instead of discussing "What should be done about juvenile delinquency in our community?" the group might discuss (after having been given the facts in a case) "What should Joe do about his delinquent son?" In either event the discussion is followed by analysis and evaluation.

Cases may be prepared in advance by the instructor or written and submitted by the students out of their own personal experiences. They may have to do with an incident or problem in such fields as politics, business, civil liberties, and psychology, or they may be examples of breakdowns in group or interpersonal communication. Usually the participants do no research other than to read and think about the facts in the case.

The advantage of the case method over the use of general topics is that there seems to be less difficulty in developing involvement in the subject among the participants—a problem that is always troublesome in any educational endeavor. The concreteness of a specific human situation is more easily gotten ahold of by a group, and besides, say the advocates of the case method, this is the way discussion topics arise in real life. There are, however, good counterarguments. First, it is not true that groups in real life always start their work with a case. As we saw in Chapter 4, often discussion will not take place until a number of events have occurred which finally become generalized into a major problem. Furthermore, while it is true that broad topics sometimes permit participants to escape into vague generalities, case discussions tend to suffer from the complaint that "we don't have enough facts." And no matter how many more facts are included in the original story, there are always those who insist that the problem cannot be solved "until we know more." It is our feeling that both the case method and the general topic approach each have their values and limitations, and that a rounded program might well consist of both techniques. . . .

Laboratory Method

The basic idea of the laboratory method of training in group processes was first developed, so far as we are aware, at the National Training Laboratories summer sessions in Bethel, Maine. In this approach, the students come together in a small group (ideally about fifteen) with an instructor (or trainer, as he is called at Bethel—unfortunately, perhaps) who proceeds to play a highly nondirective leadership role. He may outline, in general terms, the purpose of the course and of his intended role in it, and then ask the group to take over the responsibility of planning its own procedures. The instructor also acts as an observer who stimulates the group to analyze its own processes as it struggles to organize itself and carry on whatever discussion it has chosen to undertake. So far as the teacher is concerned it is of secondary importance whether the group engages in substantive discussion (i.e., politics, religion, etc.) or spends all its time on procedural matters. The reason for this attitude is that, after all, procedure (broadly defined) is the substance of an educational program in discussion. Furthermore, regardless of what the members of the group talk about, interaction takes place, some kind of atmosphere and structure develop, and these matters can then be subjected to further analysis and evaluation. The advocates of the laboratory approach maintain that this is group behavior "in the raw" and that the way for a student to *feel* as well as *understand* group processes is to participate in the birth and early growing pains of a new group which has no superstructure imposed upon it from without.

Ordinarily, the discussion meetings are supplemented by occasional "theory sessions" (in the form of lectures, films, demonstrations, etc.) in which instructors provide the students with concepts which may help them to understand what is happening in their laboratory groups. This experience may be further supplemented with suggested reading materials about group behavior.

Part of the argument which has raged among the experts over the merit of the laboratory method is, we feel, based upon a misunderstanding. A number of its critics, perhaps with some justification based upon their personal experiences, feel that the nondirective guidance which is provided by the instructor is intended as a model for leadership in all situations—either in real life decision-making groups or in learning groups where the content is something other than discussion. It is true that many of the people who teach with the laboratory method do believe that the leadership commonly provided in most learning and decision-making groups could be considerably more nondirective than it now is. It does not necessarily follow, however, that the instructor intends the very specialized kind of behavior he exercises in the laboratory setting to serve as an example for other situations. On the contrary, it seems to us that a knowledgeable teacher who uses the laboratory method would be well aware that the kind of floundering for leadership and intense self-consciousness that characterize laboratory sessions would be quite inappropriate in a group whose goals were something other than learning about small group behavior.

We would repeat once again that the four educational methods described here are not mutually exclusive. One can employ them in various combinations and to various degrees. So far as we are concerned, the matter of most importance is that an educational program in discussion somehow contain these elements:

1. An opportunity for the learner to participate in group discussions.

2. An opportunity for the learner to analyze and evaluate the group behavior in which he has participated.
3. An opportunity for the learner to become acquainted with ideas for conceptualizing and verbalizing what takes place in a discussion.
4. An opportunity for the learner to become emotionally involved in the learning process and to help control its direction.

Recommended Readings

"Can Leadership Training Be Liberal Education?" *Adult Leadership* (June, 1953).

Cantor, Nathaniel. *The Dynamics of Learning.* Foster and Stewart, 1946.

Lippitt, Ronald, Jeanne Watson, and Bruce Westley. *The Dynamics of Planned Change.* Harcourt, Brace and Company, 1958.

BIBLIOGRAPHY
Part II
Individual and Group Operations

Allen, Louis A. "The Problem-Solving Conference," *Developing Executive Skills*, New York: American Management Association, Inc., 1958.

Allport, Floyd H. "Structuronomic Conception of Behavior: Individual and Collective," *Journal of Abnormal and Social Psychology*, 64 (Jan.-June, 1962), 3-31.

Allport, Gordon W. "The Psychology of Participation," *Psychological Review*, 52 (1945), 117-132.

Anderson, Harold Homer. *Creativity and Its Cultivation*, New York: Harper, 1959.

Argyris, Chris. "T. Groups for Organizational Effectiveness," *Harvard Business Review*, 42, 2 (Mar.-Apr., 1964), 60-75.

Bales, R.F. "A Set of Categories for the Analysis of Small Group Interaction," *American Sociological Review*, XV (1950), 257-263

———. "In Conference," *Harvard Business Review*, 32, 2 (Mar.-Apr., 1954), 37-44.

Bales, Robert F. and Fred L. Strodtbeck. "Phases in Group Problem Solving," *Journal of Abnormal and Social Psychology*, 46 (1951), 485-495.

Banks, J.A. "The Group Discussion as an Interview Technique," *Sociological Review*, 5 (1957), 461-468.

Banton, Michael P. *Roles, An Introduction to the Study of Social Relations*, New York: Basic Books, 1965.

Bavelas, A. "Role Playing in Management Training," *Sociometry*, 1 (1957), 183-191.

Bennis, Warren and others, (eds.). *The Planning of Change*, New York: Holt, Rinehart and Winston, 1966.

Berkowitz, Leonard. "Personality and Group Position," *Sociometry*, 19 (1956), 210-222.

Berkowitz, Leonard, Bernard I. Levy and Aurther R. Harvey. "Effects of Performance Evaluations on Group Integration and Motivation," *Human Relations*, 1 (1948), 195-209.

Bion, W.R. "Experiences in Groups: I," *Human Relations,* 1, 3 (1948) 314-320.

Braden, Waldo W. and Earnest Brandenburg. *Oral Decision-Making: Principles of Discussion and Debate,* New York: Harper, 1955.

Bradford, Leland P., Jack R. Gebb and Kenneth D. Benne, (eds.). *T. Group Theory and Laboratory Method,* New York: John Wiley and Sons, Inc., 1964.

Brehm, Jack and Leon Festinger. "Pressures Toward Uniformity of Performance in Groups," *Human Relations,* 10, 1 (1957) 85-91.

Brind, Anna and Noh Brind. "The Therapeutic Hour of Psychodrama," *Group Psychotherapy,* 7 (March, 1953), 76-80.

Chorness, Murray H. "Increasing Creativity in Problem Solving Groups," *The Journal of Communication,* 8, 1 (Spring, 1958), 16-23.

Cohen, Aurther M. "Changing Small Group Communication Networks," *The Journal of Communication,* 11, 3 (September, 1961), 116-124.

Collins, Barry E. *A Social Psychology of Group Process for Decision Making,* New York: Wiley, 1964.

Coon, Arthur M. "Brainstorming—A Creative Problem Solving Technique," *The Journal of Communication,* 7, 3 (Autumn, 1957), 111-118.

Corson, J.J. "Innovation Challenges Conformity," *Harvard Business Review,* 40, 3 (1962), 67-74.

Deane, Wulliam M. and Erma B. Marchall. "A Validation Study of a Psychodrama Group Experience: A Preliminary Study," *Group Psychotherapy,* 18 (December, 1965), 230-236.

Dimnet, Ernest. *The Art of Thinking,* New York: Simon and Schuster, 1928.

Elliott, H.S. *The Process of Group Thinking,* New York: Association Press, 1932.

Festinger, Leon and H.A. Hutte. "An Experimental Investigation of the Effect of Unstable Interpersonal Relations in a Group," *Journal of Abnormal and Social Psychology,* 49 (1954), 513-532.

Gage, N.L. and R.V. Exline. "Social Perception and Effectiveness in Discussion Groups," *Human Relations,* 6 (1953), 381-396.

Garland, J.V. *Discussion Methods Explained and Illustrated,* 3rd ed., New York: Wilson, 1951.

Goffman, Erving. "Alienation from Interaction," *Human Relations,* 10, 1 (1957), 85-91.

Gore, William J. and J.W. Dyson (eds.). *The Making of Decisions,* New York: Free Press of Glenco, 1964.

Guilford, J.P. "Some Recent Findings on Thinking Abilities and Their Implications," *The Journal of Communication,* 3, 1 (May, 1953), 49-59.

Greenberg, Ira. "Audience in Action Through Psychodrama," *Group Psychotherapy,* 17 (June-Sept., 1964), 120-132.

Hall, Ernest T., Jane S. Morton and Robert R. Blake. "Group Problem Solving Effective Under Condition of Pooling vs. Interaction," *Journal of Social Psychology,* 59 (1963), 147-157.

Harnack, R. Victor and Thorrel B. Fest. *Group Discussion Theory and Techniques,* New York: Appleton—Century Crofts, 1964.

Harvey, O.J. "An Experimental Approach to the Study of Status Relations in Informal Groups," *American Sociological Review,* 18 (1953), 357-367.

Hays, David G. and Robert R. Bush. "A Study of Group Action," *American Sociological Review,* 19, 6 (December, 1954), 692-702.

Hochbaum, Godfrey H. "The Relation Between Group Members' Self Confidence and Their Reactions to Group Pressures to Uniformity," *American Sociological Review*, 19, 6 (December, 1954), 678-687.

Hoffman, L.R. "Conditions for Creative Problem-Solving," *Journal of Psychology*, 52 (1961), 429-444.

Hoffman, L.R. and N.R.F. Maier. "The Use of Group Decision to Resolve a Problem of Fairness," *Personnel Psychology*, 12 (Winter, 1959), 545-559.

Johnson, David M. *Psychology of Thought and Judgment*, New York: Harper, 1955.

Karlins, Marvin. "A Note of a New Test of Creativity," *Journal of Psychology*, 67 (1967), 335-340.

Kelly, Harold H. and Martin M. Shapiro. "An Experiment on Group Norms Where Conformity Is Detremental to Group Achievement," *American Sociological Review*, 19, 6 (December, 1954), 667-677.

Kelly, Harold H. and John M. Thibaut. "Experimental Studies of Group Problem Solving and Process," in Lindzey's *Handbook of Social Psychology*, Massachusetts: Addison-Wesley Publishing Company, 1954.

Kelly, J.N. Jr. "On the Right Use of Discussion," *ETC.*, 13, 2 (Winter, 1955-1956), 124-126.

Kemp, Clarence G. *Perspectives on the Group Process: A Foundation for Counseling with Groups*, Boston: Houghton, Mifflen, 1964.

Keyes, Kenneth S. *How to Develop Your Thinking Ability*, New York: McGraw-Hill, 1950.

Kiesler, Sara B. "Stress, Affiliation and Performance," *Journal of Experimental Research*, 1 (1966), 147-157.

Klein, Alan F. *How to Use Role Playing Effectively*, New York: Association Press, 1959.

Kneller, George. *The Art and Science of Creativity*, New York: Holt, Rinehart and Winston, 1965.

Landsberger, Henry A. "Interaction Process Analysis of the Mediation of Labor-Management Disputes," *The Journal of Abnormal and Social Psychology*, LI (November, 1955), 522-558.

Lee, Irving J. "Procedure for 'Coercing' Agreement," *ETC.*, 11, 3 (1954), 193-203.

Lindgren, Henry Clay and Fredrica Lindgren. "Creativity, Brainstorming, and Onerieness: A Cross-Cultural Study," *Journal of Social Psychology*, 67 (1965), 23-30.

Lippett, Ronald, Jeanne Watson and Bruce Westly. *A Comparative Study of Principles and Techniques*, New York: Harcourt, Brace and World, Inc., 1958.

Lippett, R. *Training in Community Relations: A Research Exploration Toward New Group Skills*, New York: Harper, 1949.

Loney, Glen M. *Briefing and Conference Techniques*, New York: McGraw-Hill, 1959.

Maier, Norman R.F. "Assets and Liabilities in Group Problem Solving," *Psychological Review*, 74 (July, 1967), 239-250.

———. *Problem-Solving, Discussions and Conferences*, New York: McGraw-Hill Company Inc., 1963.

McKellar, Peter. *Imagination and Thinking: A Psychological Analysis*, New York: Basic Books, 1957.

Miller, Harry L. "Group Discussion—Specific or Panacea," *ETC.*, 11, 1 (Autumn, 1953), 49-58.

Moment, David and Abraham Zeleznik. *Role Development and Interpersonal Competence: An Experimental Study of Role Performances in Problem-Solving Groups*, Boston: Harvard University Press, 1963

Moreno, J.L. "Psychodramatic Rules, Techniques and Adjunctive Methods," *Group Psychotherapy*, 18 (March-June, 1965), 73-90.

Newell, A.N. and others. *Elements of a Theory of Human Problem-Solving*, Santa Monica, California: The Rand Corp., 1957.

Olmsted, Michael L. "Orientation and Role in the Small Group," *American Sociological Review*, 19, 6 (December, 1954), 741-750.

Osborn, Alex F. *Applied Imagination*, New York: Charles Scribner's and Sons, 1957.

Parrish, Marguetite. "Psychodrama Description of Application Review of Techniques," *Group Psychotherapy*, 17 (March 1964), 37-46.

Phillips, Gerald M. " 'PERT' as a Logical Adjunct to Group Process," *The Journal of Communication*, 15, 2 (June, 1965), 89-.

Raven, Bertram, H. and Jan Reitsema. "The Effects of Varied Clarity of Group Goal and Group Path Upon the Individual and His Relation to the Group," *Human Relations*, 10, 1 (1957).

Reisman, Frank. "Roleplaying and the Lower Socio-Economic Groups," *Group Psychotherapy*, 17 (March, 1964), 37-46.

Restle, Frank. *Psychology of Judgment and Choice: A Theoretical Essay*, New York: Wiley, 1961.

Rubin, Irwin M. "Increased Self-Acceptance: A Means of Reducing Prejudice," *Journal of Personality and Social Psychology*, 5 (1967), 233-239.

Schaftel, Fannie R. *Role-Playing for Social Values*, New Jersey: Prentice-Hall, Inc., 1967

Scheff, Thomas J. *Being Mentally Ill: A Sociological Theory*, Chicago: Aldine Publishing Company, 1966.

Seidel, George J. *The Crisis of Creativity*, Notre Dame, Indiana: University of Notre Dame Press, 1966.

Shaftel, George A. and Fannie Shaftel. *Role Playing the Problem Story: An Approach to Human Relations in the Classroom*, New York: National Conference of Christians and Jews, 1952.

Sheffield, Alfred Dwight. *Creative Discussion: A Statement of Method for Leaders of Discussion Groups and Conferences*, 2nd ed. rev., New York City: The Inquiry, Distributed by the Association Press and the Womans Press, 1927.

Shera, Jesse, Allen Kent and James W. Perry (eds.). *Documentation in Action*, New York: Rineholt Pub., 1956.

Sherif, Muzager and others. *Intergroup Conflict and Cooperation: The Roberts Cave Experiment*, University of Oklahoma: University Book Exchange, 1961.

Symonds, Percival M. *Education and the Psychology of Thinking*, New York: McGraw-Hill Book Company, 1936.

Taylor, Calvin W. (ed.). *Creativity: Progress and Potential*, New York: McGraw-Hill Book Company, 1964.

Trecker, Andry and Harleigh B. Trecker. *How to Work With Groups*, New York: Womans Press, 1952.

Vinacke, William E. *The Psychology of Thinking*, New York: McGraw-Hill, 1952.

Wasserman, Paul. *Decision Making: An Annotated Bibliography*, Ithaca, New York: Cornell University, 1958.

Werkmeister, William H. *An Introduction to Critical Thinking: A Beginners Text in Logic*, Lincoln, Nebraska: Johnson Pub. Co., 1948.

Wertheimer, Max. *Productive Thinking*, New York: Harper and Brothers, 1945.

Weschler, I. "The Self in Process: A Sensitivity Training Emphasis," in I. Weschler and E.H. Schien (eds.) *Issues in Human Relations Training*, Washington, D.C.: National Education Association, National Training Laboratories, 1962.

Wolff, Kurt H. (ed., translated). *The Sociology of Georg Simmel*, Illinois: The Free Press, 1950.

PART III

GROUP
COMMUNICATION
THEORY
AND PRACTICE

The need to accentuate the importance of communication seems truly unnecessary in a decade that is undergoing a "communication explosion." From all areas and from every direction we are being confronted with personal examples of how crucial communication is to our existence. Although much of the emphasis is on communication "hardware," such as satellites, television, computers and the like, we need only glance at our daily environments to see the role communication plays in the numerous group situations in which we find ourselves daily.

It can be generalized that the prevalence of communication in our many group activities can be considered the most significant structural property of a group as well as the most readily observable phenomenon of group life.[1]

If we are going to be able to perform effectively in small groups we must be able to communicate. Social psychologist Soloman Asch states:

> We have good reason to suppose that conditions from the wider social field reach individuals from their everyday contacts with family, friends, companions. It is in these concrete contacts that communication and discussion takes place and that decisions are reached and pressures exerted to act in given ways.[2]

Just as most organizations are initiated, perpetuated and held together by communication, so too this postulate is true in the life cycle of any group. It is through communication that we form the links that eventually fuse the individuals into what, by definition,

1. Abraham Zaleznik and David Moment, *The Dynamics of Interpersonal Behavior*, New York: John Wiley and Sons, Inc., 1964, p. 71.
2. Soloman E. Asch, *Social Psychology*, New York: Prentice-Hall, Inc., 1952, p. 502.

221

can be called a "group." Without this highly complex phenomenon we would indeed be forced into total seclusion, conscripted into isolation that would set each of us apart from our fellow human beings. In a very real sense it is communication that enables us to tell and to be told, to share our innermost feelings and ideas, to exercise some control over our environments, and to form into the countless groups that offer us the support of others, as well as the opportunity to interact and solve problems with those of similar and divergent views.

What is crucial in our view of the relationship existing between discussion and communication is the notion that man must be aware of how he influences and affects himself, as well as a knowledge of how by his manipulation of both verbal and nonverbal symbols he willingly or unwillingly affects others. His abilities to communicate to, and to be communicated with, are both cause and consequence of his unique competencies and his desires to manage himself and his interpersonal relationships in the organizations and groups, both formal and informal, to which he has some allegiance and responsibility. If man is to be successful in the many groups to which he belongs, including those highly structured as well as those that are inconspicuous and subtle, he must understand himself, how he communicates with himself, how he communicates with others, how he acts and reacts in groups, and something of the dynamics of each of these groups. In short, man must understand about communication if he is to operate to his full potential. We must know how communication works and something of the impact and influence we have over its workings. It is the intent of this section to contribute to that understanding. It is hoped that an appreciation of the communication process will evolve from this understanding.

In addition to a knowledge of some of the theory of communication we must be able to have that theory reflected in our communication behavior. Practice as well as theory should truly be the aim of each discussion participant. Being able to locate and isolate potential communication problems, and the eventual resolution of those problems is in part an important ingredient of successful small group communication. For if effective communication is not practiced within the group the final product might well be distrust, misunderstanding, apathy and the like.

This section seeks to bring together both theory and practice. Under two inter-related headings this fusion is discussed and explained. The first section attempts to offer readings that discuss interpersonal and small group communication from a theoretical point of view. The main emphasis of these six selections centers on how communication, and all of its intricate variables, operate and function. In the second portion the book seeks to set forth some selections that have the practice of communication as their main emphasis. They offer the reader some suggestions for improving his communication habits within the small group.

In the first selection Wendell Johnson suggests that to understand a process as complex as communication we must look at that process and try to discover what difficulties and disorders "beset us in our efforts to communication with one another." In this popular essay "The Fateful Process of Mr. A Talking to Mr. B," Johnson maintains that one way to examine this process (communication) is to diagram it. His contention is that "if you can't diagram it you can't understand it." What he is proposing is the construction of a communication model as a means of discussing and describing the actions and reactions during each stage of the communication act.

Daniel Katz advises yet another way of viewing the communication process. Katz indicates one should begin by examining the psychological difficulties in communication. For Katz these difficulties become barriers. These barriers and difficulties are in part a function of the very nature of language, and in part are due to the emotional limitations of human beings. Therefore, to understand how we communicate and why at times we fail to communicate, one must look at *both* language and at people. To promote this understanding he presents four obstacles that are most persistent in our communication activity.

Students of communication have long agreed with the obvious observation that communication is a two-way process—with speaker and listener sharing an equal role in this transaction. Yet even with this much stated principle appearing throughout the writings in communication, the literature seems to reveal an uneven distribution in favor of the speaker. One possible reason for this unevenness might be that scholars have long either avoided any discussion as to the nature of listening or clearly indicated their uncertainty as to the ingredients of listening. Granting the importance of listening, Charles Kelly attempts to define and examine listening, and to offer an analysis of what he refers to as "empathic listening." In his essay, written specifically for this book, Kelly not only indicates what listening is and what it is not, but he also presents some suggestions for developing those empathic listening skills that might be helpful in small group communication.

It is generally agreed upon that communication takes place on many different levels and in a variety of forms. Word-symbols are the most common symbol-system used and investigated, but they are by no means the only system we use to share our ideas and feelings. Nonverbal language is one of the forms of communication that is equally as important. As participants in any communication encounter we have certainly been aware of the fact that our response to another individual goes well beyond what he says. Our responses and interpretations are based to a large degree on messages that are both verbal and nonverbal. The importance of nonverbal language is recognized in a selection by Jurgen Ruesch. In discussing three distinct categories of nonverbal forms of language (sign, object, and action language), Ruesch points out similarities and differences between verbal and nonverbal codifications—revealing the crucial character of nonverbal communication to all human interaction.

We have already mentioned that some of the readings in this section of the book will focus on the influence of language, people, listening and the nonverbal elements in the communication process. These factors deal with only a portion of the total number of variables that can affect communication and small group activity. In practice the factors that influence the outcome are even more numerous and complex. For example, Robert Sommer, in his article, "Studies in Small Group Ecology," looks at the issue of space and seating arrangement as an element in small group communication. By reviewing both observation studies and questionnaire studies, Sommer tries to detect how people in different types of face-to-face groups arrange themselves. If, for example, it is known that one seating arrangement is more conducive to communication than another, it would seem desirable for participants in a group to arrange themselves in that setting style that most contributes to interaction.

Even the most cursory of examinations reveal that to study human communication one must seek out the principles, theories, and axioms where he may. In this sense the study of human communication is truly interdisciplinary. In an article written for this publication, Samovar and Rintye attempt to deal with this multi-dimensional aspect of communication, bringing together, in summary form, several principles of human interpersonal communication drawn from a variety of disciplines. They point out that their listening and discussion is by no means exhaustive, but rather a basic core of assumptions which requires recognition in any sound theory of human communication.

Thus far we have been talking about those selections in this portion of the book that view communication from a theoretical perspective. But anyone who has been engaged in small group activity realizes that it is the implementation of theory that accounts for the success or failure of the group. Irving Lee offers a similar generalization in his essay entitled "Why Discussions Go Astray." After studying the communication problems of thirty groups, Lee produced a descriptive listing of the kinds of misevaluations manifested in these groups. By looking at the specific communication problems in an isolated number of groups Lee believed that greater understanding, and perhaps even better communication, might result.

Jack R. Gibb suggests that one way to understand communication is to view it as a "people" process. In analyzing communication from this orientation Gibb recommends we begin with "defensive behavior." For Gibb, defensive behavior is that behavior which occurs when an individual perceives threat, or anticipates threat, in the group. If a group is going to work effectively, and engage in meaningful communication, it must work to eliminate those factors that contribute to defensive behavior. He notes that a defensive climate within a group is characterized by individual attitudes and actions that reflect evaluation, control, strategy, neutrality, superiority, and certainty. In his selection Gibb also offers a description of those elements which give rise to a supportive climate within a group. In this kind of group the members mirror attitudes of description, problem orientation, spontaneity, empathy, equality and provisionalism.

Like Lee and Gibb, Edwin Black is also concerned with the twofold issues of communication breakdowns in groups, and the subsequent remedies of those breakdowns. After reviewing thirty-five group discussions Black isolated what he considered to be rhetorical causes of breakdowns. His investigation sought to determine in what way rhetorical considerations may cause or contribute to disruptions in group discourse. He maintained that when these disruptions and breakdowns occur they are either digressions or ambiguities.

We have already noted that much of what goes on between people, both in and out of groups, involves oral discourse. By means of a word-symbol-system the participants in a group attempt to solve problems and secure mutual understanding. Accepting the importance of man's use of verbal systems, Norman Stageberg proposes that a study of the intentional and unintentional distortions of language is a prerequisite for successful group discussion. As a way of examining the most serious language problems (what Stageberg calls "obstacle words"), he recommends a brief review of the seven categories which have been drafted from linguistics and logic.

Robert Benjamin, as a linguist, is also concerned with the use and misuse of language in small groups. In a selection written for this book, Benjamin focuses on "the remarkable way language permits, even encourages, description and evaluation in the same breath." Specifically, he has collected and categorized the linguistic devices with which we praise and/or deride. It is believed that an understanding of these devices will make us more aware of the words we select to represent reality, and will also enable us to more carefully examine the verbal descriptions and accounts we hear.

In the final selection in this portion of the volume, Robert Crook speaks of communication in a more general sense than did the preceeding authors. Crook maintains that interactions, both verbal and nonverbal, are dynamic factors which influence the creation and the development of the group structure. The kinds of group communication give rise to varying networks which affect not only the structure but also the effectiveness of the group in striving towards its goals. Crook offers the reader some reasons for both ineffective ("immature group functioning") and effective ("mature group functioning") in small group discussion. His main assumptions are "that communicative behaviors are significantly related to maturing and that the development of valid communication is an essential prerequisite for group effectiveness in solving problems."

chapter 6

Theory

THE FATEFUL PROCESS OF MR. A TALKING TO MR. B
Wendell Johnson

It is a source of never-ending astonishment to me that there are so few men who possess in high degree the peculiar pattern of abilities required for administrative success. There are hundreds who can "meet people well" for every one who can gain the confidence, goodwill, and deep esteem of his fellows. There are thousands who can speak fluently and pleasantly for every one who can make statements of clear significance. There are tens of thousands who are cunning and clever for every one who is wise and creative.

Why is this so? The two stock answers which I have heard so often in so many different contexts are: (1) administrators are born, and (2) administrators are made.

The trouble with the first explanation—entirely apart from the fact that it contradicts the second—is that those who insist that only God can make a chairman of the board usually think themselves into unimaginative acceptance of men as they find them. Hence any attempt at improving men for leadership is automatically ruled out.

Meanwhile, those who contend that administrators can be tailor-made are far from omniscient in their varied approaches to the practical job of transforming bright young men into the inspired leaders without which our national economy could not long survive. Nevertheless, it is in the self-acknowledged but earnest fumblings of those who would seek out and train our future executives and administrators that we may find our finest hopes and possibilities.

This article does not propose to wrap up the problem of what will make men better administrators. Such an attempt would be presumptuous and foolhardy on anyone's part; there are too many side issues, too many far-reaching ramifications. Rather, this is simply an explo-

Author's Note: Portions of the present article are adapted from a talk I gave before a conference of the American Management Association, Chicago, Illinois, February 18, 1952.

ration into one of the relatively uncharted areas of the subject, made with the thought that the observations presented may help others to find their way a little better. At the same time, the objective of our exploration can perhaps be described as an oasis of insight in what otherwise is a rather frightening expanse of doubt and confusion.

The ability to respond to and with symbols would seem to be the single most important attribute of great administrators. Adroitness in reading and listening, in speaking and writing, in figuring, in drawing designs and diagrams, in smoothing the skin to conceal and wrinkling it to express inner feelings, and in making the pictures inside the head by means of which thinking, imagining, pondering, and evaluating are carried on—these are the fundamental skills without which no man may adequately exercise administrative responsibilities.

Many of the more significant aspects of these administrative prerequisites may be brought into focus by means of a consideration of what is probably the most fateful of all human functions, and certainly the one function indispensable to our economic life: communication. So let us go on, now, to look at the process of communication and to try to understand the difficulties and disorders that beset us in our efforts to communicate with one another.

The Process Diagramed

Several years ago I spent five weeks as a member of a group of university professors who had the job of setting up a project concerned with the study of speech. In the course of this academic exploring party we spent a major part of our time talking—or at least making noises—about "communication." By the second or third day it had become plain, and each day thereafter it became plainer, that we had no common and clear notion of just what the word "communication" meant.

After several days of deepening bewilderment, I recalled an old saying: "If you can't diagram it, you don't understand it." The next day I made a modest attempt to bring order out of the chaos—for myself, at least—by drawing on the blackboard a simple diagram representing what seemed to me to be the main steps in the curious process of Mr. A talking to Mr. B. Then I tried to discuss communication by describing what goes on at each step—and what might go wrong. Since sketching that first diagram on the blackboard eight or nine years ago, I have refined and elaborated it, and I have tried from time to time, as I shall again here, to discuss the process of communication in terms of it (see Figure 10)[1].

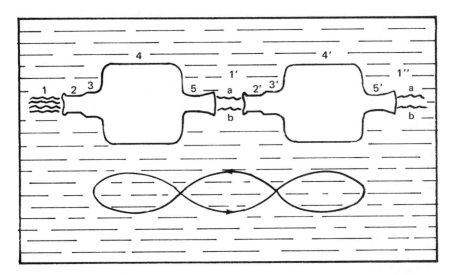

Key: Stage 1, event, or source of stimulation, external to the sensory end organs of the speaker; Stage 2, sensory stimulation; Stage 3, pre-verbal neurophysiological state; Stage 4, transformation of pre-verbal into symbolic forms; Stage 5, verbal formulations in "final draft" for overt expression; Stage 1', transformation of verbal formulations into (a) air waves and (b) light waves, which serve as sources of stimulation for the listener (who may be either the speaker himself or another person); Stages 2' through 1" correspond, in the listener, to Stages 2 through 1'. The arrowed loops represent the functional interrelationships of the stages in the process as a whole.

Figure 10. The process of communication.

Inside Mr. A

What appears to take place when Mr. A talks to Mr. B is that first of all, at Stage 1, some event occurs which is external to Mr. A's

1. The diagram, with a discussion of it, was first published in my book *People in Quandaries* (New York, Harper & Brothers, 1946), Chapter 18, "The Urgency of Paradise." I developed it further in *The Communication of Ideas*, edited by Lyman Bryson (New York, Harper & Brothers, 1948), Chapter 5, "Speech and Personality." It was also reproduced in *Mass Communications*, edited by Wilbur Schramm (Urbana, University of Illinois Press, 1949), pp. 261-274. The most recent statement is to be found in my article, "The Spoken Word and the Great Unsaid," *Quarterly Journal of Speech*, December, 1951, pp. 419-429. The form of the diagram reproduced here, together with a substantial portion of the text, are used by permission of the *Quarterly Journal of Speech*.

eyes, ears, taste buds, or other sensory organs. This event arouses the sensory stimulation that occurs at Stage 2. The dotted lines are intended to represent the fact that the process of communication takes place in a "field of reality," a context of energy manifestations external to the communication process and in major part external to both the speaker and the listener.

The importance of this fact is evident in relation to Stage 2 (or Stage 2'). The small size of the "opening" to Stage 2 in relation to the magnitude of the "channel" of Stage 1 represents the fact that our sensory receptors are capable of responding only to relatively small segments of the total ranges of energy radiations.

Sensory Limitations

The wave lengths to which the eye responds are but a small part of the total spectrum of such wave lengths. We register a sound only a narrow band of the full range of air vibrations. Noiseless dog whistles, "electronic eyes," and radar mechanisms—to say nothing of homing pigeons—underscore the primitive character of man's sensory equipment. Indeed, we seem little more than barely capable of tasting and smelling, and the narrowness of the temperature range we can tolerate is downright sobering to anyone dispassionately concerned with the efficiency of survival mechanisms.

The situation with regard to the normal individual may appear to be sufficiently dismal; let us not forget, however, how few of us are wholly normal in sensory acuity. We are familiar with the blind and partially sighted, the deaf and hard of hearing; we notice less the equally if not more numerous individuals who cannot taste the difference between peaches and strawberries, who cannot smell a distraught civet cat or feel a fly bite.

All in all, the degree to which we can know directly, through sensory avenues, the world outside (and this includes the world outside the sensory receptors but inside the body) is impressively restricted.

Any speaker is correspondingly limited in his physical ability to know what he is talking about. Relatively sophisticated listeners are likely to judge a speaker's dependability as a communicating agent by the degree to which he discloses his awareness of this limitation. The executive who demonstrates a realistic awareness of his own ignorance will in the long run acquire among his peers and subordinates a far better reputation for good judgment than the one who reveals his limitations by refusing to acknowledge them.

Pre-Verbal State

Once a sensory receptor has been stimulated, nerve currents travel quickly into the spinal cord and normally up through the base of the brain to the higher reaches of the cortex, out again along return tracts to the muscles and glands. The contractions and secretions they cause bring about new sensory stimulations which are "fed back" into the cord and brain and effect still further changes. The resulting reverberations of stimulation and response define what we may call a pre-verbal state of affairs within the organism. This state is represented at Stage 3 of the diagram.

Two statements about this pre-verbal state are fundamental: (1) we need to realize that our direct knowledge of this state is slight; (2) at the same time we are justified in assuming that it does occur.

No one has ever trudged through the spinal cord and brain with gun and camera, at least not while the owner of those organs was alive. Nevertheless, we are reasonably sure of certain facts about the nervous system. Observations have been reported by neurosurgeons, electroencephalographers, nerve physiologists, and anatomists. Thousands of laboratory animals have been sacrificed on the altars of scientific inquiry. We know that there are nerve currents, that they travel at known rates of speed, exhibit certain electrical properties, and are functionally related to specified kinds and loci of stimulation and to specified kinds and loci of response.

Thus, though our factual information is meager as yet, certainly it is sufficient to demonstrate that the nervous system is not merely a hypothetical construct. We can say with practical assurance that stimulation of our sensory end organs is normally followed by the transmission of nerve currents into the central nervous system, with a consequent reverberation effect, as described above, and the resulting state of affairs within the organism.

Two specific observations about this state of affairs are crucial: (1) it is truly pre-verbal, or silent; (2) it is this noiseless bodily state that gets transformed into words (or other symbols). Therefore—and these next few words should be read at a snail's pace and pondered long and fretfully—besides talking always to ourselves (although others may be listening more or less too), and whatever else we may also be striving to symbolize, *we inevitably talk about ourselves.*

The Individual's Filter

What the speaker—whether he be a junior executive or the general manager—directly symbolizes, *what he turns into words,* are physiological or electrochemical goings-on inside his own body. His organism, in this sense, operates constantly as a kind of filter through which facts (in the sense of things that arouse sensory impulses) must pass before they can become known to him and before they can be *communicated* by him to others in some symbolic form, such as standard English speech.

It follows, to present a single, seemingly trivial, but quite representative example, that when the junior executive says to the general manager, "It's certainly a fine day," he is exhibiting an elaborate variety of confusion; indeed, he appears literally not to know what he is talking about. In the meantime, he is talking about himself—or at least about the weather only as "filtered" by himself. He is symbolizing an inner state, first of all. In this he is the brother of all of us who speak.

I do not mean to imply that we talk solely about our inner states. We often talk about the world outside; but when we do, we filter it through our inner states. To the degree that our individual filters are standardized and alike, we will agree in the statements we make about the world outside—allowing, of course, for differences in time, place, observational set, equipment, sensory acuity, perceptive skill, and manner of making verbal reports.

The existence of the filter at Stage 3 of the process of communication is the basic fact. We may differ in our manner of appreciating and interpreting the significance of the filter, and in so doing make ourselves interesting to each other. But when the administrator—when anyone at all—simply never learns that the filter is there, or forgets or disregards it, he becomes, as a speaker, a threat to his own sanity and a potential or actual menace in a public sense.

Self-Projection

Because the filter is there in each of us, self-projection is a basic bodily process that operates not only in all our speaking but in other kinds of communicative behavior. To claim to speak literally, then, a person must always say "as I see it," or "as I interpret the facts," or "as I filter the world" if you please, or simply "to me."

An administrator whose language becomes too "is"-y tends to persuade himself that what he says the facts are is the same thing as the facts, and under the numbing spell of this illusion he may become quite incapable of evaluating his own judgments. If he is aware of projection, he must make clear, first of all to himself that he is not speaking about reality in some utterly impersonal or disembodied and "revealed" sense, but only about reality as the prism of his own nervous system projects it upon the gray screen of his own language—and he must realize that this projection, however trust-worthy or untrustworthy, must still be received, filtered, and repro-jected by each of his listeners.

Sufficient contemplation of this curious engineering scheme ren-ders one sensitive to the hazards involved in its use. As with any other possibility of miracle, one is well advised not to expect too much of it.

Patterns and Symbols

Stage 4, the first stage of symbolization, is represented in our diagram as a great enlargement in the tunnel through which "the world" passes from Stage 1 to Stage 1'. The words ultimately se-lected for utterance (at Stage 5) are a very small part of the lush abundance of possible verbalizations from which they are abstracted. Moreover, the bulge is intended to suggest that the state of affairs at Stage 3 becomes in a peculiarly human way much more significant by virtue of its symbolization at Stage 4.

At Stage 4 the individual's symbolic system and the pattern of evaluation reflected in its use come into play. The evaluative proc-esses represented at this stage have been the object of much and varied study and speculation:

Freud. Here, it would appear, was the location of Freud's chief preoccupations, as he attempted to explain them in terms of the so-called unconscious depths of the person, the struggle between the Id and the Super-Ego from which the Ego evolves, the ceaseless brewing of dreamstuff, wish and counterwish, the fabulous symbol-ism of the drama that we call the human personality.[2] Indeed, at this stage there is more than meets the eye—incredibly more so far as we may dimly but compellingly surmise.

Korzybski. Here, too, were the major preoccupations of the founder of general semantics, Alfred Korzybski: the symbol; the creation of symbols and of systems of symbols; the appalling distor-tions of experience wrought by the culturally imposed semantic crip-pling of the young through the witless and artful indoctrination of each new generation by the fateful words of the elders—the words which are the carriers of prejudice, unreasoning aspiration, delusional absolutes, and the resulting attitudes of self-abandonment. But also here we find the unencompassable promise of all that *human* can

---

2. Sigmund Freud, *A General Introduction to Psychoanalysis,* translated by Joan Riviere (New York, Liveright Publishing Corporation, 1935).

suggest, and this Korzybski called upon all men to see, to cherish, and to cultivate with fierce tenderness.[3]

Pavlov. The father of the modern science of behavior, Pavlov, also busied himself with ingenious explanations of occurrences at what we have called Stage 4.[4] In human beings, at least, the learning processes, as well as the drives and goals that power and direct them, appear to function at this stage of incipient symbolization.

It seems useful to conjecture that perhaps the general *patterns* of symbolic conditioning are formed at Stage 4 in contrast to the conditioning of specific symbolic responses (i.e., particular statements) produced at Stage 5. We may put it this way: at Stage 4 the syllogism, for example, as a *pattern* or *form* of possible symbolic response, is laid down, while at Stage 5 there occur the specific verbal responses patterned in this syllogistic mold.

Again, at Stage 4 we find the general form, "X affects Y"; at Stage 5 we see its specific progeny in such statements as "John loves Mary," "germs cause disease," "clothes make the man," and so on. In this relationship between general forms or patterns at Stage 4 and the corresponding specific utterances at Stage 5 we find the substantial sense of the proposition that our language does our thinking for us.

In fact, one of the grave disorders that we may usefully locate at Stage 4 consists in a lack of awareness of the influence on one's overt speech of the general symbolic forms operating at Stage 4. The more the individual knows about these forms, the more different forms he knows—or originates—and the more adroit he is in the selective and systematic use of them in patterning specific statements at Stage 5, the more control he exercises over "the language that does his thinking for him." The degree of such control exercised over the verbal responses at Stage 5 represents one of the important dimensions along which speakers range themselves, all the way from the naivete of the irresponsible robot—or compulsive schizophrenic patient—to the culture-shaping symbolic sophistication of the creative genius.

(Generally speaking, most of the disorders of abstracting described and emphasized by the general semanticists are to be most usefully thought of as operating chiefly at Stage 4 These disorders include

---

3. Alfred Korzybski, *Science and Sanity: An Introduction to Non-Aristotelian Systems and General Semantics* (Lancaster, Pennsylvania, Science Press, 3rd ed. 1948).

4. I.P. Pavlov, *Conditioned Reflexes: An Investigation of the Physiological Activity of the Cerebral Cortex,* translated and edited by G.V. Anrep (London, Oxford University Press, 1927).

those involving identification or lack of effective discrimination for purposes of sound evaluation.[5])

The Final Draft

The fact has been mentioned, and should be emphasized, that the "final draft" formulated at Stage 5, the words that come to be spoken, represents as a rule a highly condensed abstract of all that might have been spoken. What enters into this final draft is determined, in a positive sense, by the speaker's available knowledge of fact and relationship, his vocabulary, and his flexibility in using it, his purposes, and (to use the term in a broad sense) his habits. What enters into it is determined negatively by the repressions, inhibitions, taboos, semantic blockages, and ignorances, as well as the limiting symbolic forms, operating at Stage 4.

Mr. A to Mr. B

As the communication process moves from Stage 5 to Stage 1', it undergoes another of the incredible transformations which give it a unique and altogether remarkable character: the words, phrases, and sentences at Stage 5 are changed into air waves (and light waves) at Stage 1'. At close quarters, Mr. A may at times pat the listener's shoulder, tug at his coat lapels, or in some other way try to inject his meaning into Mr. B by hand, as it were, but this transmission of meaning through mechanical pressure may be disregarded for present purposes.

Inefficiency of Air Waves

In general, it seems a valid observation that we place an unwarranted trust in spoken words partly because we disregard, or do not appreciate, the inefficiency of air waves as carriers of information and evaluation. The reasons for this inefficiency lie both in the speaker and in the listener, of course, as well as in the air waves themselves. What the listener ends up with is necessarily a highly abstracted version of what the speaker intends to convey.

The speaker who sufficiently understands this—the wise administrator—expects to be misunderstood and, as a matter of fact, predicts quite well the particular misunderstandings with which he will need to contend. Consequently, he is able not only to forestall confusion

---

5. See Alfred Korzybski, *op. cit.,* and Wendell Johnson, *People in Quandaries,* particularly Chapters 5 through 10.

to some extent but also to give himself a chance to meet misunderstanding with the poise essential to an intelligent handling of the relationships arising out of it. A minimal requirement for the handling of such relationships is that either the speaker or the listener (or, better, both) recognize that the fault lies not so much in either one of them as in the process of communication itself—including particularly the fragile and tenuous air waves, whose cargo of meaning, whether too light to be retained or too heavy to be borne, is so often lost in transit.

Such an executive takes sufficiently into account the fact that words, whether spoken or written, are not foolproof. He will do all he can, within reason, to find out how his statements his letters and press releases, his instructions to subordinates, and so on are received and interpreted. He will not take for granted that anyone else thinks he means what he himself thinks he means. And when he discovers the misunderstandings and confusions he has learned to expect, he reacts with disarming and constructive forbearance to the resentments and disturbed human relationships that he recognizes as being due, not to men, but to the far from perfect communications by means of which men try to work and live together.

Inside Mr. B

The air waves (and light waves) that arrive at Stage 2'—that is, at the ears and eyes of the listener—serve to trigger the complex abstracting process which we have just examined, except that now it moves from 2' through 5' instead of 2 through 5. That is, the various stages sketched in the speaker are now repeated in the listener. To understand speech, or the communication process in general, is to be aware of the various functions and the disorders operating at each stage in the process—and to be conscious of the complex pattern of relationships among the various stages, as represented schematically by the double-arrowed loops in the diagram.

Effect of Feedback

Always important, these relationships become particularly significant when the speaker and listener are one and the same individual. And this, of course, is always the case, even when there are other listeners. The speaker is always affected by "feedback": he hears himself. What is significant is precisely the degree to which he is affected by feedback. It may, in fact, be ventured as a basic principle that the speaker's responsiveness to feedback—or, particularly important, the *administrator's* responsiveness to feedback—is crucial in determining the soundness of his spoken evaluations. It is crucial also, in determining his effectiveness in maintaining good working relationships with his associates.

Application to Problems

This view of the process of Mr. A speaking to Mr. B may be applied to any one of a great many specific problems and purposes. The diagram can be used especially well as a means of directing attention to the disorders of communication, such as those encountered daily in the world of trade and industry.

Preventing Troubles

In this connection, let me call attention to the fact that Professor Irving Lee of the School of Speech at Northwestern University has written a book on *How to Talk with People,*[6] which is of particular interest to anyone concerned with such disorders. Its subtitle describes it as "a program for preventing troubles that come when people talk together." The sorts of troubles with which Professor Lee is concerned in this book are among those of greatest interest and importance to personnel managers and business administrators and executives generally, and there would seem to be no better way to make my diagram take on a very practical kind of meaning than to sketch briefly what Professor Lee did and what he found in his studies of men in the world of business trying to communicate with one another.

Over a period of nearly ten years Professor Lee listened to the deliberations of more than 200 boards of directors, committees, organization staffs, and other similar groups. He made notes of the troubles he observed, and in some cases he was able to get the groups to try out his suggestions for reducing such troubles as they were having; and as they tried out his suggestions, he observed what happened and took more notes.

Among the many problems he describes in *How to Talk with People* there are three of special interest, which can be summarized thus:

(1) First of all, misunderstanding results when one man assumes that another uses words just as he does. Professor Quine of Harvard once referred to this as "the uncritical assumption of mutual under-

---

6. New York, Harper & Brothers, 1952.

standing." It is, beyond question, one of our most serious obstacles to effective thinking and communication. Professor Lee suggests a remedy, deceptively simple but profoundly revolutionary: better habits of listening. We must learn, he says, not only how to define our own terms but also how to ask others what they are talking about. He is advising us to pay as much attention to the righthand side of our diagram as to the lefthand side of it.

(2) Another problem is represented by the person who takes it for granted that anyone who does not feel the way he does about something is a fool. "What is important here," says Lee, "is not that men disagree, but that they become disagreeable about it." The fact is, of course, that the very disagreeable disagreer is more or less sick, from a psychological and semantic point of view. Such a person is indulging in "unconscious projection." As we observed in considering the amazing transformation of the physiological goings-on at Stage 3 into words or other symbols at Stage 4, the only way we can talk about the world outside is to filter it through our private inner states. The disagreeable disagreer is one who has never learned that he possesses such a filter, or has forgotten it, or is so desperate, demoralized, drunk, or distracted as not to care about it.

A trained consciousness of the projection process would seem to be essential in any very effective approach to this problem. The kind of training called for may be indicated by the suggestion to any administrator who is inclined to try it out that he qualify any important statements he makes, with which others may disagree, by such phrases as "to my way of thinking," "to one with my particular background," "as I see it," and the like.

(3) One more source of trouble is found in the executive who thinks a meeting should be "as workmanlike as a belt line." He has such a business-only attitude that he simply leaves out of account the fact that "people like to get things off their chests almost as much as they like to solve problems." Professor Lee's sensible recommendation is this: "If people in a group want to interrupt serious discussion with some diversion or personal expression—let them. Then bring them back to the agenda. Committees work best when the talk swings between the personal and the purposeful."

Constructive Factors

Professor Lee saw something, however, in addition to the "troubles that come when people talk together." He has this heartening and important observation to report:

"In sixteen groups we saw illustrations of men and women talking together, spontaneously, cooperatively, constructively. There was team-play and team-work. We tried to isolate some of the factors we found there: (1) The leader did not try to tell the others what to do or how to think; he was thinking along with them. (2) No one presumed to know it all; one might be eager and vigorous in his manner of talking, but he was amenable and attentive when others spoke. (3) The people thought of the accomplishments of the group rather than of their individual exploits."

This can happen—and where it does not happen, something is amiss. The diagram presented in *Exhibit 1,* along with the description of the process of communication fashioned in terms of it, is designed to help us figure out what might be at fault when such harmony is not to be found. And it is intended to provide essential leads to better and more fruitful communication in business and industry, and under all other circumstances as well.

Conclusion

Mr. A talking to Mr. B is a deceptively simple affair, and we take it for granted to a fantastic and tragic degree. It would surely be true that our lives would be longer and richer if only we were to spend a greater share of them in the tranquil hush of thoughtful listening. We are a noisy lot; and of what gets said among us, far more goes unheard and unheeded than seems possible. We have yet to learn on a grand scale how to use the wonders of speaking and listening in our own best interests and for the good of all our fellows. It is the finest art still to be mastered by men.

PSYCHOLOGICAL BARRIERS TO COMMUNICATION
Daniel Katz

Accurate and adequate communication between groups and peoples will not in itself bring about the millennium, but it is a necessary condition for almost all forms of social progress. Physical barriers to communication are rapidly disappearing, but the psychological obstacles remain. These psychological difficulties are in part a function of the very nature of language; in part they are due to the emotional character and mental limitations of human beings.

The Nature of Language

Much of our communication in the great society must of necessity be by formal language rather than by visual presentation or by the explicit denotation or pointing possible in small face-to-face groups. Formal language is symbolic in that its verbal or mathematical terms stand for aspects of reality beyond themselves. Though onomatopoetic words are an exception, they constitute but a small fraction of any modern language. Because of its symbolic nature, language is a poor substitute for the realities which it attempts to represent. The real world is more complex, more colorful, more fluid, more multidimensional than the pale words or oversimplified signs used to convey meaning.

Nor is there any easy solution of the problem. A language too close to perceptual reality would be useless for generalization and would, moreover, ignore complex forms of experience. Language enables us to transcend the specificity of the single event and makes possible the analysis and comparison of experiences. But the abstraction and generalization through the use of symbols which has given man his control over the natural world also makes possible the greatest distortions of reality. Many language signs may in fact be completely lacking in objective reference. The semantic movement is the current effort to cope with the woeful inadequacies inherent in the symbolic nature of language. Thus far it has contributed more to exposing the inaccuracies and weaknesses in language than to developing a science of meaning.

The imperfection of language is not due solely to the weakness of its representational quality. Viewed realistically, language as a living process has other functions than accurate communication. It

From *The Annals of the Academy of Political and Social Science,* Vol. 250, (March, 1947), pp. 17-25. Reprinted by permission.

did not arise in the history of the race, any more than in the development of the child, solely in the interest of precise interchange of information. Language as it exists is not the product of scientists trying to perfect an exact set of symbols; it is the product of the arena of everyday life, in which people are concerned with manipulating and controlling their fellows and with expressing their emotional and psychological wants. The prototype of language as a functioning process can be seen in the child's acquisition of words and phrases to extend his control of his environment beyond his limited physical reach. Similarly, adults use language to obtain sympathy, bulldoze their fellows, placate or embarrass their enemies, warm and comfort their friends, deceive themselves, or express their own conflicts. Language in operation is often intended to conceal and obscure meaning. Hence as an instrument for accurate communication it suffers from emotional loadings, polar words, and fictitious concepts.

Even the will to interchange factual information, therefore, is embarrassed by the heritage of a language developed for other purposes. This is one of the reasons for the slow growth of social science compared with natural science. Once the physical and biological sciences had got under way, their data were so far removed from everyday observation that they were free to develop scientific terminology and concepts. But this initial step is much more difficult in the social realm because we already have a well-developed popular language applying to social events and relationships. . . .

These general considerations concerning the psychological nature of language are the background against which more specific difficulties in communication can be understood. The following specific obstacles merit special attention: (1) the failure to refer language to experience and reality, (2) the inability to transcend personal experience in intergroup communication, (3) stereotypes: the assimilation of material to familiar frames of reference, and (4) the confusion of percept and concept: reification and personification.

Relation of Symbol to Fact

Psychological research abounds with illustrations of the principle that analytic thinking occurs not as the prevalent mode of human response but as a limited reaction under conditions of block or need. Men think critically and precisely only under specific conditions of motivation, and then only in reference to the particular pressing problem. Ordinarily they respond according to the law of least effort. In the field of language behavior, this appears at the most fundamental level in the tendency to confuse words with the things or processes they name. The word and its referent are fused as an unanalyzed whole in the mind of the individual. Among primitives, for example, it is not permitted to mention the name of a person recently deceased. Since there is deep fear of the spirit of the departed, it is dangerous to bring up his name, fundamentally because the name and the person named are psychologically confused. Even in our own society, many obscene and sacred words are taboo because the name is regarded as the equivalent of the object or process for which it stands.

This inability to grasp the difference between the symbol and its referent is one reason for the failure to check back constantly from language to experience and reality. Much has been said about the virtues of scientific method but one unappreciated reason for the tremendous progress in natural science has been the constant referral of scientific language to the realities which it supposedly represents. Without such an interplay between symbol and experience, distortion in the symbol cannot be corrected.

Another difficulty is that the average man has little chance, even when motivated, to check language against the facts in the real world. In our huge complex society the individual citizen often lacks the opportunity to test the language of the politicians, statesmen and other leaders by reference to the realities involved. Walter Lippmann has presented this problem brilliantly in the *Phantom Public,* in which he shows how little possibility exists for the man on the street to participate intelligently in the political process. But it is also true at the leadership level that the individual official or leader accepts reports of the working of his policies which are gross oversimplifications and even misrepresentations of the facts. The leader lives in a world of symbols, as do his followers, and he comes to rely upon what appears in newsprint for the facts instead of upon direct contact with reality. . . .

Polls and surveys have opened up new possibilities for leaders to refer words to the world of fact. During the war many governmental agencies discovered that they could learn more about the functioning of their policies through surveys using scientific samples and first-hand accounts than through press clippings or through the occasional visit of a high official to the field.

Experiential Limitation

The important psychological fact that men's modes of thinking—their beliefs, their attitudes—develop out of their ways of life is not commonly and fully appreciated. Their mental worlds derive from everyday experiences in their occupational callings, and they are not equipped to understand a language which represents a different way of life.

Because language is symbolic in nature, it can only evoke meaning in the recipient if the recipient has experiences corresponding to the symbol. It will not solve the problem of the basic difficulties in communication between the peoples of the world to have them all speak the same tongue if their experiential backgrounds differ. The individual lives in a private world of his own perception, emotion, and thought. To the extent that his perceptions, feelings, and thoughts arise from similar contacts with similar aspects of reality as experienced by others, the private world can be shared and lose something of its private character. But language itself, even if exact and precise, is a very limited device for producing common understanding when it has no basis in common experience. The linguists who argue for a world language neglect the fact that basic misunderstandings occur not at the linguistic but at the psychological level.

A dramatic example of the inability of verbal symbols to bridge the gap between different experiential worlds is the current lack of understanding between returned servicemen and civilians. Since foxhole existence has no real counterpart in unbombed America, American civilians are at a great disadvantage in understanding or communicating with returned combat servicemen.[1] In the same way the peoples of the world living under different conditions and undergoing different types of experience live in worlds of their own between which there is little communication. Even in our own society, different groups are unable to communicate. The farmer, whose way of life differs from that of the coal miner, the steel worker, or the banker, is as much at a loss to understand their point of view as they are to understand him or one another.

Labor-management controversies illustrate the gap between groups speaking different psychological languages as a result of following different ways of life. Granted that industrial disputes have as their bedrock real and immediate differences in economic interest, it is still true that these differences are augmented by the inability of each party to understand the opposing point of view. The employer, owner, or superintendent, through his executive function of making daily decisions and issuing orders and instructions, acquires a psychology of management. He can understand, though he may dislike,

---

1. The chasm between civilian and serviceman has been well described by the sociologist W. Waller in *The Veteran Comes Back* and by the novelist Z. Popkin in *Journey Home.*

a union demand for more wages. But when the union requests, or even suggests, changes in the conditions of work or changes in personnel policy, he grows emotional and objects to being told by subordinates and outsiders how to run his own plant. For their part, the workers have little understanding of the competitive position of the employer. Since the employer enjoys a way of life luxurious in comparison with their own, they find his plea of inability to pay a higher wage laughable.

The role of imagination in bridging the gap is important. This, however, is largely the function of the artist, who has the sensitivity and the willingness to seek experience beyond his own original environment. By personalizing the experiences of people in plays, novels, and pictures, the artist often does more to develop mutual understanding between groups with divergent experiences than does the social scientist, the reformer, the politician, or the educator.

More and more, however, are psychologists and practitioners coming to realize the importance of common experience as the real basis of communication. Group workers and experimental educators are emphasizing the importance of role playing in true education. By assigning a person a new experiential role to play, it is possible to increase his understanding in a fashion which no amount of preaching or book learning could do. The modern trend in education, which emphasizes learning by doing, laboratory projects, and a mixture of work experience with book learning, is a recognition of the inadequacy of language divorced from experience to achieve much success in communication.

Surmounting the Difficulty

The difficulty of communication between people of different experiential backgrounds is augmented by the distinctive jargon which seems to develop in every calling and in every walk of life. Though groups may differ in their experiences, there is generally more of a common core of psychological reality between them than their language indicates. A neglected aspect of communication is the identification of these areas of common understanding and the translation of the problems of one group into the functional language of another. It is sometimes assumed that limitations of intelligence prevent the farmer or the worker from understanding the complexities of national and international affairs. Anyone, however, who has taken the trouble to discuss with the shipyard worker or the coal miner the economic and political factors operative in the worker's immediate environment will realize the fallacy of this assumption.

Within his limited frame of reference, the coal miner, the steel worker, or the dirt farmer will talk sense. But he is unfamiliar with the language used by the professional economist or the expert on international affairs. He is capable of reacting intelligently to matters in this sphere if they are presented to him in terms of their specifics in his own experience. This translation is rarely made, because the expert or the national leader is as uninformed of the day-to-day world of the worker as the worker is of the field of the expert. . . .

Stereotypes

One aspect of the limitation imposed by one's own narrow experiences is the tendency to assimilate fictitiously various language symbols to one's own frame of reference. The mere fact we lack the experience or the imagination to understand another point of view does not mean that we realize our inadequacy and remain open-minded about it. Whether or not nature abhors a vacuum, the human mind abhors the sense of helplessness that would result if it were forced to admit its inability to understand and deal with people and situations beyond its comprehension. What people do is to fill the gap with their own preconceptions and to spread their own limited attitudes and ideas to cover all the world beyond their own knowledge.

In an older day it was popular to refer to this phenomenon through Herbart's concept of the *apperceptive mass;* later Levy-Bruhl, in his anthropological interpretations, spoke of *collective* representations; twenty years ago psychologists embraced Walter Lippmann's notion of *stereotypes;* today we speak of assimilating material to our own frame of reference. Thus the farmer who knows little about Jews save from his limited contact with a single Jewish merchant in a nearby trading center will have an opinion of all Jews, and in fact of all foreigners, based on this extremely narrow frame of reference. In the same way he will feel great resentment at the high wages paid to the city worker, without any realization of the city worker's problems. The average citizen may assimilate all discussion of the Negro-white problem to the fractional experience he has had with Negroes forced to live in slum areas.

Nor need there be even a fragmentary basis in personal experience for the stereotype. The superstitions of the culture furnish the individual ready-made categories for his prejudgments in the absence of any experience. Research studies indicate that people in all parts of the United States feel that the least desirable ethnic and racial groups

are the Japanese, the Negroes, and the Turks. When asked to characterize the Turk, they have no difficulty in speaking of him as blood-
thirsty, cruel, and dirty; yet the great majority who make this judgment not only have never seen a Turk but do not know anyone who
has. An Englishman, H. Nicolson, has written entertaining of the
stereotyped conception of his people held by the German, the
Frenchman, and the American. He writes:

> Now when the average German thinks of the average Englishman
> he . . . visualizes a tall, spare man, immaculately dressed in top hat and
> frock coat, wearing spats and an eyeglass, and gripping a short but aggres-
> sive pipe in an enormous jaw. . . . To him, the average Englishman is a
> clever and unscrupulous hypocrite; a man, who, with superhuman ingenu-
> ity and foresight, is able in some miraculous manner to be always on the
> winning side; a person whose incompetence in business and salesmanship is
> balanced by an uncanny and unfair mastery of diplomatic wiles; . . .
>
> The French portrait of the Englishman . . . is the picture of an inelegant,
> stupid, arrogant, and inarticulate person with an extremely red face. The
> French seem to mind our national complexion more than other nations.
> They attribute it to the overconsumption of ill-cooked meat. They are apt,
> for this reason, to regard us as barbarian and gross. Only at one point does
> the French picture coincide with the German picture. The French share
> with the Germans a conviction of our hypocrisy. . . .
>
> To the average American, the average Englishman seems affected, pa-
> tronizing, humorless, impolite and funny. To him also the Englishman
> wears spats and carries an eyeglass; to him also he is slim and neatly
> dressed; yet the American, unlike the German, is not impressed by these
> elegancies; he considers them ridiculous; . . . [2]

Though the oversimplified and distorted notions of racial and national groups are usually cited as examples of stereotypes, the process of assimilating material to narrow preformed frames of reference
is characteristic of most of our thinking: of our judgment of social
classes, occupational callings, artistic and moral values, and the characters and personalities of our acquaintances.

Motivation of the Stereotype

Stereotyping applies primarily to the cognitive weakness or limitation in our intellectual processes. But this stereotyped prejudgment
has an emotional dimension as well. Many of our stereotyped labels
or frames carry heavy emotional loading and so are the more resistant to fact and logic. Emotion attaches to them in many ways.
Because they give the individual a crude and oversimplified chart in
an otherwise confused universe, they afford him security. They tie in

---

2. From *Time*, July 15, 1935, p. 26.

with his whole way of thinking and feeling and acting. To abandon
them would be mental suicide. . . .

Emotion clings to words through association with emotional
events which are never dissociated from the label itself. The feeling
of dependence and affection that the child has for his mother satu-
rates the words "mother" and "home" and related phrases. These
conditioned words can then be used to call up the old emotions in
logically irrelevant situations. In the same way the child acquires
emotional content for the stereotypes of his group. If the hierarchy
of social status is built on stereotypes about Negroes, foreigners, and
the lower classes, then these stereotypes are not neutral but are
invested with the emotional color associated with the superiority of
the upper groups.

This last example suggests a further motivational basis of the stereotype. People cling to their prejudiced beliefs in labels because of the
specific psychic income to be derived from the stereotype. If people
the world over are to be judged solely on their merits as human
personalities, there is little ego-enhancement in belonging to an in-
group which bestows superiority upon its members merely through
the act of belonging. The poor whites in the South are not going to
abandon their notion of the Negro when this stereotyped belief itself
makes them superior to every member of the despised group. The
more frustrated the individual, the more emotionally inadequate and
insecure, the easier it is to channelize his dissatisfaction and aggression against a stereotyped target.

Reification and Personification

The oversimplification of the stereotype is equaled by the extraordinary opportunities which language provides for reification and personification. We easily forget the distinction between words which
refer to percepts, or aspects of perceived experience, and terms
which designate concepts and abstractions. As a result, we take a
concept like the state which stands for many complexities of human
interrelationships, and make that concept into a thing or person
possessed of all the attributes of the object or person. Thus the state,
like the individual, does things. It takes the life of a criminal, it glows
with pride at the patriotic sacrifices of its citizens; it can grow old,
become feeble, or wither away and die. When pressed, we readily
admit that we do not mean to be taken literally, but are speaking
metaphorically and analogically. Yet our thinking is so shot through
with personification and analogy that the tendency is a serious im-

pediment to our understanding and to our intelligent handling of important problems.

The problem of German war guilt is an interesting example. One school of thought made all German crimes the action of the German state; hence it was the state that should be punished, not individual Germans. The standard defense of high ranking German generals, admirals, and officials was that they were mere servants of the state, who faithfully followed its orders. An opposed school of thought, likewise accepting the fallacy of a personified German nation, identified every German as a miniature of the German nation and so considered all Germans equally guilty. Our first treatment of the Germans was based on this logic. American troops, under the fraternization ban, were forbidden so much as to speak to any German man, woman, or child. This was mild treatment for leading Nazis, but relatively harsh treatment for German children.

In the same way, the original American information policy in Germany was to hammer away at German guilt and to make the Germany people feel guilty about concentration camp atrocities. But this blanket conception of German guilt took no account of the complex realities involved. It not only failed to take into account quantitative differences in guilt between high Nazis and lesser Nazis; *qualitative* differences between active leadership in atrocities and passive acceptance of or irresponsibility about them were also ignored. The type of guilt of the Nazi leaders who set up and ran the concentration camps was of one order. The social cowardice, political passivity, and irresponsibility of the German people, who were afraid to voice objection, or who were indifferent, is guilt of another order.

Distorted Pictures

In place, then, of communication through accurate descriptions and conceptions, we reinforce and magnify for ourselves a distorted picture of the universe by our tendency to reify and personify. Perhaps the most effective account of this process is in the following by Stuart Chase:

> Let us glance at some of the queer creatures created by personifying abstractions in America. Here in the center is a vast figure called the Nation—majestic and wrapped in the Flag. When it sternly raises its arm we are ready to die for it. Close behind rears a sinister shape, the Government. Following it is one even more sinister, Bureaucracy. Both are festooned with the writhing serpents of Red Tape. High in the heavens is the Constitution, a kind of chalice like the Holy Grail, suffused with ethereal light. It must never be joggled. Below floats the Supreme Court, a black robed priesthood tending the eternal fires. The Supreme Court must be addressed

with respect or it will neglect the fire and the Constitution will go out. This is synonymous with the end of the world. Somewhere above the Rocky Mountains are lodged the vast stone tablets of the Law. We are governed not by men but by these tablets. Near them, in satin breeches and silver buckles, pose the stern figures of our Forefathers, contemplating glumly the Nation they brought to birth. The onion-shaped demon cowering behind the Constitution is Private Property. Higher than Court, Flag, or the Law, close to the sun itself and almost as bright, is Progress, the ultimate God of America.

Here are the Masses, thick black and squirming. This demon must be firmly sat upon; if it gets up terrible things will happen, the Constitution may be joggled. . . .

Capital, her skirt above her knees, is preparing to leave the country at the drop of a hairpin, but never departs. Skulking from city to city goes Crime, a red loathsome beast, upon which the Law is forever trying to drop a monolith, but its Aim is poor. Crime continues rhythmically to rear its ugly head. Here is the dual shape of Labor—for some a vast, dirty, clutching hand, for others a Galahad in armor. Pacing to and fro with remorseless tread are the Trusts and Utilities, bloated unclean monsters with enormous biceps. Here is Wall Street a crouching dragon ready to spring upon assets not already nailed down in any other section of the country. The Consumer, a pathetic figure in a gray shawl, goes wearily to market. Capital and Labor each give her a kick as she passes, while Commercial Advertising, a playful sprite, squirts perfume in her eye.[3]

The personified caricatures of popular thinking appeal not only because of their simplicity but also because they give a richness of imagery and of emotional tone lacking in a more exact, scientific description. Nor is the communication of emotional feeling to be proscribed. The problem is how to communicate emotional values without sacrificing adequacy and validity of description.

Research Needed

In brief, the psychological barriers to communication are of such strength and have such a deep foundation in human nature that the whole problem of social communication between individuals and groups needs to be re-examined in a new light. No simple formula will solve the problems arising from the many complex causes and widely ramifying aspects of the limitations of the symbolic mechanism and other psychological processes. The older attempt at any easy solution was the study of the dictionary. One instance of this type of thinking was the college faculty committee which tried to discover the dividing line between legislative matters of policy and executive matters of administration by looking up the words involved in the

---

3. *Tyranny of Words,* p. 23.

dictionary. The newer approach of the semanticists, though more sophisticated and more promising, sometimes ignores the psychological difficulties and sometimes begs the question in an uncritical operationalism.

Perhaps the whole problem of communication is inseparable from the larger context of the over-all social problems of our time. There might well be possibilities of significant advance, however, if we were to employ the research methods of science in attacking the many specific obstacles to communication. Procedures are already being worked out on the basis of research evaluation for the alleviation of minority group prejudice. Studies now in contemplation would provide functional dictionaries to supplement the standard etymological works. The process of interpersonal communication has been the subject of some research in studies of rumor.

Though the importance to accurate communication of a maximum of objective reference in language symbols has experimental support, the fact remains that such complex and involved communication is much more feasible in science than in popular discussion. It is probable that precise scientific language, with its exact reference to the objective world and objective operation, will not solve the problem of communication in practical life, where short cuts in communication are essential. But it may be possible to determine the type of short-cut symbol which conveys meaning with minimum distortion. The problem invites research.

EMPATHIC LISTENING

Charles M. Kelly

In a research project exploring listening behavior, industrial supervisors gave the following reasons for communication problems in large management-level meetings and conferences: "things discussed here are often side issues that don't interest everyone," "I think about my job upstairs," "they get off the subject," and "a lot of people like to hear themselves talk." A content analysis was made of these and other responses dealing with the perceived deficiencies of meetings and discussions. Results indicated that most of the dissatisfaction centered around the general feeling that many different issues were discussed at a typical meeting, and that usually some of these issues were not directly related to all of the participants.[1]

Complaints such as the above are not unusual, and frequently are justified. Every text of discussion and conference methodology deals with the problems of keeping the discussion on relevant and significant issues, and of motivating the participants. However, most of the emphasis in the past has dealt with the obligations of the discussants (both leaders and participants) as *speakers,* rather than as *listeners.* This unbalanced emphasis, especially as it actually affects persons in real discussions, could be an important *cause* of the problems that speaking is supposed to cure: e.g., the reason a discussion leader may have difficulty clarifying the comments of another, may be that he did not listen carefully to begin with; when one is overly concerned about what *he* is *going* to say, he really can't devote his full attention to what *is* being said by others. If a person in a group preoccupies himself by privately bemoaning the irrelevancies that inevitably occur in discussion, he may be less able to get the group back on the track; he misses opportunities for constructive action because he lacks an *accurate* analysis of the flow of ideas, even the irrelevant ones.

Of course, listening is a multi-faceted activity and it can be considered from different viewpoints, but at least two ways of categorizing listening seem especially fruitful for theoretical analysis: *deliberative listening* and *empathic listening.* Most recent writers have treated

---

Reprinted with permission of author. This original essay appears here in print for the first time.

1. Charles M. Kelly, "Actual Listening Behavior of Industrial Supervisors as Related to Listening Ability, General Mental Ability, Selected Personality Factors and Supervisory Effectiveness," Unpublished Ph.D. Dissertation, Purdue University, 1962,129.

listening as a unitary skill, i.e., as a rather definite and "deliberative" ability to hear information, to analyze it, to recall it at a later time, and to draw conclusions from it. Commercially-published listening tests and most listening training programs are based on this, the deliberative listening, viewpoint. On the other hand, empathic listening occurs when the person participates in the spirit or feeling of his environment as a communication *receiver*. This does not suggest that the listener is uncritical or always in agreement with what is communicated, but rather, that his primary interest is to become fully and accurately aware of what is going on. (See Figure 11.)

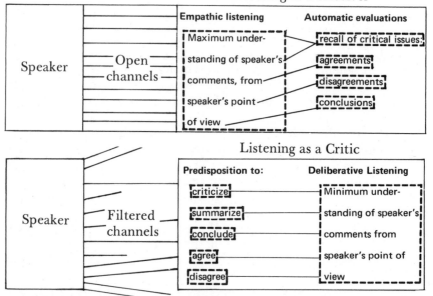

Figure 11. The differences between empathic listening and deliberative listening are primarily motivational. Both listeners seek the same objective: accurate understanding of the communication from another. The model suggests that the motivation to receive information is superior to the motivation to use critical skills. The empathic listener lets his understanding of the speaker determine his modes of evaluation, which are automatic; the deliberative listener's understanding of the speaker is filtered through his predetermined modes of selective listening, and actually spends less time as a communication receiver. The empathic listener is more apt to be a consistant listener, and is less prone to his own or other distractions. This theory is correct, only if the assumption is true that persons can and do think critically without deliberate effort—*while listening.* (Of course, if persons do not make the effort to listen *per se,* little or no understanding will occur.)

It should be observed that the terms "deliberative listening" and "empathic listening" are not mutually exclusive or exhaustive. Their main purpose is to differentiate between two basic ways of viewing the same listening activity. The desired result of both deliberative and empathic listening is identical: accurate understanding of oral communication. However, this understanding is achieved by different routes. The deliberative listener *first* has the desire to critically analyze what a speaker has said, and secondarily tries to understand the speaker (this can be the result of personal inclination or of training which emphasizes procedure at the expense of listening). The empathic listener has the desire to understand the speaker first, and, as a result, tries to take the appropriate action.

The former kind of listening is characteristic of the discussant who is predisposed to be disagreeable, or to summarize, or to clarify—even when there is little that is significant to disagree with, when there is no need to summarize, or when further clarification is a waste of the group's time. The latter kind of listening is characteristic of the person who is able to adapt quickly to the real needs of a situation because he has a presence of mind and a greater confidence in the accuracy of his awareness—he does not handicap himself by deciding in advance that he does not have to listen to a particular person who is poorly dressed, or that he must be sure to expose all faulty reasoning if he is to demonstrate his competence.

This is not to say that various skills in critical thinking are less important than emphatic listening. Without critical analysis, listening in a problem-solving discussion would be useless. The point is, however, that a person uses quite naturally whatever critical skills he has already acquired, as long as he is interested and actively listening; to the extent that he is not listening, critical skills will be of little value. Actually, a case can be made that "deliberative listening" is a self-contradiction and a misnomer—and that "empathic listening" is a redundancy. To the extent that one is deliberating (mentally criticizing, summarizing, concluding, preparing reports, etc.) he is *not listening*, but formulating his own ideas. And listening, by its very nature, *has* to be empathic; a person understands what he has heard, only to the extent that he can share in the meaning, spirit, or feeling of what the communicator has said.

There is some evidence that this line of reasoning is correct. In one experiment,[2] a researcher presented a 30-minute talk dealing with "The Supervisor and Communication" to 28 supervisors at a regularly scheduled business meeting. The supervisors were in no way led to

---

2. This study is reported in detail: Charles M. Kelly, "Mental Ability and Personality Factors in Listening," *Quarterly Journal of Speech*, XLIX, (April, 1963), 152-156.

believe that they were in an experiment or that their listening performance would be tested. Following the presentation, they were given a 30-item multiple-choice "surprise" listening test. During the following two weeks, the supervisors were given the Brown-Carlsen Listening Comprehension Test, the STEP Listening Test, the Otis Quick-Scoring Mental Ability Test, and the Cattell 16 Personality Factor Questionnaire. (Because of the nature of the Brown-Carlsen and Step listening tests, subjects have to know in advance that their listening ability is being tested.)

The results (Table 4) indicated that the supervisors' "listening ability" (as measured by the Brown-Carlsen and the STEP) was indistinguishable from general mental ability (as measured by the Otis) when they knew in advance that their listening was being tested. In fact, the listening tests correlated *lower* with each other, than each did with the test of mental ability. In other words, when the supervisors had the extra motivation of a test, or were constantly listening, they made full use of their general mental ability, and the listening tests became orally-presented tests of general mental ability, rather than of "listening." On the other hand, when the supervisors did not know their listening was being tested, their listening performance was significantly less related to general mental ability.

Table 4

Correlations (Pearson r) Among the "Surprise" Listening Test, the Brown-Carlsen Listening Test, the Step Listening Test, and the Otis Test of General Mental Ability[a]

	Brown-Carlsen	STEP	Otis
Surprise Listening test	.79	.78	.70[bc]
Brown-Carlsen		.82	.85[b]
STEP			.85[c]

[a] All correlations are significant at the .01 level.

[b] The difference between the two correlations so designated is significant at the .05 level, t = 2.205.

[c] The difference between the two correlations so designated is significant at the .05 level, t = 2.162.

Further insight can be gained by analyzing the results in terms of personality variables (Table 5). Again, the Brown-Carlsen and STEP listening tests are indistinguishable from the Otis, when compared on the basis of personality variables; the same personality factors appear about equally important (as expressed in chi square values) in the test of general mental ability as in the tests of listening ability. However, the "surprise" listening test showed significantly more substantial personality differences between good and poor listeners than did the other three tests.

The most significant differences between good and poor listeners, when they had no unusual motivation to listen because of test awareness, were that good listeners were more adventurous (receptive to new ideas), (emotionally) stable, mature, and sophisticated. Although the other six differences in Table 5 (under "surprise listening test") were not statistically significant, it is interesting to note that all were in the same direction, with the good listeners being more emotionally mature: outgoing, bright, dominant, enthusiastic, trustful and controlled (will control). The opposite ends of the personality scales, describing the poor listeners in the surprise listening test, were: aloof, dull, emotional, submissive, glum, timid, suspecting, simple, lax, and tense.

This and other studies[3] strongly indicate that when persons know that their listening comprehension is being tested, differences between individuals are primarily matters of general mental ability; when they do not know their listening performance is being tested, differences are due to personality differences (including motivation to listen), as well as general mental ability. Of these two kinds of research situations, the latter is more representative of realistic listening events.

It is likely that most communication problems arise either because of participant inattention (poor motivation), or because of a lack of general mental ability—not because of anything that can be called "listening ability." Do teachers in a faculty meeting miss the details of registration because of a lack of listening ability, or because of a lack of motivation? Does an engineer fail to understand an explanation of a new process because he lacks listening ability, or because he simply has not yet been able to visualize unfamiliar relationships? In the rare cases when a discussion is vitally important to everyone and motivation is high (as in a listening test), there is little chance of an

---

3. For a detailed analysis of this issue, see: Charles M. Kelly, "Listening: Complex of Activities—and a Unitary Skill?" *Speech Monographs,* XXXIV, (November, 1967), 455-466.

important point (or its significance) being missed, unless the listener simply lacked the mental ability to understand or appreciate it to begin with. But in most of the everyday discussions that deal with the nagging problems of industrial production, proposed new school construction, traffic safety, curriculum changes, etc., motivation to participate (and, hence, listen) is moderate at best and is not evenly distributed among the discussants—and with some persons, inattention seems to be habitual.

Table 5
Statistical Significance of Differences (Chi Square with Yates'
Correction) Between "High" and "Low" Criterion Groups (as Determined by
Scores on Each of Four Tests) on the Cattell 16 PF Scales

Cattell Scale Low Score vs. High Scores	Surprise Listening Test [bcd]	Brown- Carlsen[b]	STEP [c]	Otis[d]
Aloof vs. Outgoing	.14	.00**	.14	.00
Dull vs. Bright (intelligence factor)	.57	5.16	2.29	2.29
Emotional vs. Mature	3.57***	1.28	3.57***	1.28
Submissive vs. Dominant	.14	.00	.00	.15
Glum vs. Enthusiatic	.14	.00	.00	.00
Casual vs. Conscientious	.00	.00	.00	.00
Timid vs. Adventurous	9.19*	.57	2.29	.57
Tough vs. Sensitive	.00	.00	.00	.57 [a]
Trustful vs. Suspecting	.57 [a]	.00	.00	.00
Conventional vs. Eccentric	.00	.00	.00	.00
Simple vs. Sophisticated	3.65***	1.31	1.31	1.31
Confident vs. Insecure	.00	.57[a]	.00	.00
Conservative vs. Experimenting	.00	.59[a]	.00	.00
Dependent vs. Self-sufficient	.00	.00	.00	.00
Lax vs. Controlled	2.29	.00	.00	.00
Stable vs. Tense	7.00*[a]	.14[a]	1.31[a]	2.29[a]

*X^2 of 6.64 = 1% level.
**X^2 of 3.84 = 5% level.
***X^2 of 2.71 = 10% level.
[a] High scorers on the test scored low on the Cattell personality scale.

Using the sign test for statisitical significance, the following differences were observed between tests, on the basis of personality scales (intelligence scale, "Dull vs. Bright," was not included):

[b] difference between tests so designated was significant at p = .03
[c] p = .008
[d] p = .055

In terms of *listening* theory, it is far more important to stress empathic, rather than deliberative, listening in discussion. This observation in no way depreciates the need for education and practical experience in critical analysis, debate, general semantics—or in any of the various mental skills brought into play *while* listening. But it is a mistake to consider these skills *as* listening, since this viewpoint suggests that the listener's analysis is part of the receiving process.

The degree to which one is able to listen, and to perform other mental acts at the same time is an open question; research into the exact nature of listening, as it relates to other general mental abilities, is unclear at best. However, because of the obvious difficulties that occur in discussion when listener motivation is poor or nonexistent, and in view of the probability that problems in discussion are due to factors other than listening *ability* when participant motivation is high, the following suggestions seem warranted:

Remember the characteristics of the poor listener. It is easy to sit back in your chair and complain to yourself that the discussion is boring or unimportant. However, the description of the kind of person who habitually does this is not very flattering, and should serve as an incentive to better listening; research suggests that the poor listener is less intelligent, and less emotionally mature than the good listener. Obviously, there are times when a person may be just as well off *not* listening, but the poor listener tends to make this a crutch for the easy way out of difficult listening events.

Make a firm initial commitment to listen. Listening is hard work and it takes energy. If you have had difficulty listening in the past, and now decide merely to *try* to listen and to participate in the spirit of the discussion as long as you can, you will soon fall into old habits. Above all, don't make an initial decision *not* to listen; if discussions in the past have proved deficient, according to your standards, accurate listening will better enable you to correct them in the future.

Get physically and mentally ready to listen. Sit up, and get rid of distractions; put away paper you were reading, books, pencils, papers, etc., unless you plan to use them. Try to dismiss personal worries, fears, or pleasant reverie until a later time. Will these kinds of thoughts be more productive of personal gain than your participation in this discussion?

Concentrate on the other person as a communicator. View the others in a discussion as sources of ideas and information, not as personalities. If you are reacting to another as being dishonest, unethical, stupid, tedious—or as a college professor, or Republican, or student rioter, or disgruntled parent—it will be difficult for you to accurately perceive what he is trying to say. There is little to fear in such an open approach. Shoddy thinking or speaking needs no label to be recognized, and fewer good ideas will be discarded because they were never really listened to. Of course, it goes without saying that persons communicate with gestures as well as with their voices, and the listener is concerned with perceiving the total communication environment as accurately as possible.

Give the other person a full hearing. Avoid interrupting another person unless you are sure you understand him fully, and that it is necessary. If you feel that you aren't sure you understand him, a well phrased question is usually more appropriate than an attempt by you to clarify his position. Impatience with others can lead to false understanding or agreement, and eventually leads to greater difficulties.

Use analytical skills as supplements to, not instead of, listening. To the degree that successful participation in discussion requires your understanding of others, rather than your speaking contributions, it is important not to be distracted by our own note taking, mental review of main points, critical analysis, or preparation for argumentative "comeback." An especially dubious recommendation frequently found in articles on listening is that, since listeners can listen faster than speakers can talk, the extra time should be used to review main points, "read between the lines," etc. Whether this conscious effort is exerted between words, sentences, or major ideas is never made clear. However, interviews with subjects following "surprise" listening tests have indicated that one of the major causes of listener distraction was a speaker's previous point: "I suddenly realized that I didn't know what he was talking about, because I was still thinking about what he had said before."

Omitted from this list are the many sound suggestions that have been made by other writers about: analyzing the speaker's intent, figuring out what he is going to say or what he has not said, note-taking, mental reorganization of a speaker's comments, etc. These, and others, are perfectly valid tools to be used in an oral communication setting, but their success is due to factors other than listening. For example, a discussion leader may wisely decide to mentally review the progress of a discussion while "listening" to a certain person unnecessarily repeating himself—but the wisdom of his action is due to his prior analysis, not to "listening ability." While listening to a specific individual, he may briefly jot down the person's main ideas for future reference; if he has developed an efficient note-taking skill, he may not miss anything significant—but he is effective because he is able to take notes with very little or no conscious effort, not because note-taking is a *listening* activity. Other less talented persons may never be able to take notes without distracting them from what is truly listening.

Conclusion

Many factors make up a discussion, and listening is only one of them; however, it is an extremely important factor, and it has been diluted in the past by a shift of its meaning from one of reception to one of critical analysis.

Empathic listening cannot of itself make a good speaker out of a poor one, a clear thinker out of a dull thinker, or a good discussion out of a bad discussion. But to the extent that problems result from a lack of participant reception and understanding of the discussion interaction, empathic listening appears to be the best answer.

NONVERBAL LANGUAGE

Jurgen Ruesch

Broadly speaking, nonverbal forms of language fall into three distinct categories: *Sign language* includes all those forms of codification in which words, numbers, and punctuation signs have been supplanted by gestures; these vary from the 'monosyllabic' gesture of the hitchhiker to such complete systems as the language of the deaf. *Action language* embraces all movements that are not used exclusively as signals. Such acts as walking and drinking, for instance, have a dual function; on the one hand, they serve personal needs, and on the other, they constitute statements to those who may perceive them. *Object language* comprises all intentional and nonintentional display of material things such as implements, machines, art objects, architectural structures, and last but not least, the human body and whatever clothes it. The embodiment of letters in books and on signs has a material substance, and this aspect of words also has to be considered as object language.

Although these various forms of nonverbal codification differ somewhat from each other, they can nevertheless be considered together for comparison with verbal codifications. From the evidence presented in Table 6 and the experience gained in the construction of computers, in the study of interpersonal communication, and in the study of neuroanatomy, neurophysiology, and speech pathology, one can presume the existence of at least two principles of human symbolization, the analogic and the verbal or digital, which apply to both intraorganismic and interpersonal codifications. Since these two kinds of codification yield different types of information, the human being is faced with the task of exploiting the resulting attenuations, reinforcements, repetitions, or contradictions, in order to obtain additional knowledge about the events he is trying to understand. Indeed, the problem of coordinating information based upon different codifications—not to mention the difficulties involved in coordinating information which is contradictory because of other factors— becomes a major task. But unfortunately not all people are capable of mastering these difficulties inherent in language and human communication. The defects encountered may reflect primarily lack of mastery of nonverbal codifications, lack of mastery of verbal codifications, or deficient synchronization between the two methods of codification. But none of these disturbances is really pure and iso-

Reprinted with permission of the author and by special permission of the William Alanson White Psychiatric Foundation. From *Psychiatry*, Vol. 18 (1955) pp. 323-330.

Table 6
Similarities and Differences between Verbal and Nonverbal Codification

Nonverbal Codification	Verbal Codification

General Characteristics

The nonverbal denotation unit is a Gestalt, the appreciation of which is based on analogies.	The verbal denotation unit—either sound or its written representation—is based on phonetics.
The nonverbal denotation unit can be broken down further—for example, parts of a unit such as a photograph can be cut out and the details are meaningful in themselves.	The verbal denotation unit—spoken or written—cannot be broken down further; for example, there does not exist a meaningful fraction of the letter, word, or sound A.
Nonverbal denotation is based on continuous functions; for example, the hand is continuously involved in movement as long as the organism lives.	Verbal denotation is based on discontinuous functions; for example, sounds and letters have a discrete beginning and end.
Nonverbal denotation is governed by principles and rules which depend largely upon biological necessities—for example, the signals which indicate alarm.	Verbal denotation is governed by arbitrary, man-made principles; for example, grammatical and language rules differ in various cultural groups.
Nonverbal denotation is used as an international, intercultural, interracial, and interspecies language; it is adapted to communication with an out-group.	Verbal denotation is used as a culturally specific language; it is adapted to communication with the in-group.

Spatiotemporal Characteristics

Nonverbal denotation can indicate successive events simultaneously; for example, come and go signals can be given at the same time.	Verbal denotation must indicate simultaneous events successively; for example, a spoken or written report consists of words which are aligned serially
Nonverbal denotation is temporally flexible; for example, a movement can be carried out slowly or quickly.	Verbal denotation is temporally rather inflexible; for example, words when spoken too slowly or too quickly become unintelligible.
Nonverbal denotation is spatially inflexible; movements and objects require a known but inflexible amount of space.	Verbal denotation is spatially flexible; print may be large or small.

Methods of nonverbal denotation such as sketches, photographs, or three-dimensional models can represent space superbly.

Verbal denotation cannot indicate space successfully except for description of boundaries.

Nonverbal denotation is poor for indicating elapsed time, but good for indicating timing and coordination.

Verbal denotation is good for indicating elapsed time, but poor for indicating timing and coordination.

Characteristics Referring to Perception, Evaluation, and Transmission

Nonverbal denotation can be perceived by distance and proximity receivers alike; for example, action may be not only seen and heard, but may also produce physical impact.

Verbal denotation can be perceived by distance receivers only; that is, it can only be heard or read.

Nonverbal language influences perception, coordination, and integration, and leads to the acquisition of skills.

Verbal language influences thinking and leads to the acquisition of information.

In nonverbal language, evaluation is tied to appreciation of similarities and differences.

In verbal language, evaluation is governed by principles of logic.

In nonverbal language, expression may be skilled or unskilled, but regardless of its quality, it is usually understandable.

In verbal language, expression must be skilled; otherwise it is unintelligible.

The understanding of nonverbal denotation is based upon the participant's empathic assessment of biological similarity; no explanation is needed for understanding what pain is.

The understanding of verbal denotation is based on prior verbal agreement; the word pain differs from the German word Schmerz or the French word douleur, and the understanding of the significance of these words is bound to such previous arrangements.

Neurophysiological and Developmental Characteristics

Nonverbal denotation is tied to phylogenetically old structures of the central and autonomic nervous systems.

Verbal denotation is tied to phylogenetically younger structures, particularly the cortex.

Nonverbal denotation is learned early in life.

Verbal denotation is learned later in life.

In the presence of brain lesions, analogic understanding may be affected, while repetition of words or ability to read is retained; for example, disturbances such as aphasic alexia or transcortical sensory aphasia indicate separate neural pathways for nonverbal as opposed to verbal codification.

Nonverbal codification involves complicated networks and includes the effector organs; for example, athletes and musicians go through certain warming-up motions prior to a performance.

In the presence of brain lesions, understanding may be retained while verbal ability is impaired; for example, verbal agnosia or alexia indicate again separate neural pathways for verbal as opposed to nonverbal codification.

Verbal codification involves the central nervous system only; for example, no movements and no external perceptions are necessary in order to recall a name.

Semantic Characteristics

Actions and objects exist in their own right and usually fulfill not only symbolic but also practical functions.

Words do not exist in their own right; they are only symbols. Words, therefore, represent abstractions of aspects of events, the accuracy of which is a function of the human observer.

Nonverbal codifications permit redundancies.

Verbal codification produces fatigue when redundant.

Nonverbal codifications permit brief and succinct statements.

Verbal codification necessitates somewhat long-winded statements.

Nonverbal codifications are subject-oriented.

Verbal codification is predicate-oriented.

Nonverbal codifications have emotional appeal.

Verbal codification exerts an intellectual appeal.

Nonverbal, analogic codifications are suitable for understanding.

Verbal codification is suitable for reaching agreements.

Nonverbal codifications represent an intimate language.

Verbal codification represents a distant language.

lated; in accepting the genetic principle as a factor in the development of psychopathology one is in fact saying that earlier, nonverbal events determine later verbal and general communicative behavior.

In language development, the gradual shift from nonverbal to verbal codifications occurs in three distinct steps: The earliest forms of codification involve action signals, mediated predominantly through contraction of the smooth muscles, which appear in changes in the color and temperature of the skin, the consistency of bowel movements, the rate of breathing, and other movements, such as sucking, which are subordinated to those autonomic functions. Although such statements as can be made in early infancy usually are unintentional, they are language in the sense that the signals are understandable to both mother and child. Later on, when the child is learning to move, such somatic language is supplemented by action signals mediated through contraction of the striped muscles. The external expression of inner events through bodily manifestations of the intestinal, respiratory, and vascular systems recedes and is replaced by movements of the face and the extremities. Finally, when social action has been learned, verbal, gestural, and other symbolic forms of denotation replace some of the previously employed methods of action codification.

The consideration of language development and the relationship of nonverbal to verbal codifications sheds some light upon the shortcomings of psychotherapeutic methods. For example, when a patient verbalizes his memories or relates his dreams, a psychiatrist who attempts to reconstruct earlier events usually obtains a one-sided view. Those aspects that lend themselves most readily to verbal treatment—names of persons and places, labels of situations, and designations of stereotyped actions and unusual events—usually make up the bulk of these accounts. Every good therapist eventually arrives at the inescapable conclusion that verbal accounts cannot adequately represent analogically codified events. Furthermore, verbal denotation cannot adequately represent experiences and skills which are accessible in terms of action only. However, society, including the majority of psychiatrists, looks askance at re-enactment, action therapy, stimulation of the proximity receivers, or nonverbal exchange. When the patient has to deny himself or is denied by others nonverbal modes of exchange and analogic expression, the only solution left is a psychosis. And strangely enough, in a psychosis the nonverbal needs of a patient are acknowledged. The successful communicative therapies for acute mental illness are designed to further nonverbal expression and to stimulate the proximity receivers; among them are music therapy, psychodrama, dancing, play and occupational therapy, and such treatment methods as wet packs, continuous baths, and massage. One of the aims of therapy is to provide mentally sick patients with tasks which may develop their analogic codifications into a language which can be shared with others, but no such provisions have been made for prepsychotic conditions. Actually, by his fear that the patient may repress, the psychiatrist is likely to indicate to the patient that he does not understand the problem. He will not seem to appreciate that the patient has to gain communicative experience in the nonverbal mode before he can engage in verbal exchange.

STUDIES OF SMALL GROUP ECOLOGY
Robert Sommer

The study of ecology covers both the distribution and the density of organisms. Within the social sciences the major ecological studies have taken place at the societal rather than at the small group level (e.g., demography) although it has been known for a long time that the arrangement of individuals in face-to-face groups is not accidental. In American society, leaders tend to occupy the head positions at a table with their lieutenants at their sides, while opposition factions frequently are found at the other end of the table.[1] Numerous accounts of these phenomena are found in observational studies such as those by Whyte[2] and Wilmer.[3] Considering the number of studies concerned with small discussion groups, relatively few have made the arrangement of people a variable. The early studies by Steinzor[4] and Bass and Klubeck[5] were primarily concerned with other factors (e.g., leadership) and only afterwards was the physical arrangement of individuals examined for its effects upon interaction. This is also the procedure followed by Strodtbeck and Hook[6] who re-analyzed their jury trail data to learn the effects of table position on contribution to the discussion, and more recently Hare and Bales[7] who re-examined group discussion data for positional effects.

One of the oldest problems in social psychology concerns the classification of face-to-face groups.[8] A heuristic taxonomy of

Robert Sommer, "Further Studies of Small Group Ecology," *Sociometry*, Vol. 28, (1965) pp. 337-348. Copyright © 1965 by The American Sociological Association and reprinted by permission.

1. Edward T. Hall, *The Silent Language*, Garden City: Doubleday, 1959; Robert Sommer, "Leadership and Group Geography," *Sociometry*, 24 (March, 1961), pp. 99-110; Fred L. Strodtbeck and L. Harmon Hook, "The Social Dimensions of a Twelve-Man Jury Table," *Sociometry*, 24 (December, 1961), pp. 397-415.

2. William H. Whyte, *The Organization Man*, New York: Simon and Schuster, 1956.

3. Harry A. Wilmer, "Graphic Ways of Representing Some Aspects of a Therapeutic Community." *Symposium on Preventive and Social Psychiatry*. Washington: Government Printing Office, 1957.

4. Bernard Steinzor, "The Spatial Factor in Face-to-Face Discussion Groups," *Journal of Abnormal and Social Psychology*, 45 (July, 1950), pp. 552-555.

5. Bernard M. Bass and S. Klubeck, "Effects of Seating Arrangements in Leaderless Group Discussions," *Journal of Abnormal and Social Psychology*, 47 (July, 1952), pp. 724-727.

6. Strodtbeck and Hook, *op. cit.*

7. A. Paul Hare and Robert F. Bales, "Seating Position and Small Group Interaction," *Sociometry*, 26 (December, 1963), pp. 480-486.

8. F.H. Allport, *Social Psychology*, Boston: Houghton Mifflin, 1924; W. Moede, *Experimentelle Massenpsychologie*, Leipzig: S. Hirzel, 1920.

groups resolved some of the contradictory findings of experiments concerned with "social facilitation," some of whose results indicated a social increment while others showed a social decrement. It was Allport [9] who made the distinction between cooperating, competing, and co-acting groups. Since most of the small group research of the last decades has concerned itself with discussion groups, this distinction has been largely neglected. The goal of the present study is to learn how people in different types of face-to-face groups arrange themselves. . . .

Observational Studies

A. The Situation Where People Desire to Interact

Over a fourteen-months period, observations were made during non-eating hours in the student union cafeteria at a California university. During these hours the cafeteria is used by students for casual conversation and studying (and to a lesser extent by faculty and non-teaching staff for coffee breaks). The observations were made irregularly and there was some bias in these times in that the writer's schedule led him to pass this way at certain times rather than others but most of the daylight non-eating hours were covered. Records were kept of the seating of pairs of people. In the first series of observations, no distinction was made whether the people were conversing, studying together, or studying separately. The only category specifically excluded from the study was a pair where one or both people were eating. This cafeteria contained two different table sizes: single pedestal square tables (36 inches per side) each surrounded by four chairs, one to a side; double pedestal rectangular tables (36 × 54 inches) each surrounded by six chairs, two on the long sides and one at each end.

The 50 pairs seated at the small square tables showed a preference for corner rather than opposite seating (35 pairs sat corner to corner while 15 sat across from one another).[10] The double pedestal tables permit side-by-side and distant seating as well as corner and opposite seating. During the course of the observations, 60 pairs were observed at double tables. Table 7 shows clearly that side-by-side and distant seating were infrequent. The vast majority of pairs chose to occupy the corners or sit across from one another.

---

9. Floyd Allport, *op. cit.*
10. A similar preference for corner seating was found in a subsequent study of eating pairs in a hospital cafeteria. Of the 41 pairs, 29 sat corner-to-corner while 12 pairs sat across from one another.

Table 7
Arrangement of Pairs at Rectangular Tables
(in Per Cent)

Seating Arrangement	Series 1 (N = 50)	Series 2	
		Conversing (N = 74)	Co-acting (N = 18)
Corner	40	54	0
Across	43	36	32
Side	8	6	0
Distant	10	4	68
Total	100	100	100

It was planned to continue these observations for another six months, but in February 1965 the furniture of the cafeteria was changed. In order to accommodate more people the management moved in new tables and rearranged others. Rather than combine these new observations with the previous ones, it seemed preferable to look upon them as a new series in which additional information could be gained. In the next four months 52 additional observations were made in which the *major activity* of the people as well as their seating arrangement was recorded. A distinction was made between those pairs who were interacting (conversing, studying together) and those who were co-acting (occupying the same table but studying separately). In order to keep the data comparable to the previous observations, the present analysis focused upon the square tables (36" X 36") observed previously, as well as rectangular tables (36" X 72") which were made by pushing two of the small square tables together. The situation at the other rectangular tables (36" X 54") was confused since these tables now accommodated anywhere from four to eight people, sometimes with end chairs and sometimes without, so these are excluded from the analysis.

Of the 124 pairs seated at the small square tables, 106 were conversing or otherwise interacting while 18 were co-acting. The interacting pairs showed a definite preference for corner seating, with 70 seated corner-to-corner compared to 36 seated across from one another. However, co-acting pairs chose a very different arrangement, with only two pairs sitting corner-to-corner and 18 sitting opposite one another. These results support the previous studies in which corner seating was preferred over opposite and side-by-side seating in a variety of conditions where individuals interact. It suggests that corner seating preserves the closeness between individuals and also enables people to avoid eye contact since they do not sit face to face. The co-acting pairs use the distance across the table for books, hand-bags, and other belongings, and can avoid visual contact by looking down rather than across the table.

Seating at the rectangular tables is shown in the second and third columns of Table 1. The interacting groups prefer corner-to-corner seating, and to a lesser extent opposite seating, with little use made of side-by-side or distant seating. On the other hand, more than two-thirds of the co-acting groups chose a distant seating arrange-ment which separated the people geographically and visually.

B. The Situation Where Interaction Is Discouraged

One set of observations took place in the reading area adjacent to the reserve room of a university library. This is a large room (29' X 83') containing 33 rectangular tables (48" X 64") in the main area. Each table has a capacity of four persons, two sitting on oppo-site sides with the ends free. The room was generally quiet even when filled to capacity. This made it a good place to study how people arranged themselves when they did *not* want to interact. All observa-tions took place when the room was relatively uncrowded since this provided some choice as to seating. Due to the size of the room, it was not possible to record the arrangements at all the tables in the room without appearing conspicuous. Thus the observer randomly selected some location in the room and diagrammed the seating ar-rangments within the visible portion of the room on a prepared chart.

A pilot study[11] had shown that the majority of people who came alone sat alone if there was an empty table. This trend was more marked for the males (70%) than for the females (55%). The next largest group arranged themselves diagonally across from whoever already occupied the table. Only 10% of the students sat opposite or beside another student (i.e., in either of the two near positions) when there were empty seats available elsewhere.

Following this, there were 19 occasions when the seating patterns of those individuals presently in the reserve room were recorded, including people who came alone as well as those who came with friends. The sample consisted of 193 males and 304 women. Again it was found that a higher percentage of males (34%) than females (25%) sat alone. However, the major focus of the study was on those

---

11. This study was carried out by David Addicott.

students who sat two at a table (since there is only one possible way that people can arrange themselves three or four to a table). The results showed that 30% of the pairs sat across from one another, 15% sat side-by-side, while 56% used the diagonal or distant arrangement. Although the observations were cross-sectional and spanned only several minutes each, a record was made of any conversations at the table. Conversations were observed among 8% of the pairs sitting across from one another, 3% of those pairs sitting in a diagonal or distant arrangement, and 37% of those sitting side-by-side.

A second set of observations was made independently in the Periodical Room of the same library. The same general technique was followed in that the arrangement of all pairs was diagrammed on 14 occasions over a two month period. This room, excluding the magazine and transit areas, was 36' X 74' and contained two types of rectangular tables, one (48" X 64") with two chairs on each side and the ends free, and the other (48" X 90") with three chairs on each side and the ends free. The arrangements of pairs at the two types of tables were similar; and the pooled data show that of the 74 pairs, 19% sat across from one another, 13% sat side-by-side, and 68% sat in a distant arrangement. Conversations were noted between 14% of the people sitting opposite one another, 6% of those people sitting in a distant relationship, and 60% of those pairs sitting side-by-side.

Questionnaire Studies

A. Rectangular Table Ecology

To learn something of the way that group task influences the way people arrange themselves, a paper-and-pencil test was administered to 151 students in an introductory psychology class. Each student was asked to imagine how he and a friend of the same sex would seat themselves under four different conditions: a. To chat for a few minutes before class; b. To study together for the same exam; c. To study for different exams; and d. To compete in order to see which would be the first to solve a series of puzzles. Each time the student was asked to indicate his own seating and that of his friend on a diagram showing a table and six chairs (see Figure 12). There was one chair at the head and one at the foot and two chairs on each of the sides. In order to maximize the realism of the test, the hypothetical activity was located in the student union cafeteria during *non*-eating hours (which is, as has been noted, actively used for casual conversation, studying, etc., and has similar rectangular tables). The tasks set for the students included cooperating, co-acting, and competing activity. In addition, a distinction was made between casual interaction such as conversation and structured cooperative activity (joint study-ing for an exam). The different tasks were presented in random order in the test booklet.

Percentage of Ss Choosing This Arrangement

Seating Arrangement	Condition 1 (conversing)	Condition 2 (cooperating)	Condition 3 (co-acting)	Condition 4 (competing)
x·x□	42	19	3	7
x□x	46	25	31	41
x□·x	1	5	43	20
x□·x	0	0	3	5
xx□	11	51	7	8
x□x	0	0	13	18
TOTAL	100	100	100	99

Figure 12. Seating preferences at rectangular tables.

There were no significant differences between the sexes in seating arrangements under any of the conditions. This was unexpected, since previous studies have shown that females make greater use of side-by-side seating while males prefer to sit across from other people.

Figure 12 shows the seating preferences for the total group of 151 students. If we take "near seating" to include side-by-side, corner and opposite arrangements, and let "distant seating" refer to all other patterns, Figure 12 shows that distant seating was rarely used by casual or cooperating groups. People who want to converse or work together use the near arrangements. On the other hand distant seating is the dominant pattern in co-acting groups. The most common distant pattern shows people sitting on opposite sides of the table but not directly facing one another rather than the more physically distant head-foot arrangement. This suggests that it is the visual contact between people rather than bodily presence that is the major source of distraction in co-acting groups. Distant seating is important in competing groups although the dominant arrangement here is opposite seating.

People conversing overwhelmingly chose a corner-to-corner or opposite arrangement. On the other hand, those studying together strongly prefer to sit side-by-side. In no other condition is side seating used anywhere near this frequency. There is a metaphorical quality to these arrangements with people competing sitting "in opposition," people cooperating sitting "on the same side," people conversing sitting "in a corner" and people co-acting choosing a "distant" arrangement.

The identical questionnaire was given to 26 students in a social psychology class. After the students completed the questionnaire in the usual way, each was asked to go through his responses and explain why he chose this particular arrangement.

For the *casual group,* the dominant preference was for corner seating, and the student's explanations were: "We would be sitting close to each other and yet be able to see each person." "It's nice to be close when chatting but you should face each other instead of side-by-side." "You would be closer with only a corner than across the table, you'd have to turn less than side-by-side." "The corner arrangement is the most intimate. You wouldn't have to shout *across* the table, but, sitting adjacent you could still face the person. Sitting beside the person it is hard to look at them when you're talking." Those people who chose to sit across from one another emphasized the desirability of a direct face-to-face arrangement.

In the *cooperating group,* those people who liked the corner arrangement mentioned the ease of conversing in corner chairs ("Because we could look at each other's notes with the least change of place and effort.") while those people who chose the side arrangement emphasized the ease of sharing things in this position.

For the *co-acting group,* the dominant arrangement was a distant one and these students emphasized the need to be apart yet feel together ("This would allow for sitting far enough apart so we wouldn't interfere with each other, but if we wanted to pass comments we are close enough." "Effectively divides table into two halves yet allows brief remarks without having to raise voice. Also allows staring into space and not at neighbor's face.").

As in the previous study, opposite, distant-opposite, and distant seating were preferred by *competing groups.* The way that a face-to-face arrangement stimulates competition was frequently mentioned: e.g., "Able to see how friend is doing but there's enough room"; or, "In this situation the friend can be watched to determine his progress." The reason given most frequently by people preferring the distant-opposite arrangement was that it reduced the temptation to look at the other person's answers while the long distance aided concentration. Those people electing a distant arrangement explained that this would minimize distraction. Two of the three people preferring a side arrangement mentioned that it was easier to concentrate when not looking directly at the other person.

B. Round Table Ecology

In order to learn how the group task would affect the arrangement of people at a round table, 116 students in another introductory psychology class were asked to fill out a questionnaire similar to that of the preceding study except that the diagram showed a *round* table surrounded by six chairs. The same four situations were described (i.e., conversing with a friend, studying for the same exam, for different exams, or competing). Since the results showed no significant difference between the 65 females and 51 males, the composite totals are presented in Figure 13. People can sit in only three possible arrangements under these conditions (see Figure 13), these three arrangements comprising a rank order of physical distance.

Figure 13 shows that casual and cooperating groups made greatest use of adjacent chairs. This trend was most marked among the cooperating groups where 83% chose adjacent chairs. Although the co-acting group makes heavy use of an arrangement where one empty chair is left between the people, the majority of co-acting groups places a gap of two seats between them (i.e., sit directly opposite one another). The trend for opposite seating is most pronounced in the competing group.

Percentage of Ss Choosing This Arrangement

Seating Arrangement	Condition 1 (conversing)	Condition 2 (cooperating)	Condition 3 (co-acting)	Condition 4 (competing)
	63	83	13	12
	17	7	36	25
	20	10	51	63
TOTAL	100	100	100	100

Figure 13. Seating Preferences at Round Tables.

If we make certain assumptions on the basis of our previous study with rectangular tables, it is possible to formulate hypotheses as to how positions at a round table compare with those at a rectangular table. Adjacent seating at a round table seems somewhere between side and corner seating. Physically, it places people side-by-side at a lesser angle than in a corner arrangement. Sitting one seat away from another person at a round table does not seem to be as "distant" an arrangement as leaving the same gap at a rectangular table. This suggests that people at a round table are psychologically closer than at a corresponding position at a rectangular table. Opposite seating in the round table arrangement used here seems to serve some of the functions of both distant and opposite seating at a rectangular table.

The same questionnaire was given to 18 students who, after filling out the questionnaire in the usual way, explained why they arranged themselves as they did. Most of the students in the *converging condition* selected adjacent seats: "I want to chat with my friend, not the whole cafeteria, so I sit next to her"; "More intimate, no physical barriers between each other." In the *cooperating group,* the vast majority chose to sit in adjacent chairs. Their explanations stressed the advantages of this arrangement for comparing notes and sharing materials. Most students in the *co-acting condition* chose to sit two seats away from one another, the greatest physical distance permitted in this diagram. Of those who chose to sit one seat away, several mentioned that this "Doesn't put us directly opposite each other . . . keep looking at each other if we look up from studying," and "Not directly across from each other because we'd have more of a tendency to talk then." In the *competing condition,* most students chose to leave two seats between them which placed them directly opposite one another. The explanations emphasized the need to keep separate in order to avoid seeing each other's material. Several mentioned that opposite seating permitted them to see how the other person was doing and enhanced feelings of competition.

Discussion

These results indicate that different tasks are associated with different spatial arrangements; the ecology of interaction differs from the ecology of co-action and competition. Exactly why these particular arrangements are chosen we do not know for certain. On the basis of what our subjects report, eye contact seems an important factor in spatial arrangements. Under certain conditions direct visual contact represents a challenge to the other, a play at dominance. Among chickens and turkeys in confinement, McBride[1][2] has shown that the dominant bird in the flock has the most eye space. When he looks at a submissive bird, the latter looks away. When birds are crowded together, they stand at the wire of the coop facing outward to avoid the stress that would be generated by extended visual contact. We may only speculate as to the extent to which eye contact regulates spatial arrangements, though it is interesting to note that the only questionnaire condition in which opposite seating was chosen over other distant alternatives was in the competitive task where the sub-

---

12. Glen McBride, *A General Theory of Social Organization and Behavior,* St. Lucia: University of Queensland Press, 1964.

ject indicated a desire to "keep an eye on what the other person was doing." It is hypothesized that gestures of threat (agonistic displays) are more appropriate in competitive conditions than cooperative or strictly social tasks. On the other hand, agonistic displays are stressful to both parties, and in the animal kingdom are generally terminated by ritualized submissive behavior rather than actual combat. In a previous pilot study,[13] people were asked how they would seat themselves at a table already occupied by someone they disliked. It was found that people chose to sit at some distance from the disliked person, but *not* directly opposite him, i.e., in a distant-side position. In this way they were removed visually as well as geographically from the source of stress. The relationship between distance and aggressive behavior among chaffinches has been studied nicely by Marler.[14] Placing the cages of chaffinches various distances apart, he found the point at which aggressive displays began. Female chaffinches tolerated closer presence than males, while females whose breasts were dyed to resemble males were kept at the typical male distance by other birds.

Most stressful encounters are avoided through spatial segregation. The orbits in which people travel tend to remove them from contact with those with whom they disagree or dislike. Avoidance is the first line of defense against interpersonal stress but when this is not possible or effective, an individual develops alternate methods. Limiting the range of visual contact through social conventions or actual physical barriers are other possibilities. The present studies all took place in settings whose furnishings consisted solely of tables and chairs. No attempt was made to explore the role of physical barriers such as posts, partitions, tables, etc., in regulating interaction. The ways in which people gain privacy in public areas warrants further exploration in a society in which more and more people share a finite amount of space. In settings such as libraries, study rooms, and large open offices, it is exceedingly important to develop methods whereby unwanted or stressful interpersonal contact is avoided.

Chapin,[15] in his discussion of housing factors related to mental hygiene, indicated the importance of ease of circulation as well as areas that can be closed off from the main traffic flow. Just as people moving about a house require resting places for solitude or individual

---

13. This study was conducted by Vera Stevens and Corinne Sundberg.

14. Peter Marler, "Studies of Fighting in Chaffinches: Proximity as a Cause of Aggression," *British Journal of Animal Behavior,* 4 (1956), pp. 23-30.

15. F.S. Chapin, "Some Housing Factors Related to Mental Hygiene," *Journal of Social Issues,* 7 (1951), pp. 164-171.

concentration, people rooted to a given spot in a public area require places where their eyes can rest without stress. There is the apocryphal story of the stress produced by the newspaper strike in New York City where the seated men were unable to "retreat into" newspapers and had to look at the other occupants, particularly women standing above them. Subway officials believe that the advertisements on the wall provide safe resting places for the patron's eyes.

Since the topological similarities between different arrangements of people make it unnecessary to experiment with every conceivable physical arrangement, it seems most fruitful to isolate the socially and psychologically genotypic arrangements. The two most obvious ones are near and distant seating. In ordinary social intercourse, near seating is the rule. In American society it is only among strangers, co-acting individuals or schizophrenic mental patients that one finds distant seating patterns in any frequency.

One can divide seating patterns into several important subclasses. One possible category involves arrangements which maximize direct visual contact between individuals. According to Goffman,[16] Hall,[17] and Birdwhistell,[18] direct visual contact can be exceedingly uncomfortable and disconcerting under ordinary conditions, producing feelings of anxiety in the person upon whom the eyes are directly centered. There are cultural differences in the use of visual contact such as the middle class Southern girl described by Birdwhistell who "uses her eyes more" than does the Northern or Western girl. One can also distinguish between near arrangements according to the extent to which they facilitate tactile or olfactory contact. The number of possible arrangements is still small enough to permit clear categorization and conceptualization.

16. Erving Goffman, *Behavior in Public Places,* Glencoe: Free Press, 1963.
17. Edward T. Hall, "Silent Assumptions in Social Communication," in *Disorders of Communication,* 42 (1964), pp. 41-55.
18. Ray Birdwhistell, "Field Methods and Techniques," *Human Organization,* 11 (Spring, 1952), pp. 37-38.

INTERPERSONAL COMMUNICATION: SOME WORKING PRINCIPLES

Larry A. Samovar and Edward D. Rintye

In the age of communication hardware as sophisticated as the Telstar and global television network, perhaps it is not surprising that much intellectual energy has also been directed toward solving the mysteries of human interpersonal communication.[1] Whether or not the effort to understand the human factors in communication is equal to the intensity devoted to mastering electronic extensions of man is debatable. There is no doubt, however, that interpersonal communication is the subject of great interest to those in industry, government, and the academic world.

Yet, as one examines the literature on human communication, he may be frustrated by the realization that communication theory is not a well-defined and unified body of thought. Indeed, it is an amorphous collection of writings from disciplines as diverse as mathematics, semantics, physiology, social psychology, anthropology, rhetoric, existential philosophy, and political science.[2] Because of the interdisciplinary nature of the resource materials, it is impossible at this stage to designate any single book, department, or discipline as representative of communication theory. To study human communication, one must seek out his principles, theories, and procedures where he may; and it seems probable that many more years will elapse before any integrative theoretical framework will evolve. It is this thought which prompts the authors to offer the following summary.

The study presented is an attempt to bring together in summary form several "working principles" of human interpersonal communication. Drawn from many disciplines, these principles are by no means exhaustive of all pertinent insights in communication theory. But they do represent to the authors a basic core or foundation of

---

Reprinted with permission of authors. This original essay appears here in print for the first time.

1. "Human interpersonal communication" is used herein to refer to a process of human interaction which psychologist Carl Hovland describes as one by which "an individual (the communicator) transmits stimuli (usually verbal symbols) to modify the behavior of other individuals (communicatees)." See Carl Hovland, "Social Communication," *Proceedings of the American Philosophical Society,* XCII (November, 1948), 371.

2. Frank E.X. Dance, ed. *Human Communication Theory: Original Essays* (New York, 1967), pp. vii-viii; Floyd W. Matson and Ashley Montagu, eds. *The Human Dialogue: Perspectives on Communication* (New York, 1967), pp. viii-ix; Alfred G. Smith, ed. *Communication and Culture: Readings in the Codes of Human Interaction* (New York, 1966), p. v.

assumptions which requires recognition in any sound theory of human communication.

I. All human speech communication exhibits common elements. Berlo synthesizes the thinking of many in the communication area by identifying the following elements in any human communication situation: (1) source (sender); (2) encoding action; (3) message; (4) channel (medium); (5) decoding action; (6) receiver.[3] One additional element is necessary when considering speech communication: (7) feedback.[4] A closer look at each of these elements may be beneficial. A "source" is an individual who consciously and intentionally seeks to affect the behavior of at least one other human being through communication. To accomplish his purpose, the source must engage in some form of "encoding action" which will translate his ideas into symbols that may be combined or arranged and expressed in some form of "message." The form the message will take depends upon a host of variables, such as source self-concept, educational level, image of the receiver, status relationships, etc. This message travels to the receiver by means of a "channel." In human speech communication the two channels most commonly used—usually simultaneously—are the vocal and the visual. The receiver initiates "decoding action" in response to the message, hoping to produce approximately the same ideas encoded by the sender. It is because distortion is so probable that the last common element of human communication, called "feedback," is so important. Feedback in human communication consists of the signals sent back to the original sender by the receiver, in response to the original message.[5] These signals are the primary means by which the original sender may gage the effect of his message on the receiver, and know to make the adjustments required to clarify, elaborate, or otherwise alter subsequent messages.

II. Human attention is highly selective. People are constantly screening available stimuli in any situation, and consciously and unconsciously select some stimuli to which they will respond while at the same time ignoring others.[6] Through this selection process, and the emphasis of some details at the expense of others, "we may

---

3. David K. Berlo, *The Process of Communication: an Introduction to Theory and Practice* (New York, 1960), pp. 30-32.

4. Norbert Wiener, *Cybernetics: or Control and Communication in the Animal and the Machine* (Massachusetts, 1948), pp. 95-115.

5. *Ibid.*

6. Eugene L. Hartley and Ruth E. Hartley, *Fundamentals of Social Psychology* (New York, 1958), p. 54.

change the whole meaning of a complex pattern of stimuli."[7] In addition to his neurological limitations, man has his perceptual or attentive faculty influenced by technological, attitudinal, conceptual, and social factors.[8] Hartley and Hartley observe that "In addition to the general social directives internalized by the individual, there are many idiosyncratic pressures, internal patterns of needs and preoccupations, that emerge from the interaction between the individual's biological drives and the ways these drives are handled by his particular social group. These pressures may be seen . . . as particularized sensitivities to specific stimuli or tendencies to avoid the recognition of certain stimuli. . . . In general, people will notice things that interest them and in some way affect their own welfare. They will delegate to the background items of no direct relevance to their own needs and interests."[9] Newcomb, Turner, and Converse agree that the receiver's "pre-message motives and attitudes selectively lower certain of his thresholds. . . ."[10] It seems clear that human attention is not the result of random and incidental factors at work within the individual.

III. Man actively seeks consistency between his self-image, his behavior, and perceived information. The self-image referred to here is equivalent to the "self-concept" of Tannenbaum, Weschler, and Massarik.[11] It is a kind of psychological "base of operations."[12] Mead identifies it as characteristically being an object of itself.[13] And Carl Rogers describes the self-structure as an "organized configuration of perceptions of the self which are admissable to awareness."[14] It is composed of such elements as the perception of one's characteristics and abilities, the percepts and concepts of the self in relation to others and the environment, and the value qualities which are perceived as associated with experiences and objects.[15] Whether one refers to the self-image as man's "conscious identity,"[16] as does

7. *Ibid.,* p. 53.

8. *Ibid.,* p. 132.

9. *Ibid.,* pp. 54-55.

10. Theodore M. Newcomb, Ralph H. Turner, and Phillip E. Converse, *Social Psychology: the Study of Human Interaction* (New York, 1965), pp. 206-207.

11. Robert Tannenbaum, Irving R. Weschler, and Fred Massarik, "The Process of Understanding People," in *Interpersonal Dynamics: Essays and Readings of Human Interaction,* eds. Warren G. Bennis et al. (Homewood, Illinois, 1964), p. 732.

12. *Ibid.*

13. George H. Mead, *Mind, Self and Society* (Chicago, 1934), p. 136.

14. Carl R. Rogers, *Client-Centered Therapy: Its Current Practice, Implications, and Theory* (Boston, 1951), p. 501.

15. *Ibid.*

16. Allen Wheelis, *The Quest for Identity* (New York, 1958), p. 19.

Allen Wheelis, or prefers Burke's reference to it as the "first person addressed by a man's consciousness,"[17] there seems to be consensual agreement as to the central role of the self-image in man's attempt to communicate. Given this central role, it is not surprising that individual man seeks to behave in ways which do not threaten his self-image. Possibly more unexpected is the conclusion of research surveyed by Berelson and Steiner which states that people "tend to see and hear communications that are favorable or congenial to their predispositions; they are more likely to see and hear congenial communications than neutral or hostile ones."[18] Brown explains this phenomenon as the principle of "cognitive consistency," supporting the tendency of the human mind to seek consistency between an individual's frame of reference and available information.[19] At least three major treatments of this theme are well known in psychology: (1) congruity-incongruity (Osgood and Tannenbaum), (2) balance-imbalance (Abelson and Rosenberg), and (3) consonance-dissonance (Festinger).[20]

IV. Man maintains perceptual consistency by distorting information or by avoiding data he cannot alter. Not only does man seek consistency, as indicated by the preceding principle, but he will alter reality to maintain desired consistency. Another way of saying this is to suggest that man's psychological frame of reference determines what is perceived and how it is perceived.[21] Krech and Crutchfield contend that the ego or self has a role of unparalleled significance in the structuring of the perceptual field: "Some of the most potent of all needs and the most effective of all goals have to do with defense of the self, i.e., with the adjustment of the field in such a way as to enhance feelings of self-esteem, self-regard, etc., or to remove threats to self-esteem and self-regard."[22] S.I. Hayakawa summarizes confirming studies of Cantril, Kilpatrick, and others, when he asserts that the "self-concept is the fundamental determinant of our perceptions, and therefore of our behavior. As John Dewey said, 'A stimu-

---

17. Kenneth Burke, *A Rhetoric of Motives* (New York, 1955), pp. 38-39.
18. Bernard Berelson and Gary A. Steiner, *Human Behavior: an Inventory of Scientific Findings* (New York, 1964), pp. 529-530.
19. Roger Brown, *Social Psychology* (New York, 1965), pp. 557-609.
20. Charles E. Osgood and Percy H. Tannenbaum, "The Principle of Congruity in the Prediction of Attitude Change," *Psychological Review*, LXII (1955), 42-55; R.P. Abelson and M.J. Rosenberg, "Symbolic Psychologic: a Model of Attitudinal Cognition," *Behavioral Science*, III (1958), 1-13; Leon Festinger, *A Theory of Cognitive Dissonance* (Stanford, California, 1957).
21. David Krech and Richard S. Crutchfield, *Theory and Problems of Social Psychology* (New York, 1948), p. 94.
22. *Ibid.*, p. 69.

lus becomes a stimulus by virtue of what the organism was already preoccupied with.' "[2 3] Sherif, Sherif, and Nebergall report that an individual's own position on an issue is the *basic determinant* of whether or not he will accept a message on that issue, completely ignore the message, debunk the message, distort the message, reinforce his own position, etc.[2 4] Certainly the well-known work of Hovland, Janis, and Kelly affirms the importance of predispositional factors in perception and attitude change.[2 5] There seems little question in relevant literature that people tend to perceive information in accordance with their own predisposition, their own ego-image, and will achieve psychological consistency even though it requires them to distort or evade the true nature of the message.

V. Active participation in the communication act by the receiver tends to produce better retention of information and tends to more surely induce changes in the receiver's behavior. Speculating that ego-involvement may be the clue as to why this principle is true, Sherif, Sherif, and Nebergall maintain that experimental literature suggests that if a person is required to give a speech or write an essay or in some way physically perform a task involving information, then that information will be better retained and more completely accepted than if the person is only passively involved as a listener.[2 6] Active participation "tends to augment the effectiveness of persuasive communications."[2 7] Berelson and Steiner agree that techniques which involve people actively in dealing with information, such as discussion (as opposed to lecture), are much more effective in involving the ego and in changing attitudes and behavior.[2 8] The implication of this principle for communication seems obvious: communication acts which require overt use of message information will be more likely to be accepted and remembered by the receiver.

VI. Social roles and status systems define communication patterns within any social organization. In expressing this principle the authors assume Ralph Linton's conception of a social role, since it is undoubtedly the most widely known and influencial in the social sciences.[2 9] In Linton's view the role is the living performance of a

23. S.I. Hayakawa, *Symbol, Status and Personality* (New York, 1950), p. 38.
24. Carolyn W. Sherif, Muzafer Sherif, and Roger E. Nebergall, *Attitude and Attitude Change: the Social Judgement-Involvement Approach* (Philadelphia, 1965), pp. 219-246.
25. Carl L. Hovland, Irving L. Janis, and Harold H. Kelly, *Communication and Persuasion: Psychological Studies of Opinion Change* (New Haven, Connecticutt, 1953), pp. 175-214.
26. Sherif, Sherif, and Nebergall, *op. cit.*, p. 197.
27. Hovland, Janis, and Kelly, *op. cit.*, p. 228.
28. Berelson and Steiner, *op. cit.*, pp. 547-548.
29. Lionel J. Neuman and James W. Hughes, "The Problem of the Concept of Role—a Survey of the Literature," *Social Forces,* XXX (December, 1951), 149.

position (a status in a particular social organization), while a "status" is a collection of rights and duties distinct from the individual who occupies the position to which those rights and duties accrue.[30] For practical purposes, role and status are inseparable and may be thought of as organized patterns of expectancies related to the tasks, attitudes, behaviors, and relationships operant within a specific group.[31] Utilizing this conception of role and status, principle six expresses a well-established finding in social psychology: that social systems significantly affect how, why, to and from whom, and with what effects communication occurs.[32] Social organization limits the number of contacts, establishes the frequency of messages sent and received, and partially determines what kinds of messages will be transmitted to whom and from whom.[33] Most importantly, the status system or role organization greatly affects the manner in which members regard or perceive their messages.

VII. Speech communication is a symbolic process. Spoken words, as well as gestural, postural, facial expressions, etc., make up the "socially institutionalized sign system" used in speech communication activity.[34] Use of this sign system is a highly complex and elaborate human symbolic activity. John Carroll suggests a useful framework for discussion of this principle. He notes that any language possesses three essential properties: (1) it consists of a finite set of discrete signs, (2) those signs fulfill a reference function, and (3) the sign system is arbitrary. It is important to observe that the identifying characteristic of a sign is its use as a symbol; that is, the word or gesture serves to represent something other than itself. In so serving, the sign fulfills the second necessary property of a language, that of possessing a reference function. The sign is only a reference pointer to the thing for which it stands, and it is this referencing or pointing which is the heart of principle seven. Once this reference function is understood, it is obvious that any given linguistic-gestural system is essentially arbitrary. From a functional point of view there is no difference between "dog," "chien," "hund," or "perro"; the

---

30. Ralph Linton, *The Study of Man* (New York, 1936), pp. 113-114.

31. Carl H. Weaver and Warren L. Strausbaugh, *Fundamentals of Speech Communication* (New York, 1964), p. 187.

32. Berlo, *op. cit.,* pp. 147-152; Weaver and Strausbaugh, *op. cit.,* pp. 215-221; Bruce J. Riddle and Edwin J. Thomas, eds. *Role Theory: Concepts and Research* (New York, 1966), pp. 64-102; Newcomb, Turner, and Converse, *op. cit.,* pp. 341-345; Hartley and Hartley, *op. cit.,* pp. 148-154.

33. Berlo, *op. cit.,* p. 148.

34. John B. Carroll, *Language and Thought* (New Jersey, 1964), pp. 3-8.

referent is the same. The difference in each case is only the symbol. There is no reason, other than a historical one, why "pin" stands for a small pointed object instead of a storage receptacle.[35]

It seems apparent, then, that language is an essentially arbitrary collection of signs, discrete and referencial, to which the using community has assigned particular elements of human experience (referents).[36] As Marie Pei says it: "A language is essentially an array of words, each of which is accepted by the social group as conveying a given meaning or meanings."[37] The critical point is that the assignment of "meaning" to a specific sign is a culturally local function; a task of the particular using community, and hence, an arbitrary assignment. Carroll's three properties are present, then, in the oral-aural-gestural symbol system utilized in speech communication. Speech communication is a symbolic process.

VIII. Human communication occurs only through the use of a shared symbol system. To communicate with one another, members of the using community must use identical symbols and use them in relatively the same way.[38] The folly of attempting communication through use of uncommon symbols is apparent to anyone who has traveled abroad without a facility in the appropriate language. Yet it is not necessary to travel abroad to discover communication failures due to differing interpretation of symbols. Consider the problems inherent in the use of such symbols as "black power," "civil rights," "the free world," "conservative point of view." Although all within the family of a common language, these symbols are regarded frequently as connotative or affective; that is, the referent (object) to which they refer is not universally shared. The difference between denotation and connotation seems only a question of the extent of common agreement of the users on the symbol-to-referent relationship. Fortunately a sufficient portion of English is denotative enough to permit its users to accomplish essential "practical" daily communication.

IX. No symbol has a fixed referent. Because a large part of daily communication is accomplished through use of a restricted number of "familiar" words, many people develop the idea that the object to which a word refers is always the same; that the word's meaning is

---

35. *Ibid.,* p. 6.
36. Edward Sapir, *Language: an Introduction to the Study of Speech* (New York, 1921), p. 11.
37. Mario Pei, *The Story of Language* (New York, 1949), p. 123.
38. Stephen Ullmann, "Signs and Symbols," *Introductory Readings on Language,* eds. Wallace L. Anderson and Norman C. Stageberg (New York, 1962), pp. 198-201.

fixed and unchanging. This fallacy of "fixed referent" causes much difficulty in human communication. Ogden and Richards suggest that the "theory of direct meaning relationships between words and things is the source of almost all the difficulty which thought encounters. . . ."[39] Neither the speaker nor the listener can communicate effectively if he ignores the fact that words stand for nothing but the ideas in the mind of him who utters them. Some authorities consider it impossible to measure the meaning of linguistic elements of a message.[40] Others, such as Osgood and his associates at Illinois, believe that an instrument like the semantic differential is at least a beginning in the development of means to evaluate connotative words.[41]

X. Symbolic "meaning" is a relationship of the symbols used, the object referred to, the sender, and the receiver of the message.[42] The symbols of a message are chosen by the sender because he assumes that *he and* the receiver share approximately the same understanding of the "meaning" of those symbols. Communication is doomed if this assumption is incorrect. And there is much room for error. Both the sender and receiver confront a referent with their individual and differing backgrounds of information and attitudes. They both make assumptions about one another's information and attitudes toward themselves and the referent.[43] From the presented message the receiver selectively perceives those elements most relevant to his needs, a selection determined by his existing motives and predispositions.[44] Depending upon the congruence of the new information and the receiver's existing attitudes, he will accept, distort, or reject the substance of the message. Commenting on the complexity of attaining meaning fidelity in human communication, F.J. Roethlisberger suggests that "due to differences of background, experience, and motivation, it seems . . . extraordinary that any two persons can ever understand each other."[45] In such an abstruse, subtly varying four-fold relationship, small wonder that the symbols used, the referent, the sender, and the receiver combine only occasionally to create clear symbolic meaning.

39. C.K. Ogden and I.A. Richards, *The Meaning of Meaning* (New York, (1923), pp. 12-15.

40. Carl H. Weaver and Garry L. Weaver, "Information Theory and the Measurement of Meaning," *Speech Monographs,* XXXII (November, 1965), 447.

41. Charles E. Osgood, George J. Suci, and Percy H. Tannenbaum, *The Measurement of Meaning* (Urban, Illinois, 1957), pp. 18-25.

42. Robert Benjamin, *Semantics* (San Diego, 1965), p. 10.

43. Hartley and Hartley, *op. cit.,* pp. 36-91.

44. Berelson and Steiner, *op. cit.,* pp. 536-540.

45. F.J. Roethlisberger, "Barriers to Communication Between Men," *The Use and Misuse of Language,* ed. S.I. Hayakawa (Greenwich, Connecticutt, 1943), p. 41.

XI. All referents, references, and symbols are abstractions. The general semanticists make a major point of the idea that all human knowledge is the result of the process of faulty human perception.[46] They use the word "abstract" as an active verb referring to the selective and organizing nature of human perception.[47] In addition to the psychological factors involved in perception, some of which have been discussed, the general semanticist is concerned with the physiological limitations of the human neurological system.[48] The manner in which humans perceive with vision, touch, etc., is the result of the peculiar qualities of the individual person's nervous system, and it follows that "There are 'sights' we cannot see, and, as even children know today with their high-frequency dog whistles, 'sounds' that we cannot hear."[49] According to the general semanticist, it is not rational to suggest that human beings ever perceive anything "as it really is."[50]

In addition to using "abstraction" as a verb, the general semanticist also uses the term as a noun, to refer to "sense impressions" of a given referent at any one of four levels of abstraction (verb).[51] Four separate levels of the abstraction process may be identified: (1) the event, or sub-microscopic physical-chemical processes, (2) the ordinary object manufactured from the event by the lower nervous centers, (3) the psychological "picture" manufactured by the higher centers, and (4) the verbal label or term.[52] It may now be apparent that according to general semantics usage, one could use a term (abstraction-noun) the referent of which was identifiable at any one of the four levels of abstraction (process-verb). As the selectivity becomes more stringent, the number of characteristics remaining lessens, and the level of abstraction (process) is said to become "higher."[53]

It is clear at this point that the general semanticist sees the entire world of the human being as a series of abstractions (noun), which are the products of selective perception. If the general semanticist's thinking is valid, then all referents, all references, and all symbols are abstractions.

---

46. John C. Condon Jr., *Semantics and Communication* (New York, 1966), pp. 11-23.
47. *Ibid.*, p. 19.
48. Alfred Korzybski, *Science and Sanity: an Introduction to Non-Aristotelian Systems and General Semantics* (Lakeville, Connecticut, 1933), pp. 371-385.
49. S.I. Hayakawa, *Language in Thought and Action,* 2nd ed. (New York, 1939), p. 176.
50. *Ibid.*, p. 177.
51. Korzybski, *op. cit.*, p. 384.
52. *Ibid.*
53. Hayakawa, *op. cit.*, pp. 177-178.

XII. Non-verbal language contributes significantly to human communication. Acknowledged on a superficial level for centuries by rhetoricians, this fundamental insight gains in importance when applied to a less restrictive setting than the speaking platform. This importance is based upon the obvious fact that what a receiver sees guides his understanding of what he hears.[54] From the sender's viewpoint, visual feedback clues sent by the receiver provide an invaluable index to the effect of the message. Whichever viewpoint, however, it is true that the continuous, analogic, visual cues which accompany the discrete verbal symbols are often believed when words are not. This point gathers additional credibility when we accept the generalization that visual gestures and facial movements are "adaptive movements of the organism responding to all internal and external stimuli at once."[55] Weaver and Strausbaugh maintain that because the perception of visual language affords almost simultaneous stimulation of the brain, glands, and muscles, whereas spoken language involves discrete stimuli (words in linear presentation), visual language may have more immediate impact.[56] The visual cues which accompany spoken messages are said by Ruesch and Kees to constitute "specific instructions given by a sender about the way messages ought to be interpreted...."[57] They maintain that "the nature of interpersonal communication necessitates that these coincide in time...."[58] If both the information content of the message and the visual clues as to how the receiver should interpret the message do coincide, then the referential aspects of the statement may be clear. "But when action codifications contradict verbal codifications, then confusion is almost certain to result."[59] It appears certain that to obtain satisfactory speech communication fidelity, both the verbal and the visual messages must coincide in interpreted meaning.

The preceding pages have summarized the twelve principles felt by the authors to be basic in any consideration of interpersonal communication theory. It would be presumptuous to presume that the listing was definitive, for one might argue that the discussion should have included *all* pertinent findings of psychology, sociology, language, rhetoric, and so on. There is merit in such a position, perhaps;

---

54. Weaver and Strausbaugh, *op. cit.*, p. 260.
55. *Ibid.*, p. 261.
56. *Ibid.*
57. Jurgen Ruesch and Weldon Kees, *Nonverbal Communication: Notes on the Visual Perception of Human Relations* (Berkeley, 1956), p. 7.
58. *Ibid.*, p. 193.
59. *Ibid.*

yet this brief summary has focused not on all elements which could be included in theory building, but on those which *must* be included. The precepts discussed warrant maximum priority in any serious theory of human interpersonal communication.

chapter 7

Practice

WHY DISCUSSIONS GO ASTRAY

Irving J. Lee

The points of breakdown in group discussions are many and varied. Much of the time they coincide with the failure of participants to understand each other. Sometimes they occur when the participants understand each other too well. Very often it is by the expression of differences of opinion and interest that ideas are clarified and solutions worked out. But whenever the controversy and conflict signalize a loss of rapport, so that the participants seem to be talking at or past rather than with each other, then the differences should be recognized as disintegrative rather than productive.

A comprehensive catalogue of such disintegrative patterns is not yet available, but the following are typical: when the argument moves from the issue to the personalities; when colloquy between factions is marked by such "ego-statements" as "You're absolutely wrong," "I've had years of experience on this," "I know what I'm talking about," etc.; when a speaker identifies himself so thoroughly with an issue that criticism of it is construed as an attack on him; when one participant fails to deal with a question or argument raised by another who continues to call attention to the failure; when inaccuracy or falsification is charged; when there are discrepancies in the assertions of "the" facts, etc. It is worth noting that these do not mean that breakdown is inevitably at hand. On occasion they are manifested with maintenance of rapport.

On the assumption that the study of the sources of conflict might throw light on the processes of understanding, patterns of disintegration were looked for in fifty discussion groups. This essay summarizes some of the preliminary findings which came from focusing attention on the character of the understanding shown by the participants of what was said.

Reprinted by permission from *ETC: A review of General Semantics,* Vol. IV, No. 2, pp. 29-40. Copyright 1947, by the International Society for General Semantics.

It was realized in the early phases of the investigation that "understanding" was a many-faceted phenomenon. As a working basis, six possibilities (considered neither exclusive nor exhaustive) were isolated.

Understanding$_1$ = the following of directions. A understands$_1$ a time-table, when by following the printed instructions, he is able to board the train he wants. A understands$_1$ B when he does what B tells him to do in the way B wants it done.

Understanding$_2$ = the making of predictions. A understands$_2$ B when A is able to predict accurately what nonverbal action B will take after the utterance.

Understanding$_3$ = the giving of verbal equivalents. A understands$_3$ what B says or writes when he is able to translate the verbalization into other terms which B admits are adequate approximations. A understands$_3$ B when he is able to describe what B wants in terms admitted by or acceptable to B, whether or not A wants the same thing.

Understanding$_4$ = the agreeing on programs. A understands$_4$ B when they will undertake any agreed upon action, whether or not there is verbal agreement.

Understanding$_5$ = the solving of problems. A understands$_5$ a situation or problem when he recognizes the steps that must be taken for its solution or resolution regardless of the facilities or his ability to take such steps.

Understanding$_6$ = the making of appropriate responses. A understands$_6$ the proprieties, customs, taboos, works of art or music, poetry, architecture, etc., when his responses to them are of a sort considered appropriate by B.

Simplicity and Proper Evaluation

Much of the professional concern of those interested in the improvement of "understanding" in communication centers around the means whereby a speaker or writer can "say it clearly" or "put it into plain words" so that the processes occurring in understanding $_{1,2,3}$ can be facilitated. The effort is to reduce the verbal specialization, complexity, incoherence, compression, diffuseness, vagueness, generality, and impersonality by any or all of the known devices of reduction, amplification, concretion, iteration, variation, dramatization, and visualization.

Throughout the study an effort was made to determine the relationship between the conflicts and the degree of clarity of the statements made. The method of analysis consisted mainly of questioning the participants involved both during and after the discussion for their understanding₃ of what was being said. Despite the incompleteness of this procedure there is some evidence that, had the speakers been trained in the rhetorical techniques of simplification and attraction, a sharper understanding₃ would have resulted. As the observations continued, however, it was noticed that no matter how clearly the participants said they understood₃ the arguments, the points of conflict still remained and, indeed, were in many instances sharpened. It was as if this rhetorical emphasis dealt with a symptomatic or marginal matter rather than with the fundamental dislocation.

After twenty of the group discussions had been analyzed and after the sectors of controversy had been re-examined, another definition was added.

Understanding₇ = the making of proper evaluations.[1] A understands₇ B, a thing, a condition, a situation, a happening, a relationship, etc., (i.e., nonverbal phenomena), or what is said about each, when his response is to it rather than to something else; when his sizing-up of anything, any situation, etc., is free of identification of it with anything else; when his taking account of it is not affected by assumptions of which he is unaware; when what he says about the situation, etc., fits it, that is, neither distorts, disorders, oversimplifies, overcomplicates, overgeneralizes, negates, adds to, takes from, nor artifically separates it. A understands₇ anything, then, when his diagnosis, at any moment, is free from identifications and when he is cognizant of the structural relationships discoverable both in what is talked about and in what is said.

The emphasis in the study of the remaining thirty group discussions was turned to a descriptive listing of the kinds of misevaluations manifested. Three of the most persistent are here set out.

The Prevention of Projection

Bertrand Russell introduced the term *propositional function,* concerning which Cassius J. Keyser observed that "it is, perhaps, the weightiest term that has entered the nomenclature, in the course of a hundred years." Roughly, a *propositional function* is a statement containing one or more variables. By a variable is meant a term whose meaning or value is undetermined and to which one or more

---

1. Evaluation involves an integration of the "emotional" and "intellectual," giving an organism-as-a-whole response. This analysis of the methods of proper evaluation was based on formulations developed in Alfred Korzybski's *Science and Sanity* (2nd ed., Lancaster, Pa., 1941).

values or meanings can be assigned at will. A propositional function becomes a *proposition* when a single value is assigned to the variable.

A significant characteristic of the propositional function (e.g., "x are scarce," "Shakespeare was a great writer," "Religion is an opiate," etc.) is that such a statement is neither true nor false, but ambiguous.[2] If to x is assigned the single, more definite value "Houses for rent in 1947"[3] and we say, "Houses for rent in 1947 are scarce," the propositional function has become a one-valued true proposition. "Negroes are cowards" is to be considered a many-valued statement and therefore indeterminate. But assign to the variable "Negroes" the value "Pvt. Woodall I. Marsh of Pittsburgh, of the 92nd Div., who won the Silver Star for taking twelve wounded paratroopers out of the front line to safety, fording a raging torrent in his truck, after an officer had said it couldn't be done," and the resulting statement is a proposition, but now a false one.

A rather considerable amount of the talk in the discussions was carried on in statements containing many-valued variables *as if* they were single-valued. Much too often a permanence and a specificity were assumed in the speaking, where on closer analysis there could be found only processes and varieties, even though concealed by the terms as used. Difficulties were to be expected (and they occurred) whenever the distinction was not recognized and wherever there was confidence that single values prevailed. It should be noticed that difficulty arises not because variables are used, but only when they are presumed to be something other, i.e., identified with nonvariables.[4]

Some surprise was shown at the San Francisco Conference on World Security when the Polish question became a source of controversy, as both the American and the Russian delegates took for granted a nonexistent singularity in value in the variable "democratic."[5] Democratic$_1$, concerned with the protection of minority opin-

---

2. For a further analysis of this along with the factors of meaninglessness here omitted, see Alfred Korzybski, *op. cit.,* pp. 135-145, and Cassius J. Keyser, *Mathematics and the Question of the Cosmic Mind* (New York, 1935), pp. 4-7.

3. Of course, since there are varying degrees of rigor in the assigning of values, "Houses for rent" can be further located and specified.

4. This does not say that many-valued statements ought to be eliminated from use. It does say that for maximum "understanding," participants must know the difference and not respond as if one were the same as the other. Nor is there any reason why anyone must speak at all times in the rigorous mood of propositions. It is enough, in the present context, to recognize that the lack of rigor, when unnoticed, was a persistent source of one kind of disturbance.

5. See the statement by Dean Virginia C. Gildersleeve in *The New York Times* (Oct. 31, 1945), 21.

ions, is not democratic$_2$, the Soviet notion of racial equality and Communistic dominance. It is not argued that the awareness of the semantic distinction would have dissolved the difference in interests at the conference—but in terms of our findings it is believed that the awareness might at least have exposed the source of the friction which grew out of the belief of each delegation that the other was behaving badly, since had not both agreed on the necessity of "democracy" in Poland?

The mechanism involved here can be put in focus by comparison with the simplicity-clarity doctrine. This view would locate the trouble in the word "democratic," making it the "barrier rather than the medium of understanding." Our view suggests that it might be equally cogent to note the projection-response, i.e., the assumption of a listener that he knew how the term was being used.[6]

At the heart of the projection-misevaluation is the belief that there are values or meanings *in* terms. But values and meanings are assigned to terms by a human nervous system. But so pervasive is the unexamined notion that words can have exact meanings compounded in and of themselves, in the way a tree has branches, that it is often difficult to persuade a listener that in discussion the other fellow may be assigning a value to his variables which is not at all the one the listener would assign if he were speaking.

In the thirty group discussions the projection-developed conflicts arose mainly at three points: in the exploratory phase where the effort is to locate and expose the problem to be talked about; in the search-for-solutions phase where the conflicts of interests arise; and in the formula phase where effort is directed to the search for a program of action on which agreement can be reached. Present findings suggest that irrelevant discords which arise because of failure to uncover the individual values assigned to variables, and because of the unconscious assumption of the participants that each knows how the variables are being used by the others, are an irritating influence on the rest of the discussion.

Obstructionists, either naive or sophisticated, can readily tie up any discussion by insisting on the fixing of all variables. This is the age-old sophistry which insists that terms be defined once and for all.

---

6. John Buchan, commenting upon Marshal Haig's reserve, told the story of the latter's attempt to be friendly with a solitary private by a roadside: "Well, my man, where did you start the war?" Private (pale to the teeth): "I swear to God, Sir, I never started no war." "Start" is a "basic" word, but start with value, equivalent to a place of induction, is not start with value, equivalent to causing a war to begin. This is, of course, projection and by-passing at its simplest level.

But no definition can prevent a speaker from assigning other values to the variables, either by design or accident, as the discussion continues. In fact, the investigation revealed that there is most danger of by-passing when the members of the group hold fast to the belief that since the term has been given a definition everyone will use it in just that way. But it should be clear that no matter how terms are defined, the necessity of analysis for the values being assigned in the course of the talk still exists.

Statements of Fact and Inference

A rich source of misunderstanding[7] was the belief of many of the participants in the factuality of their assertions. It was rarely sufficiently realized that a statement of fact can be made only *after* someone observes some thing or relation. Any utterance made prior to observation or when observation is not possible involves an inference or guess. One cannot speak with more than some degree of probability about what is to happen or about what happened before records were made. Nor, because of the recalcitrance of nature and life, is it possible to be factual about a host of present perplexities. Thus, in 1947, can anyone do more than conjecture about the precise cellular functions which end in cancer?

Although in discussion people are quick to assert "the" facts on any topic, it makes more than a little difference if instead of giving statements which fit observable phenomena they give their conjectured version of what was observed. An example may make the point.

> [In an Ohio State Hospital] . . . the attendant yelled at a patient to get up off the bench so the worker-patient could sweep. But the patient did not move. The attendant jumped up with an inch-wide restraining strap and began to beat the patient in the face . . . "Get the hell up!" It was a few minutes before the attendant discovered that he was strapped around the middle to the bench and could not get up. [7]

The attendant observed one thing but assumed in his response something more, i.e., a reason for the patient's immobility. His analysis of the situation added to what could be observed and must, therefore, be considered inferential.

It seems unlikely that a discussion can be carried entirely on a factual basis using only statements based on the observations of the participants or anyone else. Any argument which seeks to prove that what is true of some, must be true of many, cases, which concludes

---

7. Albert Q. Maisel, "The Shame of Our Mental Hospitals," *Life* (May 6, 1946), 105.

that if a program did or did not work in one place, it will or will not work in an essentially similar place, which supposes that certain effects will follow from the operation of indicated causes—such typical lines of argument have an inferential basis which calls for little explication. But if conclusions and suppositions are presented *as if* they were factual and thus necessarily certain rather than tentative and probable, then an identification is at work which must affect the decisions being reached. Furthermore, if inferential utterances are passed off by participants in a discussion as if they were factual or as if they had the same degree of probability as factual statements, then there is created an atmosphere in which the search for understanding$_{4\cdot 7}$ on the issue tends to be subordinated to the vigor of the contending speakers, with the issue decided by attrition rather than by the adequacy of the assertions.

Definition-Thinking

Pete Hatsuoko had been born in this country, though one of his parents had been born in Japan. He went to the public schools and received a degree from the State University. He had never been to Japan. He could not read or write Japanese. He knew only a few Japanese phrases used in family small talk. After his induction into the Army, he was assigned to the Infantry. The orientation program included talks on the nature of the enemy. The captain in charge thought Pete should give one of the talks on "The Japanese Mentality." Pete tried in all candor to explain that he knew practically nothing about Japanese life and culture, that both his and his father's education had been received in this country. "But you're a Japanese," argued the Captain, "and you know about the Japanese. You prepare the talk." Pete did—from notes after he had read any Army handbook and a half-dozen popular magazine articles.

The evaluation of the two men may be analyzed as the prototype of a pattern which occurred frequently in the discussions. In a sense communication between them stopped when the conversation began. The issue was faced on quite different grounds by each. Pete oriented his thinking about facts. He talked in terms of them. He was, as far as is known, making statements which could have been verified or at least verified or at least investigated. The Captain, on the other hand, seemed preoccupied with associations stirred up inside his nervous system by an accident of phrasing. The verbal classification "Japanese" received his attention so that Pete's talking was neglected. It was as if the label Japanese served as a stimulus pushing off the Captain's thinking in a direction removed from the situation. The direction can be plotted by his definition: "A Japanese is a person who knows about the Japanese. It follows, therefore, that Pete Hatsuoko is a person who knows about the Japanese. It follows, therefore, that Pete Hatsuoko can give the talk. Other factors in the situation need not be considered."

The Captain's misevaluation can be viewed as a response to his private verbal definition as if it were something more. The point being made is not that there is anything sinister in the Captain's private conjuring up of images. It is enough to note that the behavior which resulted was of a kind very different from that which would have taken account of the outside phenomena. Furthermore, decisions made on the basis of verbal associations, no matter how elaborate, are not the same as nor commensurate with those derived from consideration of facts. The point, in short, is this: evaluations based on the private elaboration of verbal formulae are not the same as nor should they be equated with evaluations based on verifiable descriptions or observations.[8]

What is important here is not the particular dodging of the issue by the Captain, but that this is a type of reaction which is in evidence in a very wide variety of human situations. Two examples are given.

According to a popular account, George Westinghouse designed a train brake operated by compressed air. After it was patented he struggled to convince railroad men of his invention's value. Cornelius Vanderbilt of the New York Central is said to have replied: "Do you mean to tell me with a straight face that a moving train can be stopped with wind?"

The mechanism of the misunderstanding[7] may be generalized thus:

1. The issue was presented by reference to something nonverbal and observable.

2. The reply was oriented by a verbal definition. "What is wind? Something less solid than iron. A nonmassive thing like wind cannot stop an iron train. Therefore the proposal is to be dismissed." Our discussion experience suggests that the misunderstanding[7] would move directly to overt conflict were the conclusion to be personalized by some such assertion by Vanderbilt as, "Westinghouse, you're a fool."

---

8. An approach to (but not the same as) this distinction may be seen in the somewhat neglected insight of William James that most of the civilized languages except English have two words for knowledge, e.g., *savoir* and *connaitre, wissen* and *kennen,* or *knowledge-about* and *knowledge-of-acquaintance.* The latter is derived from direct experience of fact and situation; the former arises from reflection and abstract (i.e., verbal) thinking.

That this sort of generalized verbalistic orientation to situations is not without its significance in human affairs is, perhaps, sharply presented in Hartley's study of the attitudes of 500 students, using a slightly modified form of the Bogardus Social Distance Scale with the names of some 35 ethnic groups. In the list were included the names of three entirely imaginary nationalities: Danirean, Pirenean, Wallonian. It was found that on the average there was as much prejudice directed against the "none-such" groups as against any other. One concludes that the thinking was in terms of the words, since there were no facts on which the thinking could be based. Or as the investigator puts it: "From the point of view of the experience of students, they must represent groups completely unknown in reality. Even if some students may have chosen to consider the Pireneans to be people who live in the Pyrenees; the Wallonians, Walloons; and the Danireans something else; the fact that they tended to do this is in itself significant. In reality there are no such groups, and for the attributes an individual may assign to them, we must look to the individual for the explanation, not to the group."[9]

The identification of these two broadly characterized modes of thinking in the discussions was rarely as neatly etched or as readily explainable as in these examples, in which the point of conflict is readily evident and from which the heat of controversy is absent. For the most part the misevaluation was concealed by the complexity of the subjects under discussion. When the topics had to do with government and religious activities, labor unions, propaganda, prejudice, taxation, health and social insurance, etc., the argument on even the local and specific issues was often observed to develop around a backlog of readily defined associations which the participants had on the terms "communism," "bureaucracy," "labor racketeers," "big business," "government spending," "Wall Street," etc., quite apart from the fitness of their formulations with the immediate and particular aspect of the topic being talked about.

In one group during the course of the study an attempt was made to correct the misunderstanding[7] of the participants. That group, which was observed in five different discussions, was made up of people who manifested to an unusual degree this orientation by definition. The leader, a man of some experience, had on occasion sought to move the talk from the definition to the factual level and for his effort was accused of taking sides. In an attempt to explain the type of reaction which was producing unnecessary strains he set

---

9. Eugene Hartley, *Problems in Prejudice* (Morningside Heights, N.Y., 1946), p. 26.

up a simple demonstration by means of a conventional formula. They had been discussing the advisability of continuing the Fair Employment Practices Commission. Three recorded speeches, each favoring the continuation of the FEPC, were played. The group was then asked to rank the speakers A, B, and C according to the effectiveness, logical soundness, etc., of the argument. B was judged the best with A and C following. A month later the three speeches were replayed for the group with but one change in the instructions. It was explained that speaker B was a Negro. A was then judged the most effective with C second and B third. Such a result can, perhaps, be accounted for in many ways. But the notion that the members of the group in the second playing of the records were diverted from the speeches to a concern with the definition-associations of the word Negro is nevertheless suggestive.[10]

Conclusions

These three types of reaction which lead to misunderstanding$_7$ by no means exhaust those which have been catalogued. They are presented as indications of a source of conflict and breakdown in a rather limited series of discussion situations.

Suppose participants could be so trained that they did not project their own values into variables, did not respond inferentially as if they were responding factually, and did not identify definition with fact-thinking, etc., would it follow that problems and disagreements in discussions would be thereby solved or resolved? Little in our findings so far could either support or raise doubts about such a conclusion. What is conceivable is this: the study of the sources of misunderstanding$_7$ might, if the lessons were well learned, keep people from the moments when their talk leads to unnecessarily created controversy. Such antisepsis might, perhaps, create the atmosphere in which solutions become possible. Only then would it be desirable to explore the means leading to understanding $_{4,5}$.

It is not yet clear to what extent on-the-ground training in the patterns of proper evaluation will lead to a reduction in the points of

---

10. In this group there was an occasion when there were signs of what could be called "pathological misunderstanding$_7$." This occurred when the leader tried to account for their different responses to the same recorded speeches. A highly verbalized, aggressive member proceeded to lose his temper, even threatening the leader with physical harm for his statement that "to change one's attitude because of the word Negro was not quite sensible." Such an occurrence leads one to wonder whether a person, when unaware of the distinction, can become so immersed in definition-thinking, so habituated to identifying it with fact-thinking, that he may be rendered incapable of facing facts even when they are shown— much less talked about. In this state, identifications become evidence of a kind of unsanity.

disintegration in group discussions. The possibility of locating and charting such points, however, suggests that discussion leaders might well be made more sensitive to the signs of their development. Study might then move to the investigation of means by which such oncoming conflicts can be arrested or deflected.

One further conclusion seems inescapable. Where the basic orientation of a culture makes few semantically critical demands, it will not be surprising if men are isolated from each other by their very modes of communication. This is but a way of implying that progress in "understanding" does not require either the correction or simplification of the language in use, or the creation of special abridgments, but rather that progress depends instead on a reorientation of attitudes toward the verbalizing process itself.

The late Irving J. Lee (1909-1955) was professor of public speaking, School of Speech, Northwestern University, and author of Language Habits in Human Affairs (1941). The Language of Wisdom and Folly (1949), How to Talk with People (1952), and Customs and Crises in Communication (1954). His *posthumously published* Handling Barriers in Communication (1957), *a workbook in the application of general semantics to practical business situations, written in collaboration with Laura L. Lee, is widely used in management training programs.*

DEFENSIVE COMMUNICATION
Jack R. Gibb*

One way to understand communication is to view it as a people process rather than as a language process. If one is to make fundamental improvement in communication, he must make changes in interpersonal relationships. One possible type of alteration—and the one with which this paper is concerned—is that of reducing the degree of defensiveness.

Definition and Significance

Defensive behavior is defined as that behavior which occurs when an individual perceives threat or anticipates threat in the group. The person who behaves defensively, even though he also gives some attention to the common task, devotes an appreciable portion of his energy to defending himself. Besides talking about the topic, he thinks about how he appears to others, how he may be seen more favorably, how he may win, dominate, impress, or escape punishment, and/or how he may avoid or mitigate a perceived or an anticipated attack.

Such inner feelings and outward acts tend to create similarly defensive postures in others; and, if unchecked, the ensuing circular response becomes increasingly destructive. Defensive behavior, in short, engenders defensive listening, and this in turn produces postural, facial, and verbal cues which raise the defense level of the original communicator.

Defense arousal prevents the listener from concentrating upon the message. Not only do defensive communicators send off multiple value, motive, and affect cues, but also defensive recipients distort what they receive. As a person becomes more and more defensive, he

Dr. Gibb (Ph.D., Stanford University, 1943) is at present a private consultant to a number of national organizations. He was Professor of Psychology at The University of Colorado, and he served on the faculties of Stanford University, Michigan State University, and Brigham Young University. He has been Director of Research for the National Training Laboratories and Vice President for Research of the Society for Advancement of Management. During the period between 1953 and 1961 he directed a series of experimental and field studies designed to investigate the arousal and maintenance of defensive behavior in small groups. These studies were financed by a series of grants from the Group Psychology Branch of the Office of Naval Research. The conclusions summarized in this article were derived from analyses of the tapes of human relations training sessions in industrial, educational, and community settings and from coded observations of the sessions themselves. A major part of the data was gathered at training programs conducted by the National Training Laboratories.

Reprinted with permission from *Journal of Communication,* Vol. XI, No. 3, (September, 1961), pp. 141-148.

becomes less and less able to perceive accurately the motives, the values, and the emotions of the sender. The writer's analyses of tape recorded discussions revealed that increases in defensive behavior were correlated positively with losses in efficiency in communication.[1] Specifically, distortions became greater when defensive states existed in the groups.

The converse, moreover, also is true. The more "supportive" or defense reductive the climate the less the receiver reads into the communication distorted loadings which arise from projections of his own anxieties, motives, and concerns. As defenses are reduced, the receivers become better able to concentrate upon the structure, the content, and the cognitive meanings of the message.

Categories of Defensive and Supportive Communication

In working over an eight-year period with recordings of discussions occurring in varied settings, the writer developed the six pairs of defensive and supportive categories presented in Table 8. Behavior which a listener perceives as possessing any of the characteristics listed in the left-hand column arouses defensiveness, whereas that which he interprets as having any of the qualities designated as supportive reduces defensive feelings. The degree to which these reactions occur depends upon the personal level of defensiveness and upon the general climate in the group at the time.[2]

Table 8
Categories of Behavior Characteristic of Supportive
and Defensive Climates in Small Groups

Defensive Climates	Supportive Climates
1. Evaluation	1. Description
2. Control	2. Problem orientation
3. Strategy	3. Spontaneity
4. Neutrality	4. Empathy
5. Superiority	5. Equality
6. Certainty	6. Provisionalism

---

1. J.R. Gibb, "Defense Level and Influence Potential in Small Groups," in L. Petrullo and B.M. Bass (eds.), *Leadership and Interpersonal Behavior* (New York: Holt, Rinehart and Winston, Inc., 1961), pp. 66-81.

2. J.R. Gibb, "Sociopsychological Processes of Group Instruction," in N.B. Henry (ed.), *The Dynamics of Instructional Groups* (Fifty-ninth Yearbook of the National Society for the Study of Education, Part II, 1960), pp. 115-135.

Evaluation and Description

Speech or other behavior which appears evaluative increases defensiveness. If by expression, manner of speech, tone of voice, or verbal content the sender seems to be evaluating or judging the listener, then the receiver goes on guard. Of course, other factors may inhibit the reaction. If the listener thought that the speaker regarded him as an equal and was being open and spontaneous, for example, the evaluativeness in a message would be neutralized and perhaps not even perceived. This same principle applies equally to the other five categories of potentially defense-producing climates. The six sets are interactive.

Because our attitudes toward other persons are frequently, and often necessarily, evaluative, expressions which the defensive person will regard as nonjudgmental are hard to frame. Even the simplest question usually conveys the answer that the sender wishes or implies the response that would fit into his value system. A mother, for example, immediately following an earth tremor that shook the house, sought for her small son with the question: "Bobby, where are you?" The timid and plaintive "Mommy, I didn't do it" indicated how Bobby's chronic mild defensiveness predisposed him to react with a projection of his own guilt and in the context of his chronic assumption that questions are full of accusation.

Anyone who has attempted to train professionals to use information-seeking speech with neutral affect appreciates how difficult it is to teach a person to say even the simple "who did that?" without being seen as accusing. Speech is so frequently judgmental that there is a reality base for the defensive interpretations which are so common.

When insecure, group members are particularly likely to place blame, to see others as fitting into categories of good or bad, to make moral judgments of their colleagues, and to question the value, motive, and affect loadings of the speech which they hear. Since value loadings imply a judgment of others, a belief that the standards of the speaker differ from his own causes the listener to become defensive.

Descriptive speech, in contrast to that which is evaluative, tends to arouse a minimum of uneasiness. Speech acts which the listener perceives as genuine requests for information or as material with neutral loadings is descriptive. Specifically, presentations of feelings, events, perceptions, or processes which do not ask or imply that the receiver change behavior or attitude are minimally defense producing. The difficulty in avoiding overtone is illustrated by the problems of news reporters in writing stories about unions, communists, Negroes, and religious activities without tipping off the "party" line of the newspaper. One can often tell from the opening words in a news article which side the newspaper's editorial policy favors.

Control and Problem Orientation

Speech which is used to control the listener evokes resistance. In most of our social intercourse someone is trying to do something to someone else—to change an attitude, to influence behavior, or to restrict the field of activity. The degree to which attempts to control produce defensiveness depends upon the openness of the effort, for a suspicion that hidden motives exist heightens resistance. For this reason attempts of nondirective therapists and progressive educators to refrain from imposing a set of values, a point of view, or a problem solution upon the receivers meet with many barriers. Since the norm is control, noncontrollers must earn the perceptions that their efforts have no hidden motives. A bombardment of persuasive "messages" in the fields of politics, education, special causes, advertising, religion, medicine, industrial relations, and guidance has bred cynical and paranoidal responses in listeners.

Implicit in all attempts to alter another person is the assumption by the change agent that the person to be altered is inadequate. That the speaker secretly views the listener as ignorant, unable to make his own decisions, uninformed, immature, unwise, or possessed of wrong or inadequate attitudes is a subconscious perception which gives the latter a valid base for defensive reactions.

Methods of control are many and varied. Legalistic insistence on detail, restrictive regulations and policies, conformity norms, and all laws are among the methods. Gestures, facial expressions, other forms of nonverbal communication, and even such simple acts as holding a door open in a particular manner are means of imposing one's will upon another and hence are potential sources of resistance.

Problem orientation, on the other hand, is the antithesis of persuasion. When the sender communicates a desire to collaborate in defining a mutual problem and in seeking its solution, he tends to create the same problem orientation in the listener; and, of greater importance, he implies that he has no predetermined solution, attitude, or method to impose. Such behavior is permissive in that it allows the receiver to set his own goals, make his own decisions, and evaluate his own progress—or to share with the sender in doing so. The exact methods of attaining permissiveness are not known, but they must involve a constellation of cues and they certainly go beyond mere verbal assurances that the communicator has no hidden desires to exercise control.

Strategy and Spontaneity

When the sender is perceived as engaged in a stratagem involving ambiguous and multiple motivations, the receiver becomes defensive. No one wishes to be a guinea pig, a role player, or an impressed actor, and no one likes to be the victim of some hidden motivation. That which is concealed, also, may appear larger than it really is with the degree of defensiveness of the listener determining the perceived size of the suppressed element. The intense reaction of the reading audience to the material in the *Hidden Persuaders* indicates the prevalence of defensive reactions to multiple motivations behind strategy. Group members who are seen as "taking a role," as feigning emotion, as toying with their colleagues, as withholding information, or as having special sources of data are especially resented. One participant once complained that another was "using a listening technique" on him!

A large part of the adverse reaction to much of the so-called human relations training is a feeling against what are perceived as gimmicks and tricks to fool or to "involve" people, to make a person think he is making his own decision, or to make the listener feel that the sender is genuinely interested in him as a person. Particularly violent reactions occur when it appears that someone is trying to make a stratagem appear spontaneous. One person has reported a boss who incurred resentment by habitually using the gimmick of "spontaneously" looking at his watch and saying, "My gosh, look at the time—I must run to an appointment." The belief was that the boss would create less irritation by honestly asking to be excused.

Similarly, the deliberate assumption of guilelessness and natural simplicity is especially resented. Monitoring the tapes of feedback and evaluation sessions in training groups indicates the surprising extent to which members perceive the strategies of their colleagues. This perceptual clarity may be quite shocking to the strategist, who usually feels that he has cleverly hidden the motivational aura around the "gimmick."

This aversion to deceit may account for one's resistance to politicians who are suspected of behind-the-scenes planning to get his vote, to psychologists whose listening apparently is motivated by more than the manifest or content-level interest in his behavior, or to the sophisticated, smooth, or clever person whose "oneupmanship" is marked with guile. In training groups the role-flexible person frequently is resented because his changes in behavior are perceived as strategic maneuvers.

In contrast, behavior which appears to be spontaneous and free of deception is defense reductive. If the communicator is seen as having a clean id, as having uncomplicated motivations, as being straightforward and honest, and as behaving spontaneously in response to the situation, he is likely to arouse minimal defense.

Neutrality and Empathy

When neutrality in speech appears to the listener to indicate a lack of concern for his welfare, he becomes defensive. Group members usually desire to be perceived as valued persons, as individuals of special worth, and as objects of concern and affection. The clinical, detached, person-is-an-object-of-study attitude on the part of many psychologist-trainers is resented by group members. Speech with low affect that communicates little warmth or caring is in such contrast with the affect-laden speech in social situations that it sometimes communicates rejection.

Communication that conveys empathy for the feelings and respect for the worth of the listener, however, is particularly supportive and defense reductive. Reassurance results when a message indicates that the speaker identifies himself with the listener's problems, shares his feelings, and accepts his emotional reactions at face value. Abortive efforts to deny the legitimacy of the receiver's emotions by assuring the receiver that he need not feel bad, that he should not feel rejected, or that he is overly anxious, though often intended as support giving, may impress the listener as lack of acceptance. The combination of understanding and empathizing with the other person's emotions with no accompanying effort to change him apparently is supportive at a high level.

The importance of gestural behavioral cues in communicating empathy should be mentioned. Apparently spontaneous facial and bodily evidences of concern are often interpreted as especially valid evidence of deep-level acceptance.

Superiority and Equality

When a person communicates to another that he feels superior in position, power, wealth, intellectual ability, physical characteristics, or other ways, he arouses defensiveness. Here, as with the other sources of disturbance, whatever arouses feelings of inadequacy causes the listener to center upon the affect loading of the statement rather than upon the cognitive elements. The receiver then reacts by not hearing the message, by forgetting it, by competing with the sender, or by becoming jealous of him.

The person who is perceived as feeling superior communicates that he is not willing to enter into a shared problem-solving relationship, that he probably does not desire feedback, that he does not require help, and/or that he will be likely to try to reduce the power, the status, or the worth of the receiver.

Many ways exist for creating the atmosphere that the sender feels himself equal to the listener. Defenses are reduced when one perceives the sender as being willing to enter into participative planning with mutual trust and respect. Differences in talent, ability, worth, appearance, status, and power often exist, but the low defense communicator seems to attach little importance to these distinctions.

Certainty and Provisionalism

The effects of dogmatism in producing defensiveness are well known. Those who seem to know the answers, to require no additional data, and to regard themselves as teachers rather than as coworkers tend to put others on guard. Moreover, in the writer's experiment, listeners often perceived manifest expressions of certainty as connoting inward feelings of inferiority. They saw the dogmatic individual as needing to be right, as wanting to win an argument rather than solve a problem, and as seeing his ideas as truths to be defended. This kind of behavior often was associated with acts which others regarded as attempts to exercise control. People who were right seemed to have low tolerance for members who were "wrong"—i.e., who did not agree with the sender.

One reduces the defensiveness of the listener when he communicates that he is willing to experiment with his own behavior, attitudes, and ideas. The person who appears to be taking provisional attitudes, to be investigating issues rather than taking sides on them, to be problem solving rather than debating, and to be willing to experiment and explore tends to communicate that the listener may have some control over the shared quest or the investigation of the ideas. If a person is genuinely searching for information and data, he does not resent help or company along the way.

Conclusion

The implications of the above material for the parent, the teacher, the manager, the administrator, or the therapist are fairly obvious. Arousing defensiveness interferes with communication and thus makes it difficult—and sometimes impossible—for anyone to convey ideas clearly and to move effectively toward the solution of therapeutic, educational, or managerial problems.

A CONSIDERATION OF THE RHETORICAL CAUSES
OF BREAKDOWN IN DISCUSSION*

Edwin Black

Group discussion, as an object of study, presents as varied and complex a phenomenon as appears on the human scene. Scholars from diverse disciplines have investigated it with their sights on the personalities of the participants, on its educative and persuasive effects, and on a number of other aspects of the process. Each point of view, as it has been brought more sharply into focus, has provided an enriched understanding of group discourse.

This study was motivated by the question of whether there is a body of characteristics common to discussion and to public address; whether, indeed, one can intelligently use the language of rhetorical theory in talking about group discourse. Casual reflection, at least, justifies the assumption of some relationship between rhetoric and discussion, since an essential feature of each is the manipulation of language symbols. A long history of practical application further indicates the utility of rhetorical theory. These considerations, insofar as they are valid, point to the conclusion that an investigation of some aspect of group discussion conducted from a specifically rhetorical point of view should prove fruitful. Induced by this expectation, the primary concern of the present study was with the rhetorical causes of breakdown in discussion. Rhetorical considerations were taken to be those affecting the choice of the available means of persuasion and exposition, and the investigation sought to determine whether, and in what ways, these may cause or contribute to disruptions in group discourse.

Once an investigator has crystallized the questions which he wishes to answer, his next problem is the selection of relevant and meaningful data for his inquiry. The raw materials for this study were assembled by auditing some thirty-five classroom discussions recorded over a period of several years at Cornell University. All major types of discussion were represented in the sampling, including closed-group discussions, public discussions, and colloquies. Portions of these discussions which made no discernible contribution to group understanding or to the co-operative deliberation of a problem were defined as breakdowns. These breakdowns were isolated and submitted to three judges for verification as meeting the terms of the definition.

Reprinted with permission of the *Speech Association of America.* From *Speech Monographs,* Vol. XXII, No. 1 (March, 1955), pp. 15-19.
*Based upon M.A. thesis, Cornell University, 1953, directed by Carroll C. Arnold.

Nineteen passages of discussion, each containing one or more break-downs, were retained for detailed analysis, each having been unanimously confirmed by the judges. These were the materials studied for rhetorical factors or configurations occurring frequently enough to suggest causes of the disruptions. The examination of these passages was analytical, not experimental, since *its object was to discover hypotheses rather than to test them.*

When the portions of unproductive discussions were compared, it appeared that some key contributions, while continuous, fluent, and coherent, seemed to contribute nothing to the purposes of the discussions. These irrelevancies were, of course, *digressive* breakdowns. There were other individual contributions which did not initiate a futile line of inquiry, but which seemed discontinuous, which were ignored by the group, apparently misunderstood by the group, or which the group explicitly refused to consider. These comments were, in short, *ambiguous.*

There seemed to be distinct differences in the rhetorical character of the *digressive* and the *ambiguous* contributions. While there was some overlapping, most of the breakdowns fitted rather clearly into one or the other classification. So neat a dichotomy is certainly open to suspicion, but it proved to be convenient for this study. The implications of this dichotomy's having some basis in reality as well as in convenience will be discussed later.

Beyond suggesting a possible way of classifying disruptions, detailed examination of the breakdowns gave rise to several tentative hypotheses concerning the rhetorical causes of unsuccessful communication in discussion. Some of these hypotheses were obvious and are familiar to all who study group discussion. That failure to agree upon the meaning of a term and that lack of an objective referent for a term may lead to confusion in discussions are typical of the commonly accepted and familiar hypotheses supported by this research. However, three other hypotheses concerning causes of breakdown in discussion, perhaps less familiar to students of the process, also emerged; it is to these that the remainder of this essay will be devoted.

When the digressive breakdowns were examined, they were found, without exception, to be preceded by contributions which ended on a level of communication which was less abstract than the level on which the discussion had been proceeding. Hence, this hypothesis was suggested: *An individual contribution which ends on a level of communication less abstract than the level on which the discussion had been proceeding is likely to cause a breakdown.*[1] What this hypothesis says, in effect, is: when a discussant descends from the general to the specific without returning to the general, a digression is likely to result. The members of the group become involved in particulars, frequently allowing minutes to obscure the ultimate aims of the discussion.

The configuration described by this hypothesis was present in all cases of digression studied. Assuredly, this is not to say that every time such a configuration occurs, a digression will inevitably follow: but, the fact that each digression was preceded by verbal communication which descended from the abstract to the specific without returning to the abstract strongly suggests that here may be a contributing cause of digressive disruptions.

An especially interesting pattern also recurred among the digressive breakdowns. Often the absence of a suitable general term by which to denote, abstractly, a complicated concept or process forced discussants to become bogged down in a mass of inutile details. Perhaps the following example from one of the discussions will serve to clarify the difficulty under consideration here.

The discussants were trying to find the best means of correcting inflation. They were concerned with the economic system: a dynamic process. The discussion flowed from a consideration of dollar value to government spending, to credit, to consumer spending, to taxes, with few questions being resolved. The discussants were virtually drowning in a sea of detail because, among other reasons, it is the peculiar nature of an economic process that no single element in it can be entirely understood apart from its function in the process as a whole. The alteration of any of the variables affects the process and all other variables within the process. The discussants could not surmount this difficulty. They had no terms with which to denote the entire process on which the discussion was centered. Hence, while the discussants seemed to be aware that there is an interaction between dollar value and government spending, their common vocabulary did not permit them to denote this interaction in a way which all would understand; they were compelled to discuss dollar value and government spending as two disparate variables. The result was a preoccupation with details to the detriment of the discussion.

This example illustrates one pattern of digression. Its repeated appearance supported the hypothesis that: *The absence in a discussion of a commonly accepted and sufficiently inclusive term to de-*

---

1. Those familiar with the Process of Abstraction described by general semanticists will recognize that I have been influenced in phrasing by this concept.

*note a relevant abstract process or complex ideological structure is
likely to cause a breakdown.*

If this hypothesis should be true, it would have some interesting
implications for students and teachers of group discussion. Like the
earlier hypothesis, this, too, intimates that verbal concreteness can,
under certain circumstances, be just as destructive as excessive abstraction, and both suggest important qualifications of our injunction
against abstraction and in favor of concrete terminology. Also, they
suggest a re-examination of traditional modes of attacking problems
in discussion.

The presently proposed hypothesis, especially, indicates that there
must be some modification of the customary stress on analyzing,
before solutions are considered, as many aspects of a problem as
come within the awareness of the group. Perhaps there is a point
beyond which problem analysis becomes detrimental to discussion.
Even so prosaic a question as whether to put on a blue or a brown
suit in the morning could, if one would let it, quite logically lead to a
consideration of social mores, aesthetics and epistemology. Indeed,
one could very conceivably spend the rest of his life analyzing the
problem without exhausting the topics relevant to the decision he
must make, and die aged, wise, and undressed. Thus, the point at
which analysis of the problem ceases and deliberation of solutions
begins will be an arbitrary point. The hypothesis suggests that the
extent of problem analysis in discussion should be conditioned by
the quantity of data which the discussants can manipulate.

In addition to the suggestions that unrecovered descent from abstraction and lack of comprehensive terminology may cause discussions to falter, the passages of discussion studied hint at a third
hypothesis, describing a rhetorical cause of ambiguity.

One way of seeking the source of ambiguity or loose thinking in
general is to look at logic. In an effort to discern whether any of the
logical constructions in discussion contributions caused breakdowns,
an attempt was made to analyze the materials of the study by the
standards of formal, Aristotelian logic. The attempt yielded nothing.
Not a single syllogism was to be found in the passages, and none of
the cases of induction met the ordinary tests of formal validity, even
when the contribution proved helpful in the discussion. The conclusion, then, was that discussion, like public speaking, rarely utilizes
formal logic.

A positive finding was that the rhetorical counterparts of induction and deduction—example and enthymeme, respectively—
appeared as the basic logical elements of the discussions. The sugges-

tion of a common logical system in public speaking and discussion points to a more than adventitious relationship between traditional rhetoric and discussion.

The very use of enthymemes instead of scientific syllogisms introduces the hazard of ambiguity. More than this, the use of enthymemes in discussions concerning human affairs appears to introduce some special problems related to the clarification of values. It seemed to be characteristic of the discussions studied that the major premise of each enthymeme stated a value, while the minor premise defined a specific instance and the conclusion applied the value to the specific instance. Rarely were the conclusion and both premises explicated; usually, they were left for the listeners to infer from only one of the premises. It would, of course, make no difference whether the premises were stated or whether one or both were tacitly understood. The argument would be an enthymeme in either case, since authorities now seem generally agreed that truncation is not the distinctive factor differentiating an enthymeme from a scientific syllogism.[2]

But what occurs when the value premise is not perceived or accepted by listeners? One would suppose that collaborative thinking must break down. This is, in fact, precisely what happened in some of the discussions audited, and this pattern of breakdown occurred frequently enough to suggest the following hypothesis: *The failure to explicate the major premise of an enthymeme when the premise is not perceived to be a value of the discussants is likely to cause a breakdown.*

Not only did misunderstanding of value premises cause breakdowns, but divergence of values also contributed to ambiguity, particularly when the divergence was not recognized by discussants. The data employed in this study, as well as theoretical considerations, make it appear that a certain minimum of agreement on values is necessary in a discussion. Unless discussants have at least this minimal consonance of values, they are unable even to agree that the problem which they are to deliberate exists.

All of these considerations seem to mean, for discussion, that the failure to explicate the first premise of an enthymeme, either when the value contained therein is not recognized or when it is not shared by the discussants, can cause a breakdown characterized by ambiguity.

---

2. Edward H. Madden, "The Enthymeme: Crossroads of Logic, Rhetoric, and Metaphysics," *The Philosophical Review,* LXI (1952), 368-376; James H. McBurney, "The Place of the Enthymeme in Rhetorical Theory," *Speech Monographs,* III (1936), 49-74.

In summary, an attempt was made to detect sources of disruption in the rhetorical elements of group discourse. The study indicated that breakdowns have their sources in, among other things, a descent in verbal abstraction without a subsequent ascent, the lack of comprehensive terminology to denote a complex of ideas or a process, and the failure to verbalize value premises which are not perceived or shared by the listeners. How many of these and other concepts of traditional rhetoric and how much of its vocabulary are capable of being transferred to discussion? The query has never been answered, and studies leading to its determination might prove profitable. Certainly the conclusions from this investigation cannot be taken as final; they are untested and, hence, but tentative. However, should experimentation validate these hypotheses, we shall have advanced another step toward a rhetorical theory for group discussion.

An especially intriguing problem raised by this research is that of the relationship between discussion and rhetorical logic. The data indicated that breakdowns following from misused examples are digressive, and that breakdowns following from misused enthymemes are characterized by ambiguity. May it not be significant that the two types of breakdowns should seem to bear so close a relation to the two types of proofs in rhetoric? The Aristotelian formula is: "Whenever men in speaking effect persuasion through proofs, they do so either with examples or enthymemes; they use nothing else."[3] The formula suggested by this study is: Whenever breakdowns occur in discussion, they occur either as digressions or ambiguities, and nothing else. Some of the questions raised when these two propositions are contemplated side by side are: Is there a consistent relationship obtaining between the forms of rhetorical reasoning and the types of breakdown in discussion? Do misuse of example and misuse of enthymeme produce distinctive types of breakdown? Do all breakdowns in group deliberation have misuses of rhetorical logic at their source? Here, certainly, are problems enough for several inquiries concerned with the relationship between rhetoric and discussion—inquiries which might, in time, lead to the delineation of a systematic rhetoric of discussion, a theoretical formulation to guide future research.

---

3. Lane Cooper, trans., *The Rhetoric of Aristotle* (New York, 1932), p. 10.

OBSTACLE—WORDS IN GROUP CONFERENCE

Norman C. Stageberg

Since group discussions involve oral discourse, they face the pit-falls common to communication by verbal symbols. Both intentional and unintentional distortions of a conferee's statements seem almost inevitable and unintentional rational but highly emotional human beings gather around the conference table. Single words frequently seem to be obstacles to the forward movement of the discussion. Such obstacle-words cause delay and confusion. Particular kinds seem to be especially obstructive, and an understanding of these necessary to straighten out the snarls that often entangle discussion. We purpose here to offer a brief account of these offenders, dealing with seven categories which have been drafted from linguistics and logic. The illustrative examples are drawn mainly from the military because the material is a part of the language instruction that has been given to group-conference classes at the Air Command and Staff School of the Air University.

The kinds of obstacle-words that seem to have special importance in group conference are these: equivocal words, relative words, classi-fiers, fictions, emotive words, projective adjectives, and incomplete terms. These categories are functional, and it is understood that a word may cross boundary lines.

Equivocal Words

Equivocal words are those which, in a speech situation, may be interpreted in more than one sense. Most words in English, as a glance through a dictionary will show, have numerous meanings. But when a word is used in speech it is usually intended to have a single meaning. It is given this singleness of meaning by the context, which cuts off inappropriate senses and limits our understanding to the meaning intended by the speaker. The context must be so limitary that only one of the lexical meanings of the word is communicated to the mind of the listener. A limitary context that is not sufficiently restrictive will result in equivocal words. For example, the word student is equivocal in this sentence: "Rating scales are useful for student evaluation." This conference member might be referring to

Reprinted with permission from *The Journal of Communication*, Vol. II, No. 1, (May, 1952) pp. 82-87.

Norman C. Stageberg—Captain United States Air Force, Air University, Maxwell AFB, Montgomery, Alabama. On leave-of-absence from his position as Professor of English at Iowa State Teachers College, Cedar Falls.

evaluation of students by instructors, or to evaluation of instructors or the course by students. It is possible, however, that the context of this sentence, that is, the sentences which preceded it in discussion, might have been limitary enough to obviate the equivocation that we find in the isolated sentence.

In discussion, equivocal words can cause trouble in two kinds of verbal situations. The first is when a single occurrence of a word may have more than one meaning. For example, we might find on the agenda this proposition to be considered: "Lack of uniform discipline is detrimental to a military school." Here, uniform might mean consistent or it might refer to the care and wearing of the uniform. If, however, the sentence were spoken there would be no equivocation, for the stress would bring out the desired meaning.

The second kind of verbal situation in which equivocal words can cause trouble occurs when a word is repeated with a meaning different from its meaning in a previous context. This example is from a staff conference: "We have all agreed that we want a more business-like administration in our headquarters. I therefore suggest that we bring in officers and airmen who have had business experience." In this quotation the word business-like means efficient; but the second time that business is used it has an entirely different meaning: it means pertaining to commerce, trade, buying and selling. What the officer was really saying was, "Men with experience in buying and selling will give us an efficient administration." This, we know, is not necessarily true. The weakness in the argument was concealed by the equivocal term business. Recently a chairman of a curriculum board prevented equivocation trouble very simply: "We have been using the word block to refer to both the long and short segments of instruction. Should we reserve the word block for the long and find another word, perhaps, unit, for the short segment?"

Relative Words

Relative words are words whose meanings are vague and fluctuating, and depend on what the word is related to or compared with. Take, for example, the adjectives tall and short. Is a six-story building tall or short? If it is located in a town of 4,000 and related to the one-and two-story buildings of the community, it will probably be called tall. If, however, the same building is located in a metropolis of 5,000,000 and is related to the surrounding skyscrapers, it will be considered short. Likewise, all opposite relative adjectives, e.g., fast and slow, heavy and light, hot and cold, can be used to describe exactly the same thing. Our indispensible good is a relative adjective.

When it is stamped in purple on beef in "U.S. grade good," it means the second best of four grades. But in some mail-order catalogues, when applied to articles for sale, it means the lowest of three grades, the others being better and best. Here, then, good means poorest.

In discussion, we can avoid the imprecision of relative words in two ways. The first is by substituting figures for relative words. Instead of saying, "The students in our radio mechanics school need a heavy schedule," we can substitute figures, like "The students in our radio mechanics school need a schedule of 40 classroom hours a week." By such precision, conferees will not lose time debating the meaning of a relative word. A second way to avoid the imprecision of relative words is to substitute a description of observable behavior. As an example let us listen to a conference on promotions.

Master Sergeant Jenkins: "Sir, I don't believe that Corporal Brown deserves a promotion this month. He's been pretty undependable around the hangar."

Capt. Johnson: "Just what has he done that indicates he is undependable?"

Master Sergeant Jenkins: "Well, sir, he was late to work five times in the last two weeks. Then, before the colonel took off for Randolph last week, Brown forgot to check the radio, and the colonel couldn't call in to report his position. And the last two radios he installed were put in wrong because he hadn't read the new tech order."

Capt. Johnson: "I guess that covers it. We'll pass him by this time."

The captain, we see, has had the relative word undependable translated into terms of observable behavior and is therefore in a better position to make his judgment.

Classifiers

All nouns except proper names are classifiers. This is to say, they denote a class of objects or situations. The noun sergeant, for example, denotes a class, of which thousands of individuals are members. Classifiers differ in their breadth, their degree of generality. For instance, F-86 denotes a rather narrow class of objects. The term jet-fighter is broader, more inclusive, fighter plane is still more inclusive; and the broadening of meaning continues through airplane, instrument of war, material.

In group discussion, difficulty of interpretation most frequently occurs when we use classifiers that are too broad, that include too much. Let us illustrate with the very general classifier, instructional devices. The situation is a conference of supervisors in an Air Force technical school for the purpose of improving instruction, and the following conversation takes place:

Sgt. Dick: "I think we need to encourage our instructors to make more use of instructional devices."

Sgt. O'Hara: "I don't think that's necessary. The instructors in my section are constantly making use of examples and comparisons and figures to make clear what they're trying to get across."

Sgt. Nally: "My instructors are using the blackboard all the time. They even complain that there isn't enough board space."

Chairman: "We evidently are not clear on the meaning of 'instructional aids.' Sgt. Dick, can you tell us what you meant by that term?"

Sgt. Dick: "I guess it's too broad. What I meant was visual aids, like the opaque projector and mockups."

We observe here that the chairman quickly brought the discussion to heel by spotting the classifier that was too general and getting it replaced with a narrower word.

Fictions

Fictions are extremely general words like liberty, justice, truth, democracy, communism, socialism, officialdom, American way. Fictions are hard to communicate with because they can mean so many different things. They often refer in a general way to ideas and ideals, but they are also used to label a host of varying objects, acts, and situations. What, for example, does democracy mean? To an American, a Swiss, a Dane, and Russian it would probably mean four different things. What does the American way mean? To a Russian, fed upon anti-American propaganda, it might mean all the objectionable things that he believes Americans do: it would include lynchings, acts of government corruption, lavish living, gangster activities, oppression of the working man, and many others. But to an American it might mean all of the good things that we do: voting at the polls in secret, giving free education to all, allowing private citizens to speak their minds freely in public, giving voluntarily to charitable organizations, and so on. Because the term can include so many thousands of specific acts, it is extremely vague. It is meaningless because it is so meaningful. Often it is used merely as an emotive word, applied to some act because we approve or wish to gain approval of that act.

Suppose, in a policy conference, a staff member wished to substitute sports for a compulsory program of calisthenics. He might offer this reason, "It is the American way to participate in competitive sports, whereas regimented calisthenics smack of Fascism. I suggest, therefore, that we make available to our airmen and officers a rich and varied program of athletics to replace the standardized program of calisthenics that we now have." To this statement a cogent reply would be, "After all, the expression American way covers everything done in the United States; it certainly includes calisthenics. Perhaps we can best discuss this proposal by omitting reference to the American way and Fascism and considering the question itself."

Emotive Words

Emotive words are words which not only communicate a meaning but also express or arouse a feeling.

Many non-verbal symbols are cold and devoid of feeling—those for instance that we see on weather maps and radio facility charts—because we have usually met them before in unemotional situations. But the symbols that we call words are sometimes alive with feeling and suggestiveness and memories because we have experienced them in human and personal situations that have been charged with feeling and emotion for us. The recurrence of a particular word is likely to revive in our consciousness the feelings and associations of the past situations with which it has been associated. Moreover, we all, as members of one country and culture, have a common core of experience—in addition to experiences which are uniquely our own. Hence, there is a relative constancy in our feeling-response to many words that make possible their use in the expression, arousal, and communication of feelings.

Here is an example. We might call a certain pilot self-confident to denote a quality that he possesses and to express our feeling of approval of this quality. But if we wished to describe the same quality and express a feeling of disapproval we could call him cocky or conceited or overbearing. Similarly, many synonymous words differ mainly in the feeling they suggest about what they name or describe. Here are a few pairs: brave-reckless; careful-cowardly; statesman-politician; socialized (medicine)-public (education); leader of the people-rabble-rouser. In the everyday jargon of the military we use hundreds of terms to express a feeling of scorn or of good-natured depreciation, e.g., trigger-happy, scrambled eggs, paddlefoot pilot in the chairborne command, belly-robber, sacked out, and so on.

Emotive words inevitably enter discussion, especially when critical issues are at stake. Sometimes two disputants will bandy back and forth opposing emotive words like those paired together in the preceding paragraph. These words merely express opposite feelings while naming the same things; hence the disputants are really saying only "I like this" or "I don't like this" and are conveying no information. As an example, let us listen in on a flare-up during a meeting of a curriculum board. The background of the situation is this. The present curriculum contains many learning activities that have been planned by teacher-student cooperation. Considerable use is made of panels, committee projects, individualized staff studies, and the like. The program is a flexible one, designed to meet better the needs of the particular individuals in the course. One officer breaks out in rebellion against the program, and the following conversation ensues.

Lt. White: "This Dewey hooey that we've got in our course is nothing but a new-fangled fad."

Capt. Perro: "You're all wrong. The philosophy of Dewey is not a new-fangled fad; it's an up-to-date and progressive movement."

Lt. White: "Dewey is nothing but an educational crackpot who wants to let the rabble run the roost."

Capt. Perro: "Is that so! Dewey is an outstanding educational leader who rightly believes that the people should ascertain their own educational needs."

Lt. White: "Well, I suggest, Mr. Chairman, that we go back to the well-established and time-tried lecture method."

Capt. Perro (interrupting): "You can't call the lecture method well-established and time-tried. It's really antiquated and out-of-date."

Chairman: "Lt. White has suggested that we give up our activities program and use instead the lecture method in our course."

The chairman acted wisely: he ignored the emotive language and stuck to the facts. Such action seems to be the best course, both for chairmen and conference participants, in handling electric words that are charged with feeling.

Projective Adjectives

Projective adjectives are a type of emotive words. These adjectives differ from the emotive words described above in that they really do not describe an object at all; instead they merely reveal the speaker's feeling of approval or disapproval of the object. The feelings of the speaker are projected by the adjective into the object. Projective adjectives of approval and disapproval are frequent in our daily speech, for example in expressions like "The T-47 is a wonderful rifle" and "It's a lousy idea."

By remembering that projective adjectives describe feelings, not objects, we can avoid fruitless arguments in discussion. If, for instance, a conferee should say, "Your plan is cock-eyed," we should understand it merely as an expression of disapproval. The best reply to such a statement is to bypass the adjective and ask for the grounds of disapproval; for example, "What are the objectionable features of my plan?" In this way, the discussion can be moved forward.

Incomplete Terms

Incomplete terms are words which require further elaboration and qualification to be meaningful in a useful way. As an example, let us consider a staff meeting convened to draw up a training program. A member might make this proposal: "I believe that physical training should be required of all officers and airmen on this base because it will be beneficial to them." Beneficial is the incomplete term and must be elaborated upon before the proposal can be intelligently discussed. Beneficial to whom? To the young who are in the pink of condition? To the old whose hearts are conditioned to a sedentary life? Beneficial in what way? To improve health? To increase physical endurance? To provide an outlet for excess energy? To fill up the day?

In discussion, the danger of using incomplete terms is that they may lead to confused thinking. To overcome this danger we must make sure that all such terms are completed by the needed elaboration and qualification.

The give-and-take of discussion gives rise to countless problems in verbal communication—those involving economy of statement, interpretation of figurative language, inference, value-judgment, analogical reasoning, definition, hidden assumptions, and the like. We have dealt briefly above with but one of these problems—the understanding of obstacle-words. An understanding of these will not cure all the ills that talk is heir to, but it may help to untangle some of the backlashes in discussion.

THE LANGUAGE OF VALUE
Robert Benjamin

The ancients often spoke and wrote of the True, the Good and the Beautiful as though these functions were separate and never intruded one on another. Thoughtful communicators of those times usually left no doubt as to whether they were describing a thing, praising or condemning it, or telling how they felt about it. With today's emphasis on dyadic and group communication we are discovering how often two—or even all three—of these functions may be wrapped up in the same utterance. And with these discoveries the spotlight has been turned on language—English, in our case—and on the remarkable ways it permits, even encourages, description and evaluation in the same breath.

Small group research has been quick to pinpoint the concommitance of communication breakdown and what has been loosely termed "loaded language." Talk fails, we are told, when language we expect to be neutral takes on an unannounced slant and parenthetically cheers or boos its object. We now have instruments to measure isolated language segments for their good-or-bad impact. But I think we have nowhere collected and categorized the *linguistic devices* with which we praise or deride. Such a classification will be undertaken in the following pages.

Pure Value Assertions

Absolute Value Assertions

Let us for the moment define "evaluative" as "expressive of approval of disapproval." Thus an evaluative assertion is one in which the formulator approves or disapproves of something (or, in rare cases, places that something on the neutral mark of his approval-disapproval continuum). When we pick pure absolute examples, the distinction seems quite manageable:

(A) "John is red-headed."   (Descriptive)
(B) "John is good."   (Evaluative)

The form in example (B) is called "pure" because it contains no element of description; it voices none of the descriptive predications—if indeed there were any—on which the evaluation may have

Reprinted with permission of author. Professor Benjamin is a Professor of Speech-Communication at San Diego State College. This original essay appears here in print for the first time.

been based.[1] And the distinction between it and the description above seems clear-cut: the first gives a partial description of an object; the second expresses some sort of approval of the object. That John is red-headed (or, more precisely, red-haired) can be verified by direct examination of the object (John), without recourse to any outside factors. But no examination of John can reveal his goodness; it exists somehow *between* his character (the sum of his words, deeds, and predictable behavior) and the approval of the evaluator.

Surely this is distinction enough to justify a linguistic class called "Pure Value Assertions." Note that such assertions normally predicate *properties* ("John has the property called 'good' ") or *class membership* ("John is a good person"). Our classification of value language, then, would start out like this:

Value Assertions

Classification	Linguistic Form(s)
1. Pure value assertions	1. Property or class predication

Value assertions like "John is good," while common enough, rarely ask for an argument. When I turn the final page and say "That was a good book!" I am probably doing one of two things. Either I am (A) uttering a substitute for "I liked it"—which cannot sensibly be denied by anyone but me—or I am, in a manner suggested by Hare,[2] (B) conveying to my wife, who knows my standards for goodness in books, that this book meets some or all of those standards. In this case, my listener could scarcely deny that I hold these standards; and (since she hasn't read it) for her to argue that the book doesn't meet the standards would be senseless.

Relative Value Assertions

On occasion one may hear two persons, both of whom have read a given book, argue (?) over its merits. One must in this case distinguish contentions concerning the wisdom or validity of certain standards (a value-matter) from contentions purporting to measure the

---

1. Note that this "pure" classification does not require that the assertion have no descriptive function, merely that there be no description perceivable in the assertion itself. "John brushes his teeth regularly" (descriptive) may be among the thoughts of the speaker who says "John is good;" but no description is present in the evaluation itself.
2. R.M. Hare: *The Language of Morals* (Oxford, 1962) pp. 112-113.

book against these standards (a fact-matter).[3] But this argument cannot long survive without "good" and "bad" becoming "better than" or "worse than." For by most evaluative standards no book is completely good or bad.[4] So our diagram must distinguish:

Value Assertions

Classification	Linguistic Form
1. Pure value assertions	
a. Absolute value assertions	a. Property or class predication
b. Relative value assertions	b. Relation predication: "X better than Y"

Mixed Value Assertions

When the formulator describes and evaluates in the same sentence, however, some new problems arise.

Value-Predications

Suppose we start with the time-worn "should" and "ought to" assertions. What is John asserting when he says "The U.S. should recognize Communist China"? One possibility is the pure imperative: "Let us recognize Communist China." If we settle for this, no further cognitive analysis is necessary: the proposal stands without external support, and its negation has equal validity. But a second notion seems more plausible: that the formulator is (A) predicting (describing) the results of such action, and (B) *evaluating* these results in the same breath. Schematically:

(A) If we recognize Communist China,
     x, y and z will result.   } **Descriptive**
     If we don't recognize Communist China,
     p, q, and r will result.

(B) x, y, z (the combination) *is better*
     than p, q, r.   **Evaluative**

---

3. Literary critics will undoubtedly object to calling the measurement of literature a fact-matter. The non-factual aspect of criticism, however, can probably in every instance be attributed to disagreement over standards or to vagueness of wording. Once the critical value—standards have been agreed upon, the critical judgments concern only matter of fact.
4. In a land where most men murder, he who merely steals might be called "good." Yet by the same standards a thief is not a good man. Goodness or badness must in the end be measured against expectation or desire, and thus (short of metaphysics) must finally convert to betterness or worseness.

The nature of x, y, z and p, q, r must be found by examining the context surrounding the "should" assertion. (If there is no such context, presumably we revert to the "pure imperative" interpretation.)

One may argue that we have put too many words in John's mouth. But I find no other way to assign to his assertion a validity which I'm sure he expects. In other words, unless he is willing to have his "should" assertion weighed both for probable accuracy of prediction and for acceptability of evaluation, I am—and should be—unwilling to pay it any attention at all.[5]

We are ready, then, for a new category:

Classification	Linguistic Form(s)
1. Pure value assertions	
a. Absolute value assertions	a. Property or class predication
b. Relative value assertions	b. Relation predication: "X *better than* Y"
2. Mixed value assertions	
a. Value-predictions	a. "Should" or "ought to" (occasionally "belongs")[6]

Goal-Oriented Language

Closely resembling the value-prediction is a tangled complex of discourse which may best be called "goal-oriented language." Here one or more mixed value assertions presuppose a goal, purpose, or objective. Because the goal is presupposed and not stipulated, the assertions take on the appearance of pure description. Examples:

(A) "The Negative Income Tax is a progressive step."
(B) "The Negative Income Tax costs too much."
(C) "The Negative Income Tax is an important proposal."

The presence of "progressive" in (A) should warn all but the linguistically naive that an evaluation is involved. For though the genus of progress is change—which can be measured and described—progress must entail a goal or set of goals by which the change may be evaluated and declared (more or less) progressive. All instances of change, that is, are not progressive—only those leading in directions or exhibiting criteria deemed by the formulator to be desirable. This mixed evaluation may be separated into components as follows:

---

5. I might, for example, find his predictions probably, but myself prefer p, *q*, r to x, y, z. Or conversely, I might accept his implied relative evaluations but deny his predictions. It is in this latter instance that most practical debating should occur.

6. E.g., "The teaching of religion *belongs in* the home."

Negative Income Tax will produce x, y, z	Descriptive
Non Negative Income Tax will produce p, q, r	
x, y, z (the combination) *is better than* p, q, r	Evaluative

In (B) the culprit is the adverb "too." If I ask how much the Negative Income Tax will cost annually and someone answers "$14 billion," I have a (predicted) description of an aspect of The Tax (its cost). But what can "too much" mean? How do I examine the Negative Income Tax's predicted cost for suspected too-muchness? Again:

Negative Income Tax will cost $14 billion	(Descriptive)
Not to spend $14 billion for this purpose *is* better than to spend it.	(Evaluative)

The value component in (C) is not immediately apparent. Surely to call the Negative Income Tax "important" isn't to approve or disapprove of its passage. But importance is here predicated not of its passage, but of the proposal itself. And again, we can examine a proposal for its provisions but not for its importance. The latter is a measure of the proposal against other proposals, or of problems it purports to solve against other problems—all ranked along some important-unimportant continuum known to the formulator. And in this continuum lies the pure value element: without it "important" has limited meaning.[7]

Students of discussion are familiar also with such phrases as "the point is. . ." or "the question is. . ." or "that's not the point!," usually serving to direct attention toward one truth and away from another. Such phrases as "important" and "crucial," then, when used as above, must be included as goal-oriented mixed value language.

Classification	Linguistic Form(s)
1. Pure value assertions	
a. Absolute value assertions	a. Property or class predication
b. Relative value assertions	b. Relation predication: "x *better than* y"
2. Mixed value assertions	
a. Value-predictions	a. "Should" or "ought to" (occasionally "belongs")
b. Goal-Oriented Language	b. Normally property or class predication

7. Importance can, of course, be dejectified by certain special definitions of "important." But one must beware of such definitions as "important" "historically significant"; for here one quite likely replaces one's own value-scale with somebody elses.

Even to exemplify the incredible varieties of goal-oriented language would be too much to do here. "Success-failure," "proper," "penalize," "appropriate," "distorted," "improved," "degenerated," and "lost"[8] are but a few. Note that goal-oriented assertions, along with most other value language, seem to predicate properties. Indeed, it appears to be common practice to foist our feelings about a thing onto the thing itself: our adjectival predications merely reflect an understandable reluctance to admit that our views of a thing are not universally held.

This evasive device has a remarkable prototype in the participial "_____ing" form. Examples:

(A) "...a *cooling* effect..."
(B) "...a *receding* hairline..."
(C) "...a *disgusting* exhibition..."

(A) is an apparent exception to the "almost invariably" relational function of participial adjectives. But in (B) a relation is inescapable; there is no way to examine a hairline for its recedingness without comparing it to the same head a while ago, or with one's exceptions regarding hairlines.

Neither (A) nor (B), however, give any hint as to how the author feels about these events. In (C) the author is clearly disapproving, almost to the exclusion of any description: disgustingness is plainly not a part of the performance, but rather relates the performance to an author's evaluation of it. Mixtures of description and evalutation are also found in "stultifying," "enlivening," "widening" (horizons), etc. Thus:

Classification		Linguistic Form(s)
1. Pure value assertions		
a. Absolute value assertions	a.	Property or class predication
b. Relative value assertions	b.	Relation predication: "x *better than* y"
2. Mixed value assertions		
a. Value-predictions	a.	"Should" or "ought to" (occasionally "belongs")
b. Goal-oriented language	b.₁	Normally property or class predication
	b.₂	Participial adjective[9]

8. Like many others "lost" (or "loses") can be purely descriptive. But when a person is said to have lost in an argument or a bargaining session, the goal-expectation tie becomes inescapable.

9. An interesting half-brother is the "_____able" form; e.g., "commendable." Etymologically, "commendable" might mean "capable of being commended;" in practice, it means "ought to be commended." The "_____able" form mirrors the "_____ing" form in disguising an approval behind the formal attribution of a property.

Slanted Language

So-called "slanted" or "loaded" designators, so extensively studied and discussed in recent years are (normally) property or class designators which describe and approve (or condemn) in the same breath. Examples: "stubborn" (for "firm"), "fussy" (for "fastidious" or "precise"), "crackpot" (for "unorthodox").[10] A single replacement will in most instances eliminate (or add) the value element without changing the descriptive component. Further, the value components are temporal and can disappear on reverse through fad, fiat, or erosion. To be square used to require good character, integrity, and candor; now a square (person) enjoys Bach and dislikes rock-and-roll. Language popularly called "loaded" or "slanted," then, does indeed describe and evaluate in one breath, and must be included!

Classification		Linguistic Form(s)
1. Pure value assertions		
a. Absolute value assertions	a.	Property or class predication
b. Relative value assertions	b.	Relation predication: "x *better than* y"
2. Mixed value assertions		
a. Value-predictions	a.	"Should" or "ought to" (occasionally "belongs")
b. Goal-oriented language	b_1.	Normally property or class predication
	b_2.	Participial adjective
c. Slanted language	c.	(?)

Evaluative

When slanting loses its impact, we resort to metaphor.[11]

(A)	"The President notified the Congressional Committee that Executive files would no longer be open to committee investigators."	Description
(B)	"The President took punitive action against the Committee."	Mixed Evaluation (Slanting)
(C)	"The President pulled the rug out from under the Committee."	Mixed Evaluation (Metaphor)

10. Linguistics are familiar with the parlor games, usually attributed to Bertrand Russell, in which designators are conjugated in first, second, and third person with increasing approval or disapproval. Thus: "I am firm, you are stubborn, he is pig-headed"; "I am precise, you are fussy, he is an old woman." (S.I. Hayakawa, *Language in Thought and Action*, Harcourt, Brace and World, N.Y., 1944, pp. 95-97.)
11. A detailed explanation of the metaphorical process is out of place here; see Robert Brown: *Words and Things*, Chapter IV, for a fine discussion.

Of course, all metaphors are not evaluative. Even (C) gets its evaluative component in part from context. One could surely find a context in which even this colorful expression could be uttered by an observer with no interest in the proceedings. Thus:

Classification	Linguistic Form(s)
1. Pure value assertions	
a. Absolute value assertions	a. Property or class predication
b. Relative value assertions	b. Relation predication: "x *better than* y"
2. Mixed value assertions	
a. Value-predictions	a. "Should" or "ought to" (occasionally "belongs")
b. Goal-oriented language	b_1. Normally property or class predication
	b_2. Participial adjective
c. Slanted language	c. (?)
d. Evaluative Metaphor	d. Metaphor

Sentential Evaluation: Evaluative Conjunctions

So far we have looked at evaluative *assertions*. But sentential *connectors* also evaluate. "And" conjoins impartially. "Or," "implies," "because" and a few other logical connectors hitch two assertions together without favoring either. But the word "but," the commonest replacement for "and," usually favors its consequent over its antecedent. "Tom is faster, but Jim is a better passer," usually signifies (or defends) the coach's intention to use Jim rather than Tom. Reverse the assertions—"Jim is a better passer, but Tom is faster," and one tends to place Tom above Jim on the momentary value-scale.

"But" evaluates more markedly in an argument: A asserts something B can't deny; so B supplies a truth of his own preceded by . . . That may be true, *but*. . ." Similar evaluations are suggested by "although," "even though," and "while it is true that. . ., it must be remembered that. . ." In each case one assertion purports to assert a truth somehow more important than that asserted by the other. And, as noted earlier, importance is not a property of a truth or a proposition, but rather someone's evaluation of it.

Classification	Linguistic Form(s)
1. Pure value assertions	
a. Absolute value assertions	a. Property or class predication
b. Relative value assertions	b. Relation predication: "x *better than* y"
2. Mixed value assertions	
a. Value-predictions	a. "Should" or "ought to" (occasionally "belongs")
b. Goal-oriented language	b_1. Normally property or class prediction
	b_2. Participial adjective
c. Slanted language	c. (?)
d. Evaluative metaphor	d. Metaphor
e. Sentential evaluation	e. Conjunctions or conjunctive phrases

Unfortunately[12]—for the receiver, at least—the evaluative conjunction is unnecessary if the truths are selected carefully. Propaganda analysts have long lamented the bland series of carefully selected descriptions—all true—which collectively praise or damn their object as surely as all the linguistic evaluators we can find. Even single descriptions—"Uncle Al is sober tonight"—may imply enough to lead to unfavorable evaluation.[13] But such matters are outside a study of value language: for the language itself is purely descriptive.

The above classification of value language, even in its present tentative form, perhaps warrants a few observations:

(1) The classification is indeed tentative, its coverage incomplete, and its categories subject to question. One might easily argue that "John is good" is fully as mixed as "we should recognize Communist China," and that the schematic separation of descriptive from evaluative components should apply to the former as well as to the latter. (Objectors in this vein would probably prefer "To love your neighbor is good" as illustrative of the pure form.)

(2) One must be struck by the size of the value component in our everyday language. When one removes the evaluations, the commands, the emotive ejaculation, etc., there is not much pure description left. And Toulmin[14] notes that much of what we call "description" is actually definitive in function. Perhaps all this reflects an age where mass media report the world to us all at once; and soon each

12. The reader may enjoy classifying "unfortunately" in this context.

13. C. Roland Hall: "Excluders," *Analysis,* 20 (1959), 1-7.

14. S.E. Toulmin and H. Baier: "On Describing," *Mind* LXI (1952), 13-18.

of us knows what the other knows. To describe to one another in such a world is largely redundant.

(3) The form in which mixed evaluations occur—with traditional value words such as "good," "right," and "just," conspicuous by their absence—confirms a reluctance to own up to the value components of our mixed value assertions. "Pass the salt" is the best way to get salt; why should disapproval of the skate dance be hidden in such ostensible descriptions as, "that disgusting performance" or "degenerate dancing"? The traditional notion suggested earlier—that we tend to project our passions onto their objects—is perhaps an over-simplification. More probably our natural wish to clothe in respectable objectivity our feelings about the world, is interwoven with an instinctive understanding that our evaluations are *not entirely* about ourselves and our descriptions *not entirely* about their object. Surely the continuum approach to the descriptive-evaluative complex deserves closer scrutiny.

(4) Finally, the uneasy edges on all my categories leave me at best skeptical of the final classification chart. I hope the fuzziness is due in large part to the limited skill of the classifier rather than to the ideas involved. But surely any attempt to reduce evaluative discourse to strict categories must contend in the end with overlap and blur. For language has a way of hewing to the needs of its users. And in the present state of human response, what we think, what we feel, what we like, what we want and what we demand are very much mixed up. It should not surprise us to find our language reflecting that mixture.

What is the participant in group deliberation to make of all this? Surely he cannot carry these categories in his head. And even if he could, he would be unable to divorce his own descriptions from his evaluations (even if this were desirable!). Perhaps the most he can expect is to use language much as he has in the past, but *with a greater realization of what he is about.* With some or all participants alert to the hidden evaluations, group discourse runs less risk of needless breakdown: listening becomes more creative, speech more pliant, and hope for consensus more credible.

COMMUNICATION AND GROUP STRUCTURE
Robert B. Crook *

The ideas in this paper are limited to those which the writer considers basic to the understanding of the development of a small face-to-face discussion group from an immature to a mature level of functioning. The assumptions are (1) that communicative behaviors are significantly related to maturing[1] and (2) that the development of valid communication is an essential prerequisite for group effectiveness in solving problems.

Not only do group dynamics contribute to the understanding of communication, but also an analysis of communication helps one to comprehend the dynamics of a group's development. Interactions, both verbal and nonverbal, are dynamic factors which influence the creation and the development of the group structure. The kinds of communications give rise to varying networks which affect not only the structure but also the effectiveness of the group in striving toward its goals.

Immature Group Functioning

Before a group can function effectively it must overcome the semantic confusion which emotional coloring causes. Such a statement as "Let's stop this nonsense and get down to the problem we're here to work on" is interpreted according to the climate of the meeting and the emotional set of the individual. No two persons perceive such a statement in the same way, and highly complex reactions and interactions may result from the diverse perceptions.

Ineffective group functioning is a phenomenon far too complicated for any quick, easy explanation. A consideration of a series of facets of the whole, however, provides an introduction.

Reprinted with permission from *Journal of Communication*, Vol. XI, No. 3, (September, 1961), pp. 136-140.

*Assistant Dean, Teacher Education, Queens College, The University of the City of New York.

1. George C. Homans sees a group as "a number of persons who communicate with one another often over a span of time, and who are few enough so that each person is able to communicate with all the others, not at second hand, through other people, but face-to-face."—*The Human Group* (New York: Harcourt, Brace and Co., 1950), p. 1.
Josephine Klein also regards communication as an essential element in group structure. "The basic elements of the description of group structure are the group members and the communication or 'links' between them. These channels determine the network and the structure of the group."—*The Study of Groups* (London: Routledge & Kagan Paul, Ltd., 1956), p. 41.

Levels of Threat and Difficulty

Among the factors affecting the individual's actions and reactions is the level of threat and difficulty which he perceives in a situation.[2] Sharing information, evaluating alternatives, making recommendations, and solving problems are four levels which are successively more threatening.

The reason that each of these levels is increasingly serious is that as the degree of involvement and commitment becomes greater the threat to satisfaction regarding outcomes and personal enhancement becomes more intense. Gulley clarifies this point when he states that to attain the group goal of enlightenment members must only define, analyze, and exchange information, whereas to solve problems they must define, analyze, evaluate possible solutions, and agree upon one or more decisions to which all or the majority are committed.[3]

The perceptions of the members toward one another, the action demanded, and their involvement and commitment with regard to the action, then, become more sharply delineated as the group moves toward the problem-solving and decision-making level of participation. What the persons are able to communicate about the problem becomes highly charged with emotional feelings and reactions. These emotions, in turn, interfere with constructive thought, for the defenses which individuals erect cause omissions and inaccuracies in the messages which they receive. "Individuals learn to anticipate what is going to be said and therefore not to listen well. They will respond not to what is being said but to their own thoughts. A participant tends to listen only for what fits into his purposes."[4] Moreover, since no two listeners ever have identical perceptual reactions, each member of a group receives a different message whenever someone speaks.

Since the effective functioning of a group thus is closely related to the perceptual aspects of the communicative acts,[5] whatever affects perception adversely must be considered detrimental to valid communication. The perceptual field of the individual is not static; changing from moment to moment, it is a product both of the on-

---

2. Rensis Likert and Samuel P. Hayes, Jr. (eds.), *Some Applications of Behavioral Research* (New York: UNESCO, 1957), pp. 86-88.

3. Halbert E. Gulley, *Discussion, Conference, and Group Process* (New York: Henry Holt & Co., 1960), p. 4.

4. Robert L. Kahn and Charles F. Cannel, *The Dynamics of Interviewing: Theory, Techniques, and Cases* (New York: John Wiley & Sons, Inc., 1957), p. 6.

5. Combs and Snygg believe that communication is possible only through that part of the perceptual field that is common to two or more persons. Thus, communication is an attempt to understand the perceptual field of another.—Arthur Combs and Donald Snygg, *Individual Behavior: A Perceptual Approach to Behavior* (New York: Harper & Brothers, 1959), p. 31.

going interactions among the members of the immediate group and of the past experiences of the individuals.

Dependence and Interdependence

Dependence (authority relations) and interdependence (personal relations)[6] provide a second vantage point for examining immature group functioning. These two orientations are seen in the ways members perceive the handling and distributing of power or authority in the group and in how they perceive one another. Both orientations determine the early behaviors observed in newly formed bodies—for example, rebelliousness, submissiveness, withdrawal, or other similar responses to authority figures. In a beginning group a person may see his colleagues as potential threats in a power struggle and may regard their actions as attempts to dominate and exploit.

The needs are to define the hierarchial status and the role relationships, to develop a set of norms to regulate relations of individuals within the group, and to attain perceptual interdependence. Because of the members' perceptions of authority and its meanings, the attainment of these objectives is difficult. The need for stabilization, however, is one which persons feel, and in the first phase of group development the participants quickly attempt to establish their customary places in the leadership hierarchy.[7] Previous experiences within similar bodies determine how persons see themselves in relation to others and how they feel that the group should function.

Dependency, Pairing, and Fight-Flight

A third set of concepts for examining the immature phase in group development consists of three categories of group interactions: (1) Individuals tend to seek support and direction according to prior experiences and perceptions pertaining to the kind of leader, norms, and procedures which they should have. (2) Participants tend to seek strength and support by pairing with those who seem to agree with them. (3) Persons tend to avoid the unpleasant either by fighting it or by fleeing from it.

These three tendencies, of course, occur in combination, and their relative strengths vary from one situation to another. They also are

---

6. "The core of the theory of group development is that the principal obstacles to the development of valid communication are to be found in the orientations toward authority and intimacy that the members bring to the group."—Warren Bennis and Herbert A. Shepard, "A Theory of Group Development," *Human Relations,* IX (1956), 415-437.

7. Herbert Thelen and Watson Dickerman, "Stereotypes and the Growth of Groups," *Educational Leadership,* VI (Feb., 1949), 309-316.

interrelated to the conflicting desires for dependency upon strong leadership on the one hand and for independence of authority on the other. Thus the dependent and counterdependent behaviors of members come sharply into focus and conflict.

Mature Group Functioning

Change in member perception concerning authority in the group situation must be made if the group is to move to subsequent phases of development and if it is eventually to reach the mature level of high productivity, effectiveness, and morale. Bennis and Shepard[8] describe this final stage as one of valid communication—a level at which the members understand what they are doing, resolve internal conflicts, mobilize their resources, make intelligent decisions, identify and accept group goals, establish and maintain effective leadership, engage in meaningful exchanges of ideas, and develop methods for achieving and testing understanding. This perceptual change regarding authority seems to occur when members begin to grasp the futility of their struggle to achieve leadership structure on an either-or basis—a strong leader versus no leader. Leadership becomes the group's problem and is openly identified and worked out in terms of needed functions.

In mature interaction the individual relates his personal satisfactions and need gratifications to a framework of group achievement and functioning. In respect to atuhority he sees that he can become influential at certain times according to the requirements of the moment.

Perceptual interdependence among its members is still another characteristic of the mature group. It is possible through perceptual interdependence for members to move more directly and with greater clarity to the goal orientation which is necessary for group maintenance and success. Hare, Borgatta, and Bales make the following statement:

> One result of interaction is the mutual adjustment of individual perspectives toward a similarity in certain respects, and toward a knowledge of similarity. The content of this overlap in perspectives and expectations we can call the common culture of the group. Another result of interaction, however, is that the members of the group become more differentiated from each other, both as to what kind of thing overtly and when, and also as to the picture of the group that each individual carries in his mind.[9]

8. *Loc. cit.*
9. Paul Hare, Edgar F. Borgatta, and Robert F. Bales, *Small Groups: Studies in Social Interaction* (New York: Alfred A. Knopf, Inc., 1955), p. 345.

Conclusion

Communications or interactions are the critical links among the members of a group. They permit the development and the maintenance of a common group culture or structure. The most critical barriers to mature group functioning are the orientations toward leadership or authority and toward intimacy. Awareness concerning these two problems is necessary before a group can undertake goal clarification and orientation. To have valid communication is to have a group that has integrated both work and emotional activities in such a way that neither is denied and both are mutually supportive. To have effective communications, then, is to have an effective group.

BIBLIOGRAPHY
Part III
Group Communication: Theory and Practice

Agyris, Chris. *Interpersonal Competence and Organization Effectiveness*, Homewood, Ill.: Dorsey Press, 1962.
———. "The Individual and Organization: Some Problems of Mutual Adjustment," *Administrative Science Quarterly* (June, 1957).
American Management Association. *Are You A Good Listener?*, New York: 1955.
Anshen, Ruth Nanda (ed.). *Language: An Enquiry into Its Meaning and Function*, New York: Harper and Row, Publishers, 1957.
Asch, Solomon E. *Social Psychology*, New York: Prentice-Hall, 1952.
Babcock, C. Merton. *Ideas in Process: An Anthology of Readings in Communication*, London: Martin Secker and Warburg, 1955.
Bach, Robert O. *Communication: The Art of Understanding and Being Understood*, New York: Hastings House, 1963.
Bales, Robert F., Fred L. Strodtbeck, Theodore M. Mills and Mary Roseborough. "Channels of Communication in Small Groups," *ASR*, 16 (1951), 75-84.
Bass, Bernard M. and G. Dunteman. "Behavior in Groups as a Function of Self, Interaction, and Task Orientation." *Journal of Abnormal and Social Psychology*, 66 (1963), 419-428.
Bennis, Warren G., Kenneth D. Benne and Robert Chin. *The Planning of Change: Readings in Applied Behavioral Sciences*, New York: Holt, Rinehart and Winston, 1961.
Berlo, David K. *The Process of Communication*, New York: Holt, Rinehart and Winston, 1960.
Birdwhistell, Ray L. *Introduction to Kinesics*, Washington, D.C.: Department of State, Foreign Service Institute, 1952.
Black, Max (ed.). *The Importance of Language*, Englewood Cliffs, N.J.: Prentice-Hall, Inc., 1962.
Blackmur, R.P. *Language as Gesture*, New York: Harcourt, Brace and Company, 1952.

Blake, Robert R. and Jane S. Mouton. *Group Dynamics: Key to Decision Making*, Houston, Texas: Gulf Publishing Company, 1961.

Bois, J. Samuel. *The Art of Awareness*, Dubuque, Ia.: William C. Brown Company, Publishers, 1966.

Brennan, Lawrence D. *Modern Communication Effectiveness*, Englewood Cliffs, N.J.: Prentice-Hall, 1963.

Broadbent, Donald E. *Perception and Communication*, New York: Pergamon, 1958.

Brown, Roger. *Words and Things*, New York: The Free Press, 1958.

Campbell, James H. and Hal W. Hepler (eds.). *Dimensions in Communication: Readings*, Belmont, Calif.: Wadsworth Publishing Company, Inc., 1965.

Chase, Stuart. *The Tyranny of Words*, New York: Harcourt, Brace and World, 1954.

Cherry, Colin. *On Human Communication*, New York: Science Editions, Inc., 1961.

Church, Joseph. *Language and the Discovery of Reality*, New York: Random House, 1961.

Condon, John C. Jr. *Semantics and Communication*, New York: The Macmillan Company, 1966.

Cortright, Rupert and George Hinds. *Creative Discussion*, New York: Macmillan Company, 1959.

Crook, Robert B. "Communication and the Group Structure," *The Journal of Communication*, XI, 3 (September, 1961), 136-140.

Crowell, Laura, Allan Katcher and S. Frank Migamoto. "Self Concepts of Communication Skill and Performance in Small Group Discussion," *Speech Monographs*, XXII (March, 1955), 31-38.

Dance, Frank E.X. (ed.). *Human Communication Theory: A Book of Readings*, New York: Holt, Rinehart and Winston, Inc., 1966.

Deutsch, M. "Some Factors Affecting Membership Motivation and Achievement Motivation in a Small Group," *Human Relations*, 12 (1959), 81-95.

Dewey, John. *How We Think*, Boston: D.C. Health and Company, 1933.

Dowe, Clyde W. "Communication as Interaction and Transaction: A Behavioral Description," *ETC.*, XV (Summer, 1958), 274-282.

Duker, Sam. *Listening: Readings*, New York: Scarecrow Press, Inc., 1966.

Duncan, Hugh Dalziel. *Communication and the Social Order*, New York: Bedmunster, 1962.

Ekman, Paul. "Differential Communication of Affect by Head and Body Cues," *Journal of Personality and Social Psychology*, 2 (1965), 726-735.

Endler, Norman S. "The Effects of Verbal Reinforcement on Conformity and Deviant Behavior," *Journal of Social Psychology*, 66 (1965), 147-154.

Fearnside, W. Ward and William B. Holther. *Fallacy*, Englewood Cliffs, N.J.: Prentice-Hall, Inc., 1959.

Festinger, Leon. *A Theory of Cognitive Dissonance*, Evenstein: Row, Peterson and Company, 1957.

Festinger, L., S. Schachter and K. Back. *Social Pressure in Informal Groups*, New York: Harper and Brothers, 1950.

Fries, C.C. *Linguistics and Reading*, New York: Holt, Rinehart and Winston, 1962.

Guetzkow, Harold and H.A. Simon. "The Impact of Certain Communication Nets Upon Organization and Performance in Task-Oriented Groups," *Management Science*, 1 (1955), 233-250.

Hall, D.M. *Dynamics of Group Action,* Danville, Ill.: Interstate Printers and Publishers, 1957.

Hall, Edward T. *The Silent Language,* Garden City: Doubleday, 1959.

Haney, William V. *Communication and Organizational Behavior,* rev. ed., Homewood, Ill.: Richard D. Irwin, Inc., 1967.

———. *Communication: Patterns and Incidents,* Homewood, Ill.: Richard D. Irwin, Inc., 1960.

Hartley, E.H. and R.E. Hartley. *Fundamentals of Social Psychology,* New York: Knopf, 1952.

Hayakawa, S.I. *Language, Meaning and Maturity,* New York: Harper, 1954.

———. *Symbol Status and Personality,* New York: Harcourt, Brace and World, 1963.

———. *The Use and Misuse of Language,* New York: Fawcett World Library: Crest, Gold Medal and Premier Books, 1962.

Heider, Friz. *The Psychology of Interpersonal Relations,* New York: Wiley, 1958.

Jenkins, David H. "Predictions in Interpersonal Communication," *The Journal of Communication,* XI (September, 1961), 129-135.

Jenkens, Russell L. "Discussion Procedures in Communication," *The Journal of Communication,* II, 2 (November, 1952), 26-30.

Johnson, Wendell. *People in Quandaries,* New York: Harper and Brothers, 1946.

———. *Your Most Enchanted Listener,* New York: Harper, 1956.

Korzybski, Alfred. *Science and Sanity: An Introduction to Non-Aristotelian Systems and General Semantics* (1933), Lakeville, Conn.: Institute of General Semantics, 1948.

Leavitt, Harold J. "Some Effects of Certain Communications Patterns on Group Performance," *Journal of Abnormal and Social Psychology,* 46 (1951), 38-50.

Lee, Irving. *Customs and Crises in Communication,* New York: Harper and Brothers, 1954.

———. *How to Talk With People,* New York: Harper and Brothers, 1952.

———. *Language Habits in Human Affairs,* New York: Harper and Brothers, 1941.

———. *The Language of Wisdom and Folly,* New York: Harper and Brothers, 1949.

Lerea, Louis and Alvin Goldberg. "The Effects of Socialization Upon Group Behavior," *Speech Monographs,* XXVIII (March, 1961), 60-64.

Lewis, G.W. (ed.). *Resolving Social Conflicts: Selected Papers on Group Dynamics,* New York: Harper and Brothers, 1948.

Maier, Norman R. *Principles of Human Relations: Applications to Management,* New York: Wiley, 1952.

Maslow, Abraham H. *Motivation and Personality,* New York: Harper and Row, Publishers, 1954.

Maslow, Abraham H. *Toward a Psychology of Being,* Princeton, N.J.: D. Van Nostrand Company, Inc., 1962.

Maslow, Abraham H. *The Psychology of Science,* New York: Harper and Row, 1966.

Mason, Stella E. *Signs, Signals, and Symbols,* Springfield, Ill.: Charles C. Thomas, 1963.

Matson, F.W. and A. Montague (eds.). *The Human Dialogue: Perspectives on Communication,* New York: Free Press, 1967.

Meerloo, J.A.M. *Conversation and Communication: A Psychological Inquiry Into Language and Human Relations,* New York: International Universities Press, 1952.

Menninger, Karl A. *The Human Mind,* New York: Alfred A Knopf, Inc., 1945.

Miyamoto, S. Frank, Laura Crowell and Allan Katcher. "Communicant Behavior in Small Discussion Groups," *Journal of Communication,* VII (Winter, 1957), 151-160.

Moment, David and Abraham Zaleznik. *Role Development and Interpersonal Competence—An Experimental Study of Role Performances in Problem-Solving Groups,* Boston: Harvard University, 1963.

Mullahy, Patrick. *Study of Interpersonal Relations,* New York: Hermitage House, 1949.

Murray, Elwood. "Self-Guidance Through Group Approaches and General Semantics," *Education,* 70, 8 (April, 1950), 501-505.

Nichols, Ralph G. and Leonard A. Stevens. *Are You Listening?* New York: McGraw-Hill Book Company, 1957.

———. "Listening to People," *Harvard Business Review,* 35, 5 (Sept.-Oct., 1964), 85-93.

Norfleet, Bobbie. Interpersonal Relations and Group Productivity," *Journal of Social Issues,* 4, 2 (1948), 66-69.

Ogden, C.K. and I.A. Richards. *The Meaning of Meaning,* New York: Harcourt, Brace and World, Inc., 1952.

Payne, Stanley LeBaron. *The Art of Asking Questions,* Princeton, N.J.: Princeton University Press, 1951.

Piaget, Jean. *The Language and Thought of the Child,* New York: Merridian Books, 1955.

Pierce J.R. *Symbols, Signals and Noise,* New York: Harper and Row, 1961.

Rapoport, Anatol. *Science and the Goals of Man: A Study in Semantic Orientation,* New York: Harper and Row, Publishers, 1950.

Redding, W. Charles and George Sanborn (eds.). *Business and Industrial Communication: A Source Book,* New York: Harper and Row, Publishers, 1964.

Roethlisberger, F.J. "Barriers to Communication Between Men," *ETC.,* IX (Winter, 1952), 89-93.

Rogers, Carl R. *Client-Centered Therapy,* Boston: Houghton Mifflin, 1951.

———. *Counseling and Psychotherapy,* Boston: Houghton Mifflin, 1942.

Rosenberg, B.G. and Jonas Langer. "A Study of Postural-Gestural Communication," *Journal of Personality and Social Psychology,* 2 (1965), 593-597.

Ruesch, Jurgen. *Therapeutic Communication,* New York: W.W. Norton and Company, Inc., 1961.

Ruesch, Jurgen and Weldon Kees. *Nonverbal Communication,* Berkeley: University of California Press, 1956.

Salomon, Louis B. *Semantics and Common Sense,* New York: Holt, Rinehart and Winston, 1966.

Schachter, Stanley. "Deviation, Rejection and Communication," *Group Dynamics,* (1953), 223-248.

Scheidel, Thomas and Laura Crowell. "Feedback in Small Group Communication," *Quarterly Journal of Speech,* 52 (1966), 271-278.

———. "Idea Development in Small Discussion Groups," *Quarterly Journal of Speech,* L (April, 1964), 140-145.

Schultz, William C. *FIRO: A Three Dimensional Theory of Interpersonal Behavior*, New York: Rinehart, 1958.

Sherif, Muzafer and Carolyn W. Sherif. *An Outline of Social Psychology*, Rev. ed., New York: Harper, 1956.

Skinner, B.F. *Verbal Behavior*, New York: Appleton-Century-Crofts, 1957.

Smith, Alfred G. (ed.). *Communication and Culture*, New York: Holt, Rinehart and Winston, Inc., 1966.

Stageburg, Norman C. "Obstical-Words in Group Conference," *The Journal of Communication*, II, 1 (May, 1952), 82-87.

Taguiri, Renate and Luigi Petrullo (eds.). *Person Perception and Interpersonal Behavior*, Stanford: Stanford University Press, 1958.

Thayer, L. *Communication: Theory and Research*, Springfield, Ill.: Charles C. Thomas, 1967.

———. (ed.). *Communication: Concepts and Perspectives*, Washington, D.C.: Spartan Books, Inc., 1967.

Thompson, Loring M. "Meaning in Space," *ETC.*, XIII (Spring, 1951), 193-201.

Torrance, E. Paul. "The Behavior of Small Groups Under the Stress Conditions of 'Survival,'" *American Sociological Review*, 19, 6 (December, 1954), 751-758.

Webb, Wilse B. "Elements in Individual to Individual Communication," *The Journal of Communication*, VII, 3 (Autumn, 1957), 119-124.

Weinberg, Harry L. *Levels of Knowing and Existence*, New York: Harper and Brothers, 1959.

Whorf, Benjamin. *Language, Thought, and Reality*, Massachusetts: The Technology Press, Massachusetts Institute of Technology, 1956.

Zaleznik, Abraham. *The Dynamics of Interpersonal Behavior*, New York: John Wiley and Sons, Inc., 1964.

Zelko, H.P. *Successful Conference and Discussion Techniques*, New York: McGraw-Hill Book Company, 1958.

PART IV

GROUP LEADERSHIP

One of the most intriguing human behaviors is the leadership-followership phenomena. Who are our leaders and what makes them leaders are fascinating questions which man has been seeking answers to since the beginning of civilization. We know there were tribal leaders before recorded history, and we know history is mostly a description of those who sought power and influence and those who were influenced. Yet, we are still uncertain why and under what circumstances some of us become leaders and others remain followers. Despite the extensive literature on leaders and leadership produced by philosophers, political scientists, and psychologists, we have no agreed upon theory of leadership and no formula for producing leaders.

Plato believed that only a select few men with superior wisdom should be leaders. St. Paul said only those appointed by God could truly lead. Machiavelli felt that only those princes who demonstrated ability to organize knowledge and power to meet political and military challenge should be followed. Thomas Carlyle held that certain men were born with superior courage and insight which caused them to rise to leadership positions. Hegel and Marx doubted that any individuals had superior strength and influence, but rather, some men understood history and the power of events and were able to lead by making people aware of the direction and force of socio-economic changes. John Stuart Mill saw leaders as naturally endowed great men who used their powers of persuasion to enlighten groups and their political skill to bring followers to greater achievement. William James held that leaders arose out of moments or events that brought their genius to the fore; a genius not based on personal power but on the ability to help the group resolve the problems of the moment.

Elton Mayo exemplifies the contemporary "impersonal leadership" school, holding that power and wisdom reside within groups and it is the leader's function to provide effective conditions for group interaction rather than impose his stamp on the group. This obviously oversimplified description of various theories of leadership serves only to show why it has been so difficult to arrive at a theory of leadership or agree upon the qualifications for a leader.

Not only have we been unable to agree on a theory of leadership, but there are those who argue that we have reached a leadership crisis. They believe that our present desire for individual liberty and democratic rights is at odds with out traditional reliance on strong leaders. Some people would purposely avoid leadership positions because they think it means manipulating other people and limiting their freedom of choice. These persons tend to associate leadership with autocracy and the kind of power seeking which has frequently led to corruption of group goals and unnecessary intergroup conflict. Some would go so far as to say that modern education and mass communication make leadership unnecessary. As yet, there is no lack of leaders or leadership and apparently no successful groups without leadership. Even when some members of a group consciously avoid leader roles, others arise to fill the void. The question then becomes not one of whether there should or should not be leaders but what constitutes the most effective and desirable leadership for a given group.

Some of the confusion about leadership can be traced to our failure in the past to distinguish between "leadership" and "the leader." If nothing else, twentieth century research into the leader-follower phenomena has established that leadership is a function of group process rather than a series of isolated traits residing in an individual. It is clear now that there is no such thing as "the leader" apart from some particular group. We have come to realize that individuals are in groups to satisfy needs that cannot otherwise be satisfied, and they accept direction for the same reason. Therefore, leaders arise because in groups there are practical problems of ordering and maintaining. The main characteristic of a leader is that he represents a means of getting the group's needs fulfilled better than other members. The leader leads because it is a means of satisfying his and the group's needs. In this frame of reference it is impossible to describe a leader qua leader or to describe the ideal leader. We can describe leadership functions or leadership roles and we can find which persons perform these functions. In this way it is possible to

distinguish between "leadership"—the function, and "the leader"—
the person who is performing that function at a given time.

A focus on leadership functions as part of group process is the
basis for the selections which appear in this final chapter. Each piece
has been chosen because it sheds some light on the leadership needs
created by group behavior and the means of satisfying these needs.
The prevailing concepts of group leadership are presented in Chapter
8, Theories and Concepts, and leadership types and roles are discussed in Chapter 9, Types and Performance.

Robert A. Nisbet begins our series of selections on Theories and
Concepts with a discussion of the social crisis in Western civilization
brought on by the advent of an impersonal industrial society. He
believes we are faced with a transfer of allegiances as the old social
structures of the family, the church, the local community give way
to the impersonal and formal business and industrial institutions. As
man has become more free from social restrictions in this impersonal
urban society he has sought new sources of security and new forms
of leadership. As Nisbet states, "if social stability is rooted in personal identification and in small groups and associations small
enough to provide a sense of participation, then, plainly, there is a
serious problem presented by the vast increase of forces of impersonality and anonymity; especially when in these forces there are lodged
the basic economic and political decisions affecting the individual's
existence." He would have us seek out leadership that is close to the
people and their psychological needs and warns of the stifling effects
of centralization upon leadership.

Dominance and submission are basic facts of life according to
Franklyn Haiman in our second selection, "The Dynamics of Leadership." An understanding of what constitutes dominance and/or submission will not explain leadership but it enables us to know how
and why we are being controlled and directed. Through such a study
we can come to know more about the sources of leadership and how
psychological needs and environmental forces play a part in producing leadership. Haiman holds that as people become more knowledgeable about group process and more skillful in group participation
they are less dominated by those who seek status and prestige and
more influenced by those who possess the skills the group needs for
the successful accomplishment of its tasks.

One of the foremost contributors to leadership theory over the
past three decades has been Cecil A. Gibb. Being a social psychologist, he studied leadership as a psychological phenomena and came to

the conclusion that "leadership is not a quality which a man possesses; it is an interactional function of the personality and of the social situation." How he arrived at this theory is explained in his now famous article from the *Journal of Abnormal and Social Psychology* presented in this chapter in shortened form. He explains why leadership is only one role in a particular social system. He shows how cultural norms determine the emergence of leadership and why the leader must embody many of the same qualities as the followers. He points out how a person can be a leader at one time and a follower at another time in the same group. And, he draws a most useful distinction between leadership and headship. Gibb considers headship to be the same as domination. It is imposed and maintained from outside the group and it maintains a social distance between the head and the group for purposes of domination. It is the antithesis of *group* leadership.

If there are not universal traits of leadership to guide us in the selection of leaders then we must have other means by which to select and train persons for leadership roles. E.P. Hollander suggests in our next selection the way to meet this problem is to examine the requisites for effective leadership. He maintains that no matter what the group, there are factors which determine a differentiation of status allowing for potential influence, and factors which interrelate to yield acceptance of that influence. If we understand these factors we can apply them as the requisites for leadership effectiveness. They will always be relevant to the attainment of group goals within the context of a given group. Hollander explains these influence factors at length giving us insights into how influence operates in groups and into the crucial part that communication plays in the acceptance of influence.

Our last section of readings on leadership—Types and Performances—begins with Sol Levine's article, "Four Leadership Types: An Approach to Constructive Leadership." He stresses the paramount importance of the interaction between leadership and membership for he believes that people have lost sight of the mutual responsibility shared by leaders and members. He describes the four culturally prescribed leader roles, e.g., the Charismatic Leader, the Organizational Leader, etc., which have tended to circumscribe leadership behavior. He prescribes leadership therapy for breaking out of these binding non-constructive roles.

What is the leader's function is the question that William Schutz addresses himself to in an excerpt from his essay, "The Ego, FIRO Theory and the Leader as Completer." He stresses the application of

FIRO Theory to group behavior and derives a leadership role based upon this application. FIRO Theory "states that there are three fundamental interpersonal needs—inclusion, control, and affection—and in order for an individual (or group) to function optimally he [the leader] must establish and maintain a satisfactory relation in all three areas, with other people or with symbols of people." This to Schutz means that leadership is the act of guiding a group to optimal development in these three areas of interpersonal need. This approach establishes the leader as *completer*. He observes which functions are not being performed optimally and enables the group to accomplish optimal functioning. Whatever is needed that the group is not doing, he must do. When the group is functioning optimally, there is no function for the leader.

In an essay expressly written for this book, Laura Crowell, author of *Discussion: Method of Democracy,* concentrates on one particular operation of the leader, the act of speaking. At a time when the writing and research on leadership is concentrated on the psychological and interpersonal aspects of leadership, Crowell reemphasizes the role of the leader as speaker. She examines the fourfold function of speech in the act of leadership and the conditions which promote effective leader communication. She concludes with the admonition that, "To the extent . . . that the leader violates these conditions imposed by the very nature of small-group discussion process, he will jeopardize his chances of helping the members to move together."

Turning from the types of leadership and functional roles we come next to a study of leadership in action. This unique experimental study conducted by John Geier, focuses on factors which *eliminate* persons from leadership roles rather than those which produce leaders. His study confirms earlier research which established that there are not personality traits within individuals which make them leaders. He found though that there are certain personality traits and forms of conduct which eliminate persons from leadership roles where groups are free to choose their own leaders. This study provides an important additional dimension to leadership theory.

Another experimental study of a different type has been included in our section on Leadership Types and Performance to show how experiments with leadership have been useful in developing theories about group performance. In the article by Marvin E. Shaw an experiment is described which combines knowledge derived from studies of communication nets in small groups with earlier studies of authoritarian and non-authoritarian leadership. Shaw hypothesizes about the effects on group morale and performance when authoritarian and non-authoritarian leaders are inserted in various types of group communication nets such as the wheel and the kite nets. His experimental design and results help us understand better the complex interactions among leaders, group members and group process.

The final selection in this chapter, "Elements and Problems of Democratic Leadership," is a brief excerpt from a longer speculative essay by Bernard Kutner. Drawing widely from leadership literature Kutner points out that democratic groups must have and maintain democratic leadership if they are to remain democratic. This is not easy to do because of the tension created by the natural desire of a democratic group to maintain control over its activities and the desire to operate efficiently through leadership. He finds that groups often become saddled with authoritarian leaders because of the desire "to get things done" or because they want someone to "take over" and make the difficult decisions. The basic fault he believes lay with group members who do not assume the responsibilities for the assessment and evaluation of group needs and goals which must go on continually if a democratic group is to maintain itself. This includes a continual interest in and evaluation of the group's leadership by all members of the group. Kutner maintains that, "The group, to remain truly democratic, must be the watchdog of its own leadership."

chapter 8

Theories and Concepts

LEADERSHIP AND SOCIAL CRISIS
Robert A. Nisbet

The interest in leadership, so pronounced at the present time, is a manifestation of the same intellectual pattern that contains the interest in problems of association and dissociation. And beneath this total pattern of ideas lie the psychologically and morally baffling institutional circumstances in which more and more individuals find themselves in contemporary society. These circumstances are in a real sense the very materials of the practical problem of leadership. It is important to remind ourselves continuously that leadership is inseparable from specific, environing conditions.

What Livingston Lowes has written on the creative process is relevant in a consideration of the relation between leadership and the materials of leadership. " 'Creation' like 'creative' is one of those hypnotic words which are prone to cast a spell upon the understanding and dissolve our thinking into haze. And out of this nebulous state of the intellect springs a strange but widely prevalent idea. The shaping spirit of Imagination sits aloof, like God, as He is commonly conceived, creating in some thaumaturgic fashion out of nothing its visionary world. . . . [But] we live, every one of us—the mutest and most inglorious with the rest—at the center of a world of images. . . . Intensified and sublimated and controlled though they be, the ways of the creative faculty are the universal ways of that streaming yet consciously directed something which we know (or think we know) as life. Creative genius, in plainer terms, works through processes which are common to our kind, but these processes are superlatively enhanced."[1]

In leadership there is something of the same combination of imagination and experience that goes into the creative process; Leadership indeed is one manifestation of the creative proclivity. To draw organ-

From *Studies in Leadership* edited by Alvin W. Gouldner. (Harper and Brothers, New York), 1965. Copyright © 1950 Alvin W. Gouldner. Reprinted by permission.
1. J. Livingston Lowes, *Road to Xanadu* (Boston, 1930), pp. 428, 429, 430.

ization out of the raw materials of life is as much the objective of the leader as it is of the artist. Structure or organization is the primary concern of the leader, as form is the concern of the artist. Leadership is no more comprehensible than any other type of imaginative creation except in terms of the materials. "Every great imaginative conception is a vortex into which everything under the sun may be swept. . . .For the imagination never operates in a vacuum. Its stuff is always fact of some order, somehow experienced; its product is that fact transmuted. . . .I am not forgetting that facts may swamp imagination, and remain unassimilated and untransformed."[2]

Whether we consider the leader as planner, policy maker, ideologist or as exemplar, we are dealing essentially with an imaginative conception, a vortex, into which the materials of the environing culture are swept, assimilated, and expressed. And even as the creative urge in literature, art, drama, and religion expresses itself selectively, so to speak, in history, taking note now of one theme, now of another, forming thus distinguishable ages or periods, even so does leadership. For there are configurations of leadership, from age to age, even as there are historic configurations in the arts and sciences. It is difficult not to believe that leadership presents itself, as do poetry and painting, in historical types, even given form and illumination by some distinctive theme.

Now the theoretical problem of leadership in contemporary democracy must be seen in light of the conditions which have produced the widespread scientific interest in problems of social structure and function, identification, role, and status. All of these problems are intellectualizations of a social crisis created by certain changes in the relation of individuals to institutions. From these changes has come the obsessive problem of insecurity. And, more than anything else, it is insecurity that gives the unique color to leadership in our time.

The modern release of the individual from the traditional ties of religion, class, family, and community has made him free—free at least in the negative sense of disenchantment with, and aloofness from, the old moral certainties. But for many individuals this emancipation from the traditional fetters of custom and prejudice has resulted not in a creative sense of independence but in a stultifying feeling of aloneness and irresponsibility. For generations after the dissolution of the legal bonds of medievalism the social ties remained to bind individuals. But the same forces which led to the breaking of the legal bonds began to dissolve the psychological bonds and to smash the sense of lateral and vertical interdependence.

---

2 *Ibid.,* pp. 426-427.

Our social crisis is essentially a crisis within the same order of social relationships that is undergoing disintegration in the civilizations peripheral to the West, societies indeed that have received the full impact of Western civilization. Even as the ancient loyalties and allegiances—to caste, family, village community—are weakening in such areas as India, China, and Burma, thus creating in almost painful intensity the problem of leadership, so have the analogous loyalties become weak in our own society. Basically, ours is also a crisis in transferred allegiances. In any society the concrete loyalties and devotions of individuals—and their typical personality structures—will tend to become oriented toward those institutions which in the long run have the greatest perceptible significance to the maintenance of life. In earlier times, the family, church, class, and local community drew and held the allegiances of men, not because of any indwelling instinct to associate, not because of greater impulses to love and befriend, but because these were the chief security-providing and authority-giving agencies in the personal lives of individuals.

Leadership—actual leadership—was so subtly and so delicately interwoven into the fabric of kinship, guild, class, and church that the conscious problem of leadership hardly existed. So far as the bulk of people were concerned leadership came not from distant political rulers but from the innumerable heads of families, villages, guilds, and parishes. Between the individual and the highest ruler in the land there lay a continuous hierarchy of intermediate orders and intermediate leaders. There was indeed a kind of chain of leadership in society even as in philosophic imagination there was a "great chain of Being" that connected the lowest inorganic substance to God.

Contemporary interest in leadership in mass society, like the related interest in social cohesion, has been precipitated by the growing irrelevance of traditional centers of association and authority. As modern events make plain, the older primary centers of association have been superseded in institutional importance by the great impersonal connections of property, function, and exchange in modern society. These connections have had a liberating influence upon the individual. Through them he has been able, not only in Europe but also in parts of India, China, and Latin America, to shake off the restraints of patriarchal and hierarchical servitude. But the impersonal relations have had an isolating influence, for they are in no broad sense social relationships. As Park has written: "Everywhere in the Great Society the relations of man, which were intimate and personal, have been more or less superseded by relations that are impersonal and formal. The result is that in the modern world, in contrast with earlier and simpler societies, every aspect of life seems mechanized and rationalized. This is particularly true in our modern cities, which are in consequence so largely inhabited by lonely men and women."[3]

The moral and social isolation, the increasing individual insecurities, the rash of tensions that characterize so many areas of modern life, should not be dismissed as merely urban phenomena. For, as recent studies have shown, the old stereotype of the rural area must be discarded and replaced, in the United States at least, by a picture which contains in an increasing number of localities these same phenomena. When agriculture becomes dominated by the principles of organization that have characterized industrialism, the social consequences are the same.[4]

The point that is crucial here is that the basic decisions in modern mass society have become vested increasingly in organizations and relationships that operate with technical and essentially nonsocial procedures. Vital activities have thus been removed from the competence of the older traditional areas of practical decision-making. In consequence, their sheer institutional importance has waned. Their growing economic and administrative irrelevance has been the basis of their decline in symbolic importance, a fact of the utmost significance to the social basis of leadership in modern society.

Thus in industry, as A.D. Lindsay has written, "the tendency is to specialize planning and organization in a few hands and to ask unskilled repetition work of the great mass of work-people. . . . The factory manager is primarily a technician. He has to contrive an organization of human effort which in conjunction with the operation of machinery will produce the most efficient results. He does not treat his factory as a real society, but as a collection of forces or powers. He is not a leader and does not consider the problem of leadership. A leader has power because he is trusted and believed in; no man can lead or govern without somehow winning the confidence of those whom he leads. Business management is a much more impersonal business. . . . The odd result is that 'the management—whether employers or managing directors, do not lead the men they control. They have enormous power over men's lives but they are not their leaders. The men choose their own leaders to defend them against management.' "[5]

---

3. Robert Park, "Modern Society," cited by S. de Grazia, *The Political Community* (Chicago, 1948), p. 107.
4. See the valuable study by Walter Goldschmidt, *As You Sow* (New York, 1947).
5. A.D. Lindsay, *The Modern Democratic State* (New York, 1943), pp. 184-185.

At bottom, social organization is a pattern of basic identifications in which feelings of reciprocity and intimacy are interwoven. Only thus does the individual have a sense of status. Only thus is communication established which makes effective leadership possible. But if social stability is rooted in personal identification and in groups and associations small enough to provide a sense of participation, then, plainly, there is a serious problem presented by the vast increase of forces of impersonality and anonymity; especially when in these forces there are lodged the basic economic and political decisions affecting the individual's existence.

It is a problem in security, but it is also a problem in the perspective of freedom. For there is evidence that people tend "to react favorably to authoritarian leadership when they are emotionally insecure or when they find themselves in an ambiguous and critical social position."[6] Leadership then becomes invested with a sacred significance that offers surcease from the frustrations and anxieties of society. Studies of the National Socialist movement in Germany suggest strongly that the greatest appeal of Hitler lay in those areas or spheres of society in which feelings of moral isolation and social anonymity were strong.[7] As Drucker has written: "The despair of the masses is the key to the understanding of fascism. No 'revolt of the mob,' no 'triumphs of unscrupulous propaganda,' but stark despair caused by the breakdown of the old order and the absence of a new one. . . . Society ceases to be a community of individuals bound together by a common purpose, and becomes a chaotic hubbub of purposeless isolated nomads. . . . The average individual cannot bear the utter atomization, the unreality and senselessness, the destruction of all order, of all society, of all rational individual existence through blind, incalculable, senseless forces created as result of rationalization and mechanization. To banish these new demons has become the paramount objective of European society."[8]

The leadership of Hitler was no simple revival of ancient forms of force, nor was it based upon any of the traditional ritualizations of remote mastery or domination. Kolnai has told us that the word Führer has the meaning, among others, of "guide." "The intimacy implied in modern 'Fuhrertum' corresponds to the idea that the

---

6. Krech and Crutchfield, *Theory and Problems of Social Psychology* (New York, 1948), p. 429.

7. See, for example, H. Peak, "Observations on the characteristics and distribution of German Nazis," *Psychological Monographs*, 59, No. 276. Also, Loomis and Beegle, "The Spread of German Nazism in Rural Areas," *American Sociological Review*, 1946.

8. Peter Drucker, *The End of Economic Man* (New York, 1939), p. 67.

Leader is—in a particular sense—congenial to the People, linked to it by special bonds of affinity. . . . In an address delivered by Hitler at the Nürnberg Party Congress in 1934, we find the definition: 'Our leadership does not consider the people as a mere object of its activity; it lives in the people, feels with the people, and fights for the sake of the people!. . .' It is even suggested, much in the spirit of Schmitt, that the Führer system guarantees the only real 'democracy,' for it alone secures an effective 'representation of the people.' "[9] We are deceiving ourselves if we refuse to see that behind the appearance of Nazism lay, on the one hand, widening areas of social disintegration produced by many of the individualistic forces that we ourselves celebrate, and, on the other the popularization of the State as a spiritual area of salvation for the disinherited.

The modern intellectual has been, on the whole, the political intellectual. In his eyes the apparatus of formal government has appeared the most desirable medium of social and moral reform. The result has been to throw the greater weight of attention upon the creation and utilization of *political* leadership, upon *political* administration, leaving other types of leadership in society—and their fate in modern history—unexamined. Only in the most recent years has the problem of leadership in industry, in trade unions, in all the essentially nongovernmental forms of association, come to assume respectable significance. This fact, to be sure, has various explanations, but not least among them is the suspicion that however crucial the State may be in modern civilization, political leadership is not enough. For political leadership plainly becomes capricious and inadequate to the demand of freedom and order unless it is rooted deeply in the variety of social and economic and cultural leaderships in society. . . .

To suppose that these centers of leadership will remain vital and symbolically important when they have become institutionally irrelevant in our economic and political order is to indulge in fantasy. The decline of kinship as an important psychological sphere within Western society has been, at bottom, no more than the diminution or disappearance of those institutional functions which formerly gave the kinship group centrality in the life of the individual. It would be naive not to see that the loss of institutional functions by other groups—groups now central in our industrial civilization—may have analogous consequences. Social groups thrive not upon moral fervor or ritual enchantment but upon what they can offer their members institutionally in the way of protection and well being. Thus, as more

9. Aurel Kolnai, *The War Against the West* (London, 1938), pp. 150, 153, 156.

and more liberals have come to realize, there is a profound social difference between a State that seeks to provide a legal scene within which trade unions and cooperatives themselves can raise their members' standard of living, and a State that seeks, however benevolently, to make this its own direct and exclusive responsibility.

The demands of effective leadership, like the demands of freedom and security, necessitate a large amount of autonomy and functional significance in those spheres of society which are *intermediate* to the individual and the State. In one of his most perceptive passages Tocqueville wrote: "It must not be forgotten that it is especially dangerous to enslave men in the minor details of life. For my own part I should be inclined to think freedom less necessary in great things than in little things, if it were possible to be secure of the one without the other."[10] The implications of this statement are more relevant to our own age than they were a hundred years ago when Tocqueville wrote. For it is only in the present age that the technical command of communication and the psychological knowledge of attitudes have made it possible in any full sense to invade, politically, the private areas of existence.

The assumption that centralized power must carry with it centralized administration was tenable only in a day when the range of governmental activities was limited. It is no longer tenable. As government, in its expanding range of functions, comes ever closer to the spheres of primary social existence, the need is intensified for a theory of public administration that will be alive to social and psychological values and to the relationship between political power and cultural associations and groups. In this connection, Karl Mannheim has written that "It is obvious the modern nature of social techniques puts a premium on centralization, but this is only true if our sole criterion is to be technical efficiency. If, for various reasons, chiefly those concerned with the maintenance of personality, we deliberately wish to decentralize certain activities within certain limits, we can do so."[11]

We cannot be reminded too often that the stifling effects of centralization upon leadership are as evident in large scale private industry as in political government. Big government and big business have developed together in Western society, and each has depended upon the other. To these two has been added more recently a third force in society, big labor. In all three spheres there has been a strong

10. *Democracy in America* (New York, 1945), II, 230.
11. Karl Mannheim, *Man and Society in an Age of Reconstruction* (New York, 1940), p. 319.

tendency to organize administration in terms of ideas of power inherited from the seventeenth and eighteenth centuries. In all three spheres there are perplexing problems created by the widening gulf between, on the one hand, a technically trained and experienced managerial group who lead and, on the other, the rank-and-file membership.

"Centralization in administration," David Lilenthal has written, "promotes remote and absentee control, and thereby increasingly denies to the individual the opportunity to make decisions and to carry those responsibilities by which human personality is nourished and developed.

"I find it impossible to comprehend how democracy can be a living reality if people are remote from their government and in their daily lives are not made a part of it, or if the control and direction of making a living—in industry, farming, the distribution of goods—is far removed from the stream of life and from the local community. 'Centralization' is no mere technical matter of 'management,' of 'bigness versus smallness.' We are dealing here with those deep urgencies of the human spirit which are embodied in the faith we call 'democracy.' "[1][2]

The larger problem of society and leadership at the present time is not that of the devolution of administrative authority within formal political government. It is the division of powers and responsibilities between political authority, wherever lodged, and the whole plurality of autonomous social groups in our society. These are the areas of psychological security, as they are the areas within which practical freedom unfolds. They are also the primary spheres of leadership. So long as public opinion is confronted with the choice between insecure individualism in these areas of existence and political collectivism, the trend toward centralization will not be arrested, and the moral attraction of Leviathan will become irresistible.

---

12. T.V.A. *Democracy on the March* (New York, 1944), p. 139.

THE DYNAMICS OF LEADERSHIP

Franklyn S. Haiman

Before the last echoes of the thunderous shouting, "Duce, Duce!" and "Seig Heil! Heil Hitler!" have faded altogether from our memories, it is well that we pause to inquire into the nature of man's quest for leadership. As long as men have lived together, whether in primitive families of cave-dwellers or in complex twentieth-century national communities, they have sought and found leaders. Some of their leaders have been good, others bad. Some have led to progress and others to ruin. But, always, there have been leaders.

Recognizing its grave importance to him, man has struggled with this problem of leadership for centuries. He has studied it, he has speculated about it, and he has proposed many solutions. Early in the history of our civilization, Socrates, in Plato's *Republic,* suggested an answer which has continued through the ages to provoke the thoughts of mankind:

> Until philosophers are kings, or the kings and princes of this world have the spirit and power of philosophy, and political greatness and wisdom meet in one, and those commoner natures who pursue either to the exclusion of the other are compelled to stand aside, cities will never have rest from their evils,—no, nor the human race.[1]

A more recent recommendation to exclude certain individuals from leadership was made in a joking way, but with distinct Platonic overtones, when Al Capp's L'il Abner promoted the idea that all our candidates for public office should be required to have their "haids" examined by qualified psychiatrists.

The question is not simply one of political science and public office. It permeates every aspect of our social lives. How shall our industries be managed? How shall our unions be led? How shall our schools be operated? How shall our clubs, our lodges, and our professional organizations be influenced and controlled? How shall decisions be made within the family circle? All of these questions involve the problem of leadership, for leadership is present in every social situation.

Definitions of Leadership

We begin our study with the word "leadership" and seek to understand its meaning. In the broadest sense, leadership refers to that

From, Haiman, Franklyn S., *Group Leadership and Democratic Action.* (Houghton Mifflin Co., Boston) 1950. Copyright © 1950 Franklyn Haiman. Reprinted by permission.
1. From the *Republic* of Plato, Book V. Translated by Benjamin Jowett, and reproduced by permission of the Clarendon Press, Oxford.

process whereby an individual directs, guides, influences, or controls the thoughts, feelings or behavior of other human beings. This influence may be exerted through the medium of his works—his books, his paintings, his inventions—or it may be exerted through personal face-to-face contact. The former type is known as indirect, intellectual, or creative leadership, and includes the scientists, artists, and writers whose significant products and ideas profoundly influence other men.

Direct, face-to-face leadership operates most frequently through the medium of speech, and is the type with which we are concerned in this book.

There are other important distinctions which should be recognized at the outset. The term "leadership"—as well as the terms "guidance," "influence," or "control"—implies a *purpose* on the part of the leader. Leadership is an effort on his part to direct the behavior of others *toward a particular end.* Thus, the act of a bus driver who accidentally breaks his watch, gets off schedule, and thereby causes thirty people to be late for work, though influencing and controlling human behavior, cannot be called leadership. The driver did not intend to control others, nor was the influence aimed in any particular direction. Had he deliberately broken his watch and gotten off schedule *for the purpose of* making his passengers angry with the bus company, that might be considered leadership.

This is not to say that leadership is always a carefully planned and deliberated act. Much of it is quite spontaneous and the leader may not even be consciously aware of his intentions. Nevertheless, whether planned or unplanned, conscious or unconscious, a purpose and a goal are always present.

Returning to our bus episode, let us suppose that instead of making the passengers angry with the bus company as was intended, the driver's behavior makes them angry with him; and one burly passenger puts a fist in his mouth. This is an unanticipated result of the driver's attempted influence. It is certainly not an end he would have wished for. He tried to lead in one direction but his would-be followers moved in another. We must therefore distinguish between leadership and *attempted leadership.* Leadership is an *interaction process.* There can be no leadership without followership. *Attempts* at leadership must be responded to favorably by others before they can be described as *acts* of leadership. The follower must move, to a small degree at least, in the direction indicated by the leader.

Many people tend to add their own subjective connotations to the basic definitions and distinctions given here. Some feel that the word leadership necessarily implies a *subtle method* of control. Hence, they distinguish it from "commanding," which is an overt, unabashed act of forceful control, lacking in tact and subtlety.[2] Writers who feel this way refuse to dignify leaders who operate through force and overt domination with the title of "leader." According to them the typical military officer is not a leader. This is merely a verbal preference which need not detain us long. It is a distinction which adds an evaluative flavoring to the definition and limits the field in a way which the investigator will not find particularly helpful.

Another type of connotation commonly attached to the word is the feeling that leadership implies a firmly dominant kind of influence. Persons who carry this connotation in their minds make a distinction between leadership and "guidance." To them, the moderator of discussion, the democratic teacher, or the personal counsellor is "*only* a guide, and not *really* a leader!" This is the "strong man" concept of leadership. It ignores the fact that even the most easygoing moderator, teacher, or counsellor is in a very real sense influencing and controlling the behavior of others toward some kind of a goal—whether that goal be determined by the leader alone or in collaboration with the followers. We should reject this second type of subjective verbal coloring. Granted that there may be different methods and varying degrees of directiveness involved in any situation, let us recognize that it is all leadership none the less.

Leadership and Freedom

We are much concerned these days, and rightly so, about the matter of freedom. We hear it said that a crucial issue of our times is to develop an effective "leadership of free people." To write and talk about the leadership of free people is to get perched on two horns of a dilemma. Although the phrase may sound imposing and may stir the sympathy of lovers of democracy, what does it really mean? Can people be both led and free? Is this not a contradiction in terms?

It depends, of course, on how those terms are defined, and one could define them, if he wished, in such a way as to make them appear not to be in conflict. Let us not avoid the issue by means of diluted definitions. To be free, according to Webster's dictionary, means to be independent, unconstrained, uncontrolled, unrestricted, or "not subject to external power." In short, it means *not to be led.*

---

2. Tead, Ordway, *The Art of Leadership.* New York: Whittlesey House, 1935, pp. 11-14; and Pigors, Paul, *Leadership or Domination.* Boston: Houghton Mifflin, 1935, pp. 95-99.

The issue seems clearly and simply drawn. To be led or not to be led—that would appear to be the question.

It is not. *That* question was answered for us ages ago when civilization began. It was soon learned that a leaderless society is not a society at all, for whenever two or more men form a society and live together there is no such thing as uncontrolled, unrestricted, uninfluenced behavior. There is no such thing as absolute freedom. People inevitably have an effect upon one another. Freedom in any society is relative—a matter of degree. The real issue that confronts us, therefore, is to what extent and in what way human behavior should be influenced by others. It is a question of method and of degree—in brief, *how* shall we be led? The kind of society we have and the kind of lives we live will depend, in a large measure, upon our answers to that question.

We are not ready at this point to answer the question of policy. First we must understand the nature of the problem. We must study the dynamics of leadership—the facts and theories which explain its operations—before we can sensibly discuss our ideas of how it *ought* to be. Actually there are two aspects of the problem. The first concerns the way in which leaders attain their positions. The second concerns the methods of leadership employed once they have "arrived." With help from the psychologists, sociologists, and psychiatrists we shall explore both of these phases.

Dominance and Submission

The best available evidence from psychology seems to indicate that dominance and submission are basic facts of most animal existence. Kimbal Young points out that:

> Forms as low as lizards develop a hierarchy of dominance and submission in which a stronger and older member comes to control over other members of the species within a certain area.[3]

This author also refers to an arrangement known as the "pecking order" of chickens—a system whereby the most dominant chicken in the yard pecks at all others, the second most dominant pecks all but the first, and so on down the list to the poor, scraggly fowl at the submissive end of the line that gets pecked at by all but pecks no others!

---

3. Young, Kimball, *Social Psychology.* New York: Appleton-Century-Crofts, Inc., 1944, p. 222.

With respect to human beings, Professor Young speaks for most social psychologists when he concludes that patterns of dominance and submission, whether overt or subtle, eventually emerge in all social groups. This does not mean that the pattern is always consciously recognized by the leaders and followers, or officially formalized by an election. Nor does it mean that the relationship is necessarily permanent or that it is institutionalized in the form of a presidency, a chieftainship, or parenthood. More often than not it is a highly fluid pattern which is constantly subject to alterations impelled by changing situations. Thus the leader of a movement for social reform may no longer be a dominating figure when the cause he champions ceases to exist. The leader of a political party may be deposed if his party suffers too many defeats at the polls.

It is interesting to watch the way a group will turn to a particular person for leadership—whether or not he has sought that position and whether or not he is ever formally designated as leader. It is also fascinating to watch the methods of a person who deliberately maneuvers himself into the dominating role. This is called self-constituted leadership, and is made possible only when the members of the group accept the submissive role (assuming that they have the power to do otherwise). But observations such as these do not probe to the core of the problem. They do not face the fundamental issue of dominance: Why does this man move to the top and not another? Is it simply a matter of physical supremacy, as seems to be the case in much of the animal world?

Certainly, to the degree that we are like lower animals (and that varies from time to time, and place to place, but is always present to an extent!) physical supremacy is a vitally significant factor. We might go so far as to suggest that it is potentially present in all human situations, and point to the role of the military factor in many governments of the world or to the role of physical size in the adult's relation to the child as evidence of this contention. But to proceed from there to attribute all dominance in human relations to physical supremacy is to ignore the very complexity which makes us humans and grossly to oversimplify the entire matter. As we shall see in a few moments, even the most animal-like human societies are dominated by factors other than physical prowess. Brute force does not even begin to explain the subtleties of leadership in human affairs.

Sources of Leadership

The question of what gives rise to the leadership of men has been a source of speculation for generations. There is something compelling about the problem which has attracted the time and thought of many philosophers and has inspired extensive research efforts by psychologists and sociologists. Whatever the causes of this interest the effect is clear—a vast body of literature on the subject.

From the time of Plutarch until very recently the investigations and writings on this subject have been largely in one vein. They have been concerned with discovering and listing the traits of character which make men leaders. They have attempted to do this by studying the lives of great men,[4] by observing the behavior of leaders in action,[5] or by experiments to determine the personal qualities that influence human behavior.[6] We shall discuss their findings shortly.

In the past several years another vein of thinking has emerged. The newer approach revolves around the concept that leadership is specific to differing situations and that the factors which give rise to leadership in one situation may not be the same as those required of the leader in another situation. Leadership is thus the ability to achieve in a specific area that has importance for a given group. It is recognized that various abilities are valued differently by different groups, that leaders embody the ideals of the group in which they operate or the age in which they live, and that leadership is relative and varies according to the nature and functions of the group led.

Ralph M. Stogdill typifies this approach when he summarizes the experimental literature of recent years on the subject of the personal factors associated with leadership, and arrives at these conclusions (among others):

> The qualities, characteristics, and skills required in a leader are determined to a large extent by the demands of the situation in which he is to function as a leader. . . .
>
> It is primarily by virtue of participating in group activities and demonstrating his capacity for expediting the work of the group that a person becomes endowed with leadership status. . . . The leader is a person who occupies a position of responsibility in coordinating the activities of the

4. Plutarch, *The Lives of the Noble Grecians and Romans.* Trans. John Dryden, rev. A.H. Clough. New York: Modern Library, 1932. Also Merriam, Charles E., *Four American Party Leaders.* New York: Macmillan, 1926.

5. Cowley, W.H., "Traits of Face-to-Face Leaders," *Journal of Abnormal and Social Psychology,* XXVI (Oct.-Dec., 1931), pp. 304-13.

6. Sward, Keith, *An Experimental Study of Leadership.* Ph.D. dissertation, University of Minnesota, 1929; and Haiman, Franklyn S., "An Experimental Study of the Effects of Ethos in Public Speaking," *Speech Monographs,* XVI (Sept., 1949), pp. 190-202.

members of the group in their task of attaining a common goal. . . . A person does not become a leader by virtue of the possession of some combination of traits, but the pattern of personal characteristics must bear some relevant relationship to the characteristics, activities, and goals of the followers. Thus, leadership must be conceived in terms of the interaction of variables which are in constant flux and change.[7]

By beginning our study of the sources of leadership against the backdrop of both the older and the newer concepts which have been described here we are in a position to avoid two unfortunate extremes. By adhering to the old alone, one is in grave danger of breaking completely with reality, of talking in abstract verbal generalizations which have no existence in real life, of compiling long lists of noble virtues which no fallible human being could possibly embody, and of erroneously assuming that all leaders in all situations possess the same qualities. This is a trap into which a good many authors have fallen.[8]

On the other hand, by adhering to the new alone, there is also danger of going to an extreme. There is danger of developing a point of view which holds that since leadership is specific to given situations, there are no universal principles or scientific laws which can be discovered. One can be so enamored of the concept of "interaction of variables" that it leads to the point where we can say nothing at all, in a general way, about leadership.

We take a less extreme stand. We recognize that situational differences are exceedingly important, and that any generalizations which are made about the sources of leadership must be modified according to the social values and functions of the group in which the leader operates. This does not mean, however, that general theories are useless, or that leadership cannot be discussed validly without reference to a particular group. We agree with Stogdill when, having come to the conclusions quoted above, he goes on to say:

> Must it then be assumed that leadership is entirely. . .unpredictable. Not at all. The very studies which provide the strongest arguments for the situational nature of leadership also supply the strongest evidence indicating that leadership patterns as well as non-leadership patterns of behavior are persistently and relatively stable.[9]

In short, those of us who are interested in trying to understand the sources from which leadership springs are quite justified in pointing

---

7. Stogdill, Ralph M., "Personal Factors Associated with Leadership: A Survey of the Literature," *Journal of Psychology*, XXV (January, 1948), pp. 63-64. Reprinted by permission.
8. See Casson, Herbert N., *Tips on Leadership*. New York: B.C. Forbes, 1927.
9. Stogdill, *op. cit.*, p. 65. Reprinted by permission.

to certain factors which, in general, seem to account for the phenomenon. At the same time, we must be constantly aware that every group situation is different. Each contains within itself a unique complexity of changing forces which can quickly obscure any oversimple explanation of its leadership patterns. . . .

Conditioned Needs

Far too many studies of the sources of leadership ignore one of the most basic psychological factors to be considered—the need, drive, desire or ambition of the leader to be dominant and the corresponding need or desire of the follower to be submissive. For a thorough analysis we must trace the sources of leadership back to their foundations in the personality structure of the individuals concerned. It is obvious that some people are more desirous of leadership than others, and that this desire is the major factor in the development of behavior which eventually satisfies that need for them. But what accounts for these differences in the need for dominance? Why does one person prefer to lead and another to follow? As yet we have no completely satisfactory answer for these questions. We must rely on theory. It will be useful, first, to distinguish between abnormal and normal desires for dominance.

Abnormal desires for leadership have long been recognized. We are well acquainted with the character whose feeling of insecurity causes him to want to "hog the show," to "bask in the limelight," to strive for the "center of attention." Historians have pointed out that an unusually large percentage of political tyrants (Napoleon and Mussolini, to mention just two) have been of short physical stature, and that one of the contributing factors to their drives for power may well have been the need to compensate for inferiority feelings. A leader's abnormal desire for dominance may also be the result of early childhood experiences in which he himself was unusually dominated, perhaps by a tyrannical father, and as an adult seeks opportunities to revenge that frustration and satisfy his ego by dominating others.

Normal needs for dominance are not so readily explained. We know that some individuals and some societies are more highly motivated to compete for superiority than others. We know that as a general rule, men tend to be more interested and more accepted in dominant roles than women, and as a result are more likely to be selected for leadership in mixed groups. We know that national culture has an influence—that Germans, for example, accept and expect more dominance in the father of a family than do Americans. The authors of *Naval Leadership* develop this point well:

> Take self-assertiveness—the desire to assert oneself, to obtain standing and position, to achieve superiority. In America we are likely to regard this need as a basic component of human nature. . . . But Americans weren't born that way, they learned it. . . . The prestige motive is almost universal. It is probably the most dependable of all the social needs. But there are the Zuni of New Mexico who do not go along with the majority of cultures. The Zuni do not like individual superiority. The best thing they can say about a person is that nobody hears anything about him. If a man wins a race, they will not let him run again. Competition, the thing self-assertiveness thrives on, is practically unknown.
>
> The Arapesh tribe of New Guinea has a similar distaste for competition and superiority. The tribe has leaders, but being a leader is apparently distasteful. The big man retires from office as soon as he can persuade somebody to take over for him.[10]

It would seem that all of the environmental forces which play upon us as we grow up—what our family expects of us and trains us to do, and what society demands of us and conditions us to do—will help determine the degree of our desire for leadership.

The needs for submission, both normal and abnormal, which cause people to accept and enjoy the follower roles are best understood in terms of the parent-child relationship which all of us experience. We are brought into the world as helpless and dependent creatures. The period of time that passes until we are physically and mentally capable of caring for ourselves is longer than that of any other member of the animal kingdom. Little wonder that we become so thoroughly imbued with a feeling of submission. We learn to enjoy our dependent role—we like being cared for by our parents. But as we grow we also learn the disadvantages of dependence. We get a taste of freedom and we begin to "feel our oats." Soon we are torn by the great conflict which must eventually come to all of us—whether we are consciously aware of it or not—the conflict between our desire to submit (with all its pleasant security and unpleasant limitations) and the desire to be free (with all its pleasant advantages and unpleasant responsibilities). The way in which we resolve that conflict will, if the psychoanalysts are right, depend upon the way in which our parents have dealt with us. The way in which we resolve that conflict will also determine the degree to which we seek submission in the social groups to which we become attached.

---

10. *Naval Leadership*, U.S. Naval Institute, Annapolis, Md., 1949, p. 41. Reprinted by permission.

The psychoanalytic approach to submission also helps to clarify the phenomenon of *leader-worship*. The worship of great leaders and the search for super-men to guide our destinies can best be understood as the adult expression of an infantile attitude toward one's parents. When times are difficult and crises occur, we become weighted down and overwhelmed with the responsibilities of maturity and freedom. We yearn again for the days when father or mother would protect us and "make things all right" again. We find in the leader a father figure, and we submit our burdens to him. If we rely on him for support and protection, we must also, in order to feel comfortable, make him out to be a super-man—just as we tended to do with our parents. And the same mixed feelings that parents must come to expect will also plague the leader:

> The ambivalence characteristic of father figures in general is markedly true of leaders. It is astounding to see the savageness with which a previously loved leader may be repudiated and excoriated by the group. Just as the leader may constitute an ideal object for positive emotional feelings, so may he serve as a perfect target for the aggressions of the frustrated, disappointed, disillusioned group. Group members often feel "betrayed" by a leadership that fails, as witness the violent denunciation of the Nazi leadership after the war...To the extent that the leader assumes responsibility, he may in event of failure expect blame.[11]

We may conclude, then, that the patterns of dominance and submission which appear in any group are traceable, in part, to the psychologically conditioned motivation of its members.

Specific Skills

If the careful observation of group behavior shows nothing else, it demonstrates quite clearly that as people become more mature, emotionally and intellectually, they are less influenced in their leadership choices by the determining factors discussed thus far. Although we do not yet have experimental evidence to support the point, one notices, as he watches people grow, that the steady, thinking individual is not easily swept off his feet by the would-be leader's physical prowess, verbal facility, or popularity. He is not unduly impressed by "noble birth" or years of service. He prefers not to wait for magical powers or accident to provide his group with leadership. He sees through the glittering halo of prestige and distrusts the man who is strongly motivated by a lust for power. He prefers to turn for leadership to individuals who possess specific skill in the particular jobs

11. From *Theory and Problems of Social Psychology*, by David Krech and Richard S. Crutchfield, p. 421. Copyright, 1948. Courtesy of McGraw-Hill Book Co., Inc., New York.

that need to be done. As Ordway Tead so aptly puts it, the type of leadership mature men seek

> may be roughly compared to the role of the professional guide in mountain climbing. The guide is not thought of as better than or superior to those whom he precedes up the mountain side. He is merely regarded—and this is sufficient—as superior in his knowledge and skill in reaching the top of a particular peak.[12]

It would be naive for us—the present state of social development being what it is—to believe that the possession of specific skills is a very widely accepted factor in the selection of leaders. Certainly our civilization is a long way from having achieved a high degree of emotional and intellectual maturity. One need only explore the sources of leadership on any American college campus, whether among students or faculty, to discover that even among our most educated groups the power of prestige, seniority, physical appearance, family "background," accident, and conditioned needs are much to be reckoned with. All that we are suggesting here is that rational men are potentially capable of resisting such forces, and that occasionally we have seen them do so. In such instances, the dominance-submission patterns which are established are determined by the presence or absence of specific leadership skills.

So long as the choice of leaders in our society is determined largely by factors other than skill in leadership there is little we can do to train and prepare for it. Though conceivably one might wait patiently for seniority, or take deliberate steps to enhance his prestige, there is little he can do about his parents or his physique. The advice given in this book for the development of specific leadership abilities assumes that, to an ever increasing extent, leadership patterns will be determined by mature human beings on a thoughtful and deliberate basis.

---

12. From *The Art of Leadership* by Ordway Tead, p. 269. Copyright, 1935. Courtesy of McGraw-Hill Book Co., Inc., New York.

THE PRINCIPLES AND TRAITS OF LEADERSHIP
Cecil A. Gibb

Introduction

The problem of leadership as a psychological phenomenon is closely related with considerations of the nature of personality and achieves some clarity if the relation between the two concepts is briefly considered. Psychologists have defined personality generally in one of two ways: *(a)* as the effect the individual has on other people or *(b)* as the total pattern of habits of cognition, affection, and conation. The latter use is that more frequently chosen. Personality in this sense is an abstraction from observed behavior and the apparent relations of this behavior to the individual's needs and to the environment. As Burt has recently pointed out (2),

> [the individual is never an isolated unit and] what the psychologist has to study are the interactions between a "personality" and an "environment"—the behavior of a dynamic mind in a dynamic field of which it forms a part.

"Leadership" is a concept applied to the personality-environment relation to describe the situation when one, or at most a very few, personalities are so placed in the environment that his, or their, "will, feeling, and insight direct and control others in the pursuit of a cause"(12)

Leadership has usually been thought of as a specific attribute of personality, a personality trait, that some persons possess and others do not, or at least that some achieve in high degree and others scarcely at all. The search for leaders has often been directed toward finding those persons who have this trait well developed. The truth would seem, however, to be quite different. In fact, viewed in relation to the individual, leadership is not an attribute of the personality but a quality of his role within a particular and specified social system.[1] Viewed in relation to the group, leadership is a quality of its structure. And, depending upon the definition of "group," this particular quality may become a *"sine qua non."* Without leadership, there is no focus about which a number of individuals may cluster to form a group. A group is here defined as two or more people in a

From: Cecil A. Gibb, "The Principles and Traits of Leadership," *Journal of Abnormal and Social Psychology,* 42, 1947, 267-284. Reproduced by permission.

1. "The place in a particular system which a certain individual occupies at a particular time will be referred to as his *status* with respect to that system" (II, p. 76). "In so far as it represents overt behavior, a *role* is the dynamic aspect of a status: what the individual has to do in order to validate his occupation of the status" (II, p. 77).

state of social interaction. Group activity means that individuals are acting together in some fashion; that there is some order of the different lines of individual action. There is a division of labor within a group that is accepted by all members of the group. In a discussion group, for example, the speaker performs a task different from that of other members. Both he and the members act in expected ways, and yet their behavior may be collective. The coherence occurs because of the common understandings or cultural traditions as to how they should behave. Similarly, the concept of leadership as a cultural norm plays a considerable part in the emergence of a leader. And this would seem to be the significance of Warren's parenthetic statement that "leadership depends on attitudes and habits of dominance in certain individuals and submissive behavior in others"(16). It is not implied that these are instincts variously strong in some individuals and weak in others, but that these are accepted ways of behaving within the cultural framework and that therefore they tend to determine the field forces acting in a group situation.

Leadership Theory

This dynamic conception of groups composed of dynamic entities or personalities interacting will accord well with Lewin's notion(10) that the individual's characteristics and actions change under the varying influence of "the social field." It does not seem unreasonable to claim that groups have a capacity to propel to leadership one or more of their number; and, what is more, the choice of a specific individual for the leadership roll will be more dependent upon the nature of the group and of its purpose than upon the personality of the individual; but it will be most dependent upon the relation between the personality and the group at any particular moment. That is to say, in Linton's terms, that the group choice of a leader will be determined by the status of individual members. This claim does not lose sight of the nature of the individuals who constitute the group, and it does not assert that any member may be propelled to leadership nor does it suggest that the social situation alone makes the leader. (Leadership is both a function of the social situation and a function of personality, but it is a function of these two in interaction;) no additive concept is adequate to explain the phenomenon. There is no justification for saying that personality qualities which make for leadership exist in a latent form when not being exercised in a social situation. Any qualities of personality common to leaders in varying situations may also exist in persons who never achieve leadership status. What might be called the attributes of leaders are abstracts from a total interactional situation and are qualities of a particular social role. In the absence of this kind of social situation the latent existence of the same pattern of qualities cannot be inferred. Again, this does not mean that there can be no potential leaders, but it does mean that the potentiality cannot be directly known except as a back-inference from expressed ability.

Leadership is not usually an enduring role unless an organization is built up which enables an individual to retain the role after he ceases to be qualified for it. In this case leadership becomes domination or mere headship. In the absence of such an artificial restriction, the interaction within the group is very fluid and the momentary group leader is that person who is able to contribute most to progress toward the common goal. Ten men previously unknown to each other are set a common problem, such as transporting heavy radio equipment to the top of a steep cliff. In the initial stages they are ten individuals thinking of possible solutions. One may find a solution which he communicates to the others. Usually this establishes interaction. The ten now become one group and the group focus is the man (A) who offered the solution. He is the leader at the moment. He is in the position of influencing their behavior more than they influence his. He is in the role of initiator of group action, which at this point consists of discussion. If now his plan is accepted, the group goal changes. It has been the choice of a plan and for that phase A occupied the leadership role. The goal now, however, is the execution of the plan. Two things may happen. A, by virtue of a prestige he has acquired, may continue in the role of leader or he may find another individual (B) naturally taking over. The group problem is now more practical, and B may, by virtue of his different innate capacities or previous experiences, be better able to contribute to the group project. Leadership then passes naturally to B, and, if difficulties are met and a third man (C) offers a solution, the role may pass to him. On the other hand, it is possible that all of these individuals, A, B, and C, may find their retention of the leadership role very short lived and even momentary only because another member of the group, D, rises to a more permanent occupancy of the role by virtue of his ability to translate suggestions into working orders, and by virtue of his greater social effectiveness.

Observation of group behavior in this way strongly supports the contention that leadership is not an attribute of personality or of character. It is a social role, the successful adoption of which depends upon a complex of abilities and traits. But even more, the adoption of a leadership role is dependent upon the specific situation. The same individual in the same group may alternate between the role of leader and follower as the group goal changes. Most frequently the individual is propelled into a position of leadership by virtue of his capacity for interpersonal contribution in the specific situation. There is, however, a generic aspect to leadership as Du Vall(5) has pointed out. This is indicated by the fact that the person of all-round superiority is more frequently in situations in which he is able to make a contribution.

The first main point to be made, then, in leadership theory is that leadership is relative always to the situation. Men may come together and yet not constitute a group. Until the individuals of the aggregation are given a common object or goal, there will be no social interaction and consequently no group formation. Each may face an individual problem and achieve an individual solution. But when many face a common problem and one or more of the individual solutions is communicated to others then there is interaction, and, if that interaction is focused upon one or two individuals in the group, then he or they are leaders for the time being. Clearly, in order that such a situation may develop, it is necessary that there should be a problem, and that it should be such a problem as to afford an opportunity for the play of individual differences in its solution. The circumstances must be such as to require a choice. As Schneider(13) has pointed out, it is the social circumstances which make particular attributes of personality attributes of leadership. While the social circumstances are such as to demand the original formulation of a plan, inventing ability will be an attribute of personality determining the adoption of a leadership role. But, the plan having been formulated, the social circumstances then demand not invention but social effectiveness as an attribute of personality essential for the leadership role. And, unless the same individual possesses both attributes, the leadership passes from one to another. The situation determines which of many attributes of personality will be attributes of leadership at any given moment. That is why Pigors(12) observes that, "whenever an obstacle physical or mental prevents the flow of action, the group welcomes any manifestation of individual difference that tends to resolve this uncertainty or to facilitate group action."

Leadership, then, is always relative to the situation *(a)* to the extent that a certain kind of situation is required before the leadership relation will appear at all, and *(b)* in the sense that the particular set of social circumstances existing at the moment determines which attributes of personality will confer leadership status and consequently determines which members of a group will assume the leadership role, and which qualities of personality function to maintain the individual in that role. This was one of the things indicated by Thrasher's study of juvenile gangs in Chicago. Leadership seemed to be a quality that came out as the group moved about together—it was the result of the social situation. This is, in fact, the second principle of leadership theory. It is that individual accession to the leadership role is dependent upon the group goal and upon the capacity of the individual to contribute to the achievement of the goal. Pigors says:

> It is nonsense to talk of leadership in the abstract since no one can just lead without having a goal. Leadership is always *in* some sphere of interest, and *toward* some objective goal seen by leader and follower(12).

Only in so far as the individual can contribute to group progress in the required direction has he any claim to a hearing, and, unless he can establish himself with his fellow members, he will not receive recognition as their leader. This is, of course, to raise the question whether the leader can exercise a creative influence upon the group's goals and activities or whether he can do no more than express and exemplify already accepted ideals and contribute to progress in the direction of an accepted goal perhaps by pin-pointing and clarifying a previously vague conception. Klineberg(8) suggests that a compromise is indicated in that "the leader has great influence but only on certain groups under certain conditions. Change these or change him," he says, "and the resulting behavior is markedly altered." Schneider(13), on the other hand, claims that the "new" history as written by Marx, Turner, Beard, and others, "sees leaders as a product of the times and leadership as a function of the circumstances of the moment." The problem seems to be indeterminate because there is no denying that the "great men" of history have been responsible for changes in the social situation of which they were a part but there is no way of telling to what extent these changes would have occurred anyway or under the leadership of another group-chosen personality.

The third characteristic of the leadership process to which attention may be drawn is that its basic psychology is that of social interaction. There can be no leadership in isolation, it is distinctly a quality of a group situation. There can be no leader without followers. An individual's intellectual quality may be very superior and his individual solution of a group problem may be excellent but he is not a leader until his solution is communicated, and then not until other people are associated with him in giving expression to his ideas. Leader and follower must be united by common goals and aspirations and by a will to lead, on one side, and a will to follow, on the other, i.e., by a common acceptance of one another. From this it follows that the individual must have membership character in the group which makes him its leader, because leaders and followers are interdependent. This is the first of Brown's(1) "field dynamical laws of leadership," and the first of Du Vall's(5) criteria of the leadership process. The leader must be a member of the group; he must share the group objectives and aspirations. Stated in other words, this principle of mutual interaction between the leader and the group implies that the individual chosen leader must have certain qualities of personality which, derived as they are from his group-membership-character, confer upon him a certain social effectiveness and determine his acceptability.

Having group-membership-character, it is upon individual differences that one depends for election to leadership status. It is because there are individual differences of capacity and skill that one, and usually only one, of a group emerges having a pattern of qualifications superior to others for meeting present group needs. But these "superior" persons must not be too different. Followers subordinate themselves not to an individual who is utterly different but to a member of their group who has superiority at this time and who is fundamentally the same as they are, and who at other times is prepared to be a follower just as they are.

For Jennings(7):

> Leadership is definable by a manner of interacting with others. . . . Both isolation and leadership were found to be products of interpersonal interaction and not of attributes residing within the persons. . . . No simple variable such as the length of time the individual had been in the community or his chronological age relative to other members, or his intelligence or even his greater opportunity for contacting others, appears to account for the particular choice-status accorded him. Instead the reciprocal interplay maintaining between the individual and those in the same field and constituting the individual's personality as the latter view him appears to be the underlying basic explanation of isolation and leadership.

The determination of the role to be played by the individual is the group reaction to his interpersonal contribution. The close relation between leader and followers is therefore apparent.

The leader inevitably embodies many of the qualities of the followers. Any individual's personality at a given point in time reflects the field forces with which it is interacting. The personality which most adequately reflects those forces is the one most likely to be propelled to leadership. Thus it is that La Piere and Farnsworth(9) are led to make the point that because there is such close interaction between the leader and the led it is often difficult to determine just who affects whom and to what extent. For this reason it is possible for leadership to be nominal only. This possibility is emphasized by a carry-over of prestige from one point in time to another. The fact that individual A in our earlier example was intellectually quickest with a suggested solution of the group problem established him as a focus of attention in the minds of the others. Momentarily, at any rate, he became their leader and they became followers. A definite interactional pattern was established. A social-cultural evaluation was made of him by the others. That is precisely what is meant by prestige. Prestige is a distinction attaching to a person in the minds of others. It depends, as we have now seen, on the qualities ascribed to the individual by other members of the group. As Young points out, prestige is a special case of the point

> that a man's personality reflects others' image and recognition of him. A leader's prestige rests upon the apperceptive background of the followers. The leader takes on the qualities which his adherents project on him.(17)

This, too, is Brown's(1) second "field dynamical law of leadership," that the "leader must represent a region of high potential in the social field," i.e., that he must have prestige and this he acquires by symbolizing the ideals of all members of the group. In some instances it may be said that prestige within a group is acquired by virtue of an external appointment or by virtue of a certain status in an institution which embraces that group, as in the case of a parish priest. In such a case the assumption of a leadership role is made easier, but it is still true that it will be retained only while the individual so appointed is able to symbolize the ideals of the group members. In other words, the personality thus "made" leader must so reflect the field forces within the group with which it is interacting as to have had potential leadership status if membership without leadership could have been granted by the appointment.

Reviewing leadership theory one may say, then, that its three most important principles are, first, that leadership is always relative to the situation—relative, that is, in two senses: *(a)* that leadership flourishes only in a problem situation and *(b)* that the nature of the leadership role is determined by the goal of the group; and this is, in fact, the second principle of leadership, that it is always toward some objective goal. The third principle is that leadership is a process of mutual stimulation—a social interactional phenomenon in which the attitudes, ideals, and aspirations of the followers play as important a determining role as do the individuality and personality of the leader.

These principles lead us to accept Pigors'(12) definition of leadership as a "process of mutual stimulation which, by the successful interplay of relevant individual differences controls human energy in the pursuit of a common cause." And any person may be called a leader "during the time when and in so far as, his will, feeling and insight direct and control others in the pursuit of a cause which he presents."

As Jennings says:

> the "why" of leadership appears not to reside in any personality trait considered singly, nor even in a constellation of related traits, but in the interpersonal contribution of which the individual becomes capable in a specific setting eliciting such contribution from him(7).

provided that the individual superiority is not so great as to preclude solidarity of purpose.

Such a theory of the leadership process excludes such group situations as those organized for professional tuition, expert advice, management, and the like, and excludes the concept of headship. When once the group activity has become dominated by an established and accepted organization, leadership tends to disappear. Even if this organization originally served the leadership role, any continuance of the organization as such, after the causal set of circumstances has ceased to exist, represents a transition to a process of domination or headship, where headship is regarded, as Warren(16) defined it, as "a form of authority determined by caste, class or other factors than popular selection and acceptance," and where domination is defined by Pigors(12) as

> a process of social control in which accepted superiors assume a position of command and demand obedience from those who acknowledge themselves as inferiors in the social scale; and in which by the forcible assumption of authority and the accumulation of prestige a person (through a hierarchy of functionaries) regulates the activities of others for purposes of his own choosing.

The characteristics of this process of domination as distinct from that of leadership are that: *(a)* the position of headship is maintained through an organized system and not by the spontaneous recognition of the individual contribution to the group goal; *(b)* the group goal is arbitrarily chosen by the autocratic head in his own self-interest and is not internally determined; *(c)* there is not really *a group* at all, since there is no sense of shared feeling or joint action; and *(d)* there is in this process a wide social gap between the group members and the head, who strives to maintain this social distance as an aid to his coercion of the group through fear.

This concept of domination and headship is important because it is so different from that of leadership and because so much so-called leadership in industry, education, and in other social spheres is not leadership at all, but is simply domination. It is not, however, necessary that headship should preclude leadership. This is, in fact, the assumption which underlies the selection of military officers. . . .

There is no one leadership type of personality. One man might achieve leadership status because he has superior intellectual endowments which force him consistently upon the notice of the others and make them dependent on him. A second achieves leadership because he has a quiet helpful interest in his fellow group-members and because what British psychiatrists call his "contact" is good. Leadership resides not exclusively in the individual but in his functional relation with other members of his group.

There is nothing in these results to deny and there is much in the observation of the group situations to confirm the general agreement among students of leadership that leadership and its traits are relative to the situation. There is a specificity in leadership qualities in that characteristics which cause an individual to be propelled into the leadership role depend upon the group project of the moment. If the project is to bridge a deep and swiftly flowing creek without the aid of the customary apparatus then a number of men may be thrust successively into the leadership role. First the man who most quickly gets a workable solution may take the role. Next may be a man of athletic prowess who takes the initiative in procuring the necessary material, and later still a knowledge of, or experience with, physical or engineering principles may propel yet a third to this position of social responsibility, and, finally, good "contact" may determine the occupant of the role when the problem changes to that of deciding the order in which the group members will traverse their narrow and maybe dangerous bridge. The suggestion is that leadership potential in any specific situation requires a certain amount of skill in that kind of activity as well as evidence of other traits.

There do seem to be, however, certain general characteristics of personality the possession of which does not necessarily cause a man to have leadership status conferred upon him but which does place him higher than he would otherwise be on the scale of choice in any group.

Conclusion

Leadership is not a quality which a man possesses; it is an interactional function of the personality and of the social situation. A leader is a member of a group on whom the group confers a certain status, and leadership describes the role by which the duties of this status are fulfilled. The effectiveness of the role depends upon the functional relation between the individual attributes of the man and the specific goal of the group at any moment. It is natural that some individual attributes of skill and personality will be generally effective though they will not confer upon their possessor universal leadership status.

References

1. Brown, J.F. *Psychology and the social order.* New York: McGraw-Hill, 1936.
2. Burt, C. The assessment of personality. *Brit. J. educ. Psychol.,* 1945, 15, 107-121.
3. Carr, W.G. *Educational leadership in this emergency.* (The Cubberley Lecture.) Stanford University, Calif.: Stanford University Press, 1941.
4. Coffin, T.E. A three-component theory of leadership. This Journal, 1944, 39, 63-83.
5. Du Vall, E.W. *Personality and social group work.* New York: Association Press, 1943.
6. Gulford, J.P. *Fundamental statistics in psychology and education.* New York: McGraw-Hill, 1942.
7. Jennings, Helen H. *Leadership and isolation.* London: Longmans Green, 1943.
8. Klineberg, O. *Social psychology.* New York: Holt, 1940.
9. La Piere and Farnsworth. *Social psychology.* (2nd ed.) New York: McGraw-Hill, 1942.
10. Lewin, K. *A dynamic theory of personality.* New York: McGraw-Hill, 1935.
11. Linton, R. *The cultural background of personality.* New York: Appleton-Century, 1945.
12. Pigors, P. *Leadership or domination.* London: Harrap, 1935.
13. Schneider, J. Social class, historical circumstances and fame. *Amer. J. Sociol.,* 1937, 43, 37-56.
14. Schneider, J. The cultural situation as a condition of the achievement of fame. *Amer. sociol. Rev.,* 1937, 2, 480-491.
15. Tiffin, J. *Industrial psychology.* New York: Prentice Hall, 1942.
16. Warren, H.C. *Dictionary of psychology.* Boston: Houghton Mifflin, 1934.
17. Young, Kimball. *Social psychology.* (2nd ed.) New York: Crofts, 1945.

LEADER EFFECTIVENESS AND INFLUENCE PROCESS

E.P. Hollander

Inescapably, the selecting and training of people for positions of leadership, especially within organizational settings, demand a sense of what makes leaders effective. Therefore, while there may not be "universal traits" of leadership, it is possible to speak of requisites for effective leadership. Our intent here is to consider what some of the most salient of these appear to be, recognizing that any one individual's leadership "style" may be uniquely effective for him. From this we shall go on to the more general issue of implications regarding influence process.

Clearly, various meanings can be offered for "leader effectiveness." In our view, it is best considered to be an influence process wherein the leader is able to muster willing group support, to achieve certain clearly specified group goals, with best advantage to the individuals comprising the group. Moreover, we shall not be distinguishing between emergent and imposed leadership despite our recognition that an important distinction between the two can be made. While the goals may be different, and the source of influence quite clearly is different, the operation of a group in terms of its movement toward a goal rests on characteristics which go beyond these distinctions alone. Our considerations here, therefore, have application to the organizationally imposed leader as well as to the one who emerges by group consent.

Influence Potential and Influence Acceptance

In these last chapters . . . we have covered issues which bear on considerations of leadership functioning in terms of "idiosyncrasy credit." Two aspects of leadership in particular have been given attention. These are factors which in the first place determine a differentiation of status allowing for potential influence, and second, factors which interrelate to yield acceptance of that influence. Essentially, this represents the distinction between *attaining* versus *maintaining* leadership. The effectiveness of leadership refers to the latter process.

One central aspect of the concept of "emergent leadership" is the provision it makes for talking about group structure in terms of the development of status among group members. In this conception, potential influence may be increased or diminished depending upon the effects of ongoing interactions on persons as perceivers. The essential point here is that people retain a history of what has transpired in the past, even though that process need not be confining as a determiner of behavior since new experience is continuously having its effects.

Factors Determining Leader Effectiveness

Among those factors we have thus far noted which shape the leader's effectiveness are his competence, his fulfillment of certain group expectancies for structure and action, his perceived motivation, and his adaptability to changing requirements of the situation. Before giving separate attention to each of these elements, it should be said that they are all relative rather than absolute in character. We are not reinstating certain trait conceptions of leadership but rather are pointing to qualities which have relevance to the attainment of group goals and which are defined within the context of the group's operation at a given time. As an example, we have said that status permits a degree of latitude for behavior in terms of common expectancies in a group. We have also said that there are certain restrictions imposed upon the high status person in terms of what may be thought of as particularized expectancies, that is, role behaviors. In short, the group defines which particulars have significance in terms of its context of operation.

Particularized Expectancies

Our contention has been that role behaviors of leadership tend to be more highly prescribed. Why should this be so? Two reasons seem to apply here: as a first consideration, high status carries with it the assumption of greater initiative for action, as Thibaut and Riecken (1955) have demonstrated. The leader, as an exemplification of a high status person, is assumed to be more responsible for the actions that he displays. Equally important as a second consideration is that high status makes more stringent demands for certain roles because these carry responsibilities which are greater and more likely to affect important outcomes for the members of the group. As a person's status increases, he tends to occupy more and more important roles. Consequently, his fulfillment of the leadership function becomes more crucial to the group's achievement of its goal. Another way of viewing this is in terms of a simple figure-ground phenomenon. Actions which call attention to a person may lead him to a position of influence because of favorable outcomes. Then, since his activity now becomes more crucial to the group's attainment of goals, his visibility is even further increased. . . .

Competence

An important attribute of the leader is his competence in some task which is of importance to the group's achievement of its goal, a matter we have particularly stressed in the foregoing chapters. While competence has been misinterpreted at times to mean some necessary ability on a task, in actuality there are many group situations in which the function may not be so much a task which literally produces a product as a set of characteristics which are demanded if the group is to operate smoothly in terms of its desires. In a highly sociable setting, for example, it may be that having a good sense of humor and facilitating the social interaction of members becomes important in terms of this matter of competence. Therefore we should understand the individual's functional value for the group as encompassing a wide variety of situationally determined demands for varying kinds of attributes. Competence, it is well to emphasize, is also time-bound in that what may be important to securing a goal at one juncture may no longer be important as the goal is achieved. Accordingly, re-definitions of competence may periodically occur. This may mean that as the group moves to a new set of task requirements the former leadership becomes inadequate for reasons of its incapabilities to meet these new demands. The requirement for perceptiveness in seeing these new demands is of course associated with this aspect of leadership maintenance.

Identification

In keeping with previous points, the leader must be seen by potential followers as having an identification with the group, in the sense of a clear involvement with the group's activity. Cartwright, in summarizing the implications of work on "group dynamics," has spoken of agents of change (1951). He indicates that a key characteristic of persons who are successful in this function is that they be seen to share an identification with the group in its circumstance. Apart from attributes as such, it is therefore important that the leader, by his behavior, manifest a loyalty to the needs and aspirations of group members. These things must matter to him in ways that are accessible to view because such evidences of good faith and sincere interest serve to elicit greater acceptance of influence for reasons spelled out later.

Behavioral Processes

In addition to the two attributes of competence and identification with the group, there are several behavioral processes which seem to be important in determining the effectiveness of leadership. These may be considered under three general headings: first, providing the group with structure and goal-setting, as Hemphill has suggested (1958); second, maintaining a flexibility and adaptability in handling changing requirements as new situations develop; and, third, establishing productive social relationships which arise from a predictability of behavior on the leader's part which manifests itself in emotional stability, dependability, and fairness in distributing rewards. Recognizing that these behaviors are always achieved and defined within the group's structure, and may therefore vary in specific content as well as in the goals actually sought, let us consider what some of the implications of these would be.

Communication

For the leader to establish structure, it is essential that he foster communication within the group by providing mechanisms for participation and for the need that members be informed in advance of decisions or actions that will affect them. Adaptability to new situations also requires communication within the group. Thus, several ends of effective leadership are served by facilitating an exchange of information.

The fact that groups continually face new situations which require innovation means that the effective leader, while he may be an "idea man" in his own right, recognizes the potential merit in the good ideas of others. This is, of course, part and parcel of the facilitation of communication just mentioned. The leader is willing to give new ideas a hearing and in many instances effective leaders are known for their "open-door" policy in encouraging members to present to them relevant facts and views about situations which require attention.

Restraint and Predictability

In Chapter 1 we noted the importance of restraint in the use of power. In effective leadership, this is evidenced by the necessity of the leader to display a degree of emotional balance in his relationships with others so that he is predictable in performance rather than being impulsive and given to instability. Particularly important is this in the matter of the distribution of rewards. The leader has a great deal of visibility and therefore his actions will be interpreted in some sense as signifying the "goodness" or "badness" of the actions of group members. By rewarding those actions which are in the interest of the group and judiciously avoiding the rewarding of behaviors which are inimical to the group's best interest, the leader gains respect for his fairness in this function.

A common way of referring to the matter of predictability or dependability is to ask where a person "stands" as well as what he "stands for." In any social relationship, regularities of behavior are valued for the ease with which they may be anticipated. The leader who takes a "stand" which serves as a continuing guide to his responses is more likely to maintain his position, other things equal, than he would with a characteristic tendency toward vacillation of action. This is not to be interpreted, however, as support for a maladaptive rigidity of stance.

Advocacy

The function of representation, mentioned earlier in connection with the organizational leader in Chapter 3, may be thought of as involving advocacy. By this we refer to the leader's ability to communicate to other groups and to higher authority the particular desires and needs of his group in order to facilitate its achievement of goals, as is noted by Pelz (1952). Granting that there may be an implicit conflict between the groups within an organizational structure, it is the effective leader who stands as the primary spokesman for his group's interest in such dealings. In some important ways, his functioning in that role has certain consequences to his ability to bring about a degree of goal orientation and goal attainment within his own group. Where he is seen to be loyal to the group's goals, and to be functioning in terms of the group's best interests, as against his own self-interest, the prospect is increased that he will be successful in his influence attempts within the group.

Implications for Influence Process

This enumeration of some of the characteristics associated with leader effectiveness provides us with a basis for considering how these may have generality for broader processes of influence. The essential point with which we have been concerned relates to behaviors which evoke from followers a positive response. And we take this concern to have a bearing upon other kinds of social influence relationships in terms of their having a fundamental integrity in a *general* process. Thus, while research on leadership, conformity, mass communication, and attitude change is largely fractionated, all involve a transaction, often of a reciprocal variety, between persons or groups in a co-acting relationship.

Indeed, a key approach to social psychology today rests in an understanding of three general elements which appear to be part of all of the influence relationships noted. These elements may be characterized variously but resolve down to: (1) an influence source (or agent or group or communicator) with attributes perceived from actual or implied interactions; (2) some mode of interpersonal activity or other communication; and (3) a recipient (or follower or audience) with personal motivations, perceptions, and reference group affiliations. Whatever their particular designation, all three of these elements are involved in influence process; moreover, sufficient guidelines exist from the work done under apparently diverse headings to develop a coalescence of theory using terms at a common level of abstraction.

From our considerations here, it is evident that leadership especially has produced a study of the influence process as a transaction or interplay between characteristics of the influence agent and those of respondents within a particular social structure. But a parallel development may be found in the work on attitude change. By a rather simple translation it is possible to see the leader as a communication source and to see his behaviors or attributes as communications given off to an audience of recipients within a given social situation. Rather than being passive receptacles for these communications, it would appear now that a selective processing by the recipient goes on. With reference to attitude change, for example, this point has recently been elaborated by Bauer (1964). And, though studies of conformity appear at first glance to be of a different order, they usually involve these elements as well. The difficulty in seeing this arises in part from the essentially nonfunctional groups that are contrived in many of the traditional studies of sources of conformity. Where interaction is thus limited, correspondingly little concern exists for the interplay of relationships, or for the relevance of the conforming response to a focal group activity. However, the group itself can be seen as an influence source whose characteristics—for example, in terms of attraction to members—become relevant to the acceptance of its influence by recipients.

In sum, within these areas of leadership, attitude change, and conformity, clear parallels can be seen for the operation of these three essential elements. Following through on this integration, it is convenient to employ leadership as an illustration of the general process.

The Influence Agent

Observed attributes and behaviors of the influence agent, or leader, contribute to the perception others hold of him as a communication source. What he seems to be, in the sense for example of his upholding the appropriate reference group, fits the specific condition mentioned above in connection with the attributive expectancy of identification and the behavior of advocacy. How he stands on issues, and whether dependably so or not, lends substance to his acceptance in the sense of his credibility as a source. We may in fact think of credibility as a special case of the competence variable stressed here as an attribute of leadership. Taken together with the impression that the leader identifies with group interests vital to the individual, credibility enhances influence potential. This has implications as well for the individual's conformity response to one or more members of a group where he desires their acceptance.

The Communication

An influence agent's communications can involve all of those things he presents to others, verbally or otherwise. Whether they are called "leaders" or not, influence agents communicate messages and these may be essentially of two kinds, not entirely distinct from one another. First, there may be messages of directed content concerning objects and events, e.g., value-laden statements of an attitudinal sort or "factual" statements, presumed to be less value-laden; second, there are messages in the nature of self-references by the communicator. Goffman (1959) has put the latter well in terms of his concept of "impression management." One parallel here may be seen in connection with techniques of propaganda. The propagandist would be using directed messages when employing the technique of "card-stacking" or "glittering generalities." However, by introducing a "plain-folks" theme within his appeal, he provides a self-reference aimed at placing himself within a favorable range of response by the recipient. In so doing, he wishes to increase his credibility by making known his identification with things valued by the recipient. The key then to response to the influence assertion of a communication rests in how it is processed and understood by the recipient. This takes place in the context of two kinds of need systems, his impelling personal motivations and his salient reference group affiliations, matched against what he, the recipient, has come to know about the source.

The Recipient of the Communication

What a communication evokes depends upon the recipient's perception of both the message and the source. This seems as true of direct leader-follower interaction as of propaganda effects, once certain translations are made and a common level of abstraction is attained. Each communication may be conceived as being both assessed within the framework of personal motivations and reference group affiliations of the moment as well as itself instigating for their selective operation. Thus, influence agents seek to and often succeed in playing upon these need systems in their encounters with recipients. In the sense of a change in the recipient, influence is achieved by showing direction for the attainment of goals or by enhancing the desirability of a given reference group affiliation and a degree of compliance with its social expectancies. Conformity depends especially upon the relation of these need systems under conditions where a reliance on the group is necessary to the achievement of an impelling personal motivation, e.g., for "reality" under conditions of ambiguity. In short, the message from groups as influence agents is frequently one of offering satisfaction of personal needs for the acceptance of group standards. This is an essential exchange represented in the "idiosyncrasy credit" concept.

chapter 9

Types and Performance

FOUR LEADERSHIP TYPES:
AN APPROACH TO CONSTRUCTIVE LEADERSHIP
Sol Levine

The image of the leader in American culture is that of a successful individual standing above and beyond the populace, not as one whose success is determined by interaction with those who work with him. He is a "big man" who dominates the group and makes decisions (with "dispatch and confidence") by himself; he does not have "co-workers," but "followers" who carry out his decisions. The culture prescribes a passive reaction to leadership, which is seen in the way local chapters of a large organization are used to carry out the decisions of the national office with little opportunity to share in the making of policy.[1]

A functional conception of leadership stresses the mutual responsiveness of both leadership and membership. Good leadership must be particularly sensitive to the feelings and problems of the group. Not only must the functional leader recognize and respond to these feelings, but he must also articulate them sharply and give special attention to the group aspects of individual problems and needs. He must also stimulate and help the group to find solutions, drawing upon that part of the member's experience which is related to the group goals. *The interaction between leadership and membership is of paramount importance for participation.* It is obvious that a leader cannot respond well to a group which is not responding to him, and vice versa.

Many leaders, like members, are either anarchic or formalistic, and this fact gives rise to special participation problems. The anarchic

From Sol Levine, "An Approach to Constructive Leadership," *Journal of Social Issues,* Vol. V, No. 1, pp. 46-53. Reprinted by permission.

1. See Myrdal, G., *An American Dilemma,* New York: Harper, 1944, for his discussion entitled "The American Pattern of Individual Leadership and Mass Passivity," Chapter 33, pp. 709-79. "The masses . . . do not speak for themselves: they are the listeners in America" (p. 714). "The patterns of strong and competitive personal leadership and weak followership, which we have exemplified for politics, permeate the entire social structure" (p. 718).

participant who assumes the role of a leader, for instance, has difficulty in analyzing or abstracting. In responding predominantly to the
individual as a whole and failing to abstract from the individual those
particular features which are relevant to group problems and goals,
the anarchic leader has trouble seeing the group in appropriate perspective. The formalistic participant in the role of leader, on the
other hand, abstracts artificial or formal dimensions of the members
in his effort to perceive group goals. Since this latter type of leader
does not respond emotionally to the people in his group, it is virtually impossible for him to discover what they really feel.

How do existing cultural factors distort that mutual responsiveness
between leaders and members which is necessary for functional leadership? In answer to this question, let us focus our attention on four
specific leadership types: the charismatic leader, the organizational
leader, the intellectual leader, and the informal leader, recognizing
that any leader may be a combination of several types.[2] While we
will stress the way in which culturally prescribed roles affect the
behavior of these leaders, the chief aim is to indicate how their roles
may be redefined and their efforts geared toward eliciting greater
participation.

The Charismatic Leader

The charismatic or colorful leader, e.g., Winston Churchill, Marcus
Garvey, is one who affects and inspires his membership by the strong
expression of his emotionality. By perceiving and responding to the
feelings of those in a large group, and heightening and dramatizing
the significant emotional aspects of large-group feeling, the charismatic leader is able to express group goals and group solidarity vividly,
dramatically and emotionally. This leader stimulates solidarity by
emphasizing the strength and commonness of feeling which serve as
symbols of that group solidarity. Inclined to express feelings and
problems rather than to develop solutions, the charismatic leader
nevertheless can, when solutions are suggested, make them stand out
vividly. Thus he can serve a vital group function.

---

2. The four divisions of leadership used here are ideal types each corresponding to unique
functions which, in an organizational framework, promote participation. Characteristically,
particular leaders usually play one of the indicated roles more than the others, and their
effects on the group spring essentially from their central role. This would appear to be due
to special personality, training, and skill variables which, over a lifetime, constrain the
various leaders to adopt more specialized leadership roles (though their specialization does
not prevent them from accepting other leadership functions to a lesser degree).

Unfortunately, the colorful leader frequently does not appropriately see his own role in relation to the total goals of his group. Under the pressures of our culture he too often tends to rigidify his mode of presentation. He may cease to react to group feelings and may begin to manipulate these feelings and responses in demagogic fashion. He then uses catch words and slogans, carelessly banalizing them. He will often induce false optimism among the members because his emotionality makes him particularly vulnerable to the temptation to exaggerate the possibility of success, and because his *distorted* charismatic role makes him feel that he is performing successfully only when he stimulates "hopped-up" action and enthusiasm among the members.

The charismatic leader's role must be redefined so that he sees that it is not an individualistic role, filled with uniqueness and mystery. Nor should he believe that his success is conditioned simply by his ability to excite the membership. Rather, he should constructively view his role in its relationship to other leadership roles and to the democratic ends of his group.

In the main, the charismatic leader performs three key functions, which must be clearly defined, if his characteristic culturally produced errors are to be avoided:

Cohesion. In large organizations, face-to-face relationships among all members are impossible. The members are reinforced in their own work if they know that other people elsewhere are engaged in related activity. The charismatic leader, bringing to people a greater awareness of this type of cohesion, stimulates increased participation. Functional organizational leadership requires emotional involvement and it is the charismatic leader who can light the spark among the group members. But, in order to be healthily stimulating, he must avoid the "canned emotion" often characteristic of colorful leaders in our society. By relating himself to the informal leader, he can greatly increase his responsiveness.

Interpretation. The colorful leader is especially qualified to help members see the relation between their specific roles and the attainment of organizational objectives. This is accomplished through dramatic interpretations of what the members themselves are doing. The colorful leader heightens the excitement, meaning, and goal orientation in their work. Such reinforcement is tremendously important in the present apathetic period, for initial stimulation is necessary for participation at this stage. Integrating his functions with the intellectual leadership can give the charismatic leader better perspective of the broader group orientation, so that he can communicate these aims more meaningfully. As a by-product, his interaction with the intellectual leader will give the latter a greater emotional understanding of the daily concrete problems of group activity.

Channelization. The charismatic leader can direct participation toward group goals instead of stimulating a diffuse excitement. He has to stimulate members to be creative and productive in the working-out stage, so that the participation he engenders is not of a static, "carrying-out" variety. The channeling should lead to the development of means and ends and the active growth of members, since functional, productive participation, not formal activity, is the desired outcome. On the other hand, the charismatic leader can be actually harmful to membership morale, if mechanisms for the expression of the members' enthusiasm and action potential are not provided. Leadership in general should make sure that the enthusiasm of the members is not blocked by the absence of means for expression.

The Organizational Leader

The organizational leader (e.g., Donald Nelson) is concerned with the day-to-day functioning of the administrative, technical processes of organizational activity. In our culture the organizational leader is especially prone to judge his success by pragmatic criteria, and his role has probably been more distorted than that of any of the other types. Typically, he utilizes various superficial indices of success, such as speed and quantity. His concern is primarily with formal organization, in regard to which he has a mysterious, compelling "know-how." This emphasis often causes him to lose sight of the purpose of an undertaking, as he sanctifies the use of certain specified means. Action and the effect of action are, to him, often one and the same.

Conceiving of himself as an "executor" of action, he emphasizes "carrying out a job." He underestimates the role of discussion and thinking ("We don't have time for that!") and he frequently has a strong anti-intellectual bent. This type of leader, with his tremendous emphasis on getting something done, drives members to action; he pressures them into rigidly following the established formal (hack) procedures, which emanate from his organizational "know-how." The action which results is, of course, static and unsatisfying. Naturally, the members have little or no incentive to perform the technically necessary jobs of the group; it is not surprising, therefore, that the organizational leader often protests that he "does all the work."

Redefined in a positive way, the most important function of an administrative leader in a participation-deficient group is to improve planning and the development of functional means. Generally, the organizational leader can be most useful in the processes of analyzing, planning, and integrating. Ideally, he can contribute greatly to the human efficiency of group and organizational activity if he avoids the pragmatic "mechanical efficiency" prescribed by the culture.

To overcome his lack of sensitivity to the members, the administrative leader would do well to adopt a system of two-way communication to insure greater awareness of the feelings and abilities of the group membership. The typical organizational leader responds more easily to a few people, such as informal leaders, than to the whole group. By developing a close relationship with informal leaders, he can begin to develop emotional relationships with the group as a whole. An important function of the organizational leader should be to encourage potential informal leaders; he should not, however, attempt to fit informal leaders into the mold of the organizational type, nor choose new leaders on the basis of this image.

To curb the organizational leader's over-concern with formal participation, a closer integration with the intellectual leader is advisable. The expert's theoretical orientation may stimulate the other's interest in the broader goals, so that he may begin to question his formal means, paving the way for the emergence of more functional means. This interaction between the intellectual and the organizational leader will narrow the gap between the daily, concrete means of the organizational leader and the far more general perspective of the intellectual, producing a more integrated over-all strategy.

Some well-known organizational leaders are George Marshall, Clement Atlee, James A. Farley, and William Green.

The intellectual or expert type of leader, (e.g., Harold Laski), is a key figure in an effective organization: able to provide perspective, especially in the interpretation of less immediate goals, he can see with a minimum of bias the relationship of various aspects of a problem. Adept at the definition and discussion stages of participation, he is unfortunately often quite inadequate at the "working out" stage.

One major drawback hampers the work and weakens the ability of the American intellectual to develop participation among people: like the organizational leader he does not share, or respond sensitively to, the daily feelings of the members. He can only perceive the group's *objective* needs, since he rarely feels the members' unarticulated subjective attitudes to the group goals and to their own problems. Consequently, he seldom has deep rapport with the membership. Characteristically, the intellectual leader's understanding of group goals is based on minimal personal experience; consequently, he fails to communicate readily with the membership, relying, as he often does, on the cold, formal terminology of the academic or legal world.

The intellectual's global and idealistic statements (which are among the central components from which the cultural stereotype of the intellectual leader is derived) result from his individualistic separation from people and his culturally prescribed suppression of emotion. Typically, his use of high sounding statements and declarations fails to produce participation; anarchic workers, especially, often do not know what he is talking about. It is not surprising, therefore, that the intellectual plays such a piddling role in American organizations. All too often he is used either for specific research or as a prestige symbol on the organization's stationery or speaking platforms. Consequently, many intellectuals, not content with their token intellectual role, are out to "prove" themselves and frequently they turn to detailed organizational work as a compromise solution. Genuine participation by the intellectual would require that he think in the process of acting, thereby making a positive contribution in the "working out" stage. Unfortunately, he often works and thinks as atomistically and uncreatively as the typical formal participant, without contributing his real intellectual abilities to the group needs.

A functional intellectual role embodies an interpretation of ideas and of action, and of the interrelation of these. For this satisfying integration to become a reality, the intellectual must be an organic part of the group instead of a sporadic consultant. He needs to continuously interact with other group members, especially in the "working out" stage. Closer relationships with the charismatic and informal leaders, who are more directly and more emotionally related to the group, are crucial for increasing the expert's sensitivity, sharpening his broad perspective, and reducing his over-abstractness.

Various intellectual leaders who have been connected with action groups are Laski, Cord Meyer, Jr., Tugwell, Paul Douglas. W.E.B. DuBois, Einstein, Niebuhr, Nehru, and Jefferson. Professor Laski has actively enunciated and elaborated the broad goals of the British Labor Party. He has provided theoretical rationales for the program of his party. Nehru has given ideological direction to a significant democratic movement.

The intellectual leader can contribute to the participation of the group only by combining his overall perspective with the specific feelings of the group members. His interpretive functions are most constructive only when they are derived from, and tested by, group experience.

The Informal Leader

The role of the informal leader, often a non-office holding person who is close to the rank-and-file and is an unobtrusive grass roots opinion leader, has been not so much distorted as it has been neglected or undefined. (Many images of Lincoln—receiving people informally in the White House, his anecdotal way of communicating to people, his simplicity, etc.—are characteristic of what we mean by the informal leader).

When the informal leader is recognized as a leader, he is, typically, directed into one of the other leadership roles and forced to attempt activities alien to his personality and values. More often, he is not even recognized as a leader because of his inarticulateness, his closeness to the membership, his lack of individualism or driving ambition.

The special leadership contribution of the informal leader lies in *his acute sensitivity to the feelings of the members and his ability to work with people in a warm, flexible way.* Actually, he is an anarchic participant with deep insight, and his most crucial limitation stems from his inability to abstract. This defect leaves him fairly static, for though he responds well to what is in the present situation, he sees little beyond the concrete. This tendency is particularly reinforced by his characteristic failure to recognize himself as a leader. He tends to accept the cultural conception of the leader-as-father-figure (dynamic, verbal, godlike), and he cannot therefore envision himself as fitting the role as defined.

In order to have the members and other leaders really appreciate the value of the informal leader, it is necessary for the entire cultural conception of what a leader should be to be redefined in terms of the following basic tenets: (1) leaders are regular people, not one-man dynamos who know all the answers and do all the work; (2) leadership is developed; people aren't born with a mysterious leadership ability; (3) people who like to work with and are sensitive to other people are the best potential leaders; and (4) good leaders don't need to keep up a front of always being poised, independent, and decisive. If leadership is understood in these terms, informal leaders will not be forced into other molds which they cannot easily fill and which prevent them from making the most of their own special functions.

The primary function of the informal leader relates to communication. Because of his emotional responsiveness (he is keenly sensitive to the various shades of other people's feelings and to subtle changes in their responses), he is able to communicate to other leaders the desires of the members, as well as their probable reactions to the ideas and proposals of the leadership. Often, the informal leader can predict the elements in a plan which will appeal the least (or most) to grass roots people (the "barometer" function). Informal opinion leaders are also excellent in ferreting out the new ideas of the rank-and-file, and they can pass these along to those centralized leaders in national organizations who are not in face-to-face contact with the local membership. Finally, informal leaders help adapt the broad plans for more effective local action. These functions are the core of two-way communication.

By and large, the informal leader has been passed by in our culture, which looks to the articulate, self-confident individual for guidance and direction. Hence the student of leadership experiences difficulty in citing models of this type, a fact which reflects the dominant cultural ideal. The image of informality is connected with the name of Lincoln, the relaxed personality of Will Rogers, Bing Crosby, and Ernie Pyle. It was the genius of Rogers to have always maintained human, personal contact with the people and to have expressed their hopes and sentiments. Responsive to others, sensitive to their feelings, this type of person is potentially a superb democratic action group leader.

Leadership Therapy

The basis for change in leadership patterns depends to a large extent on the counter trends which already exist. One of the more important grounds for hope lies in the ambivalence of large numbers of people towards leadership. Krech and Crutchfield point out that many people deeply distrust leadership.[3] This attitude represents an unmistakable antagonism to the usual conception of leaders as superior, dominating figures. The ambivalence toward this kind of leader is demonstrated in the conflict between the desire for dependence upon an all-powerful leader and the widely held belief that power

---

3. Krech, D. & Crutchfield, R.S., *Theory and Problems of Social Psychology*. New York: McGraw-Hill, 1948, Chap. XI.

corrupts, i.e., that when the leader becomes powerful he will misuse power and betray his people.[4] Cynicism toward leadership does not appear to be directed toward leadership *per se,* but toward those culturally produced aspects of leadership which emphasize individualistic dominance. Anarchic workers especially reject manipulative leadership behavior. A parallel cultural trend of less significance is anti-expertism. A striking example is the public's overwhelmingly negative reaction to the 1948 Presidential predictions of the public opinion polls. The tremendous pleasure with which almost everyone attacked the pollsters points to the strong ambivalence toward the very same experts who a few days earlier were accepted as infallible.

Another potential basis for change stems from the fundamental American values relating to the common man and the underdog. The tradition of Jackson, Lincoln, and Roosevelt shows clearly that the American people are ready to reward leaders who are sensitive to the common man and who do not emphasize dominance and power over him. There seems to be a strong desire for more informal leaders, who are inclined to have a greater identification with the underdog. People like to see informal leaders accept leadership roles without giving up any of their warm, informal characteristics. The popular image of Lincoln symbolically expresses this positive attitude toward leadership. It is especially important, then, to emphasize a clearer definition of informal leadership in order to remove it from its present residual role.

Finally, in considering positive factors in leadership therapy, the conflicts within the leader himself cannot be ignored. Many a leader has adopted, with mixed feelings, formal practices which he believes are necessary for carrying out his role. He accepts these norms because he feels insecure and threatened in his position. He is continually judged by those above him in the hierarchy, the cultural conception assumes that *the* leader is entirely responsible for the group, and new functional forms have not been worked out for ready use. He uses formal pragmatic methods because they appear to be functional. If their dysfunctional elements can be shown to him, there is a strong possibility that he will accept a redefinition of his role which is more consistent with his feelings for people.

Additional conditions for his accepting a new role are: he must learn, not only theoretically but in practice, that the new role will work; he must acquire new standards for judging the success of the role, because the old formal, pragmatic criteria are not adequate

---

4. Myrdal, G., *op. cit.,* Ch. 33.

measures of functionality; the group structure must be changed so that the continuous threatening pressures which result in formalism will be relieved; the group as a whole has to accept and understand his new role in order to produce the reinforcement necessary for the change.

THE LEADER AS COMPLETER
William C. Schutz

The suggested framework for integrating group roles consists of listing all those things needed for a group to cope successfully with outer reality, interpersonal needs, and conflict-free factors. It is at this point that the FIRO theory of interpersonal behavior seems to offer a method of enumerating the necessary behaviors for coping with at least two of the three spheres. This theory states that there are three fundamental interpersonal needs—inclusion, control, and affection—and in order for an individual (or group) to function optimally he [the leader] must establish and maintain a satisfactory relation in all three areas, with other people or with symbols of people. The application of these notions to each area of influence of ego and leader development will now be pursued. The totality of requirements in these three areas may be considered necessary group functions for optimal group performance within the ego psychology—FIRO theoretical framework.

Outer Reality

The kinds of things that may go wrong in outer reality, the things that make it necessary for the leader to take some kind of action, are those in which the interpersonal needs of the group are not compatible with the requirements of external reality, or where somehow outer reality does not enhance (or even inhibits) the expression of the conflict-free area of the group. This suggests a way of categorizing outer reality for groups. FIRO describes various types of compatibility holding between people and suggests that this type of analysis can be expanded to include situations. Types of incompatibilities that can exist between the group and external reality may be described, parallel to person-person incompatibilities. Since, according to FIRO theory, individuals have three basic interpersonal needs—inclusion, control, and affection—there may be an incompatibility between a group and its environment in any of these three areas.

In the area of inclusion, a group can be incompatible with outer reality in that it wants either more or less contact and interaction with outer reality than it has. Too little contact is exemplified by military groups that live at isolated outposts. If such a group, as a whole, wants more interaction with people than the setting provides, this dissatisfaction may be the source of incompatibility between the group and its environment. On the other hand, a family group for example, including a famous person, may be constantly besieged by invitations, visitors, and by other experiences that do not permit them to maintain sufficient privacy. In this case, outer reality becomes incompatible with the group by not allowing them sufficient withdrawal from interaction with their environment.

In the area of control, outer-reality incompatibility means that the group either has too little or too much control over its environment. Too little control is exemplified by a group living at the foot of an irregularly erupting volcano. Here, there is a fundamental incompatibility between the group and outer reality because the group has too little control. On the other hand, a group that is forced to control its outer reality too much is likely to feel it has more responsibility than it can handle. For example, in wartime, aboard key ships, young, inexperienced tactical radar teams have the enormous responsibility of controlling the actions of planes in combat with the enemy. In this case control is sometimes too great, and these groups would often be quite happy to be relieved of much of their control.

In the area of affection, a group may be incompatible with outer reality because it has too few or too many affectional ties with the environment. It often happens that a particular kind of group such as the Central Intelligence Agency is required to act in a very dignified and secret manner. This group is not allowed to become intimate with any other group because of the nature of its work. This aspect of too few ties may be unsatisfactory for most group members. On the other hand, intimacy and closeness for other groups may be excessive and may be forced upon them by the external situation. This is true of certain families living in suburbia, where the great closeness of their living forces them to become close and intimate with many people in their surroundings in ways they do not desire.

The above, then, are examples of a way in which, if one accepts the FIRO framework, all possible incompatibilities between a group and outer reality might be categorized. An area of influence on ego development as elaborated by FIRO theory indicates the following.

Leadership Functions Re Outer Reality

(1) Establish and maintain sufficient contact and interaction with outside groups and individuals to avoid isolation of the group, but not so much contact that the group loses its privacy.

(2) Establish and maintain sufficient control over outer reality that the group can function satisfactorily without outside interference, and yet not so much control that the group is forced to undertake more responsibility than it desires.

(3) Establish and maintain sufficient closeness and intimacy with outside reality that the group can feel the pleasures of friendship and affection, and yet not so much intimacy with outside reality that the actions of the group become distorted and detrimental to group objectives.

Interpersonal Needs

The leader functions for establishing and maintaining satisfactory relations among members follow the same lines as those given for outer reality, except that the compatibility must be among members within the group rather than between the group and outer reality. An extensive discussion of the problems of compatibility of this type is given in FIRO (Schutz, 1958c). For the present purposes, the primary leadership functions for each area are discussed.

Satisfaction of interpersonal needs is obtained through the establishment and maintenance of an optimal relation among group members in their need areas. Hence, in order to function effectively, the group must find comfortable balance in the amount and type of contact and interaction, control and influence, and personal closeness and affection.

Leadership Functions Re Interpersonal Needs

Enough inclusion. It is necessary to maintain the group's existence. It therefore is desirable that everyone feels part of the group and to some degree knows he belongs. A desire for inclusion is motivation for efficiency in activities such as notifying members of meetings. Activities that foster these feelings include introductions and biographical stories to identify members.

Not too much inclusion. It is necessary to allow group members to maintain some degree of distance from other group members and some individuality. To accomplish this end groups are divided frequently into subgroups, labor is divided, and perhaps in a more subtle way differences are established between subgroups (male-female, Negro-White, Catholic-Jew, etc.).

Enough control. It is necessary for members to influence other members to some extent in order to make decisions. Without this influence or control of others no decision-making system could be effective. Techniques used to accomplish this end are election of officers, establishment of power hierarchies, employment of brute force, and so on.

Not too much control. In most groups it is necessary to establish behavior patterns leading to a restriction of the amount of control some members have over others. If this is not done, the value of the independent operation of some persons is lost, and some members acquire too much responsibility. The institutional procedures of majority rule and consensus are often used to limit control.

Enough affection. The necessity for this need is more controversial. For the present purposes it is assumed that affection is necessary for the effective functioning of a group. Hence, it is required that people relate to each other with sufficient warmth and closeness for group processes to proceed. If there is not enough freedom to express feelings among members, then the productivity suffers because of the tie-up of energy in the suppression of hostile impulses. Widely used behaviors attempting to gratify this need include side-whispers, subgrouping, after-meeting coffee, parties, bringing food to meetings and coffee breaks.

Not too much affection. Excessive intimacy and closeness may have the effect of detracting from the main purposes of the group, and also of personalizing task issues to an undesirable extent. Hence, it is necessary to limit the degree of closeness in groups. Techniques used for accomplishing this end are nepotism rules, fraternization rules, agenda and other procedural techniques, discipline and punishment for too much affectional play.

These functions constitute those of leadership in the area of interpersonal needs. The leadership function must see to their satisfaction by means acceptable to the group for the group to perform optimally.

Conflict-free Behavior

Leadership Functions Re Conflict-free Group Sphere

1. The establishment and clarification of the hierarchy of group goals and values.
2. The recognition and integration of the various cognitive styles (modes of approaching problem solving) existing within the group.
3. The maximal utilization of the abilities and capacities of the group members.

The essential difference between this area of leadership and the others is that the supposed physiological or somehow "purely" cognitive, thinking, characteristics of the group members must be mobilized. This requires assessing what they are and enabling them to be expressed fully. The area of cognitive style may also be included in this area. Measures of variables of this sort are now being developed and appear very promising. They may aid in explicating the conflict-free area and eventually lead to usable dimensions.

Rational and Irrational

The ego psychologists say that although the conflict-free ego sphere develops autonomously, it may still come under the influence of instinctual urges. This is a phenomenon widely noted in group behavior as well. Past studies (Schutz, 1955) indicate that for groups the task situation is commonly used to gratify interpersonal needs that have not been satisfied in the group. For example, a task is used to achieve prominence or withdrawal, power or dependency, emotional closeness or distance, until satisfactory resolution of these needs is made. If a member's strongest need is high inclusion, he works to the degree necessary to be an integral part of the group; if control, he attempts to gain the respect of the group by performing competently; if affection, he tries to be liked by all, perhaps by working, or by joking, or by whatever technique he has found most effective. Similarly, people respond appropriately to the task situation if their interpersonal needs are gratified in the present group. *Appropriate* means "in such a way as to gratify themselves maximally in terms of their values and goals and within the limits of their cognitive capacities."

The Leader as Completer

In summary, by using the model of ego development presented by the psychoanalytic ego psychologists and elaborated by FIRO theory, a description may be made of the leadership functions in a small group. This description indicates the sameness of the problem for both the individual ego and the group leaders. In both cases, in order for the leader—or ego-functions—to develop optimally, the problems of the group, or individual, must be resolved: to outer reality with respect to contact, control and closeness; to interpersonal needs (or instinctual urges) with respect to contact, control and closeness; and to the autonomous conflict-free abilities and properties of the group or individual. In addition, the leader- or ego-functions must lead to a resolution of the interaction of these areas, partly through clarification and operation of value and goal hierarchies.

This approach leads to a somewhat more complicated picture of the leader function than those usually given—a picture which may be called the *leader as completer*. If all the above-mentioned functions must be performed for optimal group operation, the best a leader can do is to observe which functions are not being performed by a segment of the group and enable this part to accomplish them. In this way he minimizes the areas of group inadequacy.

Specifically, whatever is required to enable the group to be compatible with outer reality and whatever is not being done by the group itself, the leader has to do or get done. If this means making contact with outer reality, or enabling others to do it, or becoming a spokesman to outer reality for the group, or absorbing the hostility of the external world heaped upon the group—an effective leader must perform these tasks. Occasionally it becomes necessary for the leader to become the scapegoat for interpersonal problems within the group because the incompatibility, leading to hostility, in the group is so great that no work can be accomplished. If the leader drains off some of this hostility by being the scapegoat, the group is able to continue to function. This conception also implies that when the group is fulfilling all its functions adequately, the most appropriate behavior for the leader is inaction.

This may be a somewhat different notion of a leader, since typically he is not looked upon as someone who puts himself in this position. From this analysis of the parallel with the psychoanalytic concept of the individual, the general properties of a leader become simply those functions required to maintain a certain kind of equilibrium between outer reality and interpersonal needs and the conflict-free functions of the group. These sometimes are very unpleasant, even "unleaderlike" activities.

One implication of this conception is that for some people, fulfilling these particular leadership functions would not be gratifying to their own interpersonal needs. For some, being the scapegoat voluntarily is not a pleasant way to interact in a group. Hence, the prime requisites for a leader are: (1) to know what functions a group needs; (2) to have the sensitivity and flexibility to sense what functions the group is not fulfilling; (3) to have the ability to get the things needed by his group accomplished; and (4) to have the willingness to do what is necessary to satisfy these needs, even though it may be personally displeasing. This whole conception of leadership is reminiscent of an old saying that "the good king is one whose subjects prosper."

THE SMALL-GROUP DISCUSSION LEADER AS SPEAKER
Laura Crowell

Small groups meeting for purposes of mutual enlightenment or of group problem solving regularly utilize the services of one person in a leadership capacity. This does not mean that they prohibit any other member from voluntarily performing some act usually thought of as a leadership function; it means rather that, in addition to this random assumption of leadership functions by members, one person is designated to see to it that essential duties of focusing the group on its task are not neglected.

Thus, the discussion leader in a decision-making group finds himself maintaining a constant watchfulness over the idea-composition and idea-correction accomplishments of the group[1] and taking steps to strengthen them at all necessary points. Further, he maintains a similar constant watchfulness over the general morale and the interpersonal relationships in the group, and acts, when necessary, to lift these into highest effectiveness for dependable progress toward the goal and for individual and group satisfaction in interaction and common achievement. As he acts on the basis of this silent scanning of the whole process and of the participants, he guides his actions by attention to the boundaries within which it is prudent for him to act. That is, his handling of specific problems of idea-development and interpersonal relationships must safeguard other values in the situation, values such as the general atmosphere and purposefulness of the group, the self-esteem of individual members, and the achievement of group accord on a reasonable resolution of its problem.

Since small-group discussion leadership is clearly a rhetorical act, it is necessary that the leader discover what ideas and attitudes the other members of this particular group hold which can be "harnassed" by the leader in his rhetorical discourse.[2] If they provide motive power for the common task—such as feelings of dedication to the group goal, of pleasure in the cooperative accomplishment, of confidence in members and leader—he can utilize them in helping the group move to its goal. If they are values which need to be conserved in the group activity—such as respect for individual self-esteem, concern for the welfare of society in general, expectations of small-group

---

Reprinted with permission of the author. Laura Crowell is Professor of Speech at the University of Washington. This original essay appears here in print for the first time.

1. Laura Crowell, *Discussion: Method of Democracy* (Chicago: Scott, Foresman and Co., 1963), 183-191.
2. Lloyd F. Bitzer lists the constraints given by the situation as "beliefs, attitudes, documents, facts, traditions, images, interests, motives and the like . . . ." See "The Rhetorical Situation," *Philosophy and Rhetoric,* 1 (January, 1968), 8.

processes and of leadership itself—he can fashion his discourse so as not to stretch these boundaries too severely.

But in addition to managing these constraints provided by the particular discussion situation there are basic conditions deriving from the very nature of the discussion process within which the leader must work to fulfill his responsibilities in the group. These conditions inherent in the structure of small-group discussion are that the leader's speaking is *face-to-face,* that it is *impromptu,* and that it is *interactive.* Each of these conditions merits careful analysis by anyone seeking to understand the small-group discussion leader as speaker.

1. His speaking is face-to-face. The leader, performing his focusing function for the group, usually does so encircled closely by his co-workers; all sit in direct view of each other—about a table, or simply in a circular arrangement. Clearly, the discussion leader's physical situation contrasts vividly with that of the public speaker, who is separated from his audience by significant space, is standing, is perhaps elevated above his hearers, and is regularly provided with specialized equipment—lectern, loud speaker, additional lighting. But the discussion leader *sits among* those with whom he is to work. He sees them at close range; actually, the members of a small problem-solving group are few enough in number that he can note the responses of each one separately. This immediacy is, understandably, both an asset and a liability to the leader in forwarding the goals of the group.

He can see as he talks (and as he listens) how they perceive the idea before them, its meaning and merit; indeed, he can see how they perceive his handling of the overall job and his handling of them as team-members on that job. He can see the degree of general acceptance of the current line of thinking and the degree of dedication to the common goal; he can see whether the cooperative spirit is general or whether there are pockets of unwillingness to join in the group effort. Knowledge of these matters is valuable to him in his task as focuser, and he runs a continuing survey on them to assist him in managing his options of action appropriately.

Whether or not the leader thinks about it, and whether or not the members realize it, this face-to-face relationship contributes to their cooperative action; the form invites the function.[3] Sitting thus together signifies an implicit agreement to work together, or at least to

---

3. It should be noted, however, that it was anticipation of the cooperative action to take place which produced the seating arrangement in the first place; anticipation of the function had produced the form.

begin by trying to do so. Each person in the circle has momentarily foregone in some measure his individual status through accepting physically the individual-in-a-group role, and correspondingly each has, while at the table, submerged his customary claim of personal separateness in the hope of achieving a group relatedness. This tacit expectation of working as a team is of great value to the leader.

But this propinquity also tends to make any strong expression of adverse opinion or of hostile attitude seem somewhat threatening to the leader, somehow like a violation of trust. In addition, the flood of responses (verbal and non-verbal) that the leader perceives may be almost overwhelming to him. (Were he farther away, he would undoubtedly perceive fewer of these reactions and feel them less personally; actually, it is likely that in a situation less demanding in its physical relationships fewer reactions would be exhibited for him to perceive.) Even when the leader construes these reactions as supportive of his efforts, yet their natural diversity may give him a seemingly unmanageable task of synthesis and interpretation. He may wish for a private moment now and then in order to make the careful judgments that his role requires of him, to maintain within this circle of common commitment but diverse contribution the specialized function that is his, that of focusing the group on its task.

Furthermore, even as the leader sees many reactions from the members directly and minutely, *they* are seeing *him* at close quarters also. Any momentary hesitation or confusion or private response on his part is perceivable by them, and this he knows full well. Even if he has no desire to hide his mental and psychological operations, he may wish to handle them more privately. The members have almost too much opportunity for close scrutiny of their leader.[4] And awareness of his continuing high visibility may well act as a handicap to the leader.

2. *His speaking is impromptu.* The leader, aware through his inner scanning of an exigence (i.e., something needing to be altered), assessing it to be an exigence that, in the best interests of the group, must be handled *by him,* and seeking to serve the group's purpose within the boundaries of his situation, speaks up in the verbal interchange. No amount of previous thinking and planning could have

---

4. That group members claim this right of observing their leader closely was demonstrated in the instance of the committee whose members nearest the leader felt baffled when he took notes in shorthand. When reporting this feeling afterward, they agreed that the leader had, however, used these notes with high effectiveness for the group and that, furthermore, they probably could not have read his notes from their angle of vision even had the notes been written in longhand. Nevertheless, they did feel uneasy; perhaps the explanation is that he had broken their group solidarity by this unintended assertion of his specialness.

apprised him of what the precise circumstance would be which constituted the exigence; both the content and the form of his resulting comment are, of necessity, spontaneous responses to the situation as he perceives it at that moment in the discussion; they cannot be preplanned, they are impromptu. This characteristic of the discussion leader's speaking contrasts importantly with the unbroken sweep of the public speaker's speaking;[5] even the most extemporaneous of public speakers commands his own line of thinking so that no idea or piece of amplification or support is impromptu unless he wishes it to be. And even then he chooses the time, the extent and the nature of that modification.

But the discussion leader must perform his task of focusing entirely by means of impromptu contributions. No matter how well-informed he is on the problem before the group and how well-acquainted he is with discussion procedures he simply cannot know ahead of time what he will need to say at any point in the discussion; his comments are shaped in substance and form and time by the needs of the group as he perceives them. To the extent that his prediscussion analysis of the problem to come before the group will have alerted him to necessary subordinate areas of consideration he will have a basic structure of inquiry in mind and will, no doubt, find it expedient to bring segments to the attention of the group at certain points. His introduction of these inherent structural items will be so conditioned, however, by the exigence which calls them forth that they may, in fact, be considered impromptu elements.

By these spontaneous comments, then, the discussion leader seeks to focus the group effectively on its task. Actually, it is an advantage to him that he must respond to the immediate, ongoing situation: he has thereby a greater purchase on what the group needs from him at that moment, what turn out of thought and phrase will be most helpful in focusing the potentialities of the group on the common task. Furthermore his spontaneous answering of the needs of the group may further strong creative efforts on the part of others; his willingness to give himself fully to the immediate situation may sponsor an investigative, open-minded feeling among all the members.

But the impromptu nature of his speaking involves difficulties also. All of the relevant canons of rhetoric must be invoked at once: the leader must cull his stock of available responses (**invention**), order and proportion the chosen ones (**disposition**), speak these to the group (**delivery**) in a way that suits the temper of the occasion

---

5. Except in cases of deliberately disruptive confrontation those listening to the speaker expect to withhold all reactions other than brief expressions of approval or disapproval until authorized to make them known.

(style). And all of this must be done spontaneously; there is no time to weigh, consider and then perform. All must be brought into play to meet the exigence. Martin Joos describes thus the work of a person speaking in a group of about six persons, that is, a "consultative" speaker:

> All [pronunciation, grammar, semantics] is adjusted by instantaneous homeostasis, and the speaker does not compose text more than two or three seconds in advance.[6]

And the degree of success which the leader (as "consultative" speaker) achieves with his impromptu offering will be vividly clear to him in the subsequent responses of the members. This is a severe time-table for the leader, but one inevitable for him.

3. His speaking is interactive. The discussion leader tries to release the creative energies of the members and to point them cooperatively toward the common goal. He does not seek to reach that goal directly through his own efforts; he works with and through the members for a team achievement. Thus, his speaking role is decidedly different from that of the public speaker, who does the creative job himself; any modifications of phrasing, amplification and delivery he makes in response to feedback from the audience are modifications he has chosen to make in the light of the audience responses as *he* perceived them; *he* is the sole architect of the communication, at least as it occurs orally.

But in small-group discussions the leader *participates* in the interaction. As the focuser of the efforts of the members, he helps them to remain aware of ideas already established in their jointly-produced line of thinking, identifies the point currently under consideration, poses further inquiries needing to be made,[7] assists them in working out differences of facts or interpretations, finds ways to iron out undue tensions among members and to build team spirit, etc. Thus he provides a base line for their efforts. The various levels of abstraction, the different rates of thought, the varying degrees of understanding and of language facility exhibited in the members' comments are built into a unified thought-line through the focusing activity initiated by the leader. Speaking then in an interruptible, open-ended style, the leader provides a steadying influence for the group by this constant attention to synthesis and redirection.

---

6. "The Five Clocks," *International Journal of American Linguistics,* 28 (April, 1962), 24.
7. I.A. Richards uses the term "feed-forward" to mean helping the group *"know* in some sense" what they "are looking for"; he says that ". . . all activity depends on, and is made into activity by feed-forward." *Speculative Instruments* (Chicago: The University of Chi-; cago Press, 1955), p. 120.

Chief among the advantages to the leader from this interactive nature of his speaking is the degree to which his comments are meaningful to his listeners. Whatever he says—to bring broader consideration of some issue, to introduce a further inquiry, to synthesize or summarize, to utilize differences constructively—has as its very basis *what his listeners have said,* the experiences and inferences they have used in building the thought-line thus far. The leader's use of these group-developed materials, then, as the basis of his comments gives the members a preliminary grip on his meaning. Furthermore, he has available to him group-derived *terms,* phrasings of key ideas whose special aptness brought their repeated use by the members; his use of this group-idiom is both helpful and pleasant to the members in their cooperative effort.

But at the same time interactive speaking brings strain upon the leader. First, it puts a high premium upon the efficaciousness of each of the leader's remarks. Although he carries specialized responsibilities in the group, yet he is **in the group** and, as a member of the group, he shares with the others the obligation of limiting himself to let others speak. In relatively brief comments, then, comments threaded into the flow of group thought, he seeks to handle the responsibilities he carries for group effectiveness. Consequently, each of his utterances must pack into small compass the fulfillment of some need—a clear, dependable recapitulation; a perceptive clarification; a probing question; a quick and accurate summary caught and delivered on-the-wing, as it were. His time is necessarily short, and he must achieve much in little, and without fumbling.[8] Part of this rapid move to the heart of the matter must come from an effective use of *ellipsis,* based on a true perception of what part of the sentence framework can be omitted and what **must be said** for ready comprehension by the group; part must come from an effective use of the group's own terms for key ideas, terms that have been used as meaningful handles in the interchange.

A second difficulty in interactive speaking lies in the leader's need to accommodate himself suitably to the *group tempo,* both the physical tempo arising from the rate of verbal utterance by the members and the intellectual tempo arising from their pace in developing a common thought-line and in moving to accord on each of its major segments. Whatever his own tendencies, he must act to serve the goals of the group, adapting himself to the pace if it is an appropriate one, seeking to modify it by his example if it is inappropriate.

---

8. Joos says that consultative speakers are "allowed only a limited number of attempts to return to their muttons before abandoning them . . ." "The Five Clocks," p. 26.

Within these three basic conditions the leader of a small problem-solving discussion group must work as **speaker**. Nevertheless, we sometimes find a leader trying to escape them. He may violate the first condition of his speaking (that it is *face-to-face*) by seating himself separately from the group—in lecture room style—often faintly and ineffectively conceding at the same time the participative nature of the discussion activity by having one member sit with him at the front to serve as recorder. Or he may so stock his end of the table with equipment that he asserts his separate status sufficiently strongly to destroy the team implication of the seating arrangements. Or he may assume so formal a demeanor and language, so formal a tone of voice that he thereby revokes the invitation to informal participation suggested by leaning upon the table together.

He may violate the second condition (that his speaking is *impromptu*) in several ways. He may use previously-prepared materials without appropriate adaptation to the ongoing work of the group; thus the members find themselves deprived of their own rightful stake in the decisions reached, and are balked of both an exercise of power and a feeling of satisfaction. Or he may reject the impromptu nature of his speaking role by adhering so rigidly to a prearranged time schedule that the passage of minutes determines the occurrence of his comments rather than the condition of the group's thinking.

He may violate the third condition (that his speaking is *interactive*) by being too authoritarian in his handling of member contributions, too arbitrary in his definition of goals or procedures, too tied to his own opinions; in these cases the members may quit interacting and virtually leave the field to him, or they may spend their force arguing with him on procedures and interpretations. He may speak when his silence would better serve the group, or go on so lengthily or confusedly that the group loses its momentum and the members feel deprived of their right to participate.

And what of the leader who realizes that his speaking must be *face-to-face, impromptu* and *interactive* but who fails to use these conditions effectively in his major task of focusing the group on its task productively and satisfyingly? Whatever he lacks in self-confidence or in knowledge of human relations that would let him see those about him in a true team relationship, this he must find a way to acquire.[9] Whatever he lacks in the ability to recognize and

9. Abraham Zaleznik, professor of Organizational Behavior at Harvard Business School, analyzes the forms that inner conflict takes and suggests guidelines for managing them in his article, "The Human Dilemmas of Leadership," *Harvard Business Review,* 41 (July-August, 1963), 49-55.

use sound movements of thought or to express his meaning with verbal and vocal skill in the service of the group, this he must find a way to develop. Only when he has himself well in hand in the requisite attitudes and skills can he do sufficiently effective *face-to-face, impromptu, interactive* speaking to focus the efforts of the group productively and satisfyingly upon their common problem. Leaders in small-group problem-solving discussions can neither escape these conditions of their speaking nor afford to handle them poorly.

A TRAIT APPROACH TO THE STUDY OF
LEADERSHIP IN SMALL GROUPS
John G. Geier

Prior to World War II, the emphasis in leadership research by psychologists, educators, and sociologists was on analyzing individual personality traits and characteristics. Numerous attempts were made to isolate various traits and characteristics, thought to be related to leadership behavior, and which also would "explain" why some persons were "leaders" and others not. Several reviews have been made of the many studies conducted in this search for an all-inclusive set of leadership traits.

One of the earliest surveys on individual traits characterizing leaders was made by Bird in 1940. He found 79 traits mentioned in 20 different studies, only five per cent of which were common to four or more investigations.(1) In a comprehensive survey made by Stogdill in 1948, the most commonly identified so-called "leadership traits" are listed as: (a) physical and constitutional factors—height, weight, physique, and appearance; (b) intelligence; (c) self-confidence; (d) sociability; (e) will—initiative, persistence, and ambition; (f) dominance; (g) surgency—talkativeness, enthusiasm, alertness, and originality.(2)

Among all these studies, the only common conclusion that receives even fair support is that leaders excel non-leaders in intelligence, scholarship, responsibility, activity, and social participation.

More recently, criticism has been aimed at this traditional approach to leadership research. This criticism is summarized by Jenkins:

> ". . . Progress has not been made in the development of criteria of leadership behavior, nor in setting up an adequate definition of the concept to guide research in isolating leadership traits."(3)

As compared with earlier studies, both the objectives and methods used in this research differ from the "classic designs" of prior leadership trait studies. First, previous research concentrated primarily on positive factors contributing to leadership behavior. The present study focuses on those factors which effectively *eliminate* an individual from the leadership role, in a group which begins without an assigned leader. Such negative factors have received little attention in prior studies.

Second, earlier studies have primarily utilized direct observation only of the leader himself. The present study focuses on *the way in*

From *Journal of Communication*, Vol. XVII, No. 4 (Dec. 1967), pp. 316-323.

which the leader is perceived by *other* members of the group. There is a great difference between a person *being* intelligent (as measured objectively through aptitude tests) and *appearing* intelligent, or being *perceived* as being intelligent by other persons. Focus is here aimed at describing individual traits as perceived by other group members— not traits as objectively measured.

Third, the methodology utilized in the present study underscores the potential usefulness of unstructured measuring instruments. In order to measure group member perceptions in relation to leadership behavior, it is necessary to observe not only an individual in a group, but also to obtain information from others who have an opportunity to perceive his behavior in relation to themselves and others in the group. Most previous small group research has made use of highly formalized data collection techniques. However, findings reported here were obtained through unstructured, introspective techniques— discussion and interviews with group participants. In a sense, it can be said that use of these more direct communication techniques has resulted in more accurate reporting of leadership functioning, through the perceptions of group members themselves, rather than through perceptions of an "outside observer."

Purpose of the Study

The purpose of this study, then, was to investigate factors affecting leadership emergence in leaderless groups, through analysis of situational perceptions of both leader and followers. More specifically, this objective raises three primary questions:

1. Do perceptions of members of leaderless groups reveal consistent patterns that help explain the process of emergent leadership?
2. As perceived by group members, are there identifiable traits that will likely eliminate an individual as a contender for leadership?
3. Can consistent and reliable data be collected through use of introspective techniques?

The Participants

Participants in the study were students enrolled in Speech 106, an upper level group discussion course offered at the University of Minnesota. No attempt was made to randomly or systematically sample a given population. All participants were either seniors or graduate students who selected the course as an elective subject. Fifty-nine of the 80 subjects were men.

The 80 participants were not all in one class, but were studied over a two-year period. Each class contained no more than 25 students and, at the most, only five groups were studied during any one quarter. A total of 16 groups are included in the study.

During the first two weeks of class, students were given sensitivity training and information on group interaction. These early sessions were conducted by the regular instructor, who employed the lecture-discussion method of instruction.

The Procedure

Techniques used were those that would stimulate group participants to probe and record their own perceptions of the leaderless group situation, including impressions of leadership functioning. A summary of procedures includes:

1. The 80 participants received two weeks of instruction on group interaction.
2. The participants were given instructions concerning their group task. Each student was then assigned to a group, the main task of which was to discuss a problem and to prepare a group paper presenting suggested solutions. Sixteen groups were included.
3. Group members entered the session without assigned roles. At the conclusion of the first hour-long session, each participant predicted the role(s) that each of the other group members would assume throughout the meetings. This predictive sheet, along with a diary in which each student recorded his personal expressions of the group activity, was to be turned in at the start of the second session. Observers were present periodically during the first session, although all group-member comments were recorded on tape throughout this and all other sessions.
4. The predictive sheet and diary responses were read and recorded. The speculations and reactions of group members were closely observed in the following sessions.
5. The second session was again taped and viewed occasionally by observers. Again the participants wrote their reactions in diaries, which were to be turned in at the beginning of the third session.
6. Session three was conducted in the same manner as session two.
7. Session four was conducted in the same manner as session three.
8. After each group turned in its group document and received a rank in relation to each of the other groups, each participant was then interviewed through use of the focused interview. Responses from the predictive sheets and the diaries were incorporated into the interview context.

9. Several weeks following the interview, all participants completed an open-end questionnaire relating to group interaction.
These responses were recorded in the same manner as were the
predictive sheets, diaries, and interviews.

Discussion of Method

A major concern in conducting this study was to discover a
method permitting group members to perceive their position in relation to fellow members, particularly in regard to the leadership role.
There was a need to find means to collect, classify, and evaluate
group-member responses in order to provide a meaningful approach
to studying the emergence of leadership in each of the 16 groups
observed.

Another task was to record group-member responses in such a way
that accurate conclusions might be drawn. Three primary steps were
taken:

1. A continuous collection was made of all written and tape-recorded responses as the groups were in session. These protocols
were placed in a file for each participant in a group.
2. Each participant's file was analyzed to determine the period of
the discussion to which the information related, personal characteristics discussed, and other aspects of the leadership role.
3. The focused interview described by Merton, Fiske, and Kendall
was employed.(4)

Through these methods, the hypothetically significant elements,
processes, and total structure of the observed social situation were
provisionally analyzed. Through this content or situational analysis, a
set of statements was derived concerning situational factors and outcomes. An interview guide was developed which set forth the major
areas of inquiry. The interview was then focused on the subjective
experiences of the participants exposed to the pre-analyzed situation,
in an effort to determine *their* perceptions of the situation.

The array of reported responses to group situations helped test
conclusions and, to the extent that it included unanticipated responses, gave rise to additional information on group-member perceptions. For example, the "leader" of each group studied was
identified *as that member who was perceived by a consensus of
fellow members as having made the most successful attempts to influence the group,* as exercised in the situation, and directed, through
the communication process, toward facilitating attainment of the
group goal. The word "success" is used in defining the leader to

distinguish between the ways participants separated the group "leader" from a "leader contender."

Numbers and percentages in the study were arrived at by the response of group members to interview questions such as: "What roles were obviously filled by members of the group?" Because the respondent may have mentioned the roles earlier in the interview, this question was not always asked. Instead, whenever the interviewee initially mentioned the role of "leader," he was then asked, "What attempts did the member make in assuming the role of "leader," he was then asked, "What attempts did the member make in assuming the role of leader?"

The technique of utilizing these three different sources of data to collect participant responses proved fairly successful. The procedure permits a check on any one source of data. The method has a distinct advantage over a single observational technique and may well be used to study not only aspects of leadership, but other group member roles as well.

No marked difference existed between the events as described through any one of the three sources. Instead, they generally tended to corroborate one another. This consistency of reporting among all three sources may suggest that a future study might employ only one of the measurements and reach similar conclusions. However, because this study was only exploratory, the use of any one technique alone would require refinement before reliance could be placed on a single introspective data source.

Results of the Study

The major objective of the study was to determine if patterns might be revealed through introspective data sources which would help explain the process of emergent leadership. Analysis of the perceptions of all 80 subjects showed that the pattern of leadership emergence within each of the 16 groups was almost the same.

The general pattern consisted of two stages. The first stage was characterized by elimination of leader contenders who possessed what the members perceived as negative characteristics. This rapid and relatively painless elimination process was followed by an intense struggle for leadership by the remaining contenders. This is referred to as the second stage. During this stage those members still in contention continued to make leadership moves that were either supported or rejected by those eliminated during the first stage. Throughout both stages, participants noted the types of leadership moves, the manner or "style" of each contender in relation to group goals, and their own preferences of leadership style.

Following are specific conclusions regarding these two stages in emerging leadership:

1. It seems safe to conclude that early in the first stage of leaderless group discussions, most group members show a desire to gain the role of leadership. Only two of the 80 participants indicated that they would not try for the leadership role. University students and graduate students would naturally be more likely to make a bid for leadership than would the average person. However, this does not detract from the fact that the leadership role is often sought, and that the resulting competition usually results in extreme tension.

2. Group-member response also shows a process of elimination of leader contenders in initial sessions. The sources of data indicate the presence of certain negative factors or traits that lead to rejection. These are defined as undesirable characteristics hindering group goal facilitation. Confronted with a nonstructured situation, and where the task is academically oriented, the group members tend to reject those who are not adaptable to the environment. Thus, those who were uninformed, nonparticipants, or extremely rigid, tended to be eliminated in the early group sessions. This first stage, then, may be either long or short, depending upon the length of time it takes other members to perceive these *obvious* negative traits.

3. The negative trait that eliminated the greatest number of leader contenders in the first stage was the perception of being uninformed. The data show that 38 (47.5%) of the 80 participants were perceived to be in this category. None emerged as a group leader. Actually, only one of the 38 uninformed members ever advanced to the second stage as a leader contender.

4. A second negative factor contributing to leader rejection was nonparticipation. Of the 80 participants, 17 (21.2%) were perceived to be in this category. Eleven of these 17 members were classified as nonparticipants at the close of the first session; yet at that time, all members had apparent equal information on the subject. It would appear that group members are quick to perceive nonparticipation as undesirable. Not one of these 17 persons was included as a leader contender during the second stage and, of course, not one was an emerging leader.

5. A third negative factor was extreme rigidity. Nine (11.2%) of the 80 participants were perceived to be in this category. The

rigid member was seen as a person reluctant to change either his methods or his ideas, even when they clearly conflicted with group norms or standards. Four of these nine members were eliminated from leadership contention in the first stage. The remaining five were eventually eliminated in the second stage.

6. The second stage is viewed as an intense struggle for the leadership role. Group members perceived more explicit attempts by leader contenders than during the first stage. With 42.5% of the participants still in leadership contention, and with these contenders making overt attempts at leadership function, it is not difficult to identify this period in leaderless groups.

7. The awareness of the stages is vividly described in the diaries of the group members. For example, leader contender attempts were observed in the second stage through the mannerisms which leader contenders approached fellow members for support. According to group members, these attempts were not particularly obvious in their first stage, but became so later. For example, during the second stage, leader contenders solicited lieutenants for support. Eleven of the 16 groups perceived a lieutenant role as existing in their groups. Of significance is the point that *each* leader contender who was perceived by other members as making this approach openly acknowledged the attempt in his diary. In addition, seven of the 11 lieutenants were actually leader contenders who had been eliminated earlier. This indicates that the lieutenant role is developed, generally after early elimination, and as such gives increased support to the concept of phasic development of emerging leadership.

8. The second stage, according to participant responses, showed further elimination of contenders. As the stage progressed, 10 of the 33 contenders were perceived as authoritative members. Of these 10 members, only two were eventually permitted to lead a group. With these eight rejections, it may be concluded that the authoritative members, though not eliminated in the early stage, tend to be rejected in favor of the more democratic contenders. The authoritative member is permitted to lead only in those groups which appear to have extremely inferior members.

9. Another factor accounting for elimination in the second stage is offensive verbalization. Six of the 33 contenders were rejected during this stage because fellow members simply did not like the way in which these contenders expressed themselves. The offense included such things as incessant talking and stilted speaking.

General Conclusions

On the basis of this study, it can be concluded that leadership emergence in small leaderless groups is a complex process, involving many factors. Several of these contributing factors that both affect and effect emerging leadership have been identified, but additional determinants of the role have yet to be discovered and reported.

There is value in using a functional definition of the leadership role, a definition in which the leader is perceived as that individual member who most frequently assumes leadership function. This definition permits a more constructive study than does that which regards a "leader" as any member who initiates, encourages, or facilitates group ideas.

At the same time, this study recognizes that there is no single leadership type of personality. One member might achieve leadership status because he has superior intellectual endowments which, in turn, place him considerably above his fellow members and make them depend on him. Another member might achieve leadership because he takes an interest in his fellow members and has a helpful attitude.

This research acknowledges that leadership resides not exclusively in the individual, but in his *functional relationship with fellow members and the goal accomplishment.* This factor probably contributes to the discovery that members of small leaderless groups perceive both phasic development of leaders and negative factors.

It is also important to note, however, that it was possible to classify certain factors that may be thought of as perceived traits that tend to result in leader rejection. In this sense, a trait approach to leadership may still have some merit in explaining the phenomenon of leader emergence in leaderless groups. For example, although a member may or may not have a relatively stable personality trait that can be labeled "rigid," he will tend to be eliminated in the early meetings if he is perceived by fellow members as possessing such a trait.

References

1. Bird, Charles. *Social Psychology.* New York: Appleton-Century-Croft, 1940, p. 27.
2. Stogdill, R.M. Personal Factors Associated with Leadership: A Survey of the Literature. *Journal of Psychology XXV* (1948), pp. 35-36.
3. Jenkins, W.O. A Review of Leadership Studies with Particular Reference to Military Problems. *Psychological Bulletin XXXXIIII* (1947), p. 74.
4. Merton, R.F., M. Fiske, and P. Kendall. *The Focused Interview.* Glencoe, Illinois: The Free Press, 1956, pp. 3-4.

A COMPARISON OF TWO TYPES OF LEADERSHIP IN VARIOUS COMMUNICATION NETS[1]

Marvin E. Shaw

It has been demonstrated in a number of experimental studies (4, 10, 11, 12) that the arrangement of communication channels among group members (communication nets) influences the performance and satisfaction (morale) of the group when solving problems. Another series of experiments (5, 6, 8) has demonstrated that group performance and morale are influenced by the kind of leadership operating in the group. One experiment (2) examined the effects of appointing a leader in groups which were required to solve problems in a wheel communication net. The results of this study were interpreted as showing that the effects of imposed authority are highly related to individual differences and reactions to authority. An equally probable interpretation, however, is that the assigned leaders behaved differently, depending upon the individual's perception of the kind of role that he was expected to play.

These studies reveal that at least two different variables, communication net and leadership type, influence group performance and morale. The purpose of the present experiment is to examine the effects and interaction of these two variables when operating simultaneously in small groups.

Theoretical consideration. The experiments dealing with the effects of communication nets upon group performance and morale having resulted in the formulation of a number of explanatory concepts, probably the most important ones being *independence*[2] (4, 11) and *saturation* (3, 12). Independence refers to the degree of freedom with which a group member may operate and is believed to correlate positively with efficiency and morale. Saturation is the re-

From: Marvin E. Shaw, "A Comparison of Two Types of Leadership in Various Communication Nets," *Journal of Abnormal and Social Psychology,* 50, 1955. pp. 127-134. Reproduced by permission.

1. This research was done under Contract N5-ori-166, Task Order I, between the Office of Naval Research and The Johns Hopkins University. This is Report No. 166-I-189, Project Designation No. NR 145-089, under that contract.

2. The independence of a group member permitted by the communication net is reflected (according to Leavitt [4]) by the Bavelas (1) measure of individual centrality, which is a measure of the number of transmissions and forwardings by others required for a position to transmit a unit of information to every other position in the net. A more direct expression of the independence permitted by the communication net is given by an Independence score (10) which takes into account the number of communication channels available to the individual, the total number of communication channels in the net, and the number of individuals for whom the individual in question must serve as a relayer of information. The Independence score of a position also reflects its propensity for saturation.

sult of the input and output communication requirements imposed upon a group member. It is believed that when such requirements reach a certain optimal point, the favorable effects of a high degree of independence begin to be counteracted, and the position is said to be saturated. In general, the two processes operate to produce effects which are opposite in direction; independence tends to improve performance and morale, while saturation tends to depress performance[3] and morale. However, performance and morale are affected differentially by independence and saturation; that is, morale is influenced relatively more by independence and performance is influenced relatively more by saturation.

It is reasonable to suppose that imposed leadership have an effect upon both independence and saturation and that this effect will vary with the type of imposed leadership behavior. Let us consider the expected effects of two well-publicized leadership types: authoritarian (autocratic) and nonauthoritarian (democratic). Authoritarian leadership should increase the independence of the leader himself, but should decrease the independence of the followers. This is true since the authoritarian leader would be permitted to function with little regard for the desires of the followers, while the followers would be restricted by the desires of the leader. On the other hand, nonauthoritarian leadership should increase the independence of all group members, inasmuch as its chief characteristic is that it permits each group member to have a part in deciding the *modus operandi.*

Saturation should be decreased for all group members by authoritarian leadership, since the leader may be expected to demand a minimum of participation on the part of followers and can control the communication demands upon his own position. Nonauthoritarian leadership should increase saturation for all members in the group, since coming to an agreement in a "democratic" manner will necessarily involve more communication demands upon all group members, including the leader.

To summarize, it is believed that leadership type should influence group behavior not through either independence or saturation alone, but rather through the combination of these two processes. Authoritarian leadership should decrease independence for most of its members (and hence decrease morale),[4] and should decrease saturation

---

3. Both independence and saturation correlate positively with number of messages, although, presumably, for different reasons.

4. Although independence and saturation are said to affect the performance and morale of *individuals* in the group, it is assumed that *group* performance and morale will be determined by the performance and morale of individuals combined in some manner or other.

effects for all group members (and hence improve performance). Nonauthoritarian leadership should increase independence for all group members (and hence increase morale), and should increase saturation for all group members (and hence lower performance).

It is now possible to make some predictions about the outcome of assigning authoritarian and nonauthoritarian leaders to a central position in various communication nets. First of all, authoritarian leadership should result in better group performance and lower group morale than nonauthoritarian leadership in the same communication net. Second, with a given type of leadership the relative differences among nets should be the same as in the no-leadership experiments; i.e., nets having a greater amount of independence should require less time but more messages to solve problems, make fewer errors, and indicate more satisfaction with the job than nets having lesser amounts of independence. Third, positions having the higher Independence scores should require less time and more messages to arrive at the answer, and indicate more satisfaction with the job than positions having lower Independence scores, with the difference between the leader position and the other positions being greater in the authoritarian leadership than in the nonauthoritarian leadership situation.

Method

Apparatus. The apparatus used in this experiment has been described in detail in earlier publications (10, 11). In essence, it consists of four cubicles which are connected with each other by means of slots through which messages written on 3 × 5 cards can be passed. These slots can be closed to set up different nets. Each cubicle has a work table, work materials, and a signal switch which controls a timer and a light on the Experimenter's (E's) signal panel.

Problems. Four simple arithmetic problems were used in this experiment. Each problem consisted of a statement of the problem and eight items of information. Each item of information was typed on a white card and a statement of the problem was typed on each of four white cards. Each subject (S) was given a card containing a statement of the problem and two of the information cards. The information cards were randomly distributed among the four Ss. Examples of these problems can be found in earlier reports (10, 11).

Subjects. The Ss of this experiment were all male undergraduates at The Johns Hopkins University. There was a total of 192 Ss, each of which was assigned at random to a group composed of four persons. The Ss of a given group were usually acquainted with each other prior to the beginning of the experiment, but they did not know which S was assigned to which position in the net. Each S served only once.

Experimental design. Three communication nets (the wheel, the kite, and the comcon, Fig. 1) and two types of leadership (authoritarian and nonauthoritarian) were used in this experiment. The six experimental conditions were: *(a)* authoritarian leadership in the wheel, *(b)* authoritarian leadership in the kite, *(c)* authoritarian leadership in the comcon, *(d)* nonauthoritarian leadership in the wheel, *(e)* nonauthoritarian leadership in the kite, and *(f)* nonauthoritarian leadership in the comcon. Eight groups of four Ss each were randomly assigned to each of these six conditions.

Leadership was always assigned to the position, or one of the positions, having the highest Independence score in the net (position B in Fig. 1). The two types of leadership were introduced by means of instructions to the S who was assigned to position B. The authoritarian leader was instructed to give orders to the other Ss (not suggestions), never to accept suggestions uncritically, and in general to make it clear that he was the boss. The nonauthoritarian leader was instructed to offer suggestions (not orders), to accept suggestions from other Ss if he thought they were good ones, and in general to behave in a cooperative manner. . . .

Discussion

The results generally substantiate the theoretical consideration of the effects of authoritarian and nonauthoritarian leadership upon group independence and saturation as reflected by the performance and morale of groups in various communication nets. The deviation of the groups in the kite may be at least partially explained by the kind of organization found in this net.

Evidence for the relative effectiveness of independence in determining morale and of saturation in determining performance is also found. If one assumes that type of leadership influences only independence, then authoritarian leadership would be expected to require more time, produce more errors and lower morale than nonauthoritarian leadership. The difficulty is that authoritarian leadership required *less* time and made *fewer* errors. If one assumes that type of leadership influences only saturation, then authoritarian leadership would be expected to require less time, produce fewer errors and higher morale than nonauthoritarian leadership. Here the difficulty is that authoritarian leadership produced *lower* morale. It should be clear, then, that the results from this experiment cannot be explained in terms of either independence or saturation taken alone. Also, it should be clear that independence is most effective with respect to morale, while saturation is most effective with respect to performance.

The effects of the nets variable are less clear. With the exception of the kite, however, these effects were as expected. The whole question of organizational effects produced by various communication nets needs to be examined experimentally. This will probably require that groups function in the same net for extended periods of time.

The results from this experiment also provide support for some of the findings reported by Lewin *et al.* (5, 6) in their studies of experimentally created "social climates." They reported that indications of hostility and aggression were much more frequent in the autocratic than in the democratic groups, and that their Ss liked the democratic leader better than the autocratic one. In other words, the morale of the groups was higher when they were subjected to democratic leadership than when they were subjected to autocratic leadership. This is in strict accord with the findings of this study, despite the wide differences between the two experimental situations. This agreement is of significance in that it permits wider generalization than is possible from either study taken alone. Furthermore, our use of the concept of independence refers to essentially the same kind of underlying conditions as the Lewinian concepts of "restricted space of free movement" and "rigidity of group structure."

Lewin and his students devote little space to the question of group performance in the different social climates. However, they do remark that the quantity of work output was greatest for the autocratic groups, but they hasten to add that the work of these groups was *qualitatively* inferior to that produced by the democratic groups. The general implication seems to be that in spite of the quantitative differences to the contrary, the performance of the democratic groups was better than that of the autocratic groups.[5] The results of this study agree with their findings with respect to quantitative differences; the groups with authoritarian leadership used fewer messages and less time to solve the problems than did the groups with nonauthoritarian leadership. However, the present results do not support the interpretation that the performance of democratic groups is qualitatively better than that of autocratic groups. If we accept the

---

5. The author freely admits that all of his sentiments favor this interpretation.

usual notion that number of errors in problem solving is a measure of the quality of work, then the performance of the authoritarian groups was also qualitatively superior to that of the nonauthoritarian groups.

Up to this point we have been using the "authoritarian" and "nonauthoritarian" interchangeably with the terms "autocratic" and "democratic." It should be evident that this is not strictly correct. However, the general behavior of the leaders in the two experimental situations was sufficiently similar to permit the comparisons made above. Wherever agreement is found, differences increase the generalizability of the results; when disagreement occurs, the interpretation is equivocal. The fact that in this study authoritarian leadership produced better work than nonauthoritarian leadership, whereas in the Lewin study democratic leadership produced better work than autocratic, may mean that there were significant differences in the types of leadership (i.e., authoritarian differed from autocratic and/or nonauthoritarian differed from democratic), that the two experimental designs (i.e., S population, type of problem, etc.) differed significantly, or that Lewin and his students were in error in their judgment of the quality of the work products produced by the two groups.

In conclusion, it is felt that these results support the hypothesis that authoritarian and nonauthoritarian leadership affect group performance and morale of groups in various communication nets via their influence upon group independence and saturation, and that morale is affected relatively more by independence whereas performance is affected relatively more by saturation. It is further concluded that authoritarian leadership (in agreement with Lewin's work) produces greater work output and lower morale than does nonauthoritarian leadership. The question of quality of the work as a function of type of leadership is still unsolved; no satisfactory generalization can be made at this time.

Summary

The present experiment was concerned with the effects of authoritarian and nonauthoritarian leadership upon the performance and morale of groups in various communication nets. It was predicted that (a) authoritarian leadership would result in better group performance and lower group morale than nonauthoritarian leadership in the same net; (b) with a given type of leadership, nets having the greater amount of independence would perform better (in terms of time and number of errors) and indicate more satisfaction with the job than nets having lesser amount of independence; and *(c)* positions (within nets) having the higher Independence scores would require less time and more messages to solve problems and indicate more satisfaction with the job than positions having lower Independence scores, with the difference between the leader position and the follower positions being greater with authoritarian than with nonauthoritarian leadership.

Forty-eight groups of four Ss each were required to solve simple problems. Eight groups were randomly assigned to each of the following experimental conditions: *(a)* authoritarian leadership in the wheel; *(b)* authoritarian leadership in the kite; *(c)* authoritarian leadership in the comcon; *(d)* nonauthoritarian leadership in the wheel; *(e)* nonauthoritarian leadership in the kite; and *(f)* nonauthoritarian leadership in the comcon. The leader was always assigned to the position having the highest Independence score. The two types of leadership behavior were produced by instructions to the assigned leader.

The results generally supported the predictions; exceptions were that the kite was less affected by the leadership variable than had been expected, and authoritarian leadership did not result in greater differences between the leader and follower positions as had been expected.

These results were discussed in terms of the concepts of independence and saturation, and comparisons were made with the findings reported by Lewin *et al.* It was concluded that *(a)* authoritarian and nonauthoritarian leadership affect group performance and morale via their effects upon group independence and saturation, and that morale is affected relatively more by independence while performance is affected relatively more by saturation; and *(b)* authoritarian leadership produces better performance and lower morale than does nonauthoritarian leadership.

References

1. Bavelas, A. A mathematical model for group structures. *Appl. Anthrop.*, 1948, 7, 16-30.
2. DeSoto, C.B. The effects of imposed authority status in a wheel group structure. Unpublished master's thesis, Univer. of Wisconsin, 1953.
3. Gilchrist, J.C., Shaw, M.E., & Walker, L.C. Some effects of unequal distribution of information in a wheel group structure. *J. abnorm. soc. Psychol.*, 1954, 49, 554-556.
4. Leavitt, H. J. Some effects of certain communication patterns on group performance. *J. abnorm. soc. Psychol.*, 1951, 46, 38-50.
5. Lewin, K., Lippitt, R., & White, R.K. Patterns of aggressive behavior in experimentally created "social climates." *J. soc. Psychol.*, 1939, 10, 271-299.

6. Lippitt, R., & White, R.K. The "social climate" of children's groups. In R.G. Barker, J. Kounin, & H. Wright (eds.), *Child behavior and development*. New York: McGraw-Hill, 1943. Pp. 485-508.

7. Mann, H.B., & Whitney, D.R. On a test of whether one of two random variables is stochastically larger than the other. *Ann. math. Statist.*, 1947, 18, 50-60.

8. Preston, M.G., & Heintz, R.K. Effects of participatory vs. supervisory leadership on group judgment. *J. abnorm. soc. Psychol.*, 1949, 44, 345-355.

9. Shaw, M.E. Group structure and the behavior of individuals in small groups. *J. Psychol.*, 1954, 38, 139-149.

10. Shaw, M.E. Some effects of problem complexity upon problem solution efficiency in different communication nets. *J. exp. Psychol.*, 1954, 48, 211-217.

11. Shaw, M.E. Some effects of unequal distribution of information upon group performance in various communication nets. *J. abnorm. soc. Psychol.*, 1954, 49, 547-553.

12. Shelly, M.W. The effects of problem saturation in various communication networks. Unpublished master's thesis, Univer. of Wisconsin, 1953.

13. Tukey, J.W. Comparing individual means in the analysis of variance. *Biometrics*, 1949, 5, 99-114.

ELEMENTS AND PROBLEMS OF
DEMOCRATIC LEADERSHIP
Bernard Kutner

Several assumptions are made by a group when it forms for democratic action. First, it is assumed that in organizing itself, the power and authority necessary to conduct the work of the group must be delegated to individual members or subgroups. Secondly, a leader in a democratic group is ascribed authority and invested with certain defined powers. Finally, it is deemed illegitimate for a leader to assume powers not specifically delegated by the group or its governing rules. The final authority in any democratic group thus rests ultimately with the membership. It does not merely derive from, but it is felt to maintain residence in, the group.

A group organized for action may select its leaders by democratic methods, through some form of referendum or group agreement. These may include a central organizational leader and other subleaders (e.g., committee chairman or special functionaries). However, even before leaders are selected, a group must decide upon its goals and its methods for achieving them. The leader would, in a democratic group, be an individual who serves the group in various ways but, primarily, represents the group's goals and interests. Democratic leaders, to be really democratic, would homologously reflect the group they serve and must set aside personal interests or those of some special subgroup.

Balancing Efficiency and Democracy

Leaders need authority—on this there can be little disagreement, since without authority leaders cannot carry out their functions. But the delegation of authority in a democratic group is never a mandate for any leader to employ authority without the eventual approval of the group. Where responsibility for action is not subject to critical examination, a democratic organization no longer exists. Nevertheless, some freedom of action is almost always imperative lest leadership become a sterile and unimaginative position making for red tape and unending delays. Thus, the democratic group has a two-fold responsibility in delegating authority or choosing leadership: to preserve for itself the final authority on any question and to allow a modicum of operational freedom to its leaders.

It would appear that every democratic choice of a leader involves a compromise between jealous preservation of power by the group and active, efficient performance of the group's mandate. A vigorous democratic organization must, however, constantly check its operations to make certain that it is not becoming "efficient" at the expense of its democratic methods. It is important to recognize that there is a current tendency to move from democratic to undemocratic procedures in the name of efficiency. In present-day social organizations, power easily consolidates from the many to the few—from cumbersome groups to convenient individuals.

The drive "to get things done" rather than "to do things democratically" has brought many an organization to its end. Often we suppose that because we live in the Western world where democracy is widely practiced, that it will come of its own accord—that it is "second nature." If it shows anything, much of the available evidence demonstrates the contrary, that democracy must be taught and learned to be practicable.[1] Where it is not self-consciously practiced, the tendency to accept laissez faire as the equivalent of democracy easily leads to the monopolization of authority. The perception of group goals tends to change in time, so that a passive membership may soon find that its leaders are working toward ends which it may not yet have considered or which are antagonistic to agreed-upon goals. Pigors, for example, sees the shift from democratic leadership to despotism as arising from a crisis or emergency in which autocratic measures are assumed by the leader "to save the group."[2]

It is also true that the same sort of shift may occur simply by default of the membership's interest or concern over the activities of the leader even though these may deeply involve them. Because leaders are often left in a position where they alone may serve the group's interest, they are often also the only individuals who are acquainted intimately with all of the details of the group's functioning. The larger the organization, the greater does this tendency exist. This concentration of information may have the added effect of leaving him as the only individual capable of intelligent action. Passive groups may therefore jeopardize their democratic structure unknowingly, permitting the aggregation of power, influence, and in-

---

1. See for example A. Bavelas and K. Lewin, "Training in Democratic Leadership," *Journal of Abnormal and Social Psychology,* 1942, 37, 115-119. Also L.P. Bradford and R. Lippitt, *Supervisory Training for Group Leadership* (Cambridge, Mass., Publ. Research Center Grp. Dynamics, 1945).

2. P. Pigors, *Leadership or Domination* (Boston, 1935), pp. 125-127.

formation to its leaders. Commitments in the group's name made by a leader assuming authority may embarrass the organization and threaten its members. The fault lies in two places: the leader's failure to assess correctly the relation of his action to group goals, or the tyrannical assumption of power by him, and the group's failure actively to control the limits of its leader's functions. Thus, while we must rely upon leaders, we cannot forfeit our function as policeman, censor, and supreme court without, at the same time, forfeiting our position as a member of a democratic group.

Leadership Replacement

When a discrepancy occurs between the group's goals and the leader's behavior or intentions with regard to the group's activities, the time for changing leaders has arrived. The leaders, servants of the group, must be replaceable. To retain its democratic nature a group must have a conscious awareness of the functions of its leaders so that a diagnosis for the retention or change of leadership might be made. A knowledge of leadership functions thus becomes of primary importance in assessing the democratic health of a group.

It may first be emphasized that a primary function of leadership resides in a special type of group representation.[3] The leader should represent an organization through channels specifically designed and delimited by the group itself. Specifically in terms of this representation of group interest, the leader is delegated the functions of executive administration. This involves the coordination and integration of many activities, the crystallization of group policy, and the assessment of new and diverse occurrences bearing on the group's functions. The leader serves also as a liaison between his group and outside organizations or individuals.

While a leader in a democratic group is permitted a degree of initiative and imaginative interpretation of these functions, in the final analysis the effects of his actions are subject to the approbation of the group he represents. Though a leader may also serve as a dynamic element in keeping the group functioning efficiently and may even be the "inspiring" element in the group, it is first and always the representative function of leadership which is to be considered in retaining a leader. The delicate mechanism of authority

---

3. Pigors has attempted to analyze the functions of leadership and has reduced these to one general function: representation, and three specific functions: initiation, administration, and interpretation. The author has drawn heavily upon Figors' work in the present analysis. *Op. cit.,* p. 354.

must be retractable lest a changing or unscrupulous leader is left in power so long that his authority is assumed to be permanently endowed.

Effective leadership may be said to be lost when any one of the above functions becomes impaired. Leadership in a democratic group implies that members of a group rely upon a leader to carry out the minimal functions of leadership in the hope that, through the division of labor imperative in group operation, the leader and the membership will complement each others activities to the end of group success. Leadership is, in this sense, the vehicle through which authority may be used to integrate and express the interests of the group. When it becomes an end in itself, or the vested interest of a given individual, the need for a change of leadership is apparent. It is to the group that the job of diagnosing the needs of group leadership must fall. The group, to remain truly democratic, must be the watchdog of its own leadership. . . .

Self-Examination and Democratic Leadership

Organizations established to pursue democratic action through democratic means must be constantly aware of their obligations to group interest. To this end, some form of soul-searching procedure calculated to warn itself of impending dangers seems advisable.[4] Surveillance, self-survey, self-assessment, and self-criticism are some of the methods which might achieve the goal of democratic unity. Subgroups of an organization may be set up to examine self-consciously the directions in which the organization is moving. It must weigh the apportioning of authority, the tendency of power to accumulate, the tendency for schisms between leader and group to manifest themselves, and other signs of authoritarianism characteristic of undemocratic or antidemocratic groups.

In brief, the group, to remain democratic, must make certain guarantees concerning the control of authority and the functions of leadership. It must guarantee that the group itself dispenses authority and may withdraw it at will. It must guarantee that the extension of authority to an individual or subgroup does not become a mandate for the limitless use of such authority. It must guarantee that the leaders understand their responsibility to the group and to the employment of authority for group goals. It must guarantee initiative

---

4. One such attempt, although arranged for somewhat different purposes, which might be usefully adapted by democratic-action groups may be found in H. Lasswell, *Psychopathology and Politics* (Chicago, 1930), Appendix B, pp. 277-282.

and creativity to leadership but must reserve to itself the final judgment of leader-effectiveness. It must, most importantly, guarantee that the functions of the organization, its structure, procedures, and executive personnel may be altered by democratic processes. With such flexibility and unity of purpose, the achieving of group goals, becomes more probable. It guarantees the continued active existence of the group which, while examining itself, is pursuing its ends. While some such procedure is not offered as a panacea for curing the ills of organized groups, it may be expected at least to diagnose the sources of disorganization and autocracy.

BIBLIOGRAPHY
Part IV
Group Leadership

Asch, S.E. *Groups, Leadership, and Men*, Pittsburgh: Carnegie Press, 1951.

Bass, Bernard M. "The Leaderless Group Discussion as a Leadership Evaluation Measurement," *Personal Psychology*, 7 (Winter, 1954), 470-477.

Bass, B.M. and C.R. Wurster. "Personality Variables Related to Individual Study in Leaderless Group Discussion Behavior," *The Journal of Abnormal and Social Psychology*, 48 (1953), 120-128.

Bavelos, Alex and Kurt Lewis, "Training in Democratic Leadership," *Journal of Abnormal and Social Psychology*, 37 (January, 1948), 203-208.

Belle, Wendell, Richard J. Hill and Charles R. Wright. *Public Leadership*, San Francisco: Chandler Publishing Co., 1961.

Benne, Kenneth D. "Leaders Are Made, Not Born," *Childhood Education*, 24, (January, 1948), 203-208.

Bogardus, Emory S. *Leaders and Leadership*, New York: D. Appleton-Century Co., 1934.

Browne, C.G. " 'Laissez-Faire' or 'Anarchy' in Leadership," Etc., XIII, 1 (Autumn, 1955), 61-66.

Carr, W.G. *Educational Leadership in this Emergency*, (The Cubberly Lecture), Stanford University, Calif.: Stanford University Press, 1941.

Carter, Lawnor, William Haythorn, Beatrice Shiver and John Lanzetta. "The Behavior of Leaders and other Group Members," *Journal of Abnormal and Social Psychology*, 46 (1950), 589-595.

Chowdry, K. and T.M. Newcomb. "The Relative Abilities of Leaders and Non-Leaders to Estimate Opinions of Their Own Groups," *Journal of Abnormal and Social Psychology*, 471 (1952), 51-57.

Coffin, T.E. "A Three-Component Theory of Leadership," *Journal of Abnormal and Social Psychology*, 39 (1944), 63-83.

Collier, Abraham T. "Business Leadership and a Creative Society," *Harvard Business Review*, 31, 1 (January-February, 1953), 29-39.

Cowley, W.H. "Traits of Face-to-Face Leaders," *Journal of Abnormal and Social Psychology*, XXVI (October-December, 1931), 304-313.

Crockett, W. "Emergent Leadership in Small, Decision-Making Groups," *Journal of Abnormal and Social Psychology*, 51 (1955), 378-383.

Deutsch, Morton, Albert Pepitone and Alvin Zander. "Leadership: The Small Group," *Journal of Social Issues*, 4 (Spring, 1948), 31-40.

Dooher, Joseph (ed.) *The Development of Executive Talent*, New York: American Management Association, 1952.

Feedler, F.E. "A Note on Leadership Theory: The Effect of Social Barriers Between Leaders and Followers," *Sociometry*, 20, 87-94.

Fessenden, Seth A. "Who's the Leader?" *The Journal of Communication*, VI, 1 (Spring, 1956), 4-9.

Festinger, Leon. *Conflict, Decision, and Dissonance*. Stanford, Calif.: Stanford University Press, 1964.

Fisher, Margart. *Leadership and Intelligence*, New York: Bureau of Publications, Teachers College, Comumbia University, 1954.

Fox, William M. "Group Reaction to Two Types of Conference Leadership," *Human Relations*, X,3 (1957), 279-289.

French, John. "Retraining an Autocratic Leader," *Journal of Abnormal and Social Psychology*, XXXIX (April, 1944), 224-227.

Gibb, Cecil A. "The Principles and Traits of Leadership," *Journal of Abnormal and Social Psychology*, 42 (July, 1947), 267-284.

Goldberg, S.C. "Influence and Leadership as a Function of Group Structure, *Journal of Abnormal and Social Psychology*, 49 (1954), 325-329.

Gordon, Thomas. *Group-Centered Leadership: A Way of Releasing the Creative Power of Groups*, Boston: Houghton-Mifflin Co., 1955.

Gorman, Alfred H. *The Leader in the Group*, New York: Bureau of Publications, Teachers College, Columbia University, 1963.

Gross, Neal, William E. Martin and John G. Darley. "Studies of Group Behavior: Leadership Structures in Small Organized Groups," *Journal of Abnormal and Social Psychology*, 48 (July, 1953).

Guetzkow, Harold (ed.). *Groups, Leadership and Men*, New Jersey: Carnegie Press, 1951.

Haiman, Franklyn S. "Concepts of Leadership," *Quarterly Journal of Speech*, 39 (October, 1953), 317-322.

———. *Group Leadership and Democratic Action*, Boston: Houghton-Mifflin Co., 1951.

Hare, Paul A., Edgar F. Borgatta and Robert F. Bales (ed.). *Small Groups: Studies in Social Interaction*, New York: Alfred A. Knopf, 1955.

Hamblin, Robert. "Leadership and Crises," *Sociometry*, 21 (1958), 322-335.

Hemphill, J.K. "Relations Between the Size of the Group and the Behavior of the 'Superior' Leaders," *Journal of Social Psychology*, 32 (1950), 11-12.

Jenkins, William O. "A Review of Leadership Studies with Particular Reference to Military Problems," *Psychological Bulletin*, 44, 1 (1947), 75.

Jennings, Helen. "Leadership—A Dynamic Redefinition," *Journal of Educational Sociology*, XVII (March, 1944).

———. *Leadership and Isolation*, London: Longmans Green, 1943.

Jennings, Eugene E. *An Anatomy of Leadership: Princes, Heroes, and Supermen*, New York: Harper and Brothers, 1960.

Kahn, Robert L. and Elise Boulding (eds.). *Power and Conflict Organizations*, New York: Basic Books, Inc., 1964.

Klapp, Orrin E. *Symbolic Leaders*, Chicago: Aldine Publishing Co., 1964.

Knickerbocker, I. "Leadership: A Conception and Some Implications," *Journal of Social Issues*, 4 (1948), 23-40.

Leadership in Action, National Training Laboratories, 1961.

Lewin, Kurt, "A Research Approach to Leadership Problems," *Journal of Educational Sociology*, 17 (March, 1944), 392-398.

Lippitt, Gordon L. "What Do We Know About Leadership?" *NEA*, 44 (December, 1955), 556-557.

Lippitt, Ronald. "The Psychodrama in Leadership Training," *Sociometry*, VI (August, 1933), 291.

Lippitt, Ronald, Leland P. Bradford and Kenneth Benne. "Sociodramatic Clarification of Leader and Group Roles, as a Starting Point for Effective Group Functioning," *Sociometry*, 1 (March, 1947), 82-91.

Liveright, A.A. *Strategies of Leadership in Conducting Adult Education Programs*, New York: Harper and Brothers, 1959.

Liveright, A.A. and Robert J. Blakely. *Strategies of Leadership*, New York: Harper and Brothers, 1959.

Mackenzie, Gordon N. and Stephen M. Corey. *Instructional Leadership*, New York: Bureau of Publications, Teachers College, Columbia University, 1954.

Maier, Norman R. *Problem Solving Discussions and Conferences: Leadership Methods and Skills*, New York: McGraw-Hill, 1963.

———. "The Quality of Group Decisions as Influenced by the Discussion Leader," *Human Relations*, III (1950), 155-174.

Martin, W.E.N. Gross and J.G. Darley. "Leaders, Followers and Isolates in Small Groups," *Journal of Abnormal and Social Psychology*, 47 (1952), 838-842.

Maslow, Abraham H. *Toward a Psychology of Being*, Princeton, New Jersey: D. Van Nostrand Co., Inc., 1962.

Montgomery, Field-Marshal. The Viscount. *The Path to Leadership*, New York: G.P. Putnam's Sons, 1961.

Olmsted, Donald, *Social Groups, Roles and Leadership*, Michigan: Michigan State University Press, 1961.

Pellegrin, Roland J. "The Achievement of High Statuses and Leadership in the Small Group," *Social Forces*, 32 (October, 1953), 10-16.

Petrullo, Luigi and Bernard M. Bass. *Leadership and Interpersonal Behavior*, New York: Holt, Rinehart and Winston, Inc., 1961.

Pigors, Paul. *Leadership or Domination*, Boston: Houghton-Mifflin, 1935.

Preston, M.G. and R.K. Heinz. "Effects of Participatory Versus Supervisory Leadership on Group Judgment," *Journal of Abnormal Social Psychology*, 44 (1949), 343-355.

Pryor, Margaret W. and Bernard Bass. "Group Effectiveness and Consistency of Leadership," *Sociometry*, XXV (December, 1962), 391-397.

Selvin, Hanan C. *The Effects of Leadership*, Glencoe, Ill.: The Free Press of Glencoe, Illinois, 1960.

Shaw, M. and J. Gilchrist. "Intra-group Communication and Leader Choice," *Journal of Social Psychology*, 43 (1956), 133-138.

Sherif, Muzafer (ed.). *Intergroup Relations and Leadership*, New York: John Wiley and Sons Inc., 1962, v-273.

Smelzer, Neil J. *Theory of Collective Behavior*, New York: The Free Press of Glencoe, 1963.

Stogdill, R.M. "Leadership, Membership, and Organization," *Psychology Bulletin*, 47 (1950).

———. "Personal Factors Associated with Leadership. A Survey of the Literature," *Journal of Psychology*, XXV (January, 1948), 63-64.

Stogdill, R.M. and C.L. Shartle. "Methods for Determining Patterns of Leadership Behavior in Relation to Organization Structure and Objectives," *Journal of Applied Psychology*, 32, 3 (1948), 286-291.

Tead, Ordway. *The Art of Leadership*, New York: McGraw-Hill Book Co., Inc., 1935.

Thelen, Herbert A. "The Modern View of Leadership," *Journal of National Associated Dean of Women*, 19 (October, 1955), 31-36.

Titus, Charles Hickman. *The Processes of Leadership*, Dubuque, Iowa: William C. Brown Co., 1950.

Urwick, L.F. *Leadership in the Twentieth Century*, London: Sir Isaac Pitman and Sons, Ltd., 1957.

Van Dusen, A.C. "Measuring Leadership Ability," *Personnel Psychology*, 1 (1948), 68.

Verba, Sidney. *Small Groups and Political Behavior: A Study of Leadership*, Princeton, New Jersey: Princeton University Press, 1961, viii-249.

Weber, Clarence A. and Mary E. Weber. *Fundamentals of Educational Leadership*, New York: McGraw-Hill Inc., 1955.

Whitehead, T.N. *Leadership in a Free Society*, Cambridge, Mass.: Harvard University Press, 1936.

Wilson, Woodrow. *Leaders of Men*, Princeton: Princeton University Press.

Wischmeir, Richard R. "Group and Leader-Centered Leadership," *Speech Monographs*, 22 (March, 1955), 43-48.

Zaleznik, Abraham. *Human Dilemmas of Leadership*, New York: Harper and Row, Publishers, 1966.